READINGS IN MORAL THEOLOGY
No. 7

Natural Law and Theology

edited by
Charles E. Curran
and
Richard A. McCormick, SJ

PAULIST PRESS
New York/Mahwah

Library of Congress Cataloging-in-Publication Data

Natural law and theology/edited by Charles E. Curran and Richard A. McCormick.
     p. cm.—(Readings in moral theology; no. 7)
   Includes bibliographical references.
   ISBN 0-8091-3179-X
   1. Natural law. 2. Law (Theology) 3. Christian ethics. I. Curran,
Charles E. II. McCormick, Richard A., 1922–   III. Series.
K460.N35   1991
171′.2—dc20
                                 91-4076
                                  CIP

Published by Paulist Press
997 Macarthur Boulevard
Mahwah, New Jersey 07430

Printed and bound in the
United States of America

Contents

Foreword 1
      Charles E. Curran
      Richard A. McCormick, S.J.

PART ONE:
REVELATION AND NATURAL LAW

The Natural Law in the Testimony of the Church 5
      Joseph Fuchs, S.J.

The Authority of Christian Tradition and of Natural Law .. 17
      Gerard Hughes, S.J.

Nature, Reason, and the Task of Theological Ethics 43
      Stanley Hauerwas

A Contribution to the Theological Discussion
of Natural Law 72
      Bruno Schüller, S.J.

PART TWO:
THOMAS AQUINAS ON NATURAL LAW
AND SOME CONTEMPORARY COMMENTARIES

Summa Theologiae: Question 94. Of the Natural Law 101
      Thomas Aquinas

Natural Law in Aquinas 114
      Jacques Maritain

The Originality of John Finnis' Conception
of the Natural Law 124
  Terence Kennedy, C.SS.R.

The Principles of Natural Law 139
  Ralph McInerny

The Basic Principles of Natural Law:
A Reply to Ralph McInerny 157
  John Finnis and *Germain Grisez*

PART THREE:
CONTEMPORARY REFLECTIONS
ON NATURAL LAW

The Natural Law: Recent Literature 173
  Richard A. McCormick, S.J.

The Doctrine Lives: The Eternal Return of Natural Law ... 184
  John Courtney Murray, S.J.

Rethinking Natural Law 221
  John Macquarrie

Natural Law in Moral Theology 247
  Charles E. Curran

The Pursuit of the Natural Law 296
  Michael B. Crowe

The Natural Law and Objective Morality:
A Thomistic Perspective 333
  William E. May

Natural Law Today 369
  Richard M. Gula, S.S.

Nature as the Basis of Morality 392
    Franz Böckle

Nature and Supernature 413
    John Mahoney, S.J.

List of Contributors 464

ACKNOWLEDGMENTS

The articles reprinted in Moral Theology #7 first appeared in the following publications and are reprinted with permission: "The Natural Law in the Testimony of the Church," by Joseph Fuchs, S.J. from the book *Natural Law: A Theological Investigation;* "The Authority of Christian Tradition and of Natural Law," by Gerard Hughes, S.J. from *Authority in Morals,* 1978, Georgetown University Press; "Nature, Reason, and the Task of Theological Ethics," from *The Peaceable Kingdom: A Primer in Christian Ethics* by Stanley Hauerwas, © 1983 by University of Notre Dame Press; Thomas Aquinas, *Summa Theologia of the Natural Law* from the translation of the Fathers of the English Dominion Province, 1948, Benziger Publishing Company; "Natural Law in Aquinas," Jacques Maritain from *Man and the State,* 1951, University of Chicago Press; "The Originality of John Finnis' Conception of the Natural Law," Terence Kennedy, C.SS.R. from *Euntes Docete,* 1987; "The Principles of Natural Law," Ralph McInerny, from *American Journal of Jurisprudence,* 1980, Notre Dame Law School; "The Basic Principles of Natural Law: A Reply to Ralph McInerny," John Finnis and Germain Grisez, *American Journal of Jurisprudence,* 1981, Notre Dame Law School; "The Doctrine Lives: The Eternal Return of Natural Law," John Courtney Murray, S.J., *We Hold These Truths,* 1960, Sheed and Ward; "The Natural Law and Objective Morality: A Thomistic Perspective," William E. May, *Principles of Catholic Moral Life,* 1980, Franciscan Herald Press; Franz Böckle, "Nature as the Basis of Morality," in Joseph A. Selling (ed.), *Personalist Morals: Essays in Honor of Professor Louis Janssens* (Bibliotheca Ephemeridum Theologicarum Lovaniensium, 83), Leuven University Press/Uitgeverij Peeters, Leuven, 1988, pp. 45–60; "Nature and Supernature," from *The Making of Moral Theology* by John Mahoney, S.J. (1987), Chapter 3, pp. 72–115, Oxford University Press; "A Contribution to the Theological Discussion of Natural Law," by Bruno Schüller, S.J. from *Theologie und Philosophie,* Herder and Herder; "Rethinking Natural Law," John Macquarrie from *Three Issues in Ethics,* 1970, Harper & Row; "The Pursuit of the Natural Law" by Michael B. Crowe, *Irish Theological Quarterly,* 1977.

vi

Foreword

This seventh volume in our series *Readings in Moral Theology* explores the theory of natural law which occupies a central place in the tradition of Catholic moral theology. Complications arise, however, because natural law overlaps with three topics already discussed in this series—the formation of moral norms, the distinctiveness of Christian ethics, and Catholic social teaching. In addition, natural law remains an important topic in law and jurisprudence, but such considerations lie beyond the scope of this volume.

This book brings together previously written studies on natural law under three different headings. The first part discusses the relationship between revelation and reason as sources of ethical wisdom and knowledge for moral theology. The second section discusses the natural law theory of Thomas Aquinas. The Catholic moral tradition has been significantly influenced and shaped by the thought of Thomas Aquinas. However, all recognize there are many other natural law theories. From the viewpoint of moral theology or Christian ethics anyone who admits human reason as a source of moral wisdom adopts a natural law perspective. Differences abound in the understanding of human reason and of human nature. Part three contains contemporary reflections on the meaning and application of natural law today. Different theoretical understandings of natural law are colored by the positions one takes on specific issues.

In keeping with the purpose of the series this volume tries to be representative of the discussions taking place. We hope both to acquaint a wider audience with these issues and to stimulate thinking on this important topic. We are grateful for the permission to republish here the essays which make up this volume. We apologize for the fact that the nature of the volume means that some of the older essays do not use inclusive language.

Charles E. Curran
Richard A. McCormick, S.J.

Part One

REVELATION AND NATURAL LAW

The Natural Law in the Testimony of the Church

Joseph Fuchs, S.J.

This chapter originally appeared in *Natural Law: A Theological Investigation* in 1965.

Not only philosophy but the theology of revelation itself testifies to the reality of natural right or natural law. This is not the case merely because natural law is related to supernatural and revealed realities. It is especially true because God has chosen to instruct us directly about it by supernatural Revelation. Under the influence of the Holy Spirit the Church upholds and proclaims Revelation and authentically teaches everything internally related to it. Logically then she should be heard first when this subject is discussed in a theological context. Her doctrine is the source of the *reality* which philosophical reflection recognizes as natural law. It follows for the theologian that this is not just a question of raising problems. It is primarily a task of simply listening.

DECLARATIONS OF THE CHURCH

A survey of the documents of our teaching authorities in the early centuries compared with those of the last decades points to the interesting fact that the early Church rarely referred to the natural law. Nonetheless she does so frequently today. Of course the primitive documents were less concerned with questions of moral theology than we are now. It is understandable that our secularized culture which calls fundamental natural institutions in question, but is insensible to Church doctrine or God's revelation, might yet be

5

open to consideration of the natural existence of things. The main reason, however, for the differences between the ancient and more recent treatments of natural law concepts is our modern reaction to positivism.

The Church documents of the early centuries did occasionally speak of natural law and natural rights. They spoke in a manner quite in harmony with the theology and Christian philosophy of their times, but they did not always distinguish between the two concepts in their terminology. It may be of interest if we trace the progress of this reflection of natural law in the Church's documents without making any claim to completeness in the survey.

The text of the Synod of Arles (A.D. 475),[1] which we shall consider again later, did not deal with moral theology. It was concerned with the efficacy of Christ's salvific role in the times before his coming. When treating of the era of the Mosaic Law and earlier the text speaks of the time of the natural law "which God has written into the hearts of all men" and through which salvation was possible in the hope of Christ's advent.[2]

Documents like this are rare. The use of natural law perspectives by Pius II (1359),[3] Innocent XI (1679)[4] and Alexander VIII (1690)[5] in their treatment of particular moral questions is quite evident. The fact is clear either from the actual use of the term "natural law" or because an alternative was chosen which expressed antithesis to the "divine or ecclesiastical" positive law.

It was only in the middle of the last century that references to the natural law became frequent. Pius IX turned to the natural law on the questions of neo-malthusianism,[6] the foundations of civil law[7] and the indissolubility of marriage.[8] Like the Synod of Arles he spoke about pagans who are able to attain salvation if they fulfill "the natural law and its commandments which are written in the hearts of all men."[9]

Leo XIII, even more than Pius IX, based his teaching on the laws given by nature, meaning the Creator of nature. In this way also he treated the great questions of the rights of private property, the just wage and the right to form societies and associations. He considered the problems of patriotism, the right to live, to marry etc. from the same point of view.[10]

In the period following Leo XIII it was especially Pius XI and

Pius XII who appealed to natural law in their comments on the essential questions of their times. We may indicate as an example the Encyclical of Pius XI on national-socialism[11] in which he attempted to protect the rights of man given by the Creator of nature, such as the right of parents in the education of their children or the right of free profession of faith. In *Quadragesimo Anno*[12] like Leo XIII he based his social teaching on natural law. In the Encyclical on Christian marriage he referred repeatedly to the institution itself, its values and moral orientations as having their foundations in the natural law.[13]

In times of international difficulty greater perhaps than had been experienced by any previous Pope, Pius XII[14] strove more evidently even than his predecessor to counter a positivist conception of law. His emphasis on natural law in his great public treatises is evidence of this. He explicitly grounded questions of political, social and international life as well as those of private life upon a natural moral order.

The notions and even the terms of natural law are also used in the Code of Canon Law (1918). Even more frequently, valid natural law references are recognizable in it where they are not expressly formulated.[15]

These testimonies to natural law and valid natural rights which are given by the teaching authorities of the Church put it beyond all doubt that this is a question of a truth of faith.

THE ESSENCE OF NATURAL LAW

Bearing in mind the continual progress of reflection on natural law in matters of moral theology, pre-occupations with particular problems become evident. It remains of primary importance to discover from all these numerous declarations of the Church which seldom deal purely with natural law as such, what she means explicitly by it and what precise value she attributes to it.[16]

A first series of Church texts on the essence of natural law refers to its ontological foundations. In these the being, the very essence or nature of man as composed of body and spirit appears as a norm of moral behavior and of law. There is an objective order defined by natural law and this in the final issue is based upon "being."[17] Numerous paragraphs in the texts show this clearly. Marriage is "by its nature"[18] monogamous. The attributes of the institution are "something that results from the nature of man."[19] The right to hold property is given "to us by nature itself."[20] The moral limits of medical activity result from "the teleology given by nature and existence in all things and from the order of values which results from the nature of all things."[21] The natural law is determined by the destination and nature of man;[22] it exists because of "laws written into the nature of beings"[23] which are ontologically rooted in human nature.[24] The clear meaning of all this is even more evident in such anthropomorphic phrases as: nature admonishes[25] and commands;[26] that natural law is the voice of nature[27] or that the rights of nations are dictated by nature.[28]

Another series of texts in connection with the second chapter of the Epistle to the Romans declares that natural law is found within man himself;[29] it is written in his heart.[30] By his reason man is able to read this law written in his heart,[31] at least insofar as he is not blinded by sin or passion.[32] In a sense reason itself is called natural law[33] in that it ordains that good be done and evil avoided. Reason is the voice[34] that speaks to us distinguishing between good and evil. Another term employed is the "good moral sense."[35]

These two series of texts are related. The middle term of the argument is evidently the rational cognition of man. The reality of being implies an objective assertion of the moral and juridical order. Subjectively this consists in the affirmation that rational knowledge is determined by real being. Reason reads the natural law in the nature of all things and particularly in the nature of man.[36] To say that reason is able to read the law written in the heart of man[37] means simply that reason is able to grasp the law of nature from the ontological reality of man and of all things.

This ontological aspect of natural law corresponds to its absolute value. It must not be assumed that this applies only in the case of a few of its more general norms.[38] Interpretations in a relativist sense are not to be tolerated.[39] Natural law is the superior court, so to speak, for all humanity[40] and is independent of the changing legislation of today and tomorrow.[41] It is the criterion of every law[42] and of every juridical order.[43] It follows that the State has a duty to protect natural law.[44] It must determine it more clearly by positive enactment and adapt it to concrete circumstances.[45] We have already said that the Church in her own Code emphatically refuses to recognize any legislation that contradicts the natural law. This is of special importance in any question of natural rights in the strict sense. They are understood by the Church not merely as idealistic norms but as true, valid[46] and inviolable[47] rights. Consequently they remain valid against any contrary but merely positive right.[48]

The common nucleus of all positive legislation must be similar at all times and places. This is so because it is dealing with "the exigencies derived from this nature" which are substantially the same at all times and everywhere.[49]

The noetic aspect of natural law, the fact that it is written in the heart of man and therefore naturally evident to him, ensures that the most primitive peoples are capable of a moral order and a sufficient cultural development.[50] This only serves to emphasize the necessity of fulfilling certain conditions in order that this law written in the heart (that is, the confrontation of reason and human being) can be subjectively internalized as knowledge.

It should also be obvious that the Church does not understand the natural law as a naturalistic or rationalistic creation by man in a self-sufficient world. The nature in which reason recognizes a natural order is the work of God the Creator.[51] Reason engaged upon the intelligibilities of nature must be seen as God's work. Only he has written the law of nature into man's heart when creating him.[52] The voice of nature that admonishes, orders and teaches, together with the reason that scans nature and our own hearts, are the true voices of divine reason.[53] This natural law is as certainly a manifestation of God's intellect and will as his positively revealed commandment.[54] The Code of Canon Law understands the revealed positive law, with the natural law, as being divine law.[55] Pius XII therefore said that whenever God the Creator is denied the voice of nature, too, is silenced.[56] His intention was not merely to emphasize the fact that reason, in recognizing a law in nature, needs God the Creator to support it so that it may be decisively obligatory. Rather he meant to emphasize the subjective fact that a denial of God the Creator will result in a refusal to listen to nature. It will issue ultimately in the loss of the very ability to do so.

The Natural Law and the Order of Redemption

The essence of natural law and especially the basic concept of nature as understood by the Church, becomes clearer through contrast with another divine law. The texts make a distinction between "natural" and "divine" law.[57] There is a law of nature and The Law contained in Holy Scripture[58]—and there is a law of Revelation.[59] Also there are principles of nature and the principles of Christianity.[60] Distinctions are made between natural law deriving from the Creator and the precepts of Christ[61] deriving from the Redeemer.[62] All these connote the same reality. Although the distinctions are necessary and valid it must not be forgotten that the natural law itself is divine. This is made plain in Canon 27 of the Code of Canon Law. In articulating these differences, divine law is to be understood as positive divine law whereas the law of nature exists independently of any positive historical intervention by God. Nothing else is meant by the distinction between the law of nature and the law found in Holy Scripture than this: the natural law exists without the Bible.

Fundamentally it is in this way that one should consider the contra-positions of the natural and of the revealed law. The latter includes the Old and New Testaments. Revelation is a somewhat wider concept than that of Holy Scripture. Similarly the distinctions which can be made between the principles of nature and those of Christianity and between the natural law and the teaching of Christ, differ from the preceding only in nuance. Christianity includes Scripture and the Revelations of the Old and the New Covenants. In considering Christ's teaching, of course, the Scripture and the Revelation of the New Testament come especially into the foreground. Taking all this into account there is one decisive fact found in all our texts: besides the positive divine law found in Holy Scripture, Revelation and Christianity, there is a natural law independent of these. In the contradistinction between law deriving from the Creator and that deriving from the Redeemer it must be noted that the Creator is related to the natural law and the Redeemer to Revelation.[63] A contrast of the Creator and the natural law with the Redeemer and Revelation corresponds to the distinction between nature and the supernatural.[64] Analogously the State and the family are considered as belonging to the natural order and the Church to the supernatural[65] order. It follows that these laws and rights which come from the Creator are not to be taken in the Protestant sense of the order of creation. This is understood as the order of man in his original state. They should rather be understood in the metaphysical sense as "orders" of human nature distinct from the "supernatural." Natural law is the law corresponding to this nature which is valid independently of the supernatural, of Redemption, Christianity, Revelation and Holy Scripture. At least basically it can be known without these. It is a law that truly emanates from creation *insofar* as creation is nature and not supernatural.

The natural law is thus one of two parallel streams that flow from the same source: the eternal God who is at the same Creator and Redeemer.[66] It represents an order that is valid for the state of *fallen man* and likewise for the state of *redeemed man*. Nature (the term refers to the existential essence of man and not to his state at the beginning) is not destroyed but weakened.[67] This is the Church's teaching and its sense will be precisely determined later. Man as we now know him holds the integrity of the natural faculties of intellect and will in his natural humanity. The Church knows that natural law has been confirmed by Revelation.[68] The Christian order of salvation challenges man to a permanent and ever valid natural order and not merely to a supernatural one. The Church simply does not recognize any one-sided supernaturalism which disregards the real "humanity" of man.[69] Consequently the natural law has no independent existence but belongs to the one "Christian order of salvation in which nature and grace are united."[70] Natural law achieves its fulfillment or completion in this order as Pius XI said explicitly when referring to marriage.[71] He was thinking no doubt of its evolution to the status of a sacrament and of that special stability given it by its indissolubility. He gave his Encyclical *Quadragesimo Anno* the title: "Social order, its restoration and completion according to the plan of salvation of the Gospel." In the Latin text the phrase "according to the plan of salvation of the Gospel" refers only to "completion" and not to "restoration." This clearly indicates that it is only in the spirit of the gospel that the social order achieves its completion. The particular point is not given any further precision.[72] The Church teaches that the natural law has been elevated[73] in the actual order of salvation. Now it serves not only the natural but the supernatural development of man.[74] Because of this status of the natural law within the Christian order of salvation it follows that it is not only the revealed law but also the natural norms of rights and morals which are subject to the teaching authority of the Church.[75] It is her duty within the actual order of salvation to form the consciences of all men, primarily those who are in charge of public life. She is the guardian of the Christian order of salvation and the custodian of the natural law.[76] In this the Church fulfills a duty primarily to her members but one which concerns all men even those outside the Church. All men are called to participate in grace.[77] Her activity as teacher of the natural law is all the more important when we consider that the human intellect is able to recognize this law, yet man's fallen state weakens his knowledge in various ways.

Both Pius XI in *Casti Connubii*[78] and Pius XII in his Encyclical of August 12, 1950, *Humani Generis,* drew attention as a recurrent theme to these questions of the natural cognition of morality. The relative necessity of Revelation and its proclamation by the Church[79] was repeatedly and insistently their motif.

Notes

1. 475 A.D. circa; the year is uncertain.
2. *Denz* 160 a and b.
3. *Denz* 717 g; Extra-marital intercourse is morally evil; this is quite evident not because of ecclesiastical prohibition only.
4. *Denz* 1198: Extra-marital intercourse is morally evil, not only because of positive Divine Law; and *Denz* 1199; Masturbation (mollietas) contradicts the natural law.
5. *Denz* 1292: Condemnation of the rigorist proposition that the violation of the natural law is formally sinful, even in the case of ignorance.
6. H. Batzill O.S.B., *Decisiones S. Sedis de usu et abusu matrimonii,* Taurini 1937, 15.
7. *Denz* 1756.
8. *Denz* 1767.

9. *Denz* 1677.

10. Cf. the Encyclicals of Leo XIII in ASS, especially the Encyclical *Rerum novarum,* ASS 23 (1891), 641–70. In the following pages we shall quote the Pontifical texts as given in ASS and AAS.

11. AAS 29 (1937), 145–67.

12. AAS 23 (1931), 177–228.

13. AAS 22 (1930), 539–90.

14. Already his first Encyclical *Summi Pontificatus* had *emphasized* the natural law, AAS 31 (1939), 423. This point of view is repeated most significantly in Pius XII's numerous allocutions on contemporary problems.

15. The facts in detail are these: by natural law we understand a law that cannot be changed or contradicted by positive ecclesiastical law (CIC can. 6, 6°): "From this it follows that all these dispositions do not need further positive determination by the legislative authority and are capable of being sanctioned even legally, without special intervention of the authority (cf. can. 1667, 2222 § 1)" (Ch. Lefèbvre, in DDC, vol. 4, 989). The natural law appears to limit the possible extent of legitimate customs (can. 27) much *in the same manner that loans in the ecclesiastical law* limit those of the civil law (can. 1509 and 1529). Canon law speaks in a manner similar to natural law in the realm of acquiring ownership (can. 1499, § 1). It speaks also of the natural prohibitions in reading certain books (can. 1405, § 1); of the natural obligation to denunciation (can. 1935, § 2), of the natural obligations to be observed in charitable foundations (can. 1513 § 1). It is aware likewise of the various precepts of the natural law regarding marriage and in relation to attributes derived from natural law, especially those of unity and indissolubility (can. 1110) and the impediments of natural law regarding marriage (can. 1139, § 2 and can. 1068, § 1). Cf. A Landolf, *Das Naturrecht im CIC,* Basle 1951; G. Oliviero, "Diritto naturale e diritto della chiesa," *Il diritto eccl.,* 61 (1950), 1–41.

16. In the following pages we refer principally to the Papal encyclicals but we shall also take into account the numerous allocutions of Pius XII. Insofar as these allocutions are addressed either directly to the whole Church or to a limited audience only, the latter often express the official opinion on important questions and are therefore relatively close to the encyclicals. Yet even where a lesser authority is employed, the repeated testimony, which is in accord with the teaching of the past, is of great value. This does not mean that every single statement on natural law is an article of faith, *in the same way as is the statement of the fact and value of the natural law in general. It is, perhaps, hardly necessary to remark* that in the following pages only a *selection* of Papal documents will be quoted.

17. Instruction of the Holy Office, 2 February 1956 on "Situation-ethics," AAS 48 (1956), 144.

18. Leo XIII, *Arcanum,* AAS 12 (1879 ff.), 388.

19. Pius XI, *Casti connubii,* AAS 22 (1930), 542, cf. CIC, can. 1110.

20. Leo XIII, *Quod apost. mun.,* ASS 11 (1878), 374.

21. Pius XII, Allocution, 13 September 1952, AAS 44 (1952) 784.

22. Leo XIII, *Libertas,* ASS 20 (1887) 597.

23. Pius XII, Allocution, 19 May 1956, AAS 48 (1956) 471.

24. Pius XII, Allocution, 3 October 1953, AAS 45 (1953), 739.

25. Leo XIII, *Rerum novarum,* ASS 23 (1890 ff.), 662.

26. Leo XIII, *ibid.*

27. Pius XII, *Summi Pontificatus,* AAS 31 (1939), 423.

28. Pius XII, Allocution, 6 December 1953, AAS 45 (1953), 795.

29. *Ibid.* 437. Leo XIII, *Libertas,* ASS 20 (1887 ff.), 597.

30. A frequently repeated affirmation. Cf. Pius XI, *Divini Redemptoris,* AAS 29 (1937), 76; Pius XII, Allocution, 24 December 1941, AAS 34 (1942), 16.

31. Pius XI, *Mit brennender Sorge,* AAS 29 (1937) 159.

32. *Ibid.*

33. Leo XIII, *Libertas,* ASS 20 (1887 ff.), 597.

34. *Ibid.*

35. Pius XII, Allocution, 7 September 1953, AAS 45 (1953), 606.

36. Pius XII, Allocution, 13 November 1949, AAS 41 (1949), 607; Allocution, 13 October 1955, AAS 47 (1955), 770.

37. *Ibid.*

38. Instruction of the Holy Office, 2 February 1956, AAS 48 (1956), 144 ff.

39. *Ibid.*

40. Pius XII, Allocution, 13 October 1955, AAS 47 (1955), 769.

41. Pius XII, Allocution, 19 October 1953, AAS 45 (1953), 749; Allocution, 3 October 1953, AAS 45 (1953), 739.

42. Pius XII, Allocution, 13 October 1955, AAS 47 (1955), 769.

43. Pius XII, Allocution, 13 November 1949, ASS 41 (1949), 607.

44. Leo XIII, *Rerum novarum,* ASS 23 (1890 ff.), 665.

45. Pius XII, Allocution, 6 December 1953, AAS 45 (1953), 795.

46. Pius XI, *Mit brennender Sorge,* AAS 29 (1937), 159.

47. Pius XII, Allocution, 25 September 1949, AAS 41 (1949), 556.

48. Pius XI, *Mit brennender Sorge,* AAS 29 (1937), 159.

49. Pius XII, Allocution, 3 October 1953, AAS 45 (1953), 739.

50. Pius XI, *Divini Redemptoris,* AAS 29 (1937), 76; Pius XII, *Summi Pontificatus,* AAS 31 (1939), 423.

51. A frequently emphasized idea. Cf. Pius XI, *Casti connubii,* AAS 22 (1930), 539; Pius XI, *Quadragesimo anno,* AAS 23 (1931), 191; Pius XII, Allocution, 19 October 1953, AAS 45 (1953), 749.

52. Pius XII, Allocution, 24 December 1941, AAS 34 (1942), 16. Allocution, 7 September 1953, AAS 45 (1953), 607.

53. Leo XIII, *Libertas,* ASS 20 (1887 ff.) 597.

54. Pius XII, Allocution, 1 May 1941, AAS 33 (1941), 196.

55. CIC, can. 6, 6° and can. 27; Cf. can. 1038 § 1; can. 1529; can. 1926.

56. Pius XII, *Summi Pontificatus,* AAS 31 (1939), 423.

57. One frequently meets these medieval expressions. Cf. Leo XIII, *Quod apost. mun.,* ASS 11 (1878), 374; *Rerum novarum,* ASS 13 (1890 ff.), 645; Pius X, *Singulari quadam,* AAS 4 (1912), 658; Pius XI, *Casti connubii,* AAS 22 (1930), 560; *Quadragesimo anno,* AAS 23 (1931), 193.

58. Leo XII, *Pastoralis officii* (letter to the German bishops), AAS 24 (1891 ff.), 204.

59. Leo XIII, *Rerum novarum,* ASS 23 (1890 ff.), 645; Pius XII, Allocution, 1 May 1941, AAS 33 (1941), 196; Allocution, 24 December 1944, AAS 37 (1945), 17 ff.

60. Pius XII, Allocution, 23 December 1949, AAS 42 (1950), 127; Allocution, 7 September 1953, AAS 45 (1953), 607.

61. Pius XII, Allocution, 13 October 1955, AAS 47 (1955), 768.

62. Pius XI, *Casti connubii,* AAS 22 (1930), 541; Pius XII, Allocution, 1 May 1941, AAS 33 (1941), 196 ff.

63. Pius XII, *ibid.*

64. *Ibid.*

65. Pius XI, *Divini illius magistri,* AAS 22 (1930), 52.

66. Pius XII, Allocution, 1 May 1941, AAS 33 (1941), 197.

67. Pius XII, Allocution, 25 September 1949, AAS 41 (1949), 555 ff.

68. Pius XII, Allocution, 7 September 1953, AAS 45 (1953), 607. Cf. also Leo XIII, *Rerum novarum,* ASS 23 (1891), 645; Pius XI, *Casti connubii,* AAS 22 (1930), 541.

69. Pius XII, Allocution on Christmas Day 1954, AAS 47 (1955), 25.

70. Pius XII, Allocution, 1 May 1941, AAS 33 (1941), 197.

71. Pius XI, *Casti connubii,* AAS 22 (1930), 541.

72. Cf. O. v. Nell-Breuning, S.J., *Die soziale Encyklika. Erläuterungen zum Weltrundschreiben Papst Pius XI über die gesellschaftliche Ordnung,* III, Cologne 1950, 14 ff.; J. B. Schuster, S.J., in *Scholastik* 13 (1938), 399.

73. Pius XI, *Casti connubii,* AAS 22 (1930), 541.

74. Pius XII, Allocution, 2 November 1954, AAS 46 (1954), 672 ff.

75. Pius X, *Singulari quadam,* AAS 4 (1912), 658; Pius XI, *Casti connubii,* AAS 22 (1930), 579; Pius XII, Allocution, 1 May 1941, AAS 33 (1941), 196.

76. Pius XI, *Mit brennender Sorge,* AAS 29 (1937), 160; Pius XII, Allocution, 1 May 1941, AAS 33 (1941), 196; Allocution, 2 November 1954, AAS 46 (1954), 672.

77. Pius XII, *ibid.,* 197.

78. AAS 22 (1930), 579 ff.

79. AAS 42 (1950), 561 ff.; cf. below Chapter VII.

The Authority of Christian Tradition and of Natural Law

Gerard Hughes, S.J.

This chapter originally appeared in *Authority in Morals* in 1978.

The ultimate norm for Christian belief is God's revelation of himself in Jesus of Nazareth. The contemporary Christian does not have direct access to the life and teaching of Jesus. Who Jesus was, what he did and the meaning of his life, are mediated to the Christian by the tradition of the Christian community, a tradition which consists both in the living faith handed on from believer to believer, and in the texts, starting with the Bible, in which that faith has found more permanent expression. This tradition is authoritative for Christian belief in that, somehow or other, Christian beliefs are justified in the last analysis by appeal to that tradition. The precise way in which this is done varies in different Christian communities. Some theologians would lay greater stress than others on the Bible, and especially the New Testament, somewhat at the expense of later Christian tradition, while others would wish to regard the tradition as a whole in a more unified way. Others, again, would lay more stress on the experience of the individual believer within the living tradition of the Church. Despite these variations, however, the appeal to tradition as normative for Christian belief is to be found in at any rate all the main Christian communities.

The Christian is well aware that his religious beliefs are such that he is also required to strive for moral perfection. It might well seem natural to him to suppose that the ultimate authority to which appeal is to be made in moral questions is the same tradition to which he appeals in questions of religious belief. It is this view which I shall examine in this chapter. As with questions of religious belief, the appeal to tradition to settle moral questions can take various forms according to whether the emphasis falls on the New Testament, later tradition, or the experience of the individual believer. I shall not examine these differences in detail, since I hope to show that the logic of the argument is the same in each case so far as concerns the points I wish to make.

Two qualifications will be in order. I do not intend to examine the claim that Christians come by their religious beliefs by being brought up in a believing community (which, at least in most cases, is plainly true), and come by their moral beliefs in the same way (which is at least arguable). I am not concerned with the historical, social, and personal factors which are responsible for producing the moral beliefs Christians hold. I am concerned with the way in which these beliefs are to be justified, rather than how they are to be explained. Secondly, I shall not be concerned with those moral duties which would be unintelligible apart from Christian belief as a whole. For example, Christians believe themselves to be obliged to worship God in a particular way, typically, if not in every case, by the celebration of the Eucharist. They consider themselves obliged to ask God's forgiveness for their sins, and to thank him for what he has done for them through his Son. It might be argued that these obligations are better described as religious rather than moral, though I myself would incline to think it clearer to describe them as moral obligations. Be that as it may, they are plainly obligations which would make no sense were it not for the other beliefs which Christians hold on the basis of what God revealed in Christ. I shall be concerned only with those other moral obligations which it would make sense for an unbeliever to consider himself bound by. Thus, any man might consider himself bound to keep promises, to care for his fellow men, to be faithful to his marriage, and even to give his life for others. He might argue that some of these beliefs, especially perhaps the last one, could not in the end be justified. But at least it makes sense to ask whether such beliefs can be justified without appeal to Christian revelation, in a way which would not make sense in the case of, say, the celebration of the Eucharist.

If we ask how these more general moral beliefs are to be justified, or what method is to be followed in trying to discover whether they are true or false, the Christian might adopt one or other of two basic positions. Either he will claim that some (or even all) moral problems must remain insoluble to anyone who does not hold Christian beliefs, or he will refuse to make this claim. And the positive claim might be held in a stronger form, as I have just expressed it, or in the weaker form that although the non-Christian can provide a partial justification for his moral beliefs, he cannot provide an ultimate justification for them. On this weaker view, Christian revelation would be regarded as an essential supplement to, but not as a substitute for, the arguments available to the non-believer.

Both the stronger and the weaker versions of this Christian claim hold that revelation can function as the ultimate court of appeal in moral argument, and that arguments which do not make this appeal will be either wholly or partly deficient. In harmony with this claim, a Christian might well speak of a humanist approach to moral problems in a way which implies that such an approach will be at best incomplete, and at worst will lead to false moral conclusions, precisely because it does not take any theological considerations into account.

I shall argue in the remainder of this chapter that neither the stronger nor the weaker versions of this Christian claim can be upheld consistently with other Christian beliefs about God. And I shall supplement this purely theological argument by advancing further philosophical considerations which tell against the truth of any such claim. The aims of this chapter are thus entirely negative. Nevertheless, I believe it is the right place to start, firstly because the view that I criticize here is perhaps the one which would naturally occur to the Christian, and is one which is reinforced by the habit of referring to "the Christian ethic"; and secondly because it prepares the ground for my own positive suggestions. I should also like to stress that I am endeavoring to disprove only the claim that Christian revelation functions as the *ultimate* court of appeal in morals. There may be (and, as I shall later argue, there are) other ways in which Christian tradition can be used in ethics. These uses are left wholly untouched by the arguments in this chapter.

MORALITY AND THE WILL OF GOD

Any Christian would hold that what ought to be done in any situation is also what God wills should be done, for to deny this would imply that the Christian believes in a God who is, at best, unconcerned with our moral behavior. The whole Judaeo-Christian tradition is clear that such a God is not the one in whom they believe. The Judaeo-Christian God reveals himself as a God who is most deeply concerned that his followers be just, pure, forgiving, honest, and loving. For the Christian, then, to be morally good is also to do the will of God; and to do the will of God is also to be morally good. The notions of "moral duty" and "what God wills us to do" are, in short, materially equivalent. Any instance of the one will also be an instance of the other.

That two terms are materially equivalent does not necessarily mean that one can be defined in terms of the other. For example, it may be the case that anyone who is a British citizen in good standing over the age of eighteen is also one who is eligible to vote in a British election. But "eligible to vote in a British election" does not *mean* "British citizen in good standing over the age of eighteen." Thus, from the fact that "what God wills us to do" and "moral duty" are materially equivalent expressions for the Christian, we cannot conclude that "moral duty" *means* "what God wills us to do." To hold that the two expressions are definitionally equivalent in this way is to be forced onto the horns of a most uncomfortable dilemma. On the one hand, we might have to admit that "moral duty" is to be defined in terms of the will of God because things become our moral duty only as a result of God's willing that they should be; and this is in the end a thoroughgoing voluntarist position. Alternatively, we might have to admit that "moral duty" is to be defined in terms of God's will for us because we, with our limited human understanding, are unable to give any other content to the notion of "moral duty." I shall examine, and reject, each alternative in turn.

What precisely would be the difficulty in adopting a voluntarist position? After all, there is surely a sense in which it is true that moral values and moral duties do depend on the will of God to create human beings. Had he chosen to create some other type of moral being, would not that have entailed willing them to have a different morality? Even on a Kantian view, in which morality applies to all rational agents as such, it would, I think follow that different species of moral agents would have a morality different in its content, though not in its form, from the moralities of other species. In this sense, then, it is part of Christian belief that the morality we have is what it is because of God's decision so to create us. The distinctive, and objectionable, contention of the voluntarist is that, even given the creation of man, what is right and wrong for men to do depends on a *further* act of God's will; God could have placed us under different, incompatible, obligations while leaving us unaltered. In thus severing the connection between the nature of man and the moral obligations under which God could place him, the voluntarist renders man's moral perfection unintelligible, because it is no longer related to any other facet of man's development. He therefore runs the risk of making his God arbitrary. In the main, Christian tradition has rejected this picture of God as inconsistent with his character as it has been revealed to us and with the ways in which his moral concern for us has been shown.

The other horn of the dilemma is hardly more attractive. The argument would have to run something like this: although it is of course true that God is not arbitrary in himself, and that he must have his reasons for deciding that we should be subject to certain moral obligations rather than others, nevertheless we are not in a position to know what those reasons might be. Our knowledge of ourselves might be so inadequate that we cannot grasp the relationship between what God wills us to do and the good that will result for us if we obey him. God's purposes are, after all, ultimately mysterious.

This argument does not suffice to rescue God from the charge of arbitrariness. So far as *we* are concerned, the God depicted in this argument would be indistinguishable from the God of the full-blooded voluntarist. If we can see no connection between our human fulfillment and the obligations under which God places us, then we would have no grounds for believing that our God was a moral God at all. To be sure, he might tell us that he was; but why should we believe him? Not because of his mighty deeds. Mighty deeds are no more than displays of power, and power can be misused, or can exist without any moral dimension to it whatever. Volcanoes and master criminals might both be capable of displaying great power; but they lack altogether the moral seriousness which, according to Christian tradition, we must find in God if we are to be able to recognize him *as* God. It appears that there are strong theological reasons against the view that we can never understand God's reasons for obliging us as he does, quite apart from the fact that such a view would make nonsense of our attempts to think about morality in a coherent way.

There are other equally serious difficulties against this type of position. For it to work in practice, two conditions would have to be met; firstly, it would have to be possible for us to come to know what God wills for us; secondly, it would have to be the case that, independently of what God tells us about our moral obligations, we could have no access to the basis of ethics such as, for example, a knowledge of our own nature might provide. Thus it might be the case that God's will for us was based on an anthropology which he revealed to us only in Christ, in comparison with which our own efforts to formulate an anthropology independently of revelation would be either totally false or too misleading to function as a foundation for ethics. Are there any grounds for believing that such is indeed our situation?

We may begin by inquiring what theological grounds might be urged in favor of the view that, independently of what God tells us about our moral obligations, we could have no access to the basis of ethics. At least in some passages, Karl Barth seems to come close to this kind of view.[1] A full discussion of this position is not possible here, but it appears in the end to rest on two main lines of argument, both stemming from an analysis of original sin.

The first line of argument asserts that as a result of original sin our minds are too clouded in darkness, too blinded, to be able to think properly about morality. The difficulty with this assertion, I think, lies not so much in the assertion itself, although even here there is the hint of a certain self-defeating quality about it. The main difficulty comes when it is combined with other assertions which the Christian would also wish to make, such as the assertion that man's mind is capable of responding to God's revelation when it is offered to us. It might be argued, perhaps, that we are able to accept revelation as true only by the grace of God, and that faith itself is a gift. But if grace is able to help in this case, why could it not have helped in the first place? To this in turn it might be replied that it is Christ who alone is God's grace for us, and that grace is therefore given only in connection with the response to Christ. However, I should have thought it by now a fairly well-established theological position that all men, by virtue of their being created in Christ, have grace offered to them, whether or not they ever have the opportunity to respond to revelation as such.

The rebuttal of this line of argument, then, does not depend on a kind of Pelagian position to the effect that, despite original sin, man is perfectly capable of working out his moral obligations by the light of his natural, ungraced, reason alone. I can see little theological merit in the view that there ever in fact exists such a thing as a natural reason alone, outside the order of grace. Unfortunately, the use of the term "natural" in speaking of natural law morality has given the impression that "natural" is to be contrasted with "supernatural" or "graced," and that a natural law morality is therefore a morality in which God and his grace are in no way involved. I see no reason for the Christian theologian to make this contrast, and every reason why he should not. The real focus of the discussion should not be on fallen man without grace, but rather on sinful man without explicit belief in the Christian revelation.

If we manage to remain clear on this point, I think a great deal of the force of this first line of argument from the reality of original sin is lost. Even were one to accept that the effect of original sin was totally to blind our minds to our true nature and destiny (and at least Catholic theologians would probably not accept even so much), we would have to remember that precisely because Christ died for all men we are *not* left simply with our unaided sinful minds when we come to consider morality. The grace of Christ is offered to us, even if the opportunity for explicit Christian belief is not. One would therefore require very strong *additional* arguments to show that our minds are still incapable of correct ethical reflection unless they also come to accept the teaching of the New Testament as the

Word of God. Moreover, it is far from clear how any alleged revelation could possibly commend itself to us as truly God's revelation were it to appear to us to have immoral implications. Revelation commends itself to us in part because it does harmonize with our moral aspirations. It follows that those moral aspirations must have been present antecedently (at least in a logical sense). I conclude, then, that the Christian theologian must hold not, indeed, that man has the ability to understand morality independently of God's grace, but rather that he has that ability independently of his coming to believe in Christ on the basis of God's revelation.

The same general reply is sufficient, I think, to meet the second line of argument drawn from the doctrine of original sin. On this line, it might well be conceded that man (fallen man with the help of grace, that is) has the intellectual capacity to discover and assent to moral truths; but it might be urged that he will still be seriously misled if he uses this capacity to reflect upon himself, because the desires and aspirations of his human nature are also warped by the effects of original sin. That human desires as they actually are offer no firm basis for ethics is a view with a long and distinguished history, stretching back to the Augustinian interpretation of the Fall and, behind him, to the Platonic distrust of the body in which our soul is imprisoned. One still occasionally hears echoes of the confused asceticism which speaks of the need to replace purely natural desires by supernatural ones (thus repeating the equivocation on the word "natural" to which I have already called attention). A full philosophical critique of the place of desires in ethics will be offered later, but I shall anticipate some of my remarks in order to place them here in a more theological setting.

I know of no moral philosopher who has ever maintained that living morally requires us to satisfy any and every desire that we might have. For a start, many of our desires conflict with one another, so that it is not possible in practice to satisfy them all. Furthermore, it would be widely if not universally admitted that some of our desires are irrational, or open to criticism on some other score, and that living morally requires us to forego their satisfaction in order to satisfy others. Still, even admitting all that, one might maintain that it is the desires we have which, in some fashion or other, must provide the basis of our morality, and that it simply would not make sense to say that the first step in moral thinking consists in recognizing that *all* our desires are warped, that we do not know how they are warped, and that our morality must therefore take no account of them whatever. Suppose, however, that we were to hold such a position in its extreme form. One could then easily see how the theologian could use it to argue for the absolute necessity of revelation for ethics.

But consider how revelation would strike us in such a situation. Were it the case that our desires were warped and that we could not, of ourselves, see in what way they were warped, then any alleged revelation of our moral duty would appear to us arbitrary, dehumanizing, and, ultimately, voluntarist. It would be quite unreasonable to accept such a revelation as authentic. In short, this view leads straight back to the full-blooded voluntarist position which I have already criticised. Moreover, I think it would also present a picture of a God who is most unreasonably demanding in the light of what we are able to accomplish in our fallen state. It is surely part of our normal moral view that we should not have quite unrealistic expectations of people, and that we should not place burdens upon them which they are simply incapable of bearing. On the view I am here criticizing, God must inevitably appear as demanding of us that we should live in a way which frustrates all the desires we actually have. No doubt it might be said that the point of a revealed ethic is that we should stand condemned and recognize our need of God's healing power; and, at a pinch, I can see the possibility and the value of God's revealing to us the moral dimension of life in his Kingdom even if it corresponds little or not at all to our present fallen desires and aspirations. But the point of doing Christian ethics is to try to determine how we should live here and now, as we are, in our imperfect and fallen world. It is one thing to be told that our present desires have nothing to do with the morality of the Kingdom to come (though, like Kant, I could not believe even that much); it is very much worse to be told that our present desires have nothing to do with how we ought to live here and now. A God who said *that* would be so lacking in understanding and compassion that we could have little reason to believe in him.

Up to this point, I have been arguing against the view that there are theological grounds for saying that we have no secure basis for ethics independently of revelation. In the end, my argument turns on the contention that belief in revelation is irrational unless that revelation somehow fits in with our antecedent convictions, and, in particular, with our antecedent moral convictions. This general view, commonly held by Catholic theologians, has often enough seemed Pelagian, at least in its implications, to many theologians in the Reformed traditions, and they might still incline to this view despite my efforts to show the difficulties involved in holding it consistently. Indeed, even in the Catholic tradition there are some moral theologians who hold in practice, if not in theory, that revelation is essential for our understanding of ethics. For instance, it is not uncommon to find Catholic theologians arguing that there are no conclusive arguments against the legitimacy of divorce and re-marriage unless one appeals to the New Testament teaching on the subject and to the traditional interpretation of that teaching by the Church. Sometimes, though less often, a similar position is adopted with regard to suicide, or the laying down of one's life for others. The same kind of view is implied, I believe, by any position which holds that there is a specifically Christian ethic, the conclusions of which cannot be firmly established without appeal to revelation and the tradition of the Church guided by the Holy Spirit. In my view, this position is inconsistent with the basic rationalism which underpins the whole Catholic tradition in theology, and I hope to have shown that it presents enormous difficulties for any Christian theologian. Be that as it may, however, to establish the position that revelation is the ultimate basis of Christian ethics it is not enough to show that attempts to find an alternative basis are theologically unsound. Someone who disagrees with my arguments thus far would still have established only half of his case. As I point out above, it would also be necessary to show that revelation *can* provide the ultimate basis for ethics which cannot be found elsewhere, and that appeal to revelation will enable us to solve moral dilemmas to which there is no other adequate solution. I shall now attempt to prove that this part of the case cannot be substantiated either.

THE APPEAL TO BIBLICAL TRADITION

The attempt to appeal to biblical tradition as the ultimate authority in ethics runs into several difficulties, which may be conveniently labelled exegetical, hermeneutical, and theological. I shall discuss each of these in turn.

Exegetical Difficulties

Fundamental to any proper use of the Bible is a respect for the nature of the biblical text. That means, in general, not merely that we must respect the basic Christian belief that it is inspired by God; we must also recognize the fact that the documents it contains are thoroughly human documents, written at a particular time and place with the requirements of a particular readership in mind. The fact that the biblical texts are human documents makes it at once possible, and difficult, for us to discern in them what it is that God wishes us to learn.

Any ancient culture is, and must to some extent remain, opaque to us. In particular, its language will be only imperfectly understood, and the precise flavor and overtones of its expressions may well escape us even when we are superficially able to give verbal equivalents of all its utterances. Even with a contemporary European language, it is often very difficult indeed to capture in English exactly what is being said, no matter how many dictionaries and native speakers we have at our disposal. Sometimes, indeed, there simply *is* no way of saying in English precisely what is being clearly said in the foreign language.

There are two different types of problems involved. The first is the problem of mastering a foreign language. This involves attaining a grasp of the many conventions governing the use of words, expressions, and literary forms, as well as many other conventions regarding tone of voice, context and circumstances, all of which can determine the meaning of what is said. Thus, for me to understand another English-speaker, I must know the rules governing the use of the words he employs; I must know to what words like "table" or "chair" or "shyness" refer; I must also know how to determine whether "Angela sailed into Portsmouth in great style" is to be taken metaphorically or literally; I must also be able to tell whether "John knows everything" is to be taken as a straight assertion or as a sarcastic criticism. In the case of written texts, I must know how to tell whether *Animal Farm* is a children's story or a political satire, and whether a poem is just about the changing seasons or is also about the shifting patterns of human feelings. All these points depend on the various conventions which English-speakers employ in communicating with one another. In the case of an ancient language, the evidence upon which our understanding of these conventions is based may be inadequate, or, on occasion, simply non-existent.

Secondly, it may well be the case that a written sentence, or even a series of sentences, could be ambiguous as it stands, but be quite unambiguous when spoken or written on a particular occasion. Thus, even in English, the sentence "England collapses before Australian attack" could refer to cricket, or to a military disaster; but the same sentence written on a sports' page of a newspaper could have only one meaning. By the same token, our understanding of an ancient text will depend on the amount of evidence at our disposal about the occasion and circumstances in which it was originally uttered. This evidence, too, may be seriously incomplete.

Examples of difficulties of both these kinds are not hard to find in the New Testament generally, and in New Testament ethics in particular. Kierkegaard once attacked New Testament scholars for refusing to translate *misein* as "hate" in the saying about "hating one's father and mother," and wished to insist that the word be taken in its full literal sense.[2] Scholars are still not entirely clear about what is meant by *porneia* in the exception-clause to the divorce-saying in Matthew's gospel.[3] We find it hard, on occasions, to be sure whether a contemporary would have understood that a particular saying was meant literally or as a rhetorical exaggeration. We may be fairly sure about being told to cut off a hand, or pluck out an eye, if these are sources of scandal to us—though Kierkegaard might once again accuse us of watering down the clear meaning just because we find it intolerable. But are we so sure whether the command not to resist one who is evil is to be taken as a practical guide to our behavior in the face of aggression? And is it not said in the same style, and in the same context, as the commands never to use any oath whatever, and not to get divorced and remarry? Does Luke's gospel mean to say that in order to be a disciple a rich man must sell everything that he has? Does John's gospel teach only that we must love our fellow-Christians, and not our enemies? Does Matthew's gospel require us to keep every jot and tittle of the Law of Moses? These are matters of literary convention and usage, and for many of them we simply have insufficient evidence to be sure of the answer.

In short, we are simply at too great a remove from the texts to be entirely confident that we have understood them correctly. After all, it is only in comparatively recent times that Christians (and even now, not all Christians) have recognized that the author of Genesis was not describing the process of creation. And theologians who would never dream of taking a literalist view of Genesis 1, Jonah, or Mark 13, are still perfectly capable of being quite uncritical when it comes to New Testament ethics (or, for that matter, New Testament accounts of miracles). Fundamentalism, which in the end tries to deny that exegetical problems exist, still dies hard.

The claim that the biblical tradition can function as the ultimate court of appeal in ethics would be somewhat more plausible were it the case that we could always guarantee to have properly understood the New Testament text. In fact, no such guarantee is available. And even if it were, it is quite obvious that the New Testament simply does not consider many of the moral problems with which we are faced. It is silent on the development of nuclear power stations, genetic engineering, birth control, organ transplants, and the moral dilemmas arising directly from the industrial revolution and the rise of modern capitalism. It says nothing about the proper ownership of the means of production. To be sure, texts can be found teaching that we must love others as we do ourselves, and that those are blessed who hunger and thirst after justice, or who practice the corporal works of mercy. But none of these texts will suffice as an ultimate court of appeal to settle all our ethical problems.

Hermeneutical Difficulties

Whereas exegetical problems are concerned with understanding the text, I take hermeneutical problems to be concerned with its application. Once again, the analogy with language is helpful.

Mastering a foreign language is one thing, translating it into one's own is quite another, bringing with it a new set of difficulties. Sometimes, as perhaps with the German word *Gemütlichkeit,* there may simply be no synonym in English. Sometimes, there may be an equivalent but not strictly a synonym; for example, it may be that a Spanish proverb to the effect that one cannot both toll the bells and walk in the procession is roughly an equivalent of what we (more earthy and less spiritual?) English mean by "You can't have your cake and eat it." Again, we may be deceived by etymological similarity into assuming that we have found a synonym when we have not, as when a schoolboy takes Virgil to have described Aeneas as pious. I think that the same kind of problem arises when we try to identify in one culture an action or a situation which is the same as one in another culture. Quine has, I believe, shown convincingly that problems of synonymy cannot be solved in any very simple way.[4] Though I would not subscribe to his more radical conclusions which might suggest that translation is always, and ineradicably, indeterminate, and that we might have no means of deciding between different incompatible translations, I do think he has shown that we cannot decide between them just on the evidence internal to the text itself. Assumptions have to be made which cannot of themselves be justified on the evidence of the text.

The importance of these considerations for the use of the biblical tradition as an authority in ethics is very considerable. In particular, I think it can be shown that in order to understand the import of New Testament ethics (even assuming that the exegetical problems have been successfully overcome) for the moral problems of our own day, specifically *moral* assumptions must be made which cannot themselves be justified from within the New Testament text itself. It cannot be taken for granted, and cannot be proved from the text alone, that we have found correct synonyms for the moral words which they contain, nor that we have correctly identified in our own culture the problems and situations which correspond to the problems and situations dealt with in the ethical passages in the New Testament. There are serious problems in transferring New Testament solutions straight into our own day and cultures; and these problems become quite insoluble in principle if (as is implied by the view that the New Testament is the only ultimate court of appeal) we are forbidden to make any moral assumptions not already given in the text.

Some examples may be helpful at this point. Jesus himself, and most if not all the New Testament writers, developed their teaching on marriage in the context of monogamous cultures. There is no automatic way of deciding, from this teaching alone, what they would have said in a polygamous society. Again, Jesus referred to the practice of divorce in earlier Israelite tradition and ascribed it to the necessity created by the hardness of heart of the people in question. He taught a very much stricter doctrine to his disciples. From the text alone, it remains an open question what he would have said had he been speaking to us. Similarly, it does not automatically follow that Paul would have told 19th-century plantation workers in Mississippi to be obedient to their masters, and been content simply to leave it at that, just because he was willing to take that line with the slaves of the Roman Empire. It does not automatically follow that the position of women with regard to their husbands or to their position in the Christian community should automatically remain in our day as it was at the time Paul was writing his letters. It may even be that certain elements of New Testament ethics were written in the belief that the world was shortly to come to an end. Such an *Interimsethik,* obviously, need not still apply to us who no longer share that belief.

In order even to begin to deal with questions like "What would Jesus (or Paul, or whoever) have said on this topic had he been speaking to Christians of our own day?" we have to have some way of determining which differences between New Testament times and our own are significant, and which are not. Thus, we might conclude that the differences between having several wives in contemporary West Africa and having several wives in 1st-century Palestine are important, and that the New Testament teaching on marriage would have to be expressed very differently in contemporary West African cultures. We might be of the opinion that slavery in the Roman Empire was so different from slavery as practised in 19th-century Mississippi that Paul could not possibly simply have enjoined obedience on the plantation workers. We might notice that the early Church took a very liberal line when faced with the problems of "translating" Jewish Christianity into a Gentile Greek culture, at least so far as the observance of the Mosaic Law was concerned. But even that will not suffice to prove that equally liberal solutions can be applied to the other problems I have mentioned, unless it is also proved that those problems are comparable in the relevant respects to the problems facing Paul on his missionary journeys.

Now, it is plain that the New Testament texts nowhere set out any method of deciding which circumstances are morally significant and which are not. They do not always, or even usually, set out which features of the contemporary problem were taken to be significant by the writers themselves. To decide which differences are, and which are not, significant demands further moral reflection which, without vicious circularity, cannot itself be based on the authority of the New Testament. In short, it demands the exercise of our own independent moral reasoning, no doubt assisted by grace. It is thus wholly misleading to suggest that the biblical tradition can be appealed to as the ultimate authority in ethics over and against our own moral reasoning, or that our own moral reasoning must itself be based on revelation as it is transmitted by the New Testament texts. The suggestion that, in contrast to the obscurity or futility of our own moral reasoning, we have clear and independent access to the revealed will of God in the biblical texts totally ignores the most elementary pitfalls of interpretation. Even the briefest consideration of the problems of hermeneutics makes it clear that the application of the New Testament to our own ethical problems would be quite impossible in default of other moral assumptions which could be defended on independent grounds. It follows that the authority of the biblical tradition cannot, for us, be ultimate.

Theological Difficulties

In a much more tentative way, I wish to raise a third kind of difficulty against the appeal to the New Testament as the ultimate authority in ethics. Although this difficulty is of central importance, it does not seem to me to have received the attention it deserves. I am not myself at all sure about the grounds on which it might be settled, and must content myself with an account of the issues as I see them, in the hope that others can take the matter further.

The Second Vatican Council taught that the books of the Bible are inspired, and therefore inerrant, concerning "that truth which God wanted put into the sacred writings for the sake of our salvation."[5] This is not, of course, to say that some passages of the Bible are inspired and others are not, but rather to say that in every passage we must try to discern what that truth is which God wished to be expressed there for the sake of our salvation. Now, it would be generally agreed that assertions about physics or astronomy or geography or history are not in themselves and as such instances of what I shall briefly term "salvation-truths," although they may well be made in the course of attempts by the biblical writers to communicate salvation-truths. I wish, then, to raise the question about the status of statements in the Bible about ethics.

It seems at first sight natural enough to assume that ethics is much more intimately connected with salvation than is physics or astronomy, and to conclude from this that the ethical assertions in the Bible fall under the category of teaching which is inspired and therefore inerrant. After all, as I have argued above, it is a salient characteristic of the God of the Judaeo-Christian tradition that he is morally concerned about this world, and that the response he asks for from his followers is, in part, a moral response. He does not necessarily require us to be good physicists, but he does require us to be good men.

This position is traditional, and, to my knowledge, has never been seriously challenged. It may well be correct. Still, I believe that some questions can be raised about it which need to be satisfactorily answered before the traditional position can be maintained without hesitation.

In the first place, it is clearly not traditional Christian teaching that we must all be in possession of correct answers to all our moral problems in order to be saved. If such were the case, we might also have expected the biblical writers, especially the New Testament writers, to exhibit a much greater urgency than they do about the whole range of moral problems. In fact, the impression their writings give is that morality is for the most part not their first concern, and that when they do consider moral issues it is usually because these issues have caused controversy or division in the Christian community. Occasionally, too, as in the case of Paul's teaching on the eating of meat offered to idols, the moral issue has immediate dogmatic implications. But there is in the New Testament as a whole no systematic attempt at a complete moral teaching, and little sign that the writers felt that it was particularly important that they should provide such teaching.

Moreover, it is worth looking carefully at the way in which moral issues are introduced into the New Testament writings. The impression is quite clearly given that the writers expect the Christian to take moral issues seriously. They insist that moral seriousness is a condition for entry into the Kingdom, although each individual writer tends to have his own particular emphasis on what such moral seriousness will involve. It seems to me, then, clearly to be a salvation-truth that God requires us to be morally good, and to make serious efforts to become so. Furthermore, it seems to me clearly false to say that God requires us never to make a mistake about what we ought to do. The crucial question, then, is this: are particular teachings on particular moral issues taught as salvation-truths, or are they offered simply because it is in general a salvation-truth that to take such issues seriously is required of us by our Christian belief? More detailed argument than I have seen seems to me to be required to establish that the individual moral assertions in the New Testament are salvation-truths rather than the opinions of the writers offered in the course of reinforcing the general truth that our moral behavior is intimately connected with the Kingdom. In short, I would welcome attempts to spell out in detail the traditional position that revelation is concerned with the details of morality, and not just with the general importance of being morally good. Unless this is done satisfactorily, the question of using revelation as the ultimate authority in ethics simply does not arise at all.

This issue is independent of the argument of the two preceding sections, which may now be briefly summarized. The appeal to biblical tradition as ultimately authoritative in contrast to the uncertainty or impossibility of alternative groundings for ethics cannot be justified, just because of the very nature of that tradition itself. Firstly, the biblical writings simply do not contain solutions to most of our moral problems; secondly, the evidence at our disposal for understanding the meaning of the biblical writings is not in every case adequate; thirdly, and most important of all, the process of interpreting the biblical tradition in terms which are applicable to our culture and circumstances is one which demands that further moral assumptions be made for which the text itself cannot provide any justification. This hermeneutical problem is quite a general one, and does not apply only to ethics, but to the interpretation and translation of any text from a different language or culture. Hence, the attempt to use the biblical tradition as ultimately authoritative is viciously circular, since it must invoke precisely those processes of independent moral reasoning which it is the purpose of the attempt to circumvent.

THE APPEAL TO SUBSEQUENT CHRISTIAN TRADITION

Can it be argued that the difficulties encountered in the above discussion of the biblical tradition can be overcome by appeal to subsequent tradition, and in particular by appeal to the texts in which its moral views and its interpretation of the biblical texts are expressed? It might be thought, for instance, that if we believe in the guidance of the Holy Spirit in the Church, especially if we consider the strong form of this belief in the Catholic tradition, any questions we might have about the meaning and interpretation of the biblical tradition and its applicability to our own day could be resolved by considering the way it has been understood and used by the Church throughout its history.

I do not think that this position can be maintained. There is a general reason why we should not expect it to be true. Even on the "highest" view of the guidance of the Spirit in the Church, this guidance will not be any stronger than that given by the Spirit to the inspired writers (if I may use the phrase as a convenient shorthand) of the biblical texts. If the fact that the biblical texts are inspired does not remove all our difficulties about the meaning and application of those texts to our own day, I do not see how the guidance of the Spirit in the Church will remove our difficulties in understanding and applying the documents of Christian tradition.

More specifically, the documents of Christian tradition present precisely the same problems as the biblical writings. We believe that they continue to hand down to us the revelation which God gave us in his Son. They do this by the very fact that they are the reflections of men, guided by the Spirit, on the events of the life of Jesus and on the earlier tradition in which those events were first reflected upon and interpreted. It follows that to arrive at a precise understanding of the meaning of these documents requires a study of the context, conventions, idiom, and presuppositions of their authors. This purely exegetical task is far from easy. Moreover, we are well aware that the documents of the Christian tradition are influenced also by all too human considerations. Their authors were men of their times, subject to the prejudices, cultural limitations and moral fashions of their age. Frequently, too, they had to labor under the handicap of an inadequate exegetical method so far as their interpretation of the biblical writings was concerned. Their arguments may be hard for us to grasp because they are couched in terms of philosophical positions which we might find unhelpful or confused. I myself, for instance, would not share Augustine's Platonism nor the moral and ascetical conclusions which follow from it; and although I would be much more in sympathy with Aquinas' Aristotelian approach to ethics, I feel that he, too, has been misunderstood and misrepresented by many moralists in the last hundred years or so. And in any event, Platonism, Aristotelianism, or linguistic analysis are not God's revelation. For all these reasons, it is plain that the documents of later Christian tradition will both communicate and obscure God's revelation from our point of view.

Hence, just as in the case of the biblical writings, we have the hermeneutical problem of knowing just how their authors would have expressed themselves had they been writing for us, confronted with our problems and our situation. Would they still have condemned the lending of money at interest? Would they still consider it possible to meet the conditions for a just war? Would they still have been unsympathetic to democratic forms of government? Would they still have been willing to consider abortion less reprehensible at an early stage in pregnancy? Once again, the point at issue is not directly to answer these questions one way or the other; the point is that in order to justify any answer, we need additional moral arguments, over and above the mere fact that certain views were taught at a particular time and place, or that they were generally accepted by the Christians at that time. These additional moral arguments cannot themselves, without vicious circularity, consist in further appeals to tradition. Fundamentalism with regard to subsequent Christian tradition is just as untenable, for the same reasons, as is fundamentalism with regard to the biblical writings themselves. It follows that tradition cannot legitimately be considered as the ultimate authority in ethics, or as a way of avoiding the necessity for the ordinary processes of moral reasoning.

THE APPEAL TO PERSONAL REVELATION

A discussion of the appeal to personal revelation in a chapter about the authority of Christian tradition might seem to be something of a digression. On the other hand, there are some Christian traditions where stress is laid on the personal relationship between the believer and God, and in which it is held that it is in this relationship alone that God's will is ultimately revealed. Several current discussions of Christian ethics seem to presuppose a view of this kind. In any event, it comes here in the argument, since I believe that it raises just the same kinds of issues as those we have already been considering.

The position I wish to criticize represents yet another attempt to appeal to revelation to the exclusion of ordinary moral reasoning, and relies for its theological underpinning upon the Christian belief that the Spirit is present in all believers, prompting and guiding them in their Christian vocation. This position is often reinforced, for example in Brunner[6] and to some extent in Bultmann,[7] by appeal to the biblical teaching on the New Law, or, as in some passages of Rahner,[8] by the view that discernment of spirits is to be the distinctively Christian method of deciding where our vocation lies, in contrast to the ordinary process of moral reasoning through universal principles.

The classical exposition of this view is to be found in Kierkegaard's *Fear and Trembling.* Kierkegaard considers the dilemma facing Abraham when he was called upon by God to sacrifice his son Isaac, and uses this biblical story to illustrate what he takes to be a fundamental point in Christian ethics. Kierkegaard is perfectly clear that ordinary moral reasoning would unequivocally condemn as murder the sacrifice of one's own son. But he points out that Abraham's dilemma is not that of the ordinary tragic hero, caught between conflicting moral obligations. In Abraham's case, the conflict is between morality and his duty toward God. The ethical code in which Abraham believes is precisely the source of his temptation, which Abraham can overcome only by a supreme act of faith. In his personal relationship to God in faith Abraham can see that he has a duty to transcend ordinary moral reasoning in order to do God's will. God's call to him is, in the depths of their personal relationship, self-authenticating. Abraham's greatness consists in his willingness to respond to this personal revelation of God in defiance of his ordinary moral convictions.

The logic of this position is the same as that of the two views we have already examined. It is assumed that there are some dilemmas about what we ought to do (Kierkegaard could not, for the reason just given, describe them as *moral* dilemmas) which cannot be correctly solved by the application of ordinary moral reasoning, and which are resolved only in the light of revelation. God's will cannot be reliably discovered by moral argument, but, at least in some cases, only when God explicitly discloses himself, revealing man's true destiny as he revealed Abraham's.

The problem with Kierkegaard's position, as with any position which stresses the uniqueness of the vocation of the individual Christian, is that it proves far too much, and in so doing proves nothing at all. One major check on any alleged revelation is, as I have argued above, our ordinary moral convictions. Once this check is removed, it is hard to see any reliable way of distinguishing between genuine revelations of God's will and sincere but mistaken personal convictions. If the vocation of the individual Christian is unique, then, *ex hypothesi,* there is nothing that can be said *in principle* about how he ought to live, and no way of showing that *any* decision he feels called upon to make, however outlandish it might appear to us, is not part of his unique vocation from God. Once we are asked to believe that God could will even the sacrifice of one's son as a test of faith, running counter to our deepest moral convictions, there is no limit to what such a God might not require. We are but a short step from the fully voluntarist picture of God which was rejected at the beginning of this chapter. I think this is the inevitable conclusion of locating authority ultimately in revelation rather than in the ordinary process of moral reasoning whose authority is logically prior to the acceptance and interpretation of any revelation.

CONCLUSION

We are now in a position to sum up the arguments of this chapter as a whole. Throughout, I have been arguing against the position that Christian tradition can properly be taken as the *ultimate* authoritative court of appeal in Christian ethics. I have not considered as yet other ways in which the appeal to Christian tradition might be made, or other ways in which its authority might be understood.

I have argued that it is not necessary to take revelation as ultimately authoritative just in order to avoid the Pelagian view that fallen man is perfectly capable of responding to God on his own initiative. The proponent of a natural law theory of ethics, and indeed any Christian moral philosopher, has no need to claim that his moral reflections take place independently of God and his grace. His claim is simply that his moral theory does not ultimately depend upon knowledge of the way in which God has revealed himself in Christ, as that knowledge is mediated to us by the tradition of Christian belief.

I have argued further that a correct understanding of the nature of Christian tradition, whether in the Bible or in later writings, makes it clear that this tradition cannot be ultimately authoritative for our moral reasoning. The documents of this tradition are not simply limpid expressions of the mind of God immediately accessible to all men at all times. God's revelation of himself is not fundamentally a set of utterances, but the person of his Son. The documents of tradition are interpretations of that basic revelation made by human beings under the inspiration and guidance of God, for particular audiences at particular times in history. To discover through them what God is saying to *us* in Christ, we must respond to them with our limited human minds, and with the normal means God places at our disposal. So far as morality is concerned, this response must inevitably include moral reflection which is not in turn dependent on the revelation it is trying to interpret. This moral reflection is epistemologically prior to our appeal to revelation, which cannot therefore be ultimately authoritative. To deny this is to be either voluntarist or fundamentalist or both, and, to that extent, is to subvert both the Christian picture of God and the Christian view of the human context in which he makes himself known.

The conclusion of this argument is not that the Christian moralist should not at any point consider the moral teaching of Christian tradition, nor that this tradition should in no way function as an authority for him. I believe it should, at least provided that there are good grounds for the belief that Christian revelation does contain ethical teaching. The conclusion is rather that an independent morality is an essential tool in interpreting Christian tradition, since it enables us to distinguish the voice of God from the human voices through which he speaks to us in the tradition of the Church. To the extent that we do succeed in discovering in the tradition of the

Church what God is saying to us, we shall do so by the patient methods of moral philosophy which enabled us to hear him in the first place.

I have argued, finally, that there are no good theological reasons for supposing that reflection on our human nature cannot enable us to arrive at moral truth. In particular, the Christian doctrine of original sin should not be understood in a way which makes moral reflection impossible, or in some way inherently misleading. On the other hand, although I have, as I believe, shown the necessity for independent moral reflection if there is to be a Christian ethics, I have as yet given no account of how such reflection might proceed, and on what grounds it might ultimately be based if its ultimate basis is not to be the teaching of Christian tradition.

Notes

1. Barth, ch. 8, pp. 509–732. References in the notes are to the bibliography at the end of the chapter. The bibliography is arranged alphabetically by author.
2. Kierkegaard, pp. 103–109.
3. E.g. most recently, Fitzmyer.
4. Quine, ch. 2, esp. pp. 73–79.
5. *Dei Verbum,* III, 11.
6. Brunner, pp. 78–93.
7. Bultmann, ch. 3.
8. Rahner, and the reply by Dorr.

Select Bibliography

K. Barth, *Church Dogmatics,* II, 2 (Edinburgh, T. & T. Clark, 1957).
E. Brunner, *The Divine Imperative* (London, Lutterworth Press, 1942).

R. Bultmann, *Jesus and the Word* (London, Fontana Books, 1958).

D.J. Dorr, "Karl Rahner's Formal Existentialist Ethics," *Irish Theological Quarterly* 36 (1969) pp. 221–29.

J. Fitzmeyer, "The Matthaean Divorce Texts and Some New Palestinian Evidence," *Theological Studies* 37 (1976) pp. 197–226.

J. Fuchs, *Human Values and Christianity* (London, Gill & Macmillan, 1970).

J.M. Gustafson, *Can Ethics be Christian?* (Chicago, University of Chicago Press, 1975);

———, "The Place of Scripture in Christian Ethics: A Methodological Study," *Interpretation* 24 (1970) pp. 430–55.

G.J. Hughes, "A Christian Basis for Ethics," *The Heythrop Journal* 13 (1972) pp. 27–43.

S. Kierkegaard, *Fear and Trembling,* trans. R. Payne (Oxford, Oxford University Press, 1939).

B. Lindars, "The Bible and Christian Ethics," in G. Dunstan (ed.), *Duty and Discernment* (London, S.C.M. Press, 1975) pp. 64–75;

———, "Imitation of God and Imitation of Christ," *ibid.,* pp. 100–10.

W.V.O. Quine, *Word and Object* (Cambridge, M.I.T. Press, 1960).

K. Rahner, *The Dynamic Element in the Church,* Pt. 1 (London, Burns & Oates, 1964).

N.H.G. Robinson, *The Groundwork of Christian Ethics* (London, Collins, 1971).

J.T. Sanders, *Ethics in the New Testament* (London, S.C.M. Press, 1975).

M. Simpson, "A Christian Basis for Ethics?" *The Heythrop Journal* 15 (1974) pp. 285–97.

K. Ward, *Ethics and Christianity* (London, Geo. Allen & Unwin, 1970).

Nature, Reason, and the Task of Theological Ethics

Stanley Hauerwas

This chapter first appeared in *The Peaceable Kingdom: A Primer in Christian Ethics* in 1983.

---

1. THE TASK OF CHRISTIAN ETHICS

While Christian ethics is at once descriptive and normative, the interrelation between these tasks is complex and not easily stated. However, before such questions can even be investigated we need to remind ourselves that Christian ethics is not any distinct discipline but varies from time to time and from one to another ecclesial tradition. As we shall see, how Christian ethics is understood has always been dependent on its context in a specific tradition.

The development of moral theology in Roman Catholicism through the centuries became tied to the penitential system. Moral theologians aided confessional practice as they developed the casuistical detail necessary to sustain and inform the priestly function. Thus the study of moral theology was primarily a task performed by priests and through their preaching and confessional practice they helped the community determine minimum standards of behavior. Such an approach was not minimalistic in principle but became so precisely because the primary concern of the confessional was with avoiding evil.[1]

Although moral theologians served an ecclesial function, their work was thought to be based primarily on "natural law." This may well suggest that the alleged transparency of the natural law norms reflects more the consensus within the church than the universality of the natural law itself. I suspect that "natural law," rather than indicating agreement between Christian and non-Christian, served to note agreements within a widely scattered and pluralistic Christian community. This is substantiated by the fact that the power of natural law as a systematic idea was developed in and for the Roman imperium and then for "Christendom." Thus, ironically, "natural law" became the means of codifying a particular moral tradition.

Because of the very problems it was asked to address, this form of Christian ethics tended to be act-oriented. Though it was often systemized in the language of the virtues, it evidenced little concern for or analysis of the actual development of virtue but instead concentrated on the fulfillment of specified duties. Moral theologians came to look more like lawyers than theologians. They were people skilled in adjudication of cases for the troubled conscience (no mean or small skill).

Moreover, even though they were called "theologians," these moralists seldom were required to make direct theological appeals. Theological claims set the backdrop that made their work intelligible—e.g., God is the creator of a rational universe and moral law can be thus known without the aid of revelation. Beyond that, little theological reflection was required for explicating the nature of the Christian moral life. Thus "theology" in the phrase "moral theology" denoted an unquestioned ecclesial assumption rather than an enlivening practice.

In fairness it should be said that Catholicism included other ways of thinking about the moral life, for example, spiritual and ascetical theology. Yet these forms of literature were not considered "ethics" since they did not deal with specific judgments of right and wrong. Moreover, much of the ascetical literature was devotional in character and, thus, was not meant as a means to explore systematic issues.

In contrast, theological issues always have been at the forefront of Protestant ethical reflection. In fact Protestants did not develop any specialized discipline called "Christian ethics" until recently. Of course they did not have the confessional, as did Catholics, but that was not the decisive reason for their lack of any explicit discipline called Christian ethics. Rather the Protestant emphasis on God's free grace made "ethics" an inherently doubtful enterprise, since "ethics," from such a perspective, appeared as an attempt to presumptively determine God's will or to substitute works for faith.

Indeed some could go as far as to suggest that ethics is sin insofar as it tries to anticipate God's will.[2]

This is not to say that there was no concern for ethics in the Protestant tradition; rather it was included as part of the theologians' task. Thus "ethics" involved discussion of the relation of law and gospel, creation and redemption, faith and works, the status of the orders of creation, and the nature of man as sinner and redeemed. While such problems are central to the ethical task, theological discussions of this sort often failed to deal with the kind of moral concerns and issues that constitute how men and women in fact live. Certainly individual theologians often provided compelling accounts of human existence, but they were more likely to be interested in the systematic relations between the theological concepts than in the practical force such concepts might have for directing lives. Interestingly enough, the more concrete form of analysis undertaken to guide behavior among Protestants tended to be done pastorally and, as a result, was often not informed by explicit theological convictions.

Therefore, even though Protestant ethical reflection seemed richer theologically than Catholicism's, it tended to be as culturally assimilationist as the natural law tradition. In the absence of any disciplined and practical form of ethical reflection, Protestants could only assume that "Christian ethics" was little different from the consensus of whatever culture they found themselves a part. This is most strikingly illustrated by Protestantism's inability to be more than national churches.

In fairness it ought to be said that Christian ethics appears in a more distinct light in Calvinist, Anabaptist, and Anglican traditions, due to their stress on sanctification. Each of these traditions assumes that God's activity on our behalf entails a particular way of life that can be spelled out in some detail. Yet although such an assumption often produced reflection on the moral life meant to inform Christian consciences, it rarely produced a disciplined study called "Christian ethics" in any way comparable to Catholic moral theology.

In fact the very idea of Christian ethics is a relatively new phenomenon. In America it seems to have been primarily an outgrowth of the Social Gospel movement. It occasioned courses in Protestant seminaries dealing with "Christian sociology." Soon internal criti cism of some of the enthusiasm of the Social Gospel required such courses to take a more reflective and critical standpoint. Thus the work of H. R. Niebuhr represents the attempt to make Christian ethics a discipline whose task is to clarify the moral implications of Christian theological convictions.[3] Such work is seen to be pri marily analytical and descriptive, but without explicit normative prescriptions.

This brief and inadequate attempt to characterize Christian ethics in Catholic and Protestant traditions is meant only to make us aware that the activity we call "Christian ethics" is anything but singular or clear. For example, it is very interesting that we have no "Christian ethics" in the early church. Nowhere in Scripture do we get a distinction between religious belief and behavior. The Sermon on the Mount is hardly Jesus' "ethic," but is part and parcel of his proclamation of the coming kingdom. Paul's "ethics" is not really concerned with the status of the law. Scripture creates a problem in that its integration of belief and behavior makes it difficult to de- scribe a "biblical ethic," let alone to discover in what manner it is still relevant for our current reflection.[4]

Neither is there much evidence that any of the church fathers thought it necessary to do ethics as an explicit task. Their explicit ethical reflections were primarily occasioned by their pastoral con- cerns. Thus they seldom give systematic presentations of the Chris- tian life but engage in a sort of ad hoc reflection, since their primary concern was to respond to the needs of a particular community. Indeed, there is something to be said for still labeling ethics a pas- toral discipline.

Nor do we get "ethics" as separate treatises in the highly system- atic Middle Ages. Aquinas never stopped to say: "Now I am going to do a little ethics." The "ethics" he does in the Prima-Secundae and Secunda-Secundae of the *Summa Theologica* is but the continua- tion of his theological portrayal of God's extension of himself to man so that man might have a way to God.[5] "Ethics" is not done as an independent discipline, but because such considerations are nec- essary to depict our journey with God.

So what are we to make of the fact that we now have a discipline called Christian ethics, that practitioners are armed with Ph.D.'s in the subject and are ready to apply their skills? Why should this be the case? Not every tradition feels the need to develop a distinct discipline called "ethics." Perhaps part of the reason for the concern with Christian ethics has to do with the cultural situation depicted in chapter 1. Because many of the "natural" relations that people used to assume between religious belief and behavior have been broken, we hope that if we think hard enough about those relations we can again reestablish their essential connection. Such a task is unfortunately doomed to failure. For finally these relations are not conceptual, but practical. Christian ethics, as a critical and reflective discipline, cannot restore what only a community can hold together. Christian ethics, insofar as it is an intelligible discipline at all, is dependent on a community's wisdom about how certain actions are prohibited or enjoined for the development of a particular kind of people.

That such is the case, however, helps us understand better the task of Christian ethics. For it makes clear that Christian ethics is not an abstract discipline primarily concerned with "ideas." Rather it is a form of reflection in service to a community, and it derives its character from the nature of that community's convictions. Theological claims are fundamentally practical and Christian ethics is but that form of theological reflection which attempts to explicate this inherently practical nature.

1.1 Christian Ethics Is Theology

As should be obvious from the above I have little interest in trying to claim that Christian ethics is a coherent subdiscipline within the wider discipline of theology. Indeed, I think in many ways the separation of ethics from theology has had unfortunate consequences. Ethics is but one aspect of the theological task and little hangs on whether it has integrity as a specifiable discipline.

Yet it is important not to be too humble about this. For at the same time it is crucial that Christian ethics not be understood as an afterthought to systematic theology. If theological convictions are meant to construe the world—that is, if they have the character of practical discourse—then ethics is involved at the beginning, not the end, of theology. Theological discourse is distorted when portrayed as a kind of primitive metaphysics—a view all too common among Protestants as well as Catholics. That is, Catholics often assume that one must start with fundamental theology, which investigates the conditions of truthfulness, the metaphysical presuppositions (natural theology) which make theology at all possible. Then one proceeds to systematic theology, which deals with revelational claims such as trinity, creation, redemption, Christology, church, and so on. Finally, when that work is done, one turns to ethics on the assumption that only when one's basic beliefs are clear and well-founded can one consider their moral implications. Ironically this picture usually results in a theological justification for basing ethics on a natural law methodology, with the result that theological convictions about Jesus are not directly relevant to concrete ethical analysis.

Even though Protestants have been less confident in natural theology or a natural law ethic, they also assume theology begins primarily with prolegomena. Also, especially since the nineteenth century, they have tried to prepare the way for doing theology with anthropology, attempting to show the intelligibility of theological claims. Often what was done in that respect was "ethical" insofar as ethics is understood to involve accounts of human existence, but this often resulted in theology being no more than, in Karl Barth's memorable phrase, "talking about man in a loud voice."

In contrast to both these approaches I wish to show that Christian ethics is not what one does after one gets clear on everything else, or after one has established a starting point or basis of theology; rather it is at the heart of the theological task. For theology is a practical activity concerned to display how Christian convictions construe the self and world.[6] Therefore theological claims concerning the relation of creation and redemption are already ethical claims, since they situate how one works methodologically. Put more strongly, ethics has been artificially separated from the central theological task exactly because of the abstract way in which the relation between creation and redemption, nature and grace, has been understood.

1.2 Nature and Grace: Why Being Christian
Is Not Equivalent to Being Human

The abstractions "nature" and "grace" in particular have distorted how ethics has been undertaken in the Catholic tradition. This is true despite the fact that there is a concern afoot in the Catholic Church that moral theology be more explicitly theological. For example, the "Decree of Priestly Formation" of Vatican II explicitly charged: "Its [moral theology's] scientific exposition should be more thoroughly nourished by scriptural teaching. It should show the nobility of the Christian vocation of the faithful and their obligation to bring forth fruit in charity for the life of the world."[7] Yet the theological presuppositions on which the structure of Roman Catholic ethics is built assume that is exactly what cannot be done. Unfortunately, much of contemporary Catholic ethics, while often beginning with some theological rhetoric, continues to rest finally on an anthropological foundation. For example Timothy O'Connell says,

> ... the fundamental ethical command imposed on the Christian is precisely to be what he or she is. "Be human." That is what God asks of us, no more and no less. Imitate Christ, and do this by seeking to be as faithful to the human vocation as he was. Love your neighbor as yourself. Do unto others as you would have them do unto you. Christian ethics is human ethics, no more and no less. . . . Christians are unconditionally humanists; that is our pride and our privileged vocation. . . . Thus in a certain sense, moral theology is not theology at all. It is moral philosophy, pursued by persons who are believers. Moral theology is a science that seeks to benefit from all the sources of wisdom within our world.[8]

Such a position is bound to use Christ to underwrite the integrity of the "natural," since he is seen as epitomizing the fulfillment of the human vocation. Again O'Connell says, "It is the faithful articulation of the meaning of Jesus' call that we should 'be what we are.' "[9] Apart from the fact that this seems to be very bad advice—as Mark Twain observed, the worst advice you can give anyone is to be himself—such an approach jeopardizes the attempt to make theological convictions more ethically relevant.

In fairness it should be noted that O'Connell has a chapter dealing with "elements" of a biblical morality. The covenant, kingdom, repentance, discipleship, law, and love each receive brief treatment and review. But these "elements" are not methodologically decisive for how O'Connell does ethics.[10] That such is the case, however, is not accidental, but structured into the way O'Connell understands what Christianity is about. Christian ethics is human ethics because the particularity of Jesus, his historicity as God's decisive eschatological actor, has been lost. Thus, according to O'Connell,

> What must not be debated is the fact that incarnation *could* have taken place apart from original sin. Inasmuch as this world was created as a potential receptacle for the divinity of God's Word, incarnation was possible from the first moment of creation. Therefore, even if the *function* of incarnation was (at least in part) the rectification of the evil situation of mankind, such was not the *essence* of the incarnation. No, the essence of incarnation was simply the self-gift of God to his people, the union of God, through his Word, with the good world which had come from his creative hand.[11]

Apart from the dubious wisdom of talking about the "*essence* of the incarnation," the problem with such Christology is that it results in making the events and actions of Jesus' life seem accidental. Incarnation is not an adequate summary of the story. Rather "incarnation" is but one of the conceptual reminders that the church has developed to help us tell well the story of the man who was nothing less than the God-appointed initiator of the new kingdom.

This kind of theological abstractionism is a characteristic of both Catholic and Protestant ethics. Theological concepts are reifications; they are taken as the "meat," the point, of Christian convictions. But as abstractions both "nature" and "grace" require more determinative narrative display.[12] There is no creation without the covenant with Israel, there is no redemption that does not take its meaning from Jesus' cross.[13] Neither are they general concepts that straightforwardly describe or gain their meaning from human existence per se; rather the concepts of both creation and redemption are aids to train us to be creatures of a gracious God who has called us to be citizens in a community of the redeemed.

When nature-grace, creation-redemption are taken to be the primary data of theological reflection, once they are abstracted from the narrative and given a life of their own, a corresponding distortion in moral psychology seems to follow. Since the material content —that is, the rightness or wrongness of certain behavior—is derived from nature, Christian convictions at best only furnish a motivation for "morality." As Joseph Fuchs says,

> The specific and *decisively Christian* aspect of Christian morality is not to be sought first of all in the particularity of categorical values, virtues, and norms of various human activities. Rather it resides in the believer's fundamental Christian decision to accept God's love in Christ and respond to it as one who believes and loves, as one who assumes the responsibility for life in this world in imitation of Christ, that is, as one who has died with Christ and is risen with him in faith and sacrament thus becoming a new creation.[14]

Fuchs calls this "Christian intentionality" the "deepest and most challenging element of morality, which addresses the whole person, and not only the individual deed."[15] Such intentionality "pervades" particular categorical conduct, but it does not determine its content. "This means that truthfulness, uprightness, and faithfulness are not specifically Christian, but generally human values in what they materially say, and that we have reservations about lying and adultery not because we are Christians, but simply because we are human."[16] Thus the meaning of the "Christianum" for our concrete living is to be found in its "motivating power."[17]

But to reduce the "Christianum" to the motivational distorts our moral psychology since it presupposes that virtues such as truthfulness can be "objectively" characterized abstracted from how agents must learn to be truthful. Therefore the very integrity of self, the character required for moral agency, is lost. For, as we saw in the preceding chapter, our very ability to be moral agents is dependent on our having a character that forges a link between what we do and what we are.

Likewise, when Christian convictions are relegated to the "motivational" part of our lives the historical dimension of the self is irretrievably lost. We have character just to the extent that we can claim our history as our own, but when our actions are separated from our history, when we are only the "causes" of certain pieces of behavior, we lose exactly what is necessary to be historic. There is, perhaps, a correlation between Christian ethicists' penchant for theological abstractions divorced from their narrative context and the tendency to develop a "natural law" ethic that is free from historic communities.

But it may be objected that surely I am too hard on this attempt to reinterpret natural law in terms of "humanity," for it is surely a step in the right direction. What possibly could be wrong with the claim that to be Christian is to be fully human? No one wants to maintain that there is an essential discontinuity between God's creating and redeeming work, between nature and grace. Surely what it means to be Christian is but an intensification, not a denial, of what it means to be human.

Of course that is correct, but at issue is the methodological significance it has for ethical reflection. To be Christian is surely to fulfill the most profound human desires, but we do not know what such fulfillment means on the basis of those desires themselves. It is certainly right that life in Christ makes us more nearly what we should be, but that is not to say we must start with the human to determine what it means to be a disciple of Christ. While the way of life taught by Christ is meant to be an ethic for all people, it does not follow that we can know what such an ethic involves "objectively" by looking at the human.

Moreover such a view optimistically assumes that in fact we know morally in what such a universal or objective ethic consists. As we saw above, Fuchs has an extraordinary confidence that we are, in fact, in possession of common moral intuitions and values such as truthfulness, uprightness, and faithfulness. But he does not provide a concrete analysis of those "values" sufficient to indicate why the understanding of "truthfulness" differs from society to society. I have no reason to deny that human nature may well require a fundamental orientation to truth, but I do not think it possible to abstract such truthfulness from its various narrative contexts in order to make it the basis of a "universal" and "objective" ethic.

1.3 Church and World: The Ethics of a Critical Community

The affirmation that Christian ethics is human ethics contains yet another dubious assumption, this time about the relation of church and world. Richard McCormick, a Catholic moralist like O'Connell and Fuchs, says:

> Love and loyalty to Jesus Christ, the perfect man, sensitizes us to the meaning of persons. The Christian tradition is anchored in faith in the meaning and decisive significance of God's covenant with men, especially as manifested in the saving incarnation of Jesus Christ, his eschatological kingdom which is here aborning but will finally only be given. Faith in these events, love of and loyalty to this central figure, yields a decisive way of viewing and intending the world, of interpreting its meaning, of hierarching its values. In this sense the Christian tradition only illumines human values, supports them, provides a context for their reading at given points in history.[18]

But McCormick does not tell us what, if anything, such an illumination adds to the ethical; in effect he assumes that the primary task of Christian convictions is to "support" human values. But this assumption presumes that Christians will never be radically anti-world—that is, aligned against the prevailing values of their cultures. In fact behind the emphasis on the "human" character of Christian ethics is a deep fear that there might be a radical discontinuity between Christians and their culture. The result, I fear, is that too often natural law assumptions function as an ideology for sustaining some Christians' presuppositions that their societies—particularly societies of Western democracies—are intrinsic to God's purposes.[19]

McCormick says, "If Christian faith adds new material (concrete, behavioral) content to morality, then public policy is even more complex than it seems. For example, if Christians precisely as Christians know something about abortion that others cannot know unless they believe it as Christians, then in a pluralistic society there will be problems with discussion and decision in the public forum."[20] But why does he assume that the public forum is shaped by "human" values? Why does he assume that Christians should be able to contribute to the "public forum" on its own terms? What, for example, would have been the result if Christians had approached their entry into Roman society with McCormick's presuppositions? Isn't it possible that Christians, because of the ethos peculiar to their community, might find themselves in deep discontinuity with the ethos of a particular society?

Therefore the question of the distinctiveness of Christian ethics —or as I have put it, the insistence on the significance of the qualifier—also involves questions of the relationship of church to world. Indeed, how the task of Christian ethics is to be conceived is as much an ecclesiological issue as an issue having to do with nature and grace, creation and redemption. In fact, the issues are closely interrelated, since often how church is understood in relation to world follows from how nature and grace are thought to be related.

Of the two, however, the issue of the relation of church and world is more primary.[21] By virtue of the distinctive narrative that forms their community, Christians are distinct from the world. They are required to be nothing less than a sanctified people of peace who can live the life of the forgiven.[22] Their sanctification is not meant to sustain the judgment that they are "better" than non-Christians, but rather that they are charged to be faithful to God's calling of them as foretaste of the kingdom. In this sense sanctification is a life of service and sacrifice that the world cannot account for on its own grounds.

Therefore, claims for the distinctiveness of the church, and thus Christian ethics, are not attempts to underwrite assumptions of superiority or Christian dominance. Rather they are meant to remind Christians of the radicalness of the gospel. For the gospel cannot be adequately summed up by appeals that we should love our neighbor as ourselves but is meant to transform us by teaching us to be God's peaceable people.

Emphasis on the distinctiveness of Christian ethics does not deny that there are points of contact between Christian ethics and other forms of the moral life. While such points frequently exist, they are not sufficient to provide a basis for a "universal" ethic grounded in human nature per se. Attempts to secure such an ethic inevitably result in a minimalistic ethic and often one which gives support to forms of cultural imperialism. Indeed, when Christians assume that their particular moral convictions are independent of narrative, that they are justified by some universal standpoint free from history, they are tempted to imagine that those who do not share such an ethic must be particularly perverse and should be coerced to do what we know on universal grounds they really should want to do.

I do not mean to imply that adherents of a "natural law" ethic are inherently more violent, but rather that violence and coercion become conceptually intelligible from a natural law standpoint. The universal presumptions of natural law make it more difficult to accept the very existence of those who do not agree with us; such differences in principle should not exist. For example, natural law is often expressed today in the language of universal rights—the right to be free, to worship, to speak, to choose one's vocation, etc. Such language, at least in principle, seems to embody the highest human ideals. But it also facilitates the assumption that anyone who denies such rights is morally obtuse and should be "forced" to recognize the error of his ways. Indeed, we overlook too easily how the language of "rights," in spite of its potential for good, contains within its logic a powerful justification for violence. Our rights language "absolutizes the relative" in the name of a universal that is profoundly limited and limiting just to the extent that it tempts us to substitute some moral ideal for our faithfulness to God.

To reiterate a point, recent attempts to identify Christian ethics with a universal human ethic fail to recognize that all accounts of the moral life are narrative dependent. We must recognize that, in

MacIntyre's words, "action itself has a basically historical character. It is because we all live out narratives in our lives and because we understand our own lives in terms of narratives that we live out that the form of narrative is appropriate for understanding the actions of others. Stories are lived before they are told—except in the case of fiction."[23] Moreover, we must recognize that we live out our lives in the light of certain conceptions of a possible shared future. As a result I am not a self born with no history. Rather the story of my life "is always embedded in the story of those communities from which I derive my identity. I am born with a past; and to try to cut myself off from that past, in the individualist mode, is to deform my present relationships. The possession of an historical identity and the possession of a social identity coincide."[24]

Christian ethics involves the extraordinary claim that by learning to be faithful to the way of life inaugurated by Jesus of Nazareth we have, in fact, become part of the shared history that God intends for his whole creation. But that such an eschatological view is inherent in our morality does not mean that we can assume that the "universal" inclusion of all people in God's kingdom is an accomplished fact. Rather it means that as Christians we have been given the means to recognize ourselves for what we are—historic beings who must begin our ethical reflection in the midst of history.

There is no point outside our history where we can secure a place to anchor our moral convictions. We must begin in the middle, that is, we must begin within a narrative. Christianity offers a narrative about God's relationship to creation that gives us the means to recognize we are God's creatures. Thus it is certainly true that the God we find in the story of Jesus is the same God we find in creation—namely, the God who wills us to share in his life. We have a saving God, and we are saved by being invited to share in the work of the kingdom through the history God has created in Israel and the work of Jesus. Such a history completes our nature as well as our particular history by placing us within an adventure which we claim is nothing less than God's purpose for all of creation.

This implies, moreover, that Christian ethics does not, methodologically, have a starting point. The dilemma of whether we must do Christian ethics out of a doctrine of God or of man is a false one. For Christian ethics begins in a community that carries the story of the God who wills us to participate in a kingdom established in and through Jesus of Nazareth. No matter where it begins theologically, if it tries to do more or less than remind us of the significance of that story it has lost its way. Theology has no essence, but rather is the imaginative endeavor to explicate the stories of God by showing how one claim illuminates another.

Where does this leave the issue of how best to understand the relation of creation and redemption, nature and grace? Do I mean to defend a Christian ethic that stresses redemption and grace as in essential discontinuity with creation and nature? Decidedly no! God has never been other than a saving God. That is as true of God as creator as it is of God as redeemer. By emphasizing the narrative character of our knowledge of God I mean to remind us that we do not know what it means to call God creator or redeemer apart from the story of his activity with Israel and Jesus. The language of creation and redemption, nature and grace, is a secondary theological language, that is sometimes mistaken for the story itself. "Creation" and "redemption" should be taken for what they are, namely ways of helping us tell and hear the story rightly.

Moreover, if creation and redemption are assumed to be intelligible in themselves—that is, apart from the story—the kind of "saving" that we find in the life and death of Jesus Christ is distorted. That God "saves" is not a pietistic claim about my status individually. Salvation is not fundamentally some fresh and compelling insight about my life—though such insight may be included. Rather, the God of Israel and Jesus offers us salvation insofar as we are invited to become citizens of the kingdom and thus to be participants in the history which God is creating. This does not mean that nature is only "saved" as it becomes historical, but reminds that both nature and history are abstractions. What is redeemed is this or that creature who combines aspects of nature and history.

1.4 Summary of the Argument

Thus far I have tried to argue that the "natural law" starting point for Christian ethics, even in the updated form of "Christian ethics as human ethics" has the following difficulties: (1) It creates a distorted moral psychology, since the description of act is thought to be determined by an observer without reference to the dispositions of the agent. This leads to concentration on judgments about action from an observer's standpoint that the "new Catholic moralists" at least claim they want to avoid. (2) It fails to provide an adequate account of how theological convictions are a morality, i.e., that they are meant not just to describe the world but to form the self and community. (3) It confuses the claim that Christian ethics is an ethic that we should and can commend to anyone with the claim that we can know the content of that ethic by looking at the human. (4) It fails to appreciate that there is no actual universal morality, but that in fact we live in a fragmented world of many moralities. (5) Because it seems to entail a strong continuity between church and world, natural law ethics fails to provide the critical perspective the church needs to recognize and deal with the challenges presented by our societies and the inherent violence of our world. (6) It ignores the narrative character of Christian convictions by forgetting that nature-grace, creation-redemption are secondary theological concepts only intelligible in relation to the story of the God of Abraham, Isaac, Jacob, and Jesus. (7) It tempts us to coerce those who disagree with us, since its presumptions lead us to believe that we always occupy the high ground in any dispute.

2. REASON AND REVELATION

Many would argue there is another more serious problem with my defense of a qualified ethic against natural law approaches. To emphasize the revelation within the Christian community seems to be anti-rational. For example, Richard McCormick says "if Christian faith and revelation add material content to what is knowable in principle by reason, then the churches conceivably could teach moral positions and conclusions independently of the reasons and analyses that recommend these conclusions. This could lend great support to a highly juridical and obediential notion of Christian morality."[25] At the very least his claim seems doubtful in light of the history of the use of "natural law" by church authorities to support authoritarian positions. Indeed, I would suggest that part of the difficulty with the moral reasoning supporting some of the church's sexual ethics is that by attempting to give them a "natural law" basis devoid of their theological basis they appear arbitrary and irrational —thus requiring authoritarian imposition.

Yet the question McCormick raises is an important one since it rightly concerns the questions of the kind and place of authority in Christian ethics and of the relation of that authority to reason. In his *Authority in Morals* Gerard Hughes gives a careful account of how these questions might be approached from a natural law perspective.

[The] most obvious court of appeal in moral theology is the teaching of Christian moral tradition, as this finds expression either in the Bible or in later documents of that tradition. In harmony with this approach is the view that there is a specifically Christian ethic, which it is the task of moral theology to expound by reflection on the data of the specifically Christian revelation. In so far as this revelation is taken to be authoritative in ethics, it is taken to be in some sense an ultimate, which is not open to further criticism from sources external to itself. Against this view, I propose two basic types of difficulty. The first is theological in character. I argue that the picture of God which inevitably emerges from this kind of approach is one which Christians are themselves unwilling to accept consistently. On this model, I argue God must emerge as an arbitrary figure who would have no legitimate claim on our belief or our allegiance; yet one of the clearest themes of the Judaeo-Christian tradition in the Bible is that God is someone whom man can accept as the ultimate answer to his legitimate aspirations. Any theory of revelation which denies this must in the end leave revelation itself deprived of its credentials. In particular, God must be seen as morally acceptable if we are to have any reason for believing that it is indeed God who is speaking to us. Secondly, I propose some more philosophical objections to this position. It is characteristic of the Christian religion that God reveals himself in history, and therefore in a particular culture at a particular time and place. The texts of Christian tradition in which that revelation is communicated to us are, by the same token, texts of a particular human community at different periods of its development. As such, these texts raise all the philosophical problems of interpretation and translation raised by any text. It follows that the meaning of these texts cannot simply be read off automatically from the texts themselves. In order to establish their meaning we have to have recourse to other assumptions and arguments which the texts themselves do not provide.[26]

Interestingly, Hughes advances his argument with confidence that he knows what "morality" involves. He says,

The distinctive, and objectionable, contention of the voluntarist is that even given the creation of man, what is right and wrong for men to do depends on a *further* act of God's will; God could have placed us under different, incompatible, obligations while leaving us unaltered. In thus severing the connection between the nature of man and the moral obligations under which God could place him, the voluntarist renders man's moral perfection unintelligible, because it is no longer related to any other facet of man's development. He therefore runs the risk of making his God arbitrary. In the main, Christian tradition has rejected this picture of God as inconsistent with his character that has been revealed to us and with the ways in which his moral concern for us has been shown.[27]

Now Hughes's argument against arbitrariness works only when we assume we know the nature and content of morality prior to our knowledge of God. Hence, it is odd that Hughes appeals to revelation in order to deny that Christian ethics is based on revelation— i.e., that revelation which "has been revealed to us and with the ways in which his moral concern for us has been shown." Clearly Hughes must have two different senses of revelation at work, and this is but an indication that we need to know better what he means by "revelation." In one form he seems to identify revelation as a category of knowledge that cannot be rationally justified—but that is surely a mistake.

It is a mistake because first of all the word "revelation" is not a qualifier of the epistemic status of a kind of knowledge, but rather points to the content of a certain kind of knowledge. We call knowledge about God "revelation" not because of the rationality or irrationality of such knowledge, but because of what that knowledge is about. It certainly is true that our knowledge of God may challenge certain accounts of what counts as rational, but that does not mean that revelation is thereby irrational. Revelation is properly a description of that knowledge that bears the stamp of God and God's saving intentions, but that stamp is not thereby necessarily discerned in a mysterious manner, though knowledge of revelation may well be knowledge of a mystery. To say knowledge is "revealed" marks it as being about God, in contrast to so much of our knowledge that makes no attempt to tell us about God.

It has become popular to say that revelation is not concerned with propositions, but is instead the self-disclosure of God. Thus many speak of "revelatory events"—the "Exodus event" or the "resurrection event." They often wish to suggest that revelation does not make claims about what happened, but about the meaning of what happened. In contrast, it is my contention that revelation involves propositional claims, none of which can be isolated by themselves, but are intelligible only as they form a coherent narrative.

From this perspective I find the traditional distinction between natural knowledge of God and revelation to be misleading. All knowledge of God is at once natural and revelatory. But like all knowledge it depends on analogical control. Analogies, in turn, derive their intelligibility from paradigms that draw on narratives for their rational display.[28] Our narratives of God's dealing with us inspire and control our attempt to test how what we know of God helps us understand why the world is as it is—i.e., finite.

But our knowledge of God is also moral. For example, our avowal of God's perfection is that of a being with complete integrity. Put simply, there is no underside to God's intentions. God is what God does in a manner unlike anyone or anything else. God's goodness therefore is not like our goodness, for a perfect faithfulness is

God's very nature. That God is moral in this sense is the basis for our confidence that we are more nearly ourselves when we are like God. Christian morality, therefore, cannot but require us to become faithful imitators of God.

This in fact is a familiar biblical concern. For example, consider the language of *Leviticus* 19:1–4:

> And the Lord said to Moses, "Say to all the congregation of the people of Israel, You shall be holy; for I the Lord your God am holy. Every one of you shall revere his mother and his father, and you shall keep my sabbaths: I am the Lord your God. Do not turn to idols or make for yourselves molten gods. I am the Lord your God."

Or again *Leviticus* 19:11–12:

> "You shall not steal, nor deal falsely, nor lie to one another. And you shall not swear by my name falsely, and so profane the name of your God: I am the Lord."

The biblical Commandments do not command us arbitrarily; rather they call us to be holy as God is holy, as we have learned of holiness through God's faithfulness to us. Therefore, like God we are called to be what we are and to do what we do (e.g., we leave part of our fields unharvested for the poor) because God is that kind of God. Such a morality requires no "foundation"; it is enough that we know it to reflect the very nature of God.

It may be objected that the sense of "holiness" in these verses is rather abstract, but such a charge can only be sustained by ignoring the narrative displays of God's holiness in Scripture: it is God who has brought us from the land of Egypt, who has given us the judges, prophets, and priests. As Christians we claim we learn most clearly who God is in the life and death of Jesus Christ. By learning to "imitate" Jesus we in fact become part of God's very life and therein find our true home. We become holy by becoming citizens in God's kingdom, thereby manifesting the unrelenting love of God's nature.

If we have a "foundation" it is the story of Christ. "For no other foundation can anyone lay than that which is laid, which is Jesus Christ" (1 Cor. 3:11). Here Paul speaks not of some form of individualistic perfection, but rather of the building of a community—a body of people. But such a people can survive only if their commitments to one another are built on commitment to Christ.

Such a foundation is not extra-rational; indeed, it is a claim about reality—namely, that our existence is God-given and -formed. Such a claim is properly interpreted, as are all claims, within a community that seeks to understand its world. At least the beginning of wisdom in human communities is the recognition that our lives are narrative dependent, that we are pilgrims on a journey, even if we are not sure what that journey entails. That we Christians witness to a man's life, a man called Jesus, who is the heartbeat of our life and the meaning and form of our existence becomes intelligible (and therefore rational) in the light of such narrative dependency.

It is our conviction that we are provided with a truthful account of reality that enables us to see our life as more than a succession of events when we learn to locate our story in God's story. That does not mean our life has a singular goal or meaning; rather, the story of God we learn through Christ gives us the skills to go on even when no clear goal is present. We rightly seek neither happiness nor pleasure in themselves; such entities are elusive. Rather we learn happiness and pleasure when we find in a faithful narrative an ongoing and worthy task that is able to sustain our lives.

By learning to understand ourselves as creatures, as beings open to the redemption made possible by Jesus' preaching of the kingdom, we are able to place ourselves within God's story. As creatures we learn to understand our lives as a story God is telling:

> a story which begins in the primeval creative utterance and which will one day, having reached its appointed conclusion, end. Only the Author of the drama is in a position to specify clearly the ultimate significance of the roles which particular creatures are called upon to play. Only he may finally see how the various roles make up a coherent

whole. The creature who plays his role may be very uncertain whether the story is now in its final chapters or whether the plot is really just beginning to get off the ground. In short, the creature is not responsible for the whole of the story or for all the consequences of his action. Rather, he is responsible for playing well the role allowed him. To understand ourselves as creatures is to believe that we ought not step out of the story and think of ourselves as author rather than character. We are not to orchestrate the final denouement; we are simply to be responsible.[29]

Put simply, we Christians are not called on to be "moral" but faithful to the true story, the story that we are creatures under the Lordship of a God who wants nothing more than our faithful service. By such service we become not "moral," it seems, but like God, holy.

Thus those who claim we must choose between revelation and reason in order to characterize our knowledge of God and his moral will for us are imposing foreign abstractions on the way we see the scriptural narrative work. Revelation is reasonable if we place it within the ongoing story of God's calling of Israel and his redemption wrought in Christ. The affirmation of God as creator is not the basis for establishing a "natural knowledge of God"—though certainly I would not deny that such knowledge may exist. Rather, "God as creator" is a reminder that we are creatures who are participants and actors in his world. We are such actors exactly because we have a nature that is open to historical determination.

To return to Hughes, the dichotomy between reason and revelation is particularly distorting when it is used to force claims of a "specifically religious morality" into a position of arbitrariness. He thinks that a specifically religious morality implies that we worship and serve a God who arbitrarily issues commands for no reason. Yet, as we have seen, that is not the God whom we find in Scripture calling us to be holy. To be sure God issues "commands," but God's commands make sense within his purpose of creating a people capable of witnessing in the world to the kingdom.[30]

Nor is such a God, as Hughes suggests, "someone whom man can accept as the ultimate answer to his legitimate aspirations." God's ways are not our ways. God commands us so in order to train our aspirations and desires, for we do not know what we should rightly desire. God trains us to desire rightly by calling us to be partakers and citizens in a kingdom through which we learn to be creatures, to have characters appropriate to God's Lordship, to be redeemed.

The task of Christian ethics is imaginatively to help us understand the implications of that kingdom. Or as I have said elsewhere: Christian ethics is the disciplined activity which analyzes and imaginatively tests the images most appropriate to orchestrate the Christian life in accordance with the central conviction that the world has been redeemed by the work of Jesus Christ.[31] Christian ethics as such is not in principle methodologically different from other ethics, for I suspect all accounts of the moral life require some appeal to the virtues, principles, and the narrative display of each. What makes Christian ethics Christian is not our methodology, but the content of our convictions.

Hughes is right to say that those convictions, especially as we find them in Scripture, require interpretation. But that is not, as he alleges, because we have become particularly aware of the cultural limits of the texts. Rather the texts require interpretation because they do not pretend to be self-interpreting. Scripture itself initiates us into this activity, for so much of it is interpretation on itself. For example, the New Testament is in many ways a midrash on the Hebrew Scriptures through which we Christians try to understand better what it means to be part of God's people in the light of God's presence to us in Jesus of Nazareth.[32]

But the New Testament is hardly self-interpreting. We have, after all, four Gospels, each with its own particular emphasis. These differences are not necessarily incompatible, but neither is their interrelation clear. They must be interpreted, and that requires not only careful historical research, but, even more, our willingness to be morally formed in a manner appropriate to the claims of those texts. Indeed, the diversity of Scripture is at the heart of the Christian life insofar as it requires that we be a community, a church, capable of allowing these differing texts be read amongst us with authority.

We Christians must recognize, by the very fact that we are a people of a book, that we are a community which lives through memory. We do not seek a philosophical truth separate from the book's text. Rather, we are a people of a book because we believe that "the love that moves the sun and the stars" is known in the people of Israel and the life of a particular man, Jesus. Such "truth" is inherently contingent; it can only be passed on from one generation to another by memory. We test our memory with Scripture as we are rightly forced time after time to seek out new implications of that memory by the very process of passing it on.

So memory is a moral exercise. We must be the kind of people capable of remembering our failures and sins if we are rightly to tell the story we have been charged to keep, for a proper telling requires that we reveal our sin. To acknowledge the authority of Scripture is also to learn to acknowledge our sin and accept forgiveness. It is only through forgiveness that we are able to witness to how that story has formed our lives.

Therefore, Christians claim or attribute authority to Scripture because it is the irreplaceable source of the stories that train us to be a faithful people. To remember, we require not only historical-critical skills, but examples of people whose lives have been formed by that memory. The authority of Scripture is mediated through the lives of the saints identified by our community as most nearly representing what we are about. Put more strongly, to know what Scripture means, finally, we must look to those who have most nearly learned to exemplify its demands through their lives.

I suppose Hughes could say—"Ah! But you see you still need a criterion of reason separate from the Scripture to prevent arbitrariness, for how do you know who the saints are?" There is some truth to this: we do need to try to say why some exemplify God's story better than others. However, the "reason" required is not "extra-theological." It comes from the very community formed by the memory of God's promises to us. Thus the "criterion" is not so much like a principle as it is like a story that the saints' lives exhibit. Through the lives of the saints we begin to understand how the images of Scripture are best balanced so that we might tell and live the ongoing story of God's unceasing purpose to bring the world to the peace of the kingdom.[33]

Notes

1. We still lack a good history of the development of Catholic moral theology. Though often deserving many of the criticisms made of it, the critics usually attack more a caricature rather than the practice. However, this is partly due to the fact that Catholic moral theology so often presented itself in caricature, because it lacked the means to describe its richer activity. For a short history of moral theology see Timothy O'Connell's *Principles of Catholic Morality* (New York: Seabury, 1978), pp. 10–19. James Gustafson's *Protestant and Roman Catholic Ethics* (Chicago: University of Chicago Press, 1980) is an irreplaceable source for understanding the issues between Catholic and Protestant ethics.

2. For example, see Karl Barth's *Church Dogmatics,* II/2 (Edinburgh: T. & T. Clark, 1961). There Barth maintains "that general conception of ethics coincides exactly with the conception of sin" (p. 518).

3. For a more detailed treatment of the development of Protestant Christian ethics see my article, "On Keeping Theological Ethics Theological," in *Revisions: Changing Perspectives in Moral Philosophy,* ed. Stanley Hauerwas and Alasdair MacIntyre (Notre Dame, Ind.: University of Notre Dame Press, 1983), pp. 16–42.

4. Indeed, the very phrase "biblical ethic" is as misleading as "biblical theology," for each of these phrases denotes a unity that the Scripture simply does not possess. For an important attempt to show the theological significance of the diversity of Scripture see Paul Hanson, *The Diversity of Scripture: A Theological Interpretation* (Philadelphia: Fortress Press, 1982).

5. On the structure of the *Summa Theologica* see M. Dominigu Chenu, O.P., "Introduction to the *Summa* of Saint Thomas," in *Theorist Reader: Texts and Studies* (Washington, D.C.: The Thomist Press, 1958).

6. I first learned this way of putting the matter from Julian Hartt. In particular see his *Christian Critique of American Culture* (New York: Harper & Row, 1967). The emphasis on the practical nature of Christian convictions is not meant to deny that metaphysical claims are also involved. Certainly, theological claims involve metaphysical drafts on reality—e.g., that the world is finite. By emphasizing the practical nature of languages, however, I hope to remind us that finiteness is not just an ontological, but also a moral, claim.

7. "Decree on Priestly Formation," *Documents of Vatican II,* ed. Walter Abbott (New York: American Press, 1966), p. 452.

8. O'Connell, *Principles for a Catholic Morality,* pp. 39–40.

9. Ibid., p. 40. Some may feel I have unfairly singled out O'Connell for criticism since he represents a widely shared position particularly among Catholics. I have, however, concentrated on O'Connell because he has said so well what many others only imply or say in a confused manner. Moreover the popularity of his book suggests that his position rings true to many and thus it is important that I try to state my differences with him.

10. Ibid., pp. 20–29.

11. Ibid., p. 35, his italics. O'Connell's claim in this respect is widely shared in contemporary theology. Jesus is thus the "man for others" or the paradigm of "self-giving love." The problem with such claims is that it makes it extremely hard to understand Jesus' death, since he was not put to death just because he wished to be self-giving. Surely the Romans (and some Jews) saw that he was a political threat. To place all the emphasis on Jesus as a "Christ figure" or an example of God's eternal graciousness is to lose the eschatological framework of the Gospels without which Jesus' preaching of the kingdom is unintelligible.

12. Charles Curran, in particular, tends to such abstractions by isolating what he calls the "fivefold Christian mysteries of creation, sin, incarnation, redemption, and resurrection destiny." *Moral Theology: A Continuing Journey* (Notre Dame, Ind.: University of Notre Dame Press, 1982), p. 38. Curran seems to assume that the meaning of these abstractions is clear and that the theologian's task is basically to see that some are not emphasized to the expense of others—thus it is said, "some Protestant theologians deny the goodness of creation," p. 39. But the issue is what is meant by creation, or sin, and how such notions derive their intelligibility from Christian tradition. Curran's use of these terms turns them into lifeless abstractions.

This is not to deny that "nature" is an essential category for theological reflection. But that it is so does not mean that nature has an integrity sufficient to sustain an autonomous ethic. We are "natural" to the extent that God has created us capable of receiving his grace. We thus are by nature—that is, by God's will—beings independent of God. Yet our nature must remain incomplete, since by nature we are not sufficient in ourselves. Nature as a theological concept will always be ambiguous, since it is necessary for theological reflection, yet it cannot ever be intelligibly displayed or analyzed in itself. This way of putting the matter I owe to Professor Nicholas Lash.

13. It is interesting to note that when creation-redemption, nature-grace are made primary in order to underwrite a universal ethic there is a tendency to justify violence as a legitimate form of Christian behavior. For it is alleged that Christians must take responsibility for "creation" even if it means the use of violence. Moreover the "redemption" wrought becomes

an ideal that is explicated in abstraction from Jesus' life and teaching. Thus Jesus' redemption is affirmed but not in a manner that we must take his teachings seriously for the guiding of our lives. But Jesus' "redemption" is not in discontinuity with his teaching, for unless we take the latter seriously we cannot know the meaning of the former.

14. Joseph Fuchs, "Is There a Specifically Christian Morality?" in *Readings in Moral Theology, No. 2: The Distinctiveness of Christian Ethics,* ed. Charles Curran and Richard McCormick (New York: Paulist Press, 1980), pp. 5–6.

15. Ibid., p. 7.

16. Ibid., p. 8.

17. Ibid., p. 15.

18. Richard McCormick, "Does Faith Add to Ethical Perception," in *Readings in Moral Theology, No. 2: The Distinctiveness of Christian Ethics,* ed. Charles Curran and Richard McCormick, p. 169.

19. For example, see my response to Richard Neuhaus' statement, "Christianity and Democracy," in the *Center Journal* 1/3 (Summer 1982), pp. 42–51.

20. McCormick, p. 157.

21. This is an issue largely overlooked in most Christian systematic theology. John Howard Yoder has done more than anyone to reestablish the significance and primacy of church-world categories. For example, see Yoder's *Christian Witness to the State* (Newton, Kansas: Faith and Life Press, 1977).

22. The command to forgive our enemies should surely be the most provocative reminder of how misleading is the claim that Christian ethics is human ethics. Human ethics is built on the assumption of the legitimacy of self-defense—as are also most accounts of natural law ethics that legitimate survival as the source of moral principles. On the other hand, Christian ethics severely qualifies that "desire."

23. Alasdair MacIntyre, *After Virtue* (Notre Dame, Ind.: University of Notre Dame Press, 1981), p. 197.

24. Ibid., p. 205.

25. McCormick, p. 157.

26. Gerard Hughes, *Authority in Morals* (London: Heythrop College, 1978), pp. v–vi.

27. Ibid., p. 5 (italics mine).

28. For example, see David Burrell's account of analogical argument in his "Argument in Theology: Analogy and Narrative," in *New Dimensions in Philosophical Theology,* ed. Carl Raschke (Chico, Calif.: Scholars Press, 1982). Burrell argues, "The difference between ambiguous and analo-

gous expression lies in using them systematically—that is, so as to show how the many uses can be related to one. We accomplish this, quite simply, by giving an example. Yet since examples are not ordinarily produced—as in kindergarten show-and-tell—but narrated, what we in fact do when we give an instance is tell a story."

See also Nicholas Lash, "Ideology, Metaphor, and Analogy," in *The Philosophical Frontiers of Christian Theology,* ed. B. Hebblethwaite and S. Sutherland (New York: Cambridge University Press, 1982), for an extremely nuanced account of the relation between narrative and metaphysics.

29. Gilbert Meilaender, "Against Abortion: A Protestant Proposal," *The Linacre Quarterly* 45 (May 1978), 169.

30. For some reason those concerned with the validity or invalidity of the "Divine command theory" insist on ignoring this simple fact.

31. Stanley Hauerwas, *Vision and Virtue: Essays in Christian Ethical Reflection* (reprint, Notre Dame, Ind.: University of Notre Dame Press, 1981), p. 2.

32. I am acutely aware that the issues raised here require a much fuller discussion of hermeneutics than I am able to supply. However, for a position with which I have much sympathy see Charles Wood, *The Formation of Christian Understanding: An Essay in Theological Hermeneutics* (Philadelphia: Westminster Press, 1981). Wood's discussion of the nature of canonicity seems to me to be particularly fruitful. For example, he suggests, "The form of the canon itself may indicate something of its mode of functioning. When one regards the biblical canon as a whole, the centrality to it of a narrative element is difficult to overlook: not only the chronological sweep of the whole, from creation to new creation, including the various events and developments of what has sometimes been called 'salvation history,' but also the way the large narrative portions interweave and provide a context for the remaining materials so that they, too, have a place in the ongoing story, while these other materials—parables, hymns, prayers, summaries, theological expositions—serve in different ways to enable readers to get hold of the story and to live their way into it. This overall narrative character of the canon, together with its designation as Word of God, suggests that the canon might plausibly be construed as a story which has God as its 'author.' It is a story in which real events and persons are depicted in a way that discloses their relationship to God and to God's purposes; a story that finally involves and relates all persons and events, and which, as it is told and heard in the power of God's Spirit, becomes the vehicle of God's own definitive self-disclosure. God is not only the author of this story but its chief character as well; so that as the story unfolds we come to understand

who God is. And because God is not only the chief character but also the author, the story's disclosure is God's self-disclosure. We become acquainted with God as the one who is behind this story and within it. The canon, thus construed, norms Christian witness not by providing sample statements by which to test other statements, nor by providing ideals of some other sort, but by reminding the community of the identity of the one whose word they bear" (pp. 100–101).

33. For a fuller working out of this suggestion see Patrick Sherry, "Philosophy and the Saints," *Heythrop Journal* 18 (1977), 23–37.

A Contribution to the Theological Discussion of Natural Law

Bruno Schüller, S.J.
translated by William Loewe

Anyone these days who still resolutely supports the doctrine of natural law[1] has to be seriously regarded, now even among Catholic theologians and jurists, as stuck behind the times or even reactionary. If someone dares to recall that the doctrine of natural law has, after all, a solid basis in the epistle to the Romans, especially in 2:14f, it can be objected that this passage from Romans—like other New Testament texts as well—cannot be interpreted in the sense of a philosophical natural law doctrine. One knows, of course, that Romans 2:14f has been the favorite text interpreted in a natural law sense by Catholic proponents of natural law and is still sometimes interpreted that way; but the present state of exegesis does not permit that meaning.[2] The force of this objection is supposed to be that only someone who is not up on modern exegesis or who, as a Catholic theologian, will have natural law founded on scripture at any price, even the price of unbiased exegesis, can still be tempted to read in the first two chapters of the epistle to the Romans an assertion regarding the natural law. Were this the case, the question of the existence of a natural law would certainly still not be decided negatively, from a theological viewpoint, though it would be prejudiced most unfavorably. For it is only right that it should be significantly more difficult to affirm a theological position for which a biblical foundation cannot be exhibited.

Let us suppose for the sake of argument (dato, non concesso) that at the present time the traditional doctrine of natural law really does have to come to terms with not being grounded in scripture. It can still be legitimated by adducing its indispensability for moral theology. With its axiom, ground the ought in what is, it makes a fundamental assertion about the nature of moral knowledge and ethical reasoning in general. And since scripture alone admittedly provides no adequate basis for constructing a special ethic, most people have thought up to now that this meant that even in moral theology they were directed to arguments based on natural law. But this opinion does not go uncontradicted today, for "with regard to its ethical relevance" the doctrine of natural law "has to be submitted to a relentless critique" to determine whether it really is in a position to yield "a scientifically unassailable criterion for generally binding obligations."[3]

Until now Catholic moral theology and ethics have made extensive use of natural law arguments, and they have arrived thereby, so they believed, at wholly respectable results, particularly in special ethics. Was this a matter of self-deception? But it is improbable that a dubious method should lead to quite persuasive results. To be sure. And it has happened more than once that some of its results have cast serious doubt on natural law reasoning. This has happened with traditional marital ethics, especially its evaluation of contraception; people find fault with it on numerous counts and for good reasons. But at least in recent decades this marital ethic has been constantly portrayed as secured by natural law.[4] Particularly often so-called Catholic social teaching bears the stamp of its origin in natural law. Nothing seems more obvious than to attribute doubts that arise about its correctness to the methodology that grounds it. What gets passed off as natural law, the objection goes, is patently shot through with a heavy dose of ideological elements, with ways of thinking characteristic of the enlightenment and early capitalism. The intellectual world of the middle ages also shows up, and this rests "for its part to a not inconsiderable extent on a restoration of the OT, which people used as a law book for the Christian world, for which the NT failed to provide sufficiently clear norms."[5]

Natural law reasoning is objectionable in itself and therefore necessarily leads to similarly objectionable results. In addition, it seems particularly susceptible to ideologies. If all this is so, by what other, better method should moral theology approach ethical questions whose solution, with the best will in the world, just cannot be gleaned from scripture? According to one suggestion, so long as no more reliable method has been developed, for those areas of life that have not yet been clarified ethically—biotechnology and human engineering, for example—"the step from a substantive ethic to an ethic of decision that will engage the alert conscience of the specialists [must be] risked."[6] Although it is not immediately clear just what an ethic of decision means, it still seems to have the character of a provisional emergency remedy. Another suggestion on the contrary gives the impression that it contains a different method than natural law, one that is more reliable and less susceptible to ideologies. Paradigmatically employed in social teaching, it would consist in relating "social facts" which, derived in a purely empirical manner, are therefore not of themselves normative, to "the gospel as criterion of value." Thereby they receive, or allow one to recognize, the ethical-normative character appropriate to them at the moment.[7]

All in all, it looks very bad for the doctrine of natural law. Old and venerable though it may be, its place now lies only in the history of moral theology and ethics if, really not based on scripture, it should turn out to be of dubious ethical relevance and wholly dispensable. Still and all, just as for the sake of truth the doctrine of natural law ought not be spared being "submitted to a relentless critique," so also must the objections to which it is exposed these days have their validity critically examined. It could well be that these objections sound weightier and more solid than they really are. First, then, what about scripture? Does it really provide no basis at all for the doctrine of the natural law?

I
DOES THE NT SAY ANYTHING ABOUT NATURAL LAW?

Exegetical method is "nothing but a kind of questioning," "a way of posing questions. That means that I cannot understand a given text, unless I ask it specific questions."[8] Hence it is imperative, before approaching a text, to think through as precisely as possible what you intend to ask it about. In this case the NT should be asked whether and how it takes a position on the natural law. Accordingly just what is meant by the natural law first has to be clarified, as must the question of the form in which the NT might express its position on the natural law, if it takes one, given its kerygmatic character.

By natural moral law let first of all be understood the totality of those moral norms which in principle can be apprehended in logical independence of (positive) divine revelation. This definition leaves wholly open how the intrinsic possibility of this apprehension is to be explained and what its objective and subjective cognitive basis is. Only a negative point is being made about this apprehension, namely, that it does not rest on God's revealing word and hence is not (theological) faith. The doctrine of the natural moral law, as Catholics have generally expounded it, certainly also makes a clear statement about the nature of natural moral knowledge by positing the axiom that human obligation is to be based on what human beings are. But you can separate this statement completely from the definition of the natural moral law without rendering that definition vague or meaningless. Furthermore, this separation is methodically necessary with regard to the NT. For at the outset you have to take into account the possibility that the NT ascribes a knowledge of God's moral will even to those whom God's revelatory Word has not yet reached and that the NT nonetheless offers no more precise explanation of the logical how of this knowledge. This methodical separation can also be of some importance for discussion with Protestant theology. There may well be many Protestant theologians who unhesitatingly ascribe a real knowledge of moral norms to those who do not believe in Christ, while perhaps they cannot agree to allow that every human obligation is grounded in what human beings are.[9] In sum, the concept of natural law used for the present leaves completely open how to understand the intrinsic possibility of knowing this moral law, whether it be in the sense of a pure ethics of value (M. Scheler, N. Hartmann), an ethic of being (Thomas Aquinas), or in some other sense. This also means that the natural moral law is not called natural in this context because it has its basis in the "nature" of human beings. By natural only one thing is meant: knowable in logical independence from God's verbal revelation.

The moral law, as thus knowable, is usually called natural law in contemporary theology. The reason for this is to distinguish it from the supernatural moral law. This distinction between the natural and the supernatural (nature and grace) admittedly cannot be found explicitly in scripture; rather, it is the result of later theological reflection. Hence at the outset it is not to be expected that the natural moral law should be expressed in scripture under its contemporary name. In accordance with the definition of the natural law given above, the question is much rather whether the NT ascribes a knowledge of God's will also to those whom neither Yahweh's word of revelation nor the gospel of Christ have reached, those who believe in neither Yahweh nor Christ, those who are neither Jew nor Christian but heathen.

From the standpoint of recent dogmatic theology a serious question must be faced. Is it proper to characterize pagans as such by the fact that they have become aware of God's revelatory word *in no way at all?* God really wills the salvation of all, including the salvation of pagans, but as a matter of fact this salvation only occurs in Christ, as he offers and communicates himself through his word to human beings in faith. If this is so, then it can no longer be taken for settled whether heathens in their knowledge of good and evil do not perhaps depend on Christ's revelation, whether they do not perhaps know God's precepts only because they are "anonymous Christians."[10] The grace of Christ, omnipresent among the pagans, too, seems to disallow the conclusion that the NT assumes the existence of a natural law when it ascribes real moral knowledge to pagans. Nonetheless the question remains to what extent exegesis ought to bring the theologoumenon of the "anonymous Christian" to bear on the interpretation of NT texts. This should certainly not be done where the NT itself sees what is particular to the situation of the pagans to lie in the fact that they do not live out their lives on the basis of God's (positive) revelation, either in good or evil, so that in any case their knowledge of God's moral will is not faith knowledge. It would have to be nonetheless quite different if the NT shows that in its lived experience, though this is not theologically articulated, the early community presupposes also on the part of the heathen the capacity for real moral judgment. In this case scripture presents a fact but does not explain it. Therefore in this case theology is not only permitted but even required, in the performance of its intellectus fidei, to bring the theologoumenon of the "anonymous Christian" to bear as appropriate for clarifying this fact. What this means for the question of the NT's position on the natural law is that the NT certainly acknowledges the natural law only where it not only ascribes to the heathen knowledge of moral norms but also makes it clear that this knowledge is distinct from theological faith knowledge.

That can now be said with certitude about the first two chapters of Romans, especially if you move beyond interpreting individual verses in isolation to take into account the whole context of meaning in which these chapters stand. Everything that Paul adduces from Romans 1:18 on serves to prove that "There is no distinction; all have sinned and fall short of the glory of God. They are justified by grace as a gift, on account of the redemption through Jesus Christ" (3:22ff). The sin of the Jews is exposed, because they are hearers but not followers of the torah (2:1–5, 17–22). The pagans do not have the torah, but in their reason they are brought before God through the medium of the created world, before God's eternal power and divinity, and thus they too know that they are required unconditionally to pay God honor and thanksgiving. Insofar as they fail in this, they have no excuse; they also are sinners who fall short of the glory of God. To be sure, the verses of 1:18–32 do not speak in so many words of a moral law that the pagans grasp as the binding norm of their behavior. But it is very clearly stated that heathens, inasmuch as they acknowledge God, at the same time experience the absolute claim of this God.[11] The moral law is nothing other than this claim of God on human beings, on their reverence and thankfulness. In v. 32 Paul states that heathens knew the divine ordinance that makes liable to death whoever is given over to the vices recounted in vv. 29–31. Hence he is ascribing to the pagans a knowledge of those precepts of the moral law that regulate the relationships among human beings.[12] But it is likewise clear that the moral knowledge here ascribed to heathens is of the same sort as the knowledge of God attributed to them. For it is precisely the case that the pagans indeed know God without acknowledging God, for which reason Paul holds them inexcusable (vv. 21f). But in v. 20 the pagans' knowledge of God is so described as to be clearly distinct from the proper knowledge that comes with faith. Hence Paul is saying here that heathens have a knowledge of the moral law that is (logically) independent of God's revealing word.

If Romans 1:18–32 is interpreted in context with the two following chapters, it very clearly affirms the reality of what was defined above as the natural moral law, almost with even greater clarity than Romans 2:14f, the most frequently cited verses, where Paul speaks of the "work of the law" inscribed in the hearts of the pagans. These verses can also only be understood correctly if the meaning that accrues to them in the apostle's whole line of thought receives close attention. In order to bring the Jews also to perceive their sinfulness, Paul reminds them of the canon that regulates justice before the law: God "will repay all according to their works" (2:5), the Jew no differently than the pagan. "For God is no respecter of persons" (2:11). Therefore it holds good that "All who have sinned 'without the law' will also perish 'without the law,' and all who have sinned under the law will be judged through the law" (2:12). The first half of this verse could provoke an objection. How can someone sin to whom no law is given (cf. 4:5)? To counter this objection Paul explains in 2:14f that of course the heathens do not have the torah; but since they sometimes do what the torah commands, they show that "the work of the law" is written in their hearts. This means two things. First, the pagans also experience the touch of God's moral will. Second, God's will is communicated differently to the pagans than to the Jews, to whom it is announced through the torah. Of what does this difference consist? Many well known exegetes conclude that the way in which the pagans are said to occasionally fulfill God's commands must also be the way in which they know God's commands, namely, *physei,* by nature.[13] Other exegetes will not allow this.[14] But whatever the probative force of the expression *physei,* in v. 14f Paul takes up again under a different formulation what he had already explained in 1:18–32: the pagans also have a real knowledge of God's will. But the text does not offer the slightest reason to understand the moral knowledge of the pagans affirmed in 2:14f any differently from that affirmed in 1:18–32. Therefore 2:14f also speaks about what is called natural moral law.

This interpretation of the two chapters of Romans is certainly abbreviated in the extreme. It should nonetheless be sufficient, if for its more detailed exegetical grounding we can refer to the expert analysis of the Protestant NT scholar G. Bornkamm.[15] It is by no means the case that today with the single exception of G. Bornkamm only Catholic theologians still read a statement about the natural law in Romans. H.W. Scmidt, F.J. Leenhardt, J. Murray, C.K. Barrett, H.C.G. Moule, C.H. Dodd, and R. Bultmann are Protestant theologians. They also interpret the texts in question in the sense of a natural law.[16] Any Catholic theologian who is as convinced as ever that Romans provides a scriptural basis for the doctrine of the natural moral law need not entertain the slightest fear of being subject to a typically Catholic prejudice or of being out of touch with modern exegesis.

There is a series of NT texts that make it clear that as a matter of course the early community ascribed to the pagans a proper capacity for moral judgment. Christians were encouraged to a morally blameless way of life with the thought that they ought not to discredit their Christian faith among heathens, that they had to refute the calumnies of their pagan opponents, or that they could perhaps win pagans over to the Christian faith. But all this takes for granted that despite their lack of faith heathens are quite capable of telling good from evil (cf. 1 Thes 4:12; 1 Cor 10:32; Col 4:5; 1 Tim 5:14; 6:1; Tit 2:5, 8, 10; 1 Pet 2:12, 15; 3:1, 16).[17] Meanwhile exegetes generally acknowledge that NT paranesis contains more than a few material ethical norms that it has taken over from Stoic popular philosophy, in part through the indirect route of Hellenistic Judaism. This has been demonstrated especially for the catalogues of virtues and vices as well as for the "household lists." Had the early community not been convinced that the pagans also possessed a genuine knowledge of the moral law, it would have been impossible for them to take over their ethical instructions.[18] Anyone who judges the matter on purely exegetical grounds, that is, without regard for an already elaborated systematic theology, will perceive therein without further ado an implicit acknowledgement of the natural moral law. Many Protestant exegetes also express themselves along these lines.[19] Should someone nonetheless as a Catholic theologian make use of the theory of the "anonymous Christian," they can no longer arrive at that conclusion. Then the question has to be left open, purely exegetically, whether the pagans do not perhaps know God's will solely because in a hidden manner God's word of revelation has already reached them. For as distinct from the first two chapters of Romans, Christian acceptance of originally pagan ethical norms presumes only the bare fact of moral knowledge among heathens, while the question of the nature of this knowledge does not need to be raised and therefore is also not answered. To be sure, even the bare fact of that acceptance is of no little significance. Not only does it show that as a matter of fact the material ethical norms of Christians and pagans agree to a large extent; beyond this, Christians can also learn from pagans for their knowledge of moral norms.

Let us draw a first conclusion. If by natural law is understood the totality of ethical norms that can be known at least in principle in logical independence of scripture, then the epistle to the Romans offers proof that such a natural law actually exists.

Systematic theology cannot yet acquiesce with this result. Since it consists in methodically achieved intellectus fidei, it faces the question of how it is possible for the "work of the law" to be apprehended by those who believe in neither Yahweh nor Christ. Accordingly systematic theology has to try to render explicit the subjective and the objective grounds of knowledge of the natural law. Only when it does this is it developing a theological (= scientific) doctrine of natural law. Catholic theology has reached the conclusion that reason is the subjective ground of knowledge of the natural law, while its objective ground is the "nature" of human beings. While the term reason is clear in this context, the term nature can have two different meanings, each of which can characterize the objective ground of knowing the natural law in a way that makes sense. Nature can first be understood as a counter-notion to supernatural grace and is then the objective correlate of reason insofar as reason is contrasted to theological faith. That the nature of human beings is the objective ground of knowing the natural moral law means that reason grasps the natural law in sole reliance on the humanity of human beings and in no way on their existence in Christ. This insight, however, hardly leads any further than a simple acknowledgement of a natural law. But nature can also designate human beings insofar as they are a given, as distinct from and prior to what they make of themselves on the strength of their power of free decision. That nature is the objective ground of knowing the natural law in this case means, negatively, that the natural law cannot receive its existence and specificity through the free decision of the human beings whom it concerns. Positively, it means that human beings grasp the natural law insofar as they grasp their givenness as their task, the existence bestowed on them through no effort of their own as their unconditional obligation. Should the natural law, as we defined it at the outset, now be adequately determined with regard to its objective ground, then nature has to be understood as the sheer humanness of human beings as well as in the sense of givenness: the objective basis of knowledge of the natural law is the simple humanness of human beings, and indeed, insofar as this is given over to the free decision of human beings, as that from which it proceeds.

This theological reflection intends to render the fact of the natural law intrinsically intelligible. Does it receive corroboration from scripture? Hardly, insofar as it clearly separates the sheer humanness of human beings from their existence in Christ. For, as we have already said, the distinction between nature and grace is not worked out formally in scripture. But does scripture perhaps know the concept of nature in the sense of the existence bestowed upon human beings for which they are accountable? Two texts are relevant. In Romans 1:26f Paul qualifies heterosexual intercourse as "natural," but homosexual intercourse as "unnatural" and therefore morally reprehensible. In 1 Corinthians 11:14 Paul seems to want to derive a morally significant doctrine of "nature" from the different hair lengths of men and women. In both instances the word nature designates a characteristic of human beings that is given with their humanity and which can at the same time be considered morally normative. Nonetheless, no great weight can be placed on these passages. They do indeed employ the word *physis,* but really only very incidentally, and not as a deliberate starting point for any possible basic implications. Besides, the lesson drawn from "nature" in 1 Corinthians 11:14f is certainly not persuasive.

But even if the word nature in the sense of a normative givenness plays no role in scripture, this by no means precludes the NT from expressing with different names the reality designated by the word. Nature means human beings insofar as they are always pregiven over to their own freedom, as themselves, their existence and specificity, all of which is owed wholly to their creator. Now human beings owe God wholly not only their natural human existence, but especially and before all else their supernatural life in Christ. But this supernatural life can also be entrusted to human beings only as first given by God. In other words, it has to hold for the obligation of Christians as well, that it can only be grounded in the existence of Christians. And if scripture expressed that clearly, then it would confirm what the doctrine of natural law has formulated for the natural law: that human obligation is grounded in what human beings are. The validity of this same axiom for the law of Christ as well as for the natural law rests on the fact that it characterizes the existence of human beings as the existence of a personal creature in statu viae. But human beings are personal creatures in statu viae from the perspective of their natural as well as their supernatural existence. We have already shown elsewhere that scripture really does allow the moral obligation of Christians to be grounded in the existence of Christians (Rom 6:8–13; 1 Cor 5:7; 2 Cor 5:19f; Gal 5:24; Eph 5:8–11; see also the way in which Romans 12:1 and Ephesians 4:1 ground the transition to the paranetic part of the epistles).[20] Hence the natural law axiom, ground the ought in what is, is thoroughly "scriptural." The NT not only confirms the fact of the natural law, but it also provides an account of the only way in which the natural law can be grounded objectively. Hence Catholic teaching on the natural law has a broad and solid basis in scripture.

II
CAN MORAL THEOLOGY DISPENSE WITH NATURAL LAW REASONING?

To state our position at the outset: Moral theology can *absolutely not* dispense with arguments based on natural law. We have already presented this position more fully elsewhere.[21] The decisive reason for the indispensability of this method does not lie in the fact that scripture provides practically nothing to start from in making ethical judgments in many areas of life—in politics and economics, for example. Natural law argument is not just a stopgap in moral theology. Much more is it the case that a faithful grasp of Christ's moral message is possible only to those who already experience the logically prior claim of the natural law. Now theology has the task of including within its methodical reflection on faith everything that is implied in faith itself as its presupposition (condition of possibility). Hence, as moral theology, it has to render explicit the understanding of the natural law contained in faith's law of Christ.[22]

A further development of this thesis shows that the law of Christ, insofar as it is expressed in the outer word, can contain no other ethical norms than does the natural law. To be sure, the same imperative sentences correspond only analogously, if they are expressed on the one hand as the content of the law of Christ, on the other as the content of the natural law.[23] For example, both the law of Christ and the natural law command love of neighbor. But in accordance with its essence the natural law can impose as a duty only a purely human (natural) love of neighbor, whereas the law of Christ commands a love of neighbor which surpasses all human capability, a supernatural love of neighbor. Between natural and supernatural love of neighbor there exists no univocal identity, but only an analogy. This distinction remains fully justified, even if the law of Christ can only be fulfilled insofar as the natural law is fulfilled at the same time, and if in our actual order of salvation the natural law should turn out to be capable of being fulfilled only to the extent that it is integrated into the law of Christ as the latter's presupposition.[24]

One could be tempted to test this analogous correspondence between the law of Christ and the natural law exegetically, and that means, in this case, historically, by setting up a comparison between the moral message of the NT and the moral convictions of the Hellenistic-Roman milieu. But to proceed in this manner is to choose a method which is inappropriate to the question at hand. For what would be compared with the law of Christ would be, not the natural law, but whatever moral convictions the inhabitants of the Hellenistic-Roman world happened as a pure matter of fact to have expressed. But this cannot be identified with the content of the natural law without further ado. The Greco-Roman cultural world cannot represent all of paganism. But more serious reasons weigh against such an identification. First is the possibility that the Greeks and Romans could express only incompletely or even in a distorted fashion the moral norms by which they felt bound in conscience, and then only if they were philosophers and had reflexively pondered on the phenomenon of the moral. Ethical reflection as well as ethical conceptual and linguistic material can lag completely behind the original moral experience of an individual or a cultural group. Then it should not be overlooked that the men and women of the Hellenistic-Roman world as a whole, as groups, and as individuals lived out of particular historical decisions through which they had gotten caught up in guilt, in moral bias and prejudices, without being able to free themselves at will. Hence it must be taken into account at the outset that many of the moral and legal convictions expressed in the Hellenistic-Roman world would misunderstand, twist, or even invert norms of the natural law. Finally, it must also be borne in mind that even before it was evangelized the Hellenistic-Roman world already lived under the effective redeeming grace of Christ. Hence it cannot be excluded with any certainty that in this way or that, be it ever so fragmented, the law of Christ is perhaps expressed in the moral convictions of the Greeks and Romans. As a consequence it is only possible to compare in a purely historical manner the ethic expressed in the NT with the ethic thought out and formulated in the Stoa or by Aristotle or somewhere else, but not the content of the law of Christ with the content of the natural law.[25]

Traditional scholastic moral theology affirms an extensive, though not complete, agreement of the moral precepts of the new covenant with those of the natural moral law.[26] The basis for this affirmation seems to have been the simple fact that they could not name a single moral precept incumbent upon Christians which they did not also think they could ground in the natural law. But since they were thinking primarily of the law as formulated in the outer word, they did not advert sufficiently to the fact that imperative sentences that sound alike do not have the same, univocal meaning if they are apprehended on the one hand as the content of the new law of Christ, on the other as the content of the natural law.

Protestant theology does not draw the rather ontologically oriented distinction between grace and nature or even explicitly reject it. Hence the question concerning a possibly new content of Christian ethics arises for it in a different way. Its basic comparison is drawn between the justified and the sinner, so that the question then runs: Does the justified person stand under moral claims with a new content that do not impinge on the sinner? Or do the justified and the sinner stand under the will of God with its one and the same content, the one in obedience and the other in disobedience? Opinions differ. Nonetheless it seems noteworthy that not a few Protestant theologians arrive from their own way of posing the question at a result that agrees in essence with traditional Catholic moral theology. Thus R. Bultmann writes:[27] "The ethical demand has acquired for them [i.e. believers] no new content, and their moral conduct differs from that of others only in that it bears the character of obedience. What is required of the justified is only what is good, agreeable, and perfect, what can be called virtuous and praiseworthy (Rom 12:2; Phil 4:8)."[28]

If the revealed law of Christ contains no precept to which there does not correspond analogously a similarly worded precept of the natural law, then in principle it must be possible to arrive through philosophical reflection on the natural law at a special ethic which in its material content agrees word for word with a theologically worked out ethic. In what way would the philosophically and the theologically constituted ethic differ methodically? To grasp the distinction in the most formal way possible, you can say that theology argues from the authority of the word of God. Philosophy, on the contrary, has to renounce the argument from authority and render all its ethical propositions intrinsically intelligible "ex visceribus rei." The properly theological argument for forbidding lying is that God has so ordained it. Whether or not believers grasp the intrinsic ground of this prohibition is not decisive for them. They are satisfied with the certainty that God has so disposed the matter and made it known through the word of God. Of course a believer can only accept a moral precept to the extent that he or she understands it. For example, believers have to know what lying means and what an unconditional obligation involves in order to be in a position to allow the commandment "You shall not lie" to be addressed to them as believers. But the fact that this precept really makes a claim on them, that it is in fact valid for them and does not merely present a non-contradictory and hence conceivable imperative sentence— of this they are certain insofar as they *believe* the commandment, only through the word of God. The properly philosophical argument for the prohibition of lying can only consist in demonstrating the intrinsic ground for the unlawfulness of lying. But that is also precisely what characterizes the so-called natural law argument. It does not rest on the authority of the word of God but intends to render ethical norms intrinsically intelligible through a reflexive demonstration of their basis, to produce an "evidentia intrinseca" for their real validity.

If you research Catholic and Protestant manuals of moral theology on how they approach the grounding of individual, material ethical norms, you soon notice this: Insofar as they really produce arguments, they all have a clearly discernible tendency not only to adduce the word of God as proof as often as they can, but also to exhibit whenever possible the intrinsic ground for the validity of a moral demand. Accordingly they strive to match, as it were, the faith acknowledgement of a divine commandment with an acknowledgement for which the commandment is intrinsically comprehensible. Since the law of Christ and the natural law coincide in their wording, in principle this should work out in each case. But would this not render the faith acknowledgement of a moral precept basically superfluous? Why should something be accepted in faith as God's command which is already grasped as a command of God intrinsically through the voice of conscience without any faith at all? Ought the positive revelation of moral demands have perhaps in general only a "subsidiary" function? Does it only allow people to acknowledge in faith what in principle they could know through their own insight but what for some reason or other they do not in fact apprehend, no longer apprehend, or do not yet apprehend? Not as though, in principle, faith could and should be sublated into reason's knowledge. Only the knowledge in faith of moral demands, not faith knowledge in general, is under discussion. The gospel of Christ, God's sovereignly free act of reconciliation with human beings through the Word Incarnate—human beings as wayfarers can never grasp these through a knowledge that comprehends them intrinsically, but can only acknowledge and confess them in faith. Not so the double commandment of love. Human beings are capable in principle of grasping it as a divine commandment without faith, on the basis of intrinsic evidence. True, in this fashion they grasp immediately only the content of the natural law. But insofar as in faith they know themselves called to a life in Christ, they also know at the outset that they cannot fulfill God's will except "in Christ," and thus they know that it is a matter of more than simply a precept of the natural law.

It ought to be at least worthy of serious consideration whether, not least for special ethics, the so-called natural law type of argument is not the only appropriate one, while theological reasoning can only play a subsidiary role whenever it is possible at all. In that role it would provide a supplementary certitude if this were needed or would substitute for natural law reasoning in those cases where, despite its possibility in principle, the latter will have not yet proven successful. By the power of its own dynamic, theological faith finds fulfillment in eschatological "sight." Analogously, faith knowledge of God's moral will in this wayfaring state seems to tend already to rise into a knowledge which comprehends God's will on intrinsic grounds, insofar as such an intrinsically comprehending knowledge is possible in this wayfaring condition with respect to the divine law. Should this hypothesis prove correct, theology would have to point out and elucidate from the perspective of God's word of revelation the vocation of Christians to a life of discipleship of Christ. In this connection it would have to insist on Paul's warning: "For the rest, brothers and sisters, whatever is true, whatever is honorable, whatever is just, whatever is pure, whatever is lovely, whatever is gracious, whatever is virtuous and praiseworthy, set your mind on these things" (Phil 4:8). Obviously "whatever is virtuous and praiseworthy" needs to be ascertained reflectively. To the extent that the NT has pronounced on this, it must absolutely be heard and taken seriously. But in any case moral theology would have to try to ascertain, through a knowledge that grasps the matter on intrinsic grounds, what in particular "the will of God is, what is good, what is agreeable and perfect," aware that it (like every Christian) is rendered capable of this task through the renewal of mind that Christ bestows (cf. Rom 12:2).

It is scarcely possible to find a place for this thesis within the basic direction of contemporary Catholic theology, which seems to be distancing itself more and more from philosophy and thinks it can say something pristinely theological on every conceivable topic. Yet it ought to conform very precisely to the scriptural evidence. Let someone read in all sobriety the apostolic exhortations, the catalogues of virtues and vices, the household lists, the letter of James. What moral instructions are found there that cannot in principle be grasped by anyone? If the apostolic paranesis plays a comparatively secondary role in special moral theology, the reason is not that moral theologians did not study scripture, but much more that by and large this paranesis only recalls what the whole world takes as self-evident. This statement ought not to be read as a put-down. On the contrary, by its restraint biblical paranesis offers an agreeable contrast to much that later theologians felt obliged to add to it for the sake of "deepening" or "Christianizing" it.

One final aspect of the significance of natural law reasoning. It intends to render moral precepts intelligible through a reflexive demonstration of their intrinsic ground. Thus it also has an indispensable role to play in resolving a question often raised today: How are timeless ethical norms to be methodically distinguished from temporally conditioned norms in scripture? Let us grant that the validity of a NT precept can only be grasped in faith, only through the security deposit that the word of revelation posts for it, while its intrinsic ground is hidden from the believer's understanding. In that case how would it be possible to know with certainty whether this precept was valid for Christians of all ages or only for Christians of the first century or so? That could really only be known if the precept itself contained an indication of the length of its validity. If the validity of a precept is only guaranteed by the authority of the word of God, then the duration of this validity can also only be guaranteed if it is itself an intrinsic constituent of this validity. But what NT precept contains such a designation of its timeless or merely time-bound binding force? But if a moral precept can be understood on the basis of its intrinsic ground, then one is also in a position to judge whether it binds Christians of all ages or only a particular epoch. For it is one and the same basis that constitutes the binding power of a precept in general as well as the duration of that binding force.

Let us sum up the reasons that render arguments based on natural law apparently indispensable within moral theology. First, the phenomenon of the moral itself can only be originally disclosed to human beings through their logically immediate experience of the natural law. It is from this experience that all moral concepts and ideas first acquire meaning and significance for people. But these moral concepts are the only possible medium through which God reveals in Christ the supernatural moral law, the law of Christ. Thus theology can only understand and interpret the supernatural moral law in that it also reflects methodically and critically upon its medium of revelation, the moral concepts and ideas that first receive meaning and significance from the natural law. Second, a revelation of the numerous individual precepts of the one law of Christ does not seem in principle necessary, since in their wording these individual commandments agree with those of the natural law, while the natural law is communicated to human beings chiefly through their conscience. There are really only relatively few individual precepts that the NT sets forth explicitly. To the extent that the word of revelation does contain individual precepts of the law of Christ, it probably intends to help people out at those points where they have not yet managed to apprehend moral precepts on their intrinsic grounds. Even if human beings should never manage to dispense with this assistance totally, nonetheless they should strive to require it as little as possible. They should constantly endeavor to match their faith knowledge of moral precepts as far as possible with a knowledge that grasps their intrinsic intelligibility. Finally, only the latter sort of knowledge can undertake to decide, in the interpretation of scripture and tradition, which elements of traditional morality are binding for all time and which have only temporally conditioned binding force.

One may ask what justifies calling all reflexively and critically obtained knowledge of morality based on intrinsic reasons simply *natural law* reasoning or argumentation. Now it would be a good thing if "natural law," used adjectivally, could be replaced by some other adjective developed from the phrase "natural moral law." But the German language happens not to allow such an adjective to be formed. The substantive justification for speaking about natural law reasoning is this: The primordial mode of knowledge of the natural law is knowledge that comprehends intrinsically, a knowledge of the moral law on the basis of its intrinsic ground and not by the testimony of authority. At the same time, however, the natural moral law is by definition the totality of norms that are in principle knowable in logical independence of the word of revelation, of the "auctoritas Dei revelantis." Hence knowledge of the moral on the basis of its ground and primordial knowledge of the natural moral law are one and the same. What is called natural law reasoning could also be designated with the scholastic tradition as argumentatio ex ratione (as distinct from argumentatio ex auctoritate Dei revelantis). To be sure, the adjectival use of "natural law" also intends to specify the ground rule by which alone the argumentatio ex ratione can succeed, namely that it render human obligation comprehensible on the basis of what human beings are, as what they are is given to human beings as a possibility they are free to take up. When all is said and done, the main thing in moral theology is really not words like natural law and its adjectival use. What is really important is the difference between the two kinds of knowledge, knowledge based on the testimony of authority and knowledge of the moral based on its intrinsic ground. Hence what is significant is the objective foundation of the moral, as this is characterized through the axiom: ground the ought in what is.[29]

It is unnecessary to go into the objection raised against the "ethical relevance" of natural law reasoning. But what about the reliability of such reasoning and its susceptibility to ideologies? No matter how precisely a method is matched to its object, it still leads to false results if it is applied incorrectly. Hence a contestable sexual ethic or a dubious social doctrine settles nothing with regard to the reliability or unreliability of the natural law reasoning which was used to help ground the sexual ethic or social doctrine. What would be proven would be just one thing: Natural law reasoning carries no guarantee that it will be applied correctly. And no one who is familiar with the issue of grounding ethical positions and its difficulties will be surprised in the least that he or she as well as others repeatedly fall short of the truth. In addition, theologians can take it as settled fact that for people of this epoch of salvation history a knowledge of the moral law that is free of all errors and mistakes is no real possibility but sheer illusion.[30] For the human race's past this can be proven historically. For the period with which it deals, church history could provide a wealth of material. But there are also theological proofs. Just one, by way of an argument a fortiori, can be briefly sketched. There is a so-called merely authentic pronouncement of the church's teaching office, which essentially interprets the law of

Christ correctly "as a rule" but also errs "by way of exception," so that it cannot be determined a priori how often the "exceptional case" of error actually occurs. But if even the teaching office of the church, to which the proclamation and interpretation of the law of Christ have been entrusted in a special way, is not assured of an assistance of the Holy Spirit that would operate infallibly at all times, how much the less is everyone else. The danger of erring is ever present for human beings as they actually are. What wonder is it if they succumb time and again? In the Catholic Church, natural law arguments have not always been used so consciously and deliberately as in the past one hundred years. Have sexual ethics gone from better to worse over these hundred years? Or were sexual ethics better before Aristotelian philosophy was taken over from medieval scholasticism? We do not have the expertise to judge whether or not Catholic social teaching is as permeated with ideological elements as the position cited at the beginning of this article affirms. But even if the charge were true, what would that say against natural law reasoning? The same position also has it that the middle ages basically misunderstood the OT, seeing in it "the law book of the Christian world, for which the NT did not provide sufficiently clear norms." In that case Christians are also not safe from error even if they want to stick to scripture. Protestant theology, which from its very beginnings saw itself as based solely on scripture, will confirm this ungrudgingly. It counts little against the truth of the NT that people frequently misunderstand it. Just as little does it count against natural law reasoning that people frequently err in applying it.

Can the natural law method yield "a scientifically unassailable criterion for generally valid obligations"? The question goes to the heart of natural law knowledge, indeed of moral knowledge in general. Natural law knowledge is knowledge of the moral on the basis of its intrinsic ground. But knowledge is only such insofar as it is certain of its truth. It can only be certain of its truth if it has a criterion, a measure by which truth is distinguished from error. Hence the question of an "unassailable criterion" for natural law knowledge is the same as the question whether a knowledge of the moral based on its intrinsic ground is possible at all. This fundamental question is posed too seldom in moral theology. It can be answered initially only in philosophical ethics, which for its part is thrown back on epistemology and ontology. Hence an answer cannot be fairly expected here. But one thing should be clear: The question, by means of what criterion the permissibility of contraception can be known with certainty, is basically no different than the question of what "scientifically unassailable criterion" we have by which to recognize the impermissibility of lying or slander.

Finally, what about the "gospel as criterion of value" for ethically evaluating "facts" that have been grasped by purely empirical means and that are therefore not normative in themselves? Does this criterion of value render all reflection and argument based on natural law superfluous? In any case the gospel can only be heard and understood in faith. Immediately there arises the question of the "pre-understanding" that always undergirds every faith understanding as its condition of possibility. It was already shown that human beings are only in a position to understand the gospel in faith as a "value" and "criterion of value" because they already know, logically prior to their faith and through a knowledge based on intrinsic reasons, what a value is. Now ethical value, grasped intrinsically and with logical priority to faith, is nothing else than the content of the natural law. Thus faith understanding of the gospel as a "criterion of value" always already includes the understanding of the natural law based on intrinsic reasons. Consequently in this context as well natural law is involved. Let us attend to it more precisely. What content is to be grasped in the gospel as "criterion of value"? The call to follow Christ? The double commandment to love God and neighbor? Were "gospel as criterion of value" to be given a general formulation, it would play no other role in the evaluation of empirical data than does the chief ethical principle: The good is to be done and evil avoided. But then how do you go about methodically concretizing such a general moral principle? Let us suppose that the "gospel as criterion of value" is equivalent to the whole moral message of the NT. Now, all the preceding reflections have aimed to establish precisely how the revealed moral message renders reflection and argumentation based on natural law not superfluous, but on the contrary absolutely required. "The gospel as criterion of value" offers no alternative to knowledge of the moral based on natural law because there can be no such alternative.

Things are not so bad for traditional Catholic natural law doctrine as they might seem in light of the many objections that are being raised against it of late. Doubtless these objections signal a very serious and difficult problem, the problem of moral knowledge and ethical reasoning in general. But we should not make the doctrine of natural law responsible for this problem and think that by destroying the doctrine we are solving the problem.

Notes

1. Lex naturalis, lex naturae, natural moral law and natural law are used synonymously in what follows.

2. Thus P. Mikat against B. Kötting in a discussion in connexion with a lecture of F. Wieacker on natural law. Cf. F. Wieacker, *Zum heutigen Stand der Naturrechtsdiskussion* (Cologne 1965). P. 59, P. Mikat's contribution.

3. L.M. Weber, "Ethische Probleme der Biotechnik und Anthropotechnik," *Arzt und Christ* 11 (1965) 230.

4. Cf. among others L.M. Weber, *Mysterium Magnum* (Freiburg i. Br. 1963) 9–62.

5. Thus J. Ratzinger, "Naturrecht, Evangelium und Ideologie in der katholischen Soziallehre," in Kl. von Bismarck and W. Dirks, eds., *Christlicher Glaube und Ideologie* (Stuttgart 1964) 24.

6. L.M. Weber, "Ethische Probleme der Biotechnik," 231.

7. Thus J. Ratzinger, op. cit., 27ff.

8. R. Bultmann, *Glauben und Verstehen,* Bd. IV (Tübingen 1965) 165.

9. This holds, for example, for K. Barth and J. Ellul. See B. Schüller, *Die Herrschaft Christi und das weltliche Recht* (Rome 1963).

10. Cf. Kl. Hiesenhuber, "Der anonyme Christ, nach Karl Rahner," *ZkTh* 86 (1964) 286–303; further: K. Rahner, *Schriften zur Theologie,* Bd. VI (Einsiedeln-Zurich-Cologne 1965) 545–554.

11. R. Bultmann, *Theologie des NT* (Tübingen 1953) 224: "But above all, knowledge of God as creator contains within itself knowledge of human beings, namely, of human beings in their creatureliness and in their standing beneath God's claim."

12. Cf. H.W. Schmidt, *Der Brief an die Römer* (Berlin 1963) 40; C.K. Barrett, *A Commentary on the Epistle to the Romans* (London 1962) 41; J. Murray, *The Epistle to the Romans* (Michigan 1964) 50ff; F.J. Leenhardt, *L'Epître de S. Paul aux Romains* (Neuchâtel-Paris 1957) 42; P. Althaus, *Der Brief an die Römer,* 9th edition (Göttingen 1957) 17; further, H. Schlier, *Der Brief an die Galater,* 12th edition (Göttingen 1962) 178.

13. The following understand the law written in the heart in the sense of a natural law as this was defined above: H.W. Schmidt, op. cit., 47f; F.J. Leenhardt, op. cit., 47; J. Murray, op. cit., 72f; C.K. Barrett, op. cit., 51f; Handley C.G. Moule, *The Epistle to the Romans* (Michigan n.d.) 65; C.H. Dodd, *The Meaning of Paul for Today,* 4th ed. (London 1964) 65; R. Bultmann, *Glauben und Verstehen,* Bd. II, 4th ed., 89f; 123; H. Schlier, op. cit., 178; G. Bornkamm, "Gesetz und Natur," in *Das Ende des Gesetzes,* 2nd ed. (Munich 1958) 9–33 (provides further bibliography). P. Mikat., loc. cit., says there can be no talk "of a Pauline doctrine of natural law." That is correct, if by a doctrine of natural law is understood an explicit reflection on the natural law and its conditions of possibility. But you can affirm the existence of a natural law without offering to establish its intrinsic possibility. That is what Paul does. He does not do it only incidentally, since what matters for him is to make clear how the pagans are also without exception sinners. Mikat is correct when he says that Paul is making not a "juridic-philosophical" but "a theological statement"; but it is a theological statement about the natural law, which serves the intelligibility of the proclamation of justification.

14. It is above all Karl Barth and those Protestant theologians obviously influenced by him who reject the idea that Romans 2:14f says anything about natural law. Cf. K. Barth, *KD* 1, 2, 3rd ed. (Zollikon-Zurich 1945) 332; IV, 1 (1953) 437; F. Flückiger, "Die Werke des Gesetzes bei den Heiden," *ThZ* B (1952) 17–42; B. Reike, "Syneidesis in Rom 2, 15," *ThZ* 12 (1956) 157–161; J. Ellul, *Die theologische Begründung des Rechts* (Munich 1948) esp. 46f, 68ff; further, A. Nygren, *Der Römerbrief* (Göttingen 1951) 94; O. Michel, *Der Brief an die Römer* (Göttingen 1963) 77f. Flückiger, Reike and Michel leave it unclear just what they understand by natural law. It may be that it is only the sense of natural law as interpreted by the Stoa that they refuse to discover in Paul, without intending to reject the idea that Paul ascribes to the heathen a moral knowledge that is essentially different from faith knowledge. One ought not assume that Protestant

theologians always understand natural law in the same way as Catholic theology. W. Schrage writes along these lines in *Die konkreten Einzelgebote in der paulinischen Paränese* (Gütersloh 1961) 193, on Romans 2:15: "The work of the law written in the heart is not the norm and demand of any natural law nor of an autonomous ethic, but rather the divine law." Such a contrast between natural law and divine law would be nonsensical, if Schrage understood by natural law what Catholic theology does.

15. Loc. cit.; also, "Die Offenbarung des Zornes Gottes," in *Das Ende des Gesetzes,* 2nd edition, 9–33.

16. See note 13.

17. On 1 Thessalonians 4:12, see A. Depke, *NTD,* 8; M. Dibelius, *HNT,* 11; on Colossians 4:5: M. Dibelius, *HNT,* 12; on the Pastorals: A. Schlatter, *Die Kirche der Griechen;* G. Holtz, *Theol. Hdk. z. NT,* 13; M. Dibelius–H. Conzelmann, *HNT,* 13; on 1 Peter: J. Schneider, *NTD,* 10; K. H. Schelkle, *Die Petrusbriefe.* On the whole matter, cf. W. Schrage, op. cit., 196f.

18. See also W. Schrage, op. cit., 197ff, for a list of all the pertinent literature.

19. Basically all the Protestant theologians cited in note 17.

20. B. Schüller, "Wie weit kann die Moraltheologie das Naturrecht entbehren?" in *Lebendiges Zeugnis* (March 1965), Heft 1–2, 53f; see also above all C.H. Dodd, *Gospel and Law* (Cambridge 1957).

21. B. Schüller, op. cit., 41–64 (in French translation: *NouvRevTh* 98 [May 1966] 449–475).

22. J. David, "Kirche und Naturrecht," in *Orientierung* 30 (June 1966) 133, ascribes to us the view that moral theology can "not manage without reference to the natural law, if it [wants] to construct a somewhat closed system of moral theology." He bases this on the article cited in note 21. But this is not entirely justified. For in that article it says on p. 52: "Human beings are only ready to hear the moral message of Christ and to understand it in faith because they already experience the claim of the natural law which is (logically) prior to God's Word of revelation in Christ. Therefore for Christians the message of Christ and the natural law are not alternatives. The faith understanding of Christ's precept already contains within itself, as its (transcendental) presupposition, a natural understanding of the natural law. . . . *That is the reason* why moral theology, precisely because it has as its immediate object the law of Christ accepted in faith, cannot neglect to include the natural law in its methodical reflection. The better and more clearly it understands the natural law, so much the better is it able to hear and grasp the law of Christ clearly and without distortion." Therefore any moral theological reasoning, that is, reasoning based on reve-

lation, necessarily includes as an intrinsic moment an interpretation of the natural law. And just so little can the ecclesiastical teaching office authoritatively interpret the revealed law of Christ without interpreting the natural law, at least insofar as a correct understanding of the natural law conditions a proper understanding of the law of Christ.

23. B. Häring, *Moralverkündigung nach dem Konzil* (Bergen-Enkheim 1966) 72 states with indignation that "The unbelievable idea still flits around in many heads (including Catholic theologians) that the moral teaching of the NT adds nothing new *by way of content* to the natural law; it merely brings new motivation." That may really be worse than the moral doctrine of Pelagius. Häring names no names. Hence it is not evident whether the position laid out here falls under this verdict. No matter, what Catholic theologian would not know that obedience toward God's commandment can only be salvific (salutaris) insofar as it is performed in the power of the grace of Christ, hence insofar as it is an obedience received "as a gift"? Finally, given the reformation doctrine of justification, it seems highly unlikely that Protestant theologians have been surreptitiously recommending Pelagianism in their ethics.

24. The question under discussion here regards the significance of the natural law within moral theology. This is wholly independent of the other questions whether human beings as they in fact are, were they thrown upon their natural powers alone, could fulfill the natural law or whether in our actual order of salvation a purely natural good act (actus mere honestus, non salutaris) is even possible, that is, whether perhaps fulfillment of the natural law is only possible insofar as it is an inner moment of the fulfillment of the law of Christ.

25. R. Schnackenburg, for instance, overlooks this in his article on "Die neutestamentliche Sittenlehre in ihrer Eigenart im Vergleich zu einer naturlichen Ethik," in J. Stelzenberger, ed., *Moraltheologie und Bibel* (Paderborn 1964) 39–69. He identifies the "purely natural ethic" with Greek, especially Stoic and Aristotelian ethics (40).

26. Cf. for example B. Suarez, *De legibus* 1.10 c. 2 nr. 5–12; A. Vermeersch, I., Nr. 153; M. Zalba, I, Nr. 368; Mausbach-Ermecke, I, 9th edition (Münster W. 1959) 124; K. Martin, *Lehrbuch der kath. Moral,* 2nd edition (Mainz: Kirchheim 1851) 42 writes that "Christian law" is "in its content the integration and fulfillment" of "the natural law." A. Koch, *Lehrbuch der Moraltheologie* (Freiburg i. Br. 1905) on p. 58 has an almost identical statement. But both are inadequate when it comes to specifying just what integration and fulfillment mean concretely.

27. In the article, "Das Problem der Ethik bei Paulus," in *ZNW* 23 (1924) 138; ibid., *Glauben und Verstehen* II, 125: "With regard to the con-

tent of moral demands there is no specifically Christian ethic; and if by chance you would want to designate the commandment of love as a specifically Christian commandment, you should keep in mind that Paul calls the commandment of love the summary of the precepts of the law; but these can be acknowledged before one has heard the Christian message proclaimed. In regard to ethics, genuine Christian preaching does not have special demands to produce." Cf. also R. Bultmann, *Theologie des NT* (1953) 565.

28. The following voice the same idea: H. Greeven, *ThWbNT* II, 769: "For all that the new life of Christians differs at its very core, in its foundation and the source of its strength, from any non-Christian 'morality,' agreement with the pagans reigns concerning what has to count as *euskēmōn.* . . ." O. Cullmann, *Christus und die Zeit,* 3rd edition (Zurich 1962) 201: "Early Christian ethics cannot consist in new precepts, but rather in the demand to acknowledge the precept of the hour anew in the present situation from the perspective of fulfillment and with regard to perfection, and thus to 'fulfill' the Old Law." Cf. also R. Liechtenhan, *Gottes Gebot im NT* (Basel 1942) 72f, 81; E. Dinkler, "Zum Problem der Ethik bei Paulus," in *ZThK* 49 (1952) 199.

29. Accordingly the question often posed today, whether human beings as they are can distinguish exactly between what they are because of their natural humanity and what they are because of their calling to a supernatural life in Christ, proves relatively fruitless. For this supernatural calling (grace), in the opinion of many, also stamps and deeply conditions the natural humanity (nature) of human beings. Let us accept that this imprint is really of the sort that human beings cannot know with exactitude what they are in their natural humanity. What would that mean for moral theology! For moral theology the only thing that counts is whether an ethical norm is really binding or not on human beings as they actually are and whom alone theology knows, and whether theology can ascertain that norm's binding power only through revelation or through a reflexive demonstration of its intrinsic ground.

30. For a fuller substantiation of this statement and of the explanations which follow, cf. B. Schüller, "Die Autorität der Kirche und die Gewissensfreiheit der Gläubigen," in *Der Männerseelsorger,* Heft 5 (September/October 1966) 130–143.

31. It is possible that J. Ratzinger, op. cit., does not intend to eliminate every normative use of natural law from a Christian social doctrine. His view is not too clearly put. On the one hand he explains that a Christian social doctrine is based "on the application of the gospel to the actual social situation," that it results from two "components," the "given social situa-

tion" and the gospel as "criterion of value." On the other hand, he seems not to have found fault with traditional Catholic social doctrine because it uses natural law arguments at all, but rather because it "was content" with natural law criteria and allowed them "too much space." This lack of clarity arises from Ratzinger's failure to pose the important question of how faith knowledge of the gospel as a criterion of value is related to knowledge of natural criteria.

Part Two

THOMAS AQUINAS ON NATURAL LAW AND SOME CONTEMPORARY COMMENTARIES

Summa Theologiae: Question 94. Of the Natural Law

Thomas Aquinas

This translation is that of the Fathers of the English Dominican Province, 1948.

We must now consider the natural law, concerning which there are six points of inquiry: (1) What is the natural law? (2) What are the precepts of the natural law? (3) Whether all acts of virtue are prescribed by the natural law? (4) Whether the natural law is the same in all? (5) Whether it is changeable? (6) Whether it can be abolished from the heart of man?

FIRST ARTICLE
IS THE NATURAL LAW A HABIT?

We proceed thus to the First Article:

Obj. 1. It would seem that the natural law is a habit because, as the Philosopher says, "there are three things in the soul: power, habit, and passion."[1] But the natural law is not one of the soul's powers, nor is it one of the passions, as we may see by going through them one by one. Therefore, the natural law is a habit.

Obj. 2. Further, Basil says that the conscience or "*synderesis* is the law of our mind,"[2] which can only apply to the natural law. But *synderesis* is a habit, as was shown in the First Part.[3] Therefore, the natural law is a habit.

Obj. 3. Further, the natural law abides in man always, as will be shown further on. But man's reason, to which the law pertains, does not always think about the natural law. Therefore, the natural law is not an act but a habit.

On the contrary, Augustine says that "a habit is that whereby something is done when necessary."[4] But such is not the natural law since it is in infants and in the damned who cannot act by it. Therefore, the natural law is not a habit.

I answer that A thing may be called a habit in two ways. First, properly and essentially, and thus the natural law is not a habit. For it has been stated above that the natural law is something appointed by reason, just as a proposition is a work of reason.[5] Now, that which a man does is not the same as that whereby he does it, for he makes a becoming speech by the habit of grammar. Since, then, a habit is that by which we act, a law cannot be a habit properly and essentially.

Secondly, the term "habit" may be applied to that which we hold by a habit; thus faith may mean that which we hold by faith. And accordingly, since the precepts of the natural law are sometimes considered by reason actually, while sometimes they are in the reason only habitually, in this way the natural law may be called a habit. Thus, in speculative matters, the indemonstrable principles are not the habit itself whereby we hold those principles but are the principles the habit of which we possess.

Reply Obj. 1. The Philosopher proposes there to discover the genus of virtue,[6] and since it is evident that virtue is a principle of action, he mentions only those things which are principles of human acts, viz., powers, habits, and passions. But there are other things in the soul besides these three: there are acts; thus to will is in the one that wills; again, things known are in the knower. Moreover, its own natural properties are in the soul, such as immortality and the like.

Reply Obj. 2. Synderesis is said to be the law of our mind because it is a habit containing the precepts of the natural law, which are the first principles of human actions.

Reply Obj. 3. This argument proves that the natural law is held habitually, and this is granted.

To the argument advanced in the contrary sense we reply that sometimes a man is unable to make use of that which is in him habitually on account of some impediment; thus, on account of sleep, a man is unable to use the habit of reasoning. In like manner, through the deficiency of his age, a child cannot use the habit of understanding principles, or the natural law, which is in him habitually.

SECOND ARTICLE
DOES THE NATURAL LAW CONTAIN
SEVERAL PRECEPTS OR ONE ONLY?

We proceed thus to the Second Article:
    Obj. 1. It would seem that the natural law contains, not several precepts, but one only. For law is a kind of precept, as stated above.[7] If, therefore, there were many precepts of the natural law, it would follow that there are also many natural laws.
    Obj. 2. Further, the natural law is consequent to human nature. But human nature as a whole is one, though, as to its parts, it is manifold. Therefore, either there is but one precept of the law of nature, on account of the unity of nature as a whole, or there are many by reason of the number of parts of human nature. The result would be that even things relating to the inclination of the concupiscible faculty belong to the natural law.
    Obj. 3. Further, law is something pertaining to reason, as stated above.[8] Now, reason is but one in man. Therefore, there is only one precept of the natural law.
    On the contrary, The precepts of the natural law in man stand in relation to practical matters as the first principles to matters of demonstration. But there are several first indemonstrable principles. Therefore, there are also several precepts of the natural law.
    I answer that, As stated above, the precepts of the natural law are to the practical reason what the first principles of demonstrations are to the speculative reason because both are self-evident principles.[9] Now a thing is said to be self-evident in two ways: first, in itself; secondly, in relation to us. Any proposition is said to be self-evident in itself if its predicate is contained in the notion of the subject, although, to one who knows not the definition of the subject, it happens that such a proposition is not self-evident. For instance, this proposition, "Man is a rational being," is in its very nature self-evident, since who says "man" says "a rational being,"

and yet to one who knows not what a man is, this proposition is not self-evident. Hence it is that, as Boethius says,[10] certain axioms or propositions are universally self-evident to all, and such are those propositions whose terms are known to all, as, "Every whole is greater than its part," and, "Things equal to one and the same are equal to one another." But some propositions are self-evident only to the wise who understand the meaning of the terms of such propositions; thus to one who understands that an angel is not a body, it is self-evident that an angel is not circumspectively in a place, but this is not evident to the unlearned, for they cannot grasp it.

Now, a certain order is to be found in those things that are apprehended universally. For that which, before aught else, falls under apprehension, is "being," the notion of which is included in all things whatsoever a man apprehends. Wherefore the first indemonstrable principle is that the same thing cannot be affirmed and denied at the same time, which is based on the nature of "being" and "not-being," and on this principle all others are based, as it is stated in *Metaphysics* IV.[11] Now, as "being" is the first thing that falls under the apprehension simply, so "good" is the first thing that falls under the apprehension of the practical reason, which is directed to action, since every agent acts for an end under the aspect of good. Consequently, the first principle in the practical reason is one founded on the notion of good, viz., that good is that which all things seek after. Hence this is the first precept of law, that good is to be done and pursued, and evil is to be avoided. All other precepts of the natural law are based upon this, so that whatever the practical reason naturally apprehends as man's good (or evil) belongs to the precepts of the natural law as something to be done or avoided.

Since, however, good has the nature of an end, and evil the nature of a contrary, hence it is that all those things to which man has a natural inclination are naturally apprehended by reason as being good and, consequently, as objects of pursuit, and their contraries as evil and objects of avoidance. Wherefore the order of the precepts of the natural law is according to the order of natural inclinations. Because in man there is first of all an inclination to good in accordance with the nature which he has in common with all substances, inasmuch as every substance seeks the preservation of its own being according to its nature, and by reason of this inclination, whatever is a means of preserving human life and of warding off its obstacles belongs to the natural law. Secondly, there is in man an inclination to things that pertain to him more specially according to that nature which he has in common with other animals, and in virtue of this inclination, those things are said to belong to the natural law "which nature has taught to all animals,"[12] such as sexual intercourse, education of offspring, and so forth. Thirdly, there is in man an inclination to good according to the nature of his reason, which nature is proper to him; thus man has a natural inclination to know the truth about God and to live in society, and in this respect, whatever pertains to this inclination belongs to the natural law, for instance, to shun ignorance, to avoid offending those among whom one has to live, and other such things regarding the above inclination.

Reply Obj. 1. All these precepts of the law of nature have the character of one natural law inasmuch as they flow from one first precept.

Reply Obj. 2. All the inclinations of any parts whatsoever of human nature, e.g., of the concupiscible and irascible parts, insofar as they are ruled by reason, belong to the natural law and are reduced to one first precept, as stated above, so that the precepts of the natural law are many in themselves but are based on one common foundation.

Reply Obj. 3. Although reason is one in itself, yet it directs all things regarding man, so that whatever can be ruled by reason is contained under the law of reason.

THIRD ARTICLE
ARE ALL ACTS OF VIRTUE PRESCRIBED
BY THE NATURAL LAW?

We proceed thus to the Third Article:

Obj. 1. It would seem that not all acts of virtue are prescribed by the natural law because, as stated above, it is essential to a law that it be ordained to the common good.[13] But some acts of virtue are ordained to the private good of the individual, as is evident especially in regard to acts of temperance. Therefore, not all acts of virtue are the subject of natural law.

Obj. 2. Further, every sin is opposed to some virtuous act. If, therefore, all acts of virtue are prescribed by the natural law, it seems to follow that all sins are against nature, whereas this applies to certain special sins.

Obj. 3. Further, those things which are according to nature are common to all. But acts of virtue are not common to all, since a thing is virtuous in one and vicious in another. Therefore, not all acts of virtue are prescribed by the natural law.

On the contrary, Damascene says that "virtues are natural."[14] Therefore, virtuous acts also are a subject of the natural law.

I answer that We may speak of virtuous acts in two ways: first, under the aspect of virtuous; secondly, as such and such acts considered in their proper species. If, then, we speak of acts of virtue considered as virtuous, thus all virtuous acts belong to the natural law. For it has been stated that to the natural law belongs everything to which a man is inclined according to his nature. Now each thing is inclined naturally to an operation that is suitable to it according to its form; thus fire is inclined to give heat. Wherefore, since the rational soul is the proper form of man, there is in every man a natural inclination to act according to reason, and this is to act according to virtue. Consequently, considered thus, all acts of virtue are prescribed by the natural law, since each one's reason naturally dictates to him to act virtuously. But if we speak of virtuous acts considered in themselves, i.e., in their proper species, thus not all virtuous acts are prescribed by the natural law; the many things are done virtuously to which nature does not incline at first, but which, through the inquiry of reason, have been found by men to be conducive to well-living.

Reply Obj. 1. Temperance is about the natural concupiscences of food, drink, and sexual matters, which are indeed ordained to the natural common good, just as other matters of law are ordained to the moral common good.

Reply Obj. 2. By human nature we may mean either that which is proper to man—and in this sense all sins, as being against reason, are also against nature, as Damascene states[15]—or we may mean that nature which is common to man and other animals, and in this sense certain special sins are said to be against nature; thus, contrary to heterosexual intercourse, which is natural to all animals, is male homosexual union, which has received the special name of the unnatural vice.

Reply Obj. 3. This argument considers acts in themselves. For it is owing to the various conditions of men that certain acts are virtuous for some as being proportionate and becoming to them, while they are vicious for others as being out of proportion to them.

FOURTH ARTICLE
IS THE NATURAL LAW THE SAME IN ALL MEN?

We proceed thus to the Fourth Article:

Obj. 1. It would seem that the natural law is not the same in all. For it is stated in the *Decretum* that "the natural law is that which is contained in the Law and the Gospel."[16] But this is not common to all men because, as it is written, "all do not obey the gospel." Therefore, the natural law is not the same in all men.

Obj. 2. Further, "Things which are according to the law are said to be just," as stated in *Ethics* V.[17] But it is stated in the same book that nothing is so universally just as not to be subject to change in regard to some men.[18] Therefore, even the natural law is not the same in all men.

Obj. 3. Further, as stated above, to the natural law belongs everything to which a man is inclined according to his nature. Now, different men are naturally inclined to different things, some to the desire of pleasures, others to the desire of honors, and other men to other things. Therefore, there is not one natural law for all.

On the contrary, Isidore says, "The natural law is common to all nations."[19]

I answer that, As stated above, to the natural law belong those things to which a man is inclined naturally, and among these, it is proper to man to be inclined to act according to reason. Now the process of reason is from the common to the proper, as stated in *Phys.* I.[20] The speculative reason, however, is differently situated in this matter from the practical reason. For, since the speculative reason is concerned chiefly with necessary things, which cannot be otherwise than they are, its proper conclusions, like the universal principles, contain the truth without fail. The practical reason, on the other hand, is concerned with contingent matters, about which human actions are concerned, and consequently, although there is necessity in the general principles, the more we descend to matters of detail, the more frequently we encounter deviations. Accordingly, then, in speculative matters, truth is the same for all men both as to principles and as to conclusions, although the truth is not known to all as regards the conclusions but only as regards the principles which are called common notions.[21] But in matters of action, truth or practical rectitude is not the same for all as to matters of detail but only as to the general principles, and where there is the same rectitude in matters of detail, it is not equally known to all.

It is, therefore, evident that, as regards the general principles, whether of speculative or practical reason, truth or rectitude is the same for all and is equally known by all. As to the proper conclusions of the speculative reason, the truth is the same for all but is not equally known to all; thus it is true for all that the three angles of a triangle are together equal to two right angles, although it is not known to all. But as to the proper conclusions of the practical reason, neither is the truth or rectitude the same for all, nor, where it is the same, is it equally known by all. Thus it is right and true for all to act according to reason, and from this principle, it follows as a proper conclusion that goods entrusted to another should be restored to their owner. Now this is true for the majority of cases, but it may happen in a particular case that it would be injurious, and therefore unreasonable, to restore goods held in trust, for instance, if they are claimed for the purpose of fighting against one's country. And this principle will be found to fail the more according as we descend further into detail, e.g., if one were to say that goods held in trust should be restored with such and such a guarantee or in such and such a way, because the greater the number of conditions added, the greater the number of ways in which the principle may fail, so that it be not right to restore or not to restore.

Consequently, we must say that the natural law as to general principles is the same for all both as to rectitude and as to knowledge. But as to certain matters of detail, which are conclusions, as it were, of those general principles, it is the same for all in the majority of cases both as to rectitude and as to knowledge, and yet, in some few cases, it may fail both as to rectitude by reason of certain obstacles (just as natures subject to generation and corruption fail in some few cases on account of some obstacle) and as to knowledge, since, in some, the reason is perverted by passion or evil habit or an evil disposition of nature; thus, formerly, theft, although it is expressly contrary to the natural law, was not considered wrong among the Germans, as Julius Caesar relates.[22]

Reply Obj. 1. The meaning of the sentence quoted is not that whatever is contained in the Law and the Gospel belongs to the natural law, since they contain many things that are above nature, but that whatever belongs to the natural law is fully contained in them. Wherefore Gratian, after saying that "the natural law is what is contained in the Law and the Gospel," adds at once, by way of example, "by which everyone is commanded to do to others as he would be done by."[23]

Reply Obj. 2. The saying of the Philosopher is to be understood of things that are naturally just, not as general principles but as conclusions drawn from them, having rectitude in the majority of cases but failing in a few.[24]

Reply Obj. 3. As, in man, reason rules and commands the other powers, so all the natural inclinations belonging to the other powers must needs be directed according to reason. Wherefore it is universally right for all men that all their inclinations should be directed according to reason.

FIFTH ARTICLE

CAN THE NATURAL LAW BE CHANGED?

We proceed thus to the Fifth Article:

Obj. 1. It would seem that the natural law can be changed because, on Sir. 17:9, "He gave them instructions, and the law of life," a gloss says: "He wished the law of the letter to be written in order to correct the law of nature."[25] But that which is corrected is changed. Therefore, the natural law can be changed.

Obj. 2. Further, the slaying of the innocent, adultery, and theft are against the natural law. But we find these things changed by

God, as when God commanded Abraham to slay his innocent son, and when He ordered the Jews to borrow and purloin the vessels of the Egyptians, and when He commanded Hosea to take to himself "a wife of fornications." Therefore, the natural law can be changed.

Obj. 3. Further, Isidore says that "the possession of all things in common and universal freedom are matters of natural law."[26] But these things are seen to be changed by human laws. Therefore, it seems that the natural law is subject to change.

On the contrary, It is said in the *Decretum:* "The natural law dates from the creation of the rational creature. It does not vary according to time but remains unchangeable."[27]

I answer that A change in the natural law may be understood in two ways. First, by way of addition. In this sense, nothing hinders the natural law from being changed, since many things, for the benefit of human life, have been added over and above the natural law both by the divine law and by human laws.

Secondly, a change in the natural law may be understood by way of subtraction, so that what previously was according to the natural law ceases to be so. In this sense, the natural law is altogether unchangeable in its first principles, but in its secondary principles, which, as we have said, are like certain proper conclusions closely related to the first principles, the natural law is not changed so that what it prescribes be not right in most cases. But it may be changed in some particular cases of rare occurrence through some special causes hindering the observance of such precepts, as stated above.

Reply Obj. 1. The written law is said to be given for the correction of the natural law, either because it supplies what was wanting to the natural law or because the natural law was perverted in the hearts of some men as to certain matters, so that they esteemed those things good which are naturally evil, which perversion stood in need of correction.

Reply Obj. 2. All men alike, both guilty and innocent, die the death of nature, which death of nature is inflicted by the power of God on account of original sin, according to 1 Kings: "The Lord kills and makes alive." Consequently, by the command of God, death can be inflicted on any man, guilty or innocent, without any injustice whatever. In like manner, adultery is intercourse with another's wife, who is allotted to him by the law handed down by God.

Consequently, intercourse with any woman, by the command of God, is neither adultery nor fornication. The same applies to theft, which is the taking of another's property. For whatever is taken by the command of God, to Whom all things belong, is not taken against the will of its owner, whereas it is in this that theft consists. Nor is it only in human things that whatever is commanded by God is right but also in natural things—whatever is done by God is, in some way, natural, as stated in the First Part.[28]

Reply Obj. 3. A thing is said to belong to the natural law in two ways. First, because nature inclines thereto, e.g., that one should not do harm to another. Secondly, because nature did not bring in the contrary; thus we might say that for man to be naked is of the natural law because nature did not give him clothes, but art invented them. In this sense, "the possession of all things in common and universal freedom" are said to be of the natural law because, to wit, the distinction of possessions and slavery were not brought in by nature but devised by human reason for the benefit of human life. Accordingly, the law of nature was not changed in this respect except by addition.

SIXTH ARTICLE
CAN THE LAW OF NATURE BE ABOLISHED
FROM THE HEART OF MAN?

We proceed thus to the Sixth Article:

Obj. 1. It would seem that the natural law can be abolished from the heart of man because, on Rom. 2:14, "When the Gentiles who have not the law," etc., a gloss says that "the law of righteousness, which sin had blotted out, is graven on the heart of man when he is restored by grace."[29] But the law of righteousness is the law of nature. Therefore, the law of nature can be blotted out.

Obj. 2. Further, the law of grace is more efficacious than the law of nature. But the law of grace is blotted out by sin. Much more, therefore, can the law of nature be blotted out.

Obj. 3. Further, that which is established by law is made just. But many things are legally established which are contrary to the law of nature. Therefore, the law of nature can be abolished from the heart of man.

On the contrary, Augustine says, "Thy law is written in the hearts of men, which iniquity itself effaces not."[30] But the law which is written in men's hearts is the natural law. Therefore, the natural law cannot be blotted out.

I answer that, As stated above, there belong to the natural law, first, certain most general precepts that are known to all; and secondly, certain secondary and more detailed precepts which are, as it were, conclusions following closely from first principles. As to those general principles, the natural law, in the abstract, can nowise be blotted out from men's hearts. But it is blotted out in the case of particular action insofar as reason is hindered from applying the general principles to a particular point of practice on account of concupiscence or some other passion, as stated above.[31] But as to the other, i.e., the secondary precepts, the natural law can be blotted out from the human heart either by evil persuasions, just as in speculative matters errors occur in respect of necessary conclusions, or by vicious customs and corrupt habits, as among some men theft and even unnatural vices, as the Apostle states, were not esteemed sinful.

Reply Obj. 1. Sin blots out the law of nature in particular cases, not universally, except perchance in regard to the secondary precepts of the natural law, in the way stated above.

Reply Obj. 2. Although grace is more efficacious than nature, yet nature is more essential to man and therefore more enduring.

Reply Obj. 3. The argument is true of the secondary precepts of the natural law, against which some legislators have framed certain enactments which are unjust.

Notes

1. *Eth.,* II, 5 (1105b 20).
2. Cf. *In Hexaëm.,* hom. VII (PG 29, 158); St. John Damascene, *De Fide Orth.,* IV, 22 (PG 94, 1200).
3. *S. T.,* I, q. 79, a. 12.

4. *De Bono Coniug.,* XXI (PL 40, 390).

5. Q. 90, a. 1, ad 2.

6. *Eth.,* II, 5 (1105b 20).

7. Q. 92, a. 2.

8. Q. 90, a. 1.

9. Q. 91, a. 3.

10. *De Hebdom.* (PL 64, 1311).

11. Aristotle, *Metaph.,* III, 3 (1005b 29).

12. *Dig.,* I, i, 1 (I, 29a).—Cf. O. Lottin, *Le droit naturel,* pp. 34, 78.

13. Q. 90, a. 2.

14. *De Fide Orth.,* III, 14 (PG 94, 1045).

15. *Op. cit.,* II, 4; 30; IV, 20 (PG 94, 876; 976; 1196).

16. Gratian, *Decretum,* I, i. prol. (I, 1).

17. Aristotle, *Eth.,* V, 1 (1129b 12).

18. *Op. cit.,* V, 7 (1134b 32).

19. *Etymol.,* V, 4 (PL 82, 199).

20. Aristotle, *Phys.,* I, 1 (184a 16).

21. Boethius, *De Hebdom.* (PL 64, 1311).

22. Caesar, *De Bello Gallico,* VI, 23 (I, 348).

23. *Decretum,* I, i, prol. (I, 1).

24. *Eth.,* V, 1 (1129b 12).

25. *Glossa ordin.* (III, 403E).

26. *Etymol.,* V, 4 (PL 82, 199).

27. Gratian, *Decretum,* I, v, prol. (I, 7).

28. *S.T.,* I, q. 105, a. 6, ad 1.

29. *Glossa ordin.* (VI, 7E); Peter Lombard, *In Rom.,* super II, 14 (PL 191, 1345).

30. *Confess.,* II, 4 (PL 32, 678).

31. Q. 77, a. 2.

Natural Law in Aquinas

Jacques Maritain

This chapter first appeared in *Man and the State* in 1951.

The genuine idea of natural law is a heritage of Greek and Christian thought. It goes back not only to Grotius, who indeed began deforming it, but, before him to Suarez and Francisco de Vitoria; and further back to St. Thomas Aquinas (he alone grasped the matter in a wholly consistent doctrine, which unfortunately was expressed in an insufficiently clarified vocabulary,[1] so that its deepest features were soon overlooked and disregarded); and still further back to St. Augustine and the Church Fathers and St. Paul (we remember St. Paul's saying: "When the Gentiles who have not the Law, *do by nature* the things contained in the Law, these, having not the Law, are a law unto themselves . . .");[2] and even further back to Cicero, to the Stoics, to the great moralists of antiquity and its great poets, particularly Sophocles. Antigone, who was aware that in transgressing the human law and being crushed by it she was obeying a better commandment, the *unwritten and unchangeable laws,* is the eternal heroine of natural law: for, as she puts it, they were not, those unwritten laws, born out of today's or yesterday's sweet will, "but they live always and forever, and no man knows from where they have arisen."[3]

The First Element (Ontological) in Natural Law

Since I have not time here to discuss nonsense (we can always find very intelligent philosophers, not to quote Mr. Bertrand Russell, to defend it most brilliantly) I am taking it for granted that we admit that there is a human nature, and that this human nature is the same in all men. I am taking it for granted that we also admit that man is a being gifted with intelligence, and who, as such, acts with an understanding of what he is doing, and therefore with the power to determine for himself the ends which he pursues. On the other hand, possessed of a nature, or an ontologic structure which is a locus of intelligible necessities, man possesses ends which necessarily correspond to his essential constitution and which are the same for all—as all pianos, for instance, whatever their particular type and in whatever spot they may be, have as their end the production of certain attuned sounds. If they do not produce these sounds they must be tuned, or discarded as worthless. But since man is endowed with intelligence and determines his own ends, it is up to him to put himself in tune with the ends necessarily demanded by his nature. This means that there is, by the very virtue of human nature, an order or a disposition which human reason can discover and according to which the human will must act in order to attune itself to the essential and necessary ends of the human being. The unwritten law, or natural law, is nothing more than that.

The example that I just used—taken from the world of human workmanship—was purposely crude and provocative: yet did not Plato himself have recourse to the idea of any work of human art whatever, the idea of the Bed, the idea of the Table, in order to make clear his theory (which I do not share) of eternal Ideas? What I mean is that every being has its own natural law, as well as it has its own essence. Any kind of thing produced by human industry has, like the stringed instrument that I brought up a moment ago, its own natural law, that is, the *normality of its functioning,* the proper way in which, by reason of its specific construction, it demands to be put into action, it *"should"* be used. Confronted with any supposedly unknown gadget, be it a corkscrew or a peg-top or a calculating machine or an atom bomb, children or scientists, in their eagerness to discover how to use it, will not question the existence of that inner typical law.

Any kind of thing existing in nature, a plant, a dog, a horse, has its own natural law, that is, the *normality of its functioning,* the proper way in which, by reason of its specific structure and specific ends, it *"should"* achieve fullness of being either in its growth or in its behavior. Washington Carver, when he was a child and healed sick flowers in his garden, had an obscure knowledge, both by intelligence and congeniality, of that vegetative law of theirs. Horse-breeders have an experiential knowledge, both by intelligence and congeniality, of the natural law of horses, a natural law with respect to which a horse's behavior makes him a *good horse* or a *vicious horse* in the herd. Well, horses do not enjoy free will, their natural law is but a part of the immense network of essential tendencies and regulations involved in the movement of the cosmos, and the individual horse who fails in that equine law only obeys the universal order of nature on which the deficiencies of his individual nature depend. If horses were free, there would be an ethical way of conforming to the specific natural law of horses, but that horsy morality is a dream because horses are not free.

When I said a moment ago that the natural law of all beings existing in nature is the proper way in which, by reason of their specific nature and specific ends, they *should* achieve fullness of being in their behavior, this very word *should* had only a metaphysical meaning (as we say that a good or a normal eye "should" be able to read letters on a blackboard from a given distance). The same word *should* starts to have a *moral* meaning, that is, to imply moral obligation, when we pass the threshold of the world of free agents. Natural law for man is *moral* law, because man obeys or disobeys it freely, not necessarily, and because human behavior pertains to a particular, privileged order which is irreducible to the general order of the cosmos and tends to a final end superior to the immanent common good of the cosmos.

What I am emphasizing is the first basic element to be recognized in natural law, namely the *ontological* element; I mean the *normality of functioning* which is grounded on the essence of that being: man. Natural law in general, as we have just seen, is the ideal formula of development of a given being; it might be compared with an algebraical equation according to which a curve develops in space, yet with man the curve has freely to conform to the equation. Let us say, then, that in its ontological aspect, natural law is an *ideal order* relating to human actions, a *divide* between the suitable and the unsuitable, the proper and the improper, which depends on human nature or essence and the unchangeable necessities rooted in it. I do not mean that the proper regulation for each possible human situation is contained in the human essence, as Leibniz believed that every event in the life of Caesar was contained beforehand in the idea of Caesar. Human situations are something existential. Neither they nor their appropriate regulations are contained in the essence of man. I would say that they ask questions of that essence. Any given situation, for instance the situation of Cain with regard to Abel, implies a relation to the essence of man, and the possible murder of the one by the other is incompatible with the general ends and innermost dynamic structure of that rational essence. It is rejected by it. Hence the prohibition of murder is grounded on or required by the essence of man. The precept: thou shalt do no murder, is a precept of natural law. Because a primordial and most general end of human nature is to preserve being—the being of that existent who is a person, and a universe unto himself; and because man insofar as he is man has a right to live.

Suppose a completely new case or situation, unheard of in human history: suppose, for instance, that what we now call *genocide* were as new as that very name. In the fashion that I just explained, that possible behavior will face the human essence as incompatible with its general ends and innermost dynamic structure: that is to say, as prohibited by natural law. The condemnation of genocide by the General Assembly of the United Nations[4] has sanctioned the prohibition of the crime in question by natural law—which does not mean that that prohibition was part of the essence of man as I know not what metaphysical feature eternally inscribed in it—nor that it was a notion recognized from the start by the conscience of humanity.

To sum up, let us say that natural law is something both *ontological* and *ideal.* It is something *ideal,* because it is grounded on the human essence and its unchangeable structure and the intelligible necessities it involves. Natural law is something *ontological,* because the human essence is an ontological reality, which moreover does not exist separately, but in every human being, so that by the same token natural law dwells as an ideal order in the very being of all existing men.

In that first consideration, or with regard to the basic *ontological* element it implies, natural law is coextensive with the whole field of natural moral regulations, the whole field of natural morality.

Not only the primary and fundamental regulations but the slightest regulations of natural ethics mean conformity to natural law—say, natural obligations or rights of which we perhaps have now no idea, and of which men will become aware in a distant future.

An angel who knew the human essence in his angelic manner and all the possible existential situations of man would know natural law in the infinity of its extension. But we do not. Though the Eighteenth Century theoreticians believed they did.

THE SECOND ELEMENT (GNOSEOLOGICAL) IN NATURAL LAW

Thus we arrive at the *second* basic element to be recognized in natural law, namely natural law *as known,* and thus as measuring in actual fact human practical reason, which is the measure of human acts.

Natural law is not a written law. Men know it with greater or less difficulty, and in different degrees, running the risk of error here as elsewhere. The only practical knowledge all men have naturally and infallibly in common as a self-evident principle, intellectually perceived by virtue of the concepts involved, is that we must do good and avoid evil. This is the preamble and the principle of natural law; it is not the law itself. Natural law is the ensemble of things to do and not to do which follow therefrom in *necessary* fashion. That every sort of error and deviation is possible in the determination of these things merely proves that our sight is weak, our nature coarse, and that innumerable accidents can corrupt our judgment. Montaigne maliciously remarked that, among certain peoples, incest and thievery were considered virtuous acts. Pascal was scandalized by this. All this proves nothing against natural law, any more than a mistake in addition proves anything against arithmetic, or the mistakes of certain primitive peoples, for whom the stars were holes in the tent which covered the world, prove anything against astronomy.

Natural law is an unwritten law. Man's knowledge of it has increased little by little as man's moral conscience has developed. The latter was at first in a twilight state.[5] Anthropologists have taught us within what structures of tribal life and in the midst of what half-awakened magic it was primitively formed. This proves merely that the knowledge men have had of the unwritten law has passed through more diverse forms and stages than certain philosophers or theologians have believed. The knowledge which our own moral conscience has of this law is doubtless still imperfect, and very likely it will continue to develop and to become more refined as long as humanity exists. Only when the Gospel has penetrated to the very depth of human substance will natural law appear in its flower and its perfection.

So the law and the knowledge of the law are two different things. Yet the law has force of law only when it is promulgated. It is only insofar as it is known and expressed in assertions of practical reason that natural law has force of law.

At this point let us stress that human reason does not discover the regulations of natural law in an abstract and theoretical manner, as a series of geometrical theorems. Nay more, it does not discover them through the conceptual exercise of the intellect, or by way of rational knowledge. I think that Thomas Aquinas' teaching, here, should be understood in a much deeper and more precise fashion than is usual. When he says that human reason discovers the regulations of natural law through the guidance of the *inclinations* of human nature, he means that the very mode or manner in which human reason knows natural law is not rational knowledge, but knowledge *through inclination.*[6] That kind of knowledge is not clear knowledge through concepts and conceptual judgments; it is obscure, unsystematic, vital knowledge by connaturality or congeniality, in which the intellect, in order to bear judgment, consults and listens to the inner melody that the vibrating strings of abiding tendencies make present in the subject.

When one has clearly seen this basic fact, and when, moreover, one has realized that St. Thomas' views on the matter call for an historical approach and a philosophical enforcement of the idea of development that the Middle Ages were not equipped to carry into effect, then at last one is enabled to get a completely comprehensive concept of Natural Law. And one understands that the human knowledge of natural law has been progressively shaped and molded by the inclinations of human nature, starting from the most basic ones. Do not expect me to offer an a priori picture of those genuine inclinations which are rooted in man's being as vitally permeated with the preconscious life of the mind, and which either developed or were released as the movement of mankind went on. They are evinced by the very history of human conscience. Those inclinations *were really genuine* which in the immensity of the human past have guided reason in becoming aware, little by little, of the regulations that have been most definitely and most generally recognized by the human race, starting from the most ancient social communities. For the knowledge of the primordial aspects of natural law was first expressed in social patterns rather than in personal judgments: so that we might say that the knowledge has developed within the double protecting tissue of human inclinations and human society.

With regard to the second basic element, the element of knowledge which natural law implies in order to have force of law, it thus can be said that natural law—that is, natural law *naturally known,* or, more exactly, natural law *the knowledge of which is embodied in the most general and most ancient heritage* of mankind—covers only the field of the ethical regulations of which men have become aware by virtue of knowledge *through inclination,* and which are *basic principles* in moral life—progressively recognized from the most common principles to the more and more specific ones.

All the previous remarks may help us to understand why, on the one hand, a careful examination of the data of anthropology would show that the fundamental *dynamic schemes* of natural law, if they are understood in their authentic, that is, still undetermined meaning (for instance: to take a man's life is not like taking another animal's life; or, the family group has to comply with some fixed pattern; or, sexual intercourse has to be contained within given limitations; or, we are bound to look at the Invisible; or, we are bound to live together under certain rules and prohibitions), are subject to a much more universal awareness—everywhere and in every time— than would appear to a superficial glance; and why, on the other hand, an immense amount of relativity and variability is to be found in the particular rules, customs, and standards in which, among all peoples of the earth, human reason has expressed its knowledge even of the most basic aspects of natural law: for, as I pointed out above, that spontaneous knowledge does not bear on moral regulations conceptually discovered and rationally deduced, but on moral regulations known through inclination, and, at the start, on general tendential forms or frameworks, I just said on *dynamic schemes* of moral regulations, such as can be obtained by the first, "primitive" achievements of knowledge through inclination. And in such tendential frameworks or dynamic schemes many various, still defective contents can occur—not to speak of the warped, deviated, or perverted inclinations which can mingle with the basic ones.

We may understand at the same time why natural law essentially involves a dynamic development, and why moral conscience, or the knowledge of natural law, has progressed from the age of the cave-man in a double manner: first, as regards the way in which human reason has become aware in a less and less crepuscular, rough, and confused manner, of the primordial regulations of natural law; second, as regards the way in which it has become aware— always by means of knowledge through inclination—of its further, higher regulations. And such knowledge is still progressing, it will progress as long as human history endures. That progress of moral conscience is indeed the most unquestionable instance of progress in humanity.

I have said that natural law is unwritten law: it is unwritten law in the deepest sense of that expression, because our knowledge of it is no work of free conceptualization, but results from a conceptualization *bound* to the essential inclinations of being, of living nature, and of reason, which are at work in man, and because it develops in proportion to the degree of moral experience and self-reflection, and of social experience also, of which man is capable in the various ages of his history. Thus it is that in ancient and mediaeval times attention was paid, in natural law, to the *obligations* of man more than to his *rights*. The proper achievement—a great achievement indeed— of the XVIIIth Century has been to bring out in full light the *rights* of man as also required by natural law. That discovery was essentially due to a progress in moral and social experience, through which the root *inclinations* of human nature as regards the rights of the human person were set free, and consequently, *knowledge through inclination* with regard to them developed. But, according to a sad law of human knowledge, that great achievement was paid for by the ideological errors, in the theoretical field, that I have

stressed at the beginning. Attention even shifted from the obligations of man to his rights only. A genuine and comprehensive view
would pay attention *both* to the obligations and the rights involved
in the requirements of natural law.

Notes

1. Especially because the vocabulary of the *Commentary on the Sentences,* as concerns the "primary" and "secondary" precepts of Natural
Law, is at variance with the vocabulary of the *Summa theologica* (i–ii. 94).
Thomas' respect for the stock phrases of the jurists also causes some trouble,
particularly when it comes to Ulpian.

2. Paul, Rom. 2:14.

3.   "Nor did I deem
Your ordinance of so much binding force,
As that a mortal man could overbear
The unchangeable unwritten code of Heaven;
This is not of today and yesterday,
But lives forever, having origin
Whence no man knows: whose sanctions I were loath
In Heaven's sight to provoke, fearing the will
Of any man."

                (Sophocles *Antigone* ii. 452–60,
                George Young's translation)

4. December 11, 1948.

5. Cf. Raïssa Maritain, *Histoire d'Abraham ou les premiers âges de la
conscience morale* (Paris: Desclée De Brouwer, 1947).

6. This is, in my opinion, the real meaning implied by St. Thomas,
even though he did not use the very expression when treating of Natural
Law. Knowledge through inclination is generally understood in all his doctrine on Natural Law. It alone makes this doctrine perfectly consistent. It
alone squares with such statements as the following ones: "Omnia illa ad
quae homo *habet naturalem inclinationem, ratio naturaliter apprehendit ut
bona,* et per consequens ut opere prosequenda; et contraria eorum, ut mala
et vitanda" (i–ii. 94. 2); "Ad legem naturae pertinet omne illud ad quod

homo inclinatur secundum naturam. . . . Sed, si loquamur de actibus vir-
tuosis secundum seipsos, prout scilicet in propriis speciebus considerantur,
sic *non* omnes actus virtuosi sunt de lege naturae. Multa enim secundum
virtutem fiunt *ad quae natura non primo inclinat; sed per rationis inquisi-
tionem ea homines adinvenerunt,* quasi utilia ad bene vivendum" (i–ii. 94.
3). The matter has been somewhat obscured because of the perpetual comparison that St. Thomas uses in these articles between the speculative and
the practical intellect, and by reason of which he speaks of the *propria
principia* of Natural Law as *"quasi conclusiones principiorum communium"* (i–ii. 94. 4). As a matter of fact, those *propria principia* or specific
precepts of Natural Law are in no way conclusions rationally deduced; they
play in the practical realm a part *similar* to that of conclusions in the speculative realm. (And they appear as inferred conclusions to the "after-
knowledge" of the philosophers who have to reflect upon and explain the
precepts of Natural Law.)

The Originality of John Finnis' Conception of the Natural Law

Terence Kennedy, C.SS.R.

This article first appeared in *Euntes Docete* in 1987.

John Finnis is a Catholic layman, married and with a family, who wants to rationally justify and renew the natural law tradition and so provide a sure grounding for the Church's moral teaching. His fields of competence are jurisprudence and ethics, both of which are sources for his reflection.

Born in Australia in 1940, he graduated with an honors LL.B from Adelaide University and went on to Oxford as a Rhodes scholar. He has taught there and in Malawi. He has been Fellow and Praelector in Jurisprudence of University College, and Reader in Law, University of Oxford. He specialized in constitutional law and is adviser to a number of governments in that field. He has been active in the abortion debate and on biomedical issues. He has acted as adviser to the English bishops especially on IVF.[1]

Finnis is of interest to us not so much for his conclusions as for the general framework of ethical and legal theory he sets up. The nub of his originality is his theory of the natural law. Therefore this essay shall pay attention to his magisterial exposition of the significance of natural law, the basic goods for man that ground it and the modes of responsibility that guide practical reasoning. His principal work, *Natural Law and Natural Rights,* was really addressed to the legal profession. He acknowledges his debt to Germain Grisez for the fundamental philosophy that inspired him.[2] He labors within the classic tradition of Plato, Aristotle and St. Thomas Aquinas but he does not belong to the Thomist school. He treats St. Thomas as we might expect a sympathetic lawyer would as occupying a "uniquely strategic place in the history of natural law theorizing."[3] By maintaining a critical attitude to his master he discovered the blank spaces in his theory that he filled with his own insights.

He has expounded the Rule of Law[4] in society in terms of human rights as the modern idiom for natural law. In *Fundamentals of Ethics*[5] he directs his thought to Catholic moral theology. It is a smaller philosophical work outlining the nature of practical reason, the objectivity of morality and the refutation of consequentialism. The last of these is much debated among moralists at the moment. We shall not tarry on the exact point but on the deeper reasons for Finnis's denial since right understanding is crucial here because "the Roman Catholic Church . . . is perhaps unique in the modern world in claiming to be an authoritative exponent of natural law."[6]

The Middle Ages were content to define natural law as a "participation in eternal law" but this does not satisfy contemporary questioning of the origin and apprehension of the most essential ethical and juridic principles. How does one pass from these principles to fully concrete actions? Present-day thinking is not prepared to derive human rights from eternal law. Modern logic and epistemology, anthropology and sociology must enter into consideration. Finnis therefore propounds a view of the last end of man not as the single good of the contemplation of God but as the fullness of life with all its complex and multiple goods in the Kingdom. He thus demonstrates a Christian philosopher's awareness of the contemporary humanistic demands for true autonomy and integral fulfilment for man. "Any state that would count as the 'one ultimate good for all humans' must involve a plurality of goods, such is the irreducible complexity of integral human fulfilment."[7] Instead of the traditional theme of the desire for God as the uniting factor in all moral theology he accentuates, in typically modern tones, the possibility of a personal relationship with God.[8] His search for the foundations of ethics leads him to the existential goods that man experiences now as components of final happiness. He set himself the task of exploring these goods and the responsible modes of human action in achieving them. He voyages into this "black hole" left in the moral universe mapped by previous theories and which has wrecked so many modern accounts of practical reason in ethics.

Finnis along with Grisez is notably different from other Catholic scholars writing on natural law. He uses the Aristotelian–Thomistic tradition to bolster his insights into the codification of the basic goods and the modes of practical reason. He does not see natural law in terms of affectivity and connaturality as Maritain does.[9] Nor does he share Joseph Fuchs'[10] preoccupation for method and salvation history. He believes that his stance shows the teleological and consequentialist theories so popular among Catholic moralists to be absurd.

This essay shall discuss his contribution to the understanding of natural law under three headings; I. Natural Law within the Philosophy of Law, II. Listing the Basic Goods, and III. Practical Reasoning.

I.
NATURAL LAW WITHIN THE PHILOSOPHY OF LAW

The starting-point for Finnis is a reflection on "the institutions of human law."[11] The social sciences following Bentham and Austin defined law in a univocal, value-free sense. H.L.A. Hart and J. Raz have described the functional variants that yield a "general theory of law,"[12] that can be adequately explained in terms of focal and peripheral meaning. The focal definition arises from an "internal point of view," i.e. not from external imposition or fear of punishment but as an interiorized standard for the appraisal of behavior. The legal point of view is specified as that of practical reason which is not the descriptive theory of the social scientist but the knowledge actually required in decision-making by judges, politicians, lawyers and citizens. The focal question is: why is it practically necessary to have law? Natural law gives an answer that primarily concerns the basic goods of human flourishing and the rational ways of obtaining them; secondarily with justifying legal and social theory.

Finnis schematizes the principles of natural law as: 1. a set of first principles indicating the basic goods of human flourishing; 2. the basic requirements of practical reason that distinguishes sound from unsound moral action; 3. a set of general moral standards that realize the above principles in all life's circumstances and situation.

These justify positive law even when it is not logically deduced from natural law and can show when it is defective precisely as law.

Natural law as such, he says, has no history but the theories and doctrines explaining it do have a history. He visualized growth in our comprehension of it but this cannot be identified with natural law as such. He seems to disagree with the advocates of the historicity of natural law as such and criticizes A.P. D'Entrèves for failing to make this distinction.

Lawyers object to natural law on the ground that it confuses legal validity with morality and that it does not satisfactorily explain the variety of opinions within the law. Positive law is no mere "copy" of natural law since it cannot provide all the determinations needed in an ordered community. On the question of cultural variation Finnis quotes St. Thomas' threefold distinction of principles.

1. The most general which fix the end and point of having moral principles in the goods affirmed and attained through them and which "cannot as general principles be eliminated from the human heart."[13] Finnis then connects these first general principles with Hart's list of goods that no sane person could ever deny such as knowledge, friendship, children etc. Variables such as situation, circumstances and moral demands are left apart. His classification of the basic goods satisfies the lawyer's need to identify the basis of human and legal rights not only philosophically but with practical and concrete precision. Finnis' original formulation brings the first principles of natural law into the realm of practical goods which will function as an undeniable basis for ethics and human rights. Has he, however, without noticing it slipped over into St. Thomas' second category of "*ut in pluribus*" which corresponds with what would in practice be referred to in English as "absolute" and so is seen as a truly binding value?[14] Whatever the answer to this question he has elegantly and coherently united the juridic with the ethical point of view so that the tradition of natural law reasoning can enliven modern human rights thinking.

2. At the second level, i.e., of cultural realization these principles may have their meaning obscured and their formulation may be corrupted by ignorance or prejudice. They may be falsely limited,

e.g., to interpersonal relationships alone. By recognizing the shifting quality of cultural expressions and their proneness to error Finnis emphasizes the negative quality or danger at this second level. This leads on to convictions of what we see as right and wrong in practice.

3. At the third level only the truly wise can perceive the rule to follow in the most difficult issues in human affairs. "For the real problem of morality, and of the point or meaning of human existence, is not in discerning the basic aspects of human well-being, but in integrating these various aspects into the intelligent and reasonable commitments, projects and actions that go to make up one or other of the many admirable forms of human life."[15]

The main objection to natural law is that it falls prey to the "is-ought" fallacy deriving these principles as "oughts" from the facts of human nature. However the first *per se nota* practical principles, argues Finnis, cannot be inferred from facts, metaphysics or speculative principles. "When discerning what is good, to be pursued (*prosequendum*), intelligence is operating in a different way, yielding a different logic from when it is discerning what is the case."[16] Finnis' problematic is to trace how practical moral rules of action depend on the first principles. He quotes D.J. O'Connor's charge that St. Thomas' theory can not explain "just how the specific moral rules which we need to guide our conduct can be shown to be connected with allegedly self-evident principles."[17]

The criterion of conformity with human nature is not established by a faculty-argument but by the reasonableness of the action. Here is the nub of Hume's difficulty of showing how reason could provide a reason or motivation for decision. He was heir to Suarez and Grotius who distinguished the judgment of right and wrong derived from the nature of things from the obligation to act flowing from the will of God. Thus natural law became identified with a relationship of fittingness or conformity of action to nature, and obligation with the effect of a superior's will on a subject. This is the font of a voluntaristic account of the human act and of natural law that goes contrary to St. Thomas. The key question is: what moves one to act on a decision of the will? For Suarez it is the driving or pushing force of the will as commanding this action. For St. Thomas *imperium* is an act of intelligence whereby one sees the decided and desired action as a good that will realize the person. It is thus the rational attraction of the good that motivates our decision. The reason for action is not the result of a push but it is our response to the pull of the good.[18] Finnis contends that the weakness of the tradition flowing from Suarez through Hume to the present "is-ought" objections to natural law is that it could not and did not identify the basic goods as the only valid reasons for moral activity and the pursuit of integral human fulfilment. By participating in these goods man becomes his true self in communion with his fellows and with God. Obligation arises from the necessity of certain means to desired ends. The natural law is therefore a law of reason and not an obligation of an inferior to conform himself to the imposed will of a superior. Natural law is then truly the rational rule of liberty. This high-point of morality is the intelligent objective or "good of a form of life which, by its full and reasonably integrated realization of the basic forms of human well-being, renders one a fitting subject for the friendship of the being whose friendship is a basic good that in its full realization embraces all aspects of human being, a friendship indispensible for every person."[19]

The key to a valid understanding of law and ethics is for Finnis not metaphysics or the social sciences but practical reason in pursuit of the fullness of humanity.

II.
Listing the Basic Goods

The strategy espoused by Finnis is to consider practical reason in its function of achieving human goods and making man participate in them. No human good can be had without its being recognized as desirable and fulfilling. The reasonableness of these goods is not just a universal phenomenon of human action. It is a necessary element in our happiness and constitution as persons. We do not understand human nature by deducing what is good from the abstract or speculative principles of our humanity. Rather we come to what is genuinely human by reflecting on human action and this tells us what is good for man. Our reflection moves naturally from the objective or good sought to the activity and from the activity to the nature of the agent or the person. Thus human nature is to be understood on the basis of good ethics and not vice versa. By exploring the possibilities of action we come to a comprehension of our inclinations and capacities.

By examining the activities of finding out, assessing and making true judgments it becomes obvious that these activities are justified by the value of truth or knowledge.[20] This is a non-instrumental value sought for its own sake and not because of power, pleasure or survival. Our inclination toward truth reveals knowledge as a general form of the good. A particular piece of knowledge is only an instance of our participation in the value of truth as a reason for decision and action. Even the skeptic spontaneously prefers truth to ignorance.

" 'Knowledge is something good to have' asserts a value that functions as a starting-point in reasoning to what is to be done. It is not a rule or norm of particular action. A basic practical principle serves to orientate one's practical reasoning, and can be instantiated (rather than 'applied') in indefinitely many, more specific, practical principles and premises."[21]

But particular premises are rarely logically derived from first principles. They are not inferences or conclusions but embody them as tacit presuppositions. "The good of knowledge was not for him an 'end' external to the 'means' by which he 'pursued' it or sought to 'attain' it."[22] This value is participated in by commitment, action and decision. It is never exhausted nor is the search for it ever finished. Every project and life-style has its own first principles. These are the real and intelligent reasons for action that we learn only by experience. They cannot be reduced to or explained away by the physical, social or psychological conditions that surround them.

Finnis is sensitive to the modern mind when he treats the idea of principles in any discipline. Self-evidence is not a "relic of the discredited Aristotelian conception of axiomized sciences of nature,"[23] nor the self-explanatory and self-contained idea of Euclid, nor the obvious truth of certain judgments when they are presented to the mind as in St. Thomas. An axiom is now understood as a premise which has the capacity to generate a whole system of theorems that rests, at least implicitly, on a formal logic. These premises cannot be discovered by looking at the objects studied in the science.

They become obvious through broad and long experience. They do not depend on sentiment or the feeling of certitude and together form an objective if implicit methodology for the science.[24]

The principles of practical reason underlying decision are not the same as those of logic, mathematics or science. They fulfill my desires and inclinations through my involvement in the goods of human well-being. It is better to choose knowledge than to remain in ignorance or error. A skeptic doubting the value of knowledge believes his own statements are functionally true and so defeats his own efforts. Knowledge then is an inescapable aspect of the human, what we call a basic good.

Basic values open up our horizons to the possibilities of practical action. We understand our human nature not by deducing conclusions from universal characteristics of humanity but by contemplating, from our own internal point of view, what are our deepest needs, desires and inclinations, individually and in community. These values are not good because we desire them, but we desire them because they are good.

Finnis has considered the research findings of anthropologists. A mere urge must be distinguished from an inclination to fulfilment and this from the pre-conditions for its satisfaction. He arrives at a set of basic common values after sorting through H.L.A. Hart's "natural facts and aims" and J. Rawl's "primary goods" and the main literature on variations of culture. These values are in no way specific moral rules but as universal phenomena of human society illustrate the link between human inclinations and basic goods. He thus passes from the scientific data to the ethically critical question of what are the undeniable intelligible aspects of human well-being for all men. These will be the first, self-evident and indemonstrable human goods.

They are listed and codified thus. 1. Life; vitality in all its aspects from self-preservation and health-care to the transmission of life by procreation. 2. Knowledge. 3. Play; a performance simply for its own sake and the joy it gives. 4. Aesthetic experience; beauty and its appreciation. 5. Sociability; from a minimum of peace and harmony to friendship in its fullness. 6. Practical reasonableness; to shape one's life, character and destiny by intelligence. Interiorly it means peace of heart; exteriorly it is authenticity which makes our actions truly efficacious realizations of our personality in the world, real expressions of our identity and freedom. 7. Religion; an ultimate order of things that reaches beyond death and refers all to its origin and end, God. This list seems to be as complete and exhaustive as any ever invented. Others have been suggested but Finnis challenges their authors to demonstrate they are more comprehensive.

Since each good is self-evident and cannot be reduced to any other there is no hierarchy among them. However there is a priority of values in one's life-commitments, e.g., a scholar will give preference to knowledge over sport as a personal priority. Ranking occurs because of temperament, inclination and capacity but not from any commensurability of these goods. St. Thomas says the order of the goods follows the order of the inclinations, i.e., toward self-preservation in existence, then to procreation and education of offspring and lastly to what is specifically human and rational. Finnis disagrees with this metaphysical grounding of our practical principles. He also refutes the modern desire to discover one form of well-being or experience more fundamental than all the rest. Robert Nozick's thought-experiment[25] with his "experience machine" shows how senseless this quest is.

Finnis has heralded a change in our understanding of premises and principles in modern thought and has applied this to ethics and practical reasoning. Each basic good is a unique, self-evident and indemonstrable source that generates a coherent and logically connected set of values. The distinguishing characteristic of Finnis' system is the independence of one value from another so that each value is self-asserting because of its intrinsic worth. Life as a whole is then seen as an interaction of our participation in these values through our unique commitments, actions and decisions making up our destiny.

III.
PRACTICAL REASONING

Our reflection on the basic goods uncovers a horizon of practical possibilities for action. One asks what is to be done, what left undone and what should never be done. The irreducible and inde-monstrable methodological requirements for participating in these goods thus also belong to the first principles of practical reason. Taken together they form what we call practical wisdom or pru-dence. We see the need for such principles when we think of how the Ten Commandments determine the basic goods. There are hidden premises that only great experience, balanced judgment and proven virtue can bring to light. It is an insight into what is genuinely hu-man and reasonable and not just rational. For Aristotle it meant seeking the "mean" for virtuous action.

Finnis has classified ten prudential principles of practical rea-son. 1. Reasonableness itself is a basic good that structures our pur-suit of every good. It expresses the "natural law method" that gives reasons for what is to be done and not done.[26] 2. A coherent plan of life i.e., seeing life as one whole so that our commitments and proj-ects direct our energies and inclination to our chosen destiny; the wisdom of the Gospel. 3. No arbitrary preference among values means focusing on certain values as preferences around which to weave the fabric of one's existence. This is done without reducing the worth of any of the other values as in Rawl's "thin theory of the good." 4. No arbitrary preferences among persons maintains the human dignity of each person as a participator in the basic goods. The Golden Rule furnishes a universal standard for criticizing all selfishness and double-standards. Fairness may, of course, demand that we show preference for our own health or make an option for the poor without prejudicing equality among men. 5. Detachment and commitment are complementary. The failure of any one proj-ect in life is not the collapse of one's destiny. Nor can life be success-ful without persistence, determination and efficiency in realizing one's commitments. Both fanaticism and indecision are to be avoided. 6. Consequences represent the efficiency of action and have limited relevance in the moral assessment of an action. While we must be efficient in seeking our objectives utilitarianism is irratio-nal as a philosophy of practical reason because the goods involved cannot be measured or weighed against each other. Further how can we predict the future or reasonably foresee long-term consequences? 6. Every basic value is to be respected in every act. A consequential-ist calculus holds that some good may be deliberately sacrificed for a good that is more pressing, urgent or important, e.g., deliberate, direct killing of an innocent person in order to save the life of a hostage. Since consequentialist reason is senseless as said above we must conclude that the act directly aims at hurting, damaging or destroying a basic value. This is not the same as the unintended, unavoidable side-effects of an action. We respect every basic good in every action since none of these goods can be subordinated to any other nor to any project or commitment. This leads to absolute negative prohibitions, e.g., of acts that directly kill the innocent, or anti-procreative sexual acts, or lying, or blasphemy. These are often identified with the Catholic Church's moral teaching as a natural law ethic. Finnis objects that this reduces natural law to this one principle forgetting all the other demands of prudence. 8. The requirements of the common good means that reason must provide for all the conditions needed for the human person's flourishing in the web of relationships and shared efforts that make up society. We shall not enter into Finnis' exposition of how natural law as a prudential methodology functions as a foundation for law, authority and obligation. He reflects on human rights as always being expressions of duty. They are the contemporary grammar for natural law thinking. The common good is the focal point where the rays of practical reason meet and we can see a spectrum of ethical themes emerge. The common good thus sheds its brilliance over the whole of ethics. 9. Following one's conscience means adhering to the reasonable moral judgments one believes are correct against the sway of passion or social pressure. If we were blessed with all the virtues and lived in a perfectly harmonious community our consciences would readily and spontaneously judge aright. Human dignity provides that we follow our consciences even when we may quite inculpably be in error. 10. Morality is the result of applying these nine principles to our commitments and life-projects. Terms such as "moral," "right," "ought" or "obligation" gain their significance in terms of these principles. Moral judgments do not necessarily involve every principle but at least one will have a bearing on any moral decision.

Moral arguments are generated in this form. Major: a requirement of practical reason e.g., the recognition of a basic good or harmony of purpose. Minor: this principle in these circumstances can only be realized by this act. Conclusion: therefore this act is to be done. This depth structure is mostly implicit in human activities. By recognizing it we make contact with the principles of prudence and see natural law functioning as practical reason.

In *Fundamentals of Ethics* Finnis emphasizes that ethics is not merely theoretical knowledge about human activity. Since it aims at truth it may in one way be called speculative since some knowledge gained has intrinsic worth in itself as truth. But it is properly practical because it is knowledge gained in and for the conduct of life. Ethics is practical because its objective and its matter is practical. Its purpose is not merely knowledge of the truth but our active involvement and participation in its achievement. The person is always involved as an active subject. This is known as the transparency[27] of the subject in all moral statements. So what is good for us is not only the good itself but our attaining it. Natural law is the basic human reasonableness that justifies all our life's actions and commitments as well as being the foundation for ethics and law. In the end natural law is identified with practical wisdom. "The good of extending one's reasonableness into one's decisions and actions, is (when it is itself fully pursued and participated in) the disposition which we call the virtue of practical wisdom (*prudentia*) and that virtue provides the indispensable direction needed for all the other moral virtues. Practical wisdom itself gets its indispensable direction from those other basic principles which formulate one's understanding of the other basic goods and ends on the list (life, knowledge, sociability, etc . . .)."[28]

What difference does this theory make in moral theology? It shows that all moral action springs from the pre-moral principles of practical reasonableness, i.e., the basic goods and prudence. Finnis has thus set up a philosophical framework in which one can judge all systems of what was called casuistry. While he acknowledges that he has not descended to practico-practical judgments in the circumstances he does see such decision as revolving directly from his principles. He thus has a seemingly unitary conception of ethics. Just as he does not appear to distinguish the theory of law from jurisprudence as two qualitatively distinct disciplines nor would he draw a broadly different picture of moral theology and casuistry.[29]

He has certainly set out wise principles for judging teleological and proportionalist systems in moral theology. Unfortunately his theory of equally underived and indemonstrable basic goods has been transformed into a hierarchical "association of basic goods" in Richard McCormick's mitigated teleology or proportionalism.[30] This he demonstrates to be a rationalization that overlooks the direct harm done and misidentifies the person wronged. Calculating a better proportion of benefits to harms ultimately falters on the question of whether it is better to suffer evil than to do it. His theory of the natural law which demands that we respect every basic good in every action has become the watershed in criticizing modern Catholic theories of practical reasoning.

Finnis has returned to the broad intellectualist tradition in his understanding of natural law and he has provided an original interpretation of its first principles as affirmations of the basic goods of human flourishing, and its methodology as a regime of practical wisdom. Thus the great tree of natural wisdom can blossom into moral theology when watered with the rivers of the Spirit and bear the fruits of eternal life.

Notes

1. See e.g., "Natural Law in *Humanae Vitae,*" *Law Quarterly Review* 84 (1968) 467–471; "The Abortion Act: What has changed?" *Criminal Law Review* (1971) 3–12; "IVF and the Catholic Tradition," *The Month* (1984) 55–8.

2. See *Natural Law and Natural Rights,* Clarendon, Oxford, 1980, vii, 53, 55, 76–80, 127–132. This book will be referred to as NLNR following Finnis' usage.

3. NLNR vi.

4. Finnis uses this term for institution, a state of affairs and for the legal system, NLNR 270–279.

5. *Fundamentals of Ethics,* Clarendon, Oxford, 1983, 163 pp. This is a much smaller volume than NLNR and really purposes to lay the ethical foundations for a sound moral theology. Its approach is philosophical and ends with the God-question as influencing man's destiny. It therefore shows the possibility of faith is a personal relationship with God.

6. NLNR vi. See also his "The Natural Law, Objective Morality, and Vatican II," in *Principles of Catholic Moral Life,* edited by William E. May, Franciscan Herald Press, Chicago, 1980, 113–151.

7. "Aquinas Lecture 1985; Practical Reasoning, Human Goods and the End of Man," *New Blackfriars,* Oct. 1985, 448. This lecture refutes the idea of beatitude as an isolated act of contemplation of God. Perhaps Finnis has failed to see that contemplation properly understood is man's highest achievement and that contemplation of God as perfectly fulfilled friendship with Him is the formal element in integral human flourishing in heaven. His point that the basic goods cannot be lost or superseded in the Kingdom is well-made.

8. See "The Value of the Human Person," *Twentieth Century* (Australia), 27 (1972) 126–137.

9. NLNR 255, also J. Maritain, *Nove lezioni sulla legge naturale,* Jaca, Milano, 1985 where the basic insights into natural law come through a sort of connatural and affective intuition into our humanity.

10. J. Fuchs, S.J., *Natural Law,* Sheed and Ward, London, 1965, 10–13, 29–32, 178–180.

11. NLNR 3.

12. Their point of view as evaluative jurisprudence is developed in NLNR 7–18.

13. See NLNR 33–34.

14. Josef Seifert argues that these goods "cease to assume this *absolute* character when they appear outside the context of moral action, or rather when their moral relevance is potential and does not address someone." See his "Absolute Moral Obligations," *Anthropos* 1 (1985) 88. See pp. 60 and 64 where *ut in pluribus* since it describes fundamental human values as culturally realized requires a stronger sense in English than merely "for the greater number of cases" or "for the most part" because here the value is lost sight of and appears to be reduced to statistics.

15. NLNR 31.

16. NLNR 34. This is also the theme of the opening chapter of *Fundamentals of Ethics.* See also "Natural Law and Unnatural Acts," *Heythrop Journal,* 4 (1970) 367–368. Of prime importance for his discussion of the practical quality of the first principles of human action is the article of Germain Grisez, "The First Principle of Practical Reason," *Natural Law Forum,* 10 (1965) 168–201.

17. NLNR 34.

18. NLNR 338–339.

19. NLNR 46.

20. Finnis uses knowledge as his test case to show how a basic value is

established in NLNR Chapter II and goes on in Chapter III to list them fully without repeating his argumentation.

21. NLNR 63.

22. NLNR 64.

23. NLNR 66.

24. A great contribution of Finnis is that he can conceive of natural law as methodology as well as principle. He thus distances himself from the scholastics with their emphasis on virtue, etc. He gives greater space to experience and the need for research.

25. NLNR 95, 186–187, 189, 197.

26. NLNR 103. Well-being is understood more from a moral point of view than ontologically, i.e., it comes through practical action.

27. See *Fundamentals of Ethics,* 3, 23, 27, 70–74.

28. NLNR 69.

29. Finnis does not seem to advert to the debate among moralists about whether casuistry is a science or discipline distinct from moral theology or, for the matter, from ethics. A less unitary conception of the possible disciplines of practical reason may be found in J. Maritain's *The Degrees of Knowledge.*

30. See Lisa Sowle Cahill's "Teleology, Utilitarianism, and Christian Ethics," *Theological Studies* 42 (1981) 4, 622–624 to see how Finnis' thought has been transmuted into proportionalism. An advantage of Finnis' unitary conception of the working of practical reason is that it will not allow compromise. The integration of St. Thomas' natural law theory with modern teleological thinking as proposed by a number of authors in *Sittliche Normen* (Patmos, Düsseldorf, 1981, edited by W. Kerber S.J.) would then be impossible.

The Principles of Natural Law

Ralph McInerny

This originally appeared in *American Journal of Jurisprudence* in 1980.

When I reflected on the assignment that had been given me for this occasion—to tell you about the direction discussion of natural law among philosophers has taken over the past quarter of a century —I very swiftly came to the conclusion that I did not want to conduct you on a barefoot trek over the very uneven terrain that assignment suggests. Such a survey would be a very difficult thing to do, and I fear it would not be an unqualified treat for the mind. Confirmation in this thought came when I hit upon a more manageable and, I think, far more interesting approach.

Fifteen years ago Professor Germain Grisez published an article entitled "The First Principle of Practical Reason." It appeared in *The Natural Law Forum,* since metamorphosed into *The American Journal of Jurisprudence.* On this occasion there is something especially fitting in concentrating on this essay by Grisez; the fact that he has developed and expanded the views of his article in a number of subsequent volumes published by the University of Notre Dame Press adds to that fittingness. Not that I am motivated by a sense of loyalty to the *genius loci* alone. Grisez' article was reprinted in the anthology edited by Anthony Kenney devoted to Aquinas in the *Modern Studies in Philosophy* series. Moreover, it has been warmly commended by Alan Donegan and provides the basis for the approach John Finnis takes in his recently published *Natural Law and Natural Rights.*[1] I think it is safe to say that Germain Grisez' interpretation of the key text in Thomas Aquinas' *Treatise on Law,* IaIIae, q. 94, a. 2 has become for many the definitive and authoritative one. It is certainly true that some reflections on it, even if they served only to draw yet more attention to Grisez' work, would worthily, if modestly, fulfill my assignment today.

In what follows, I shall do three main things. First, I shall recall as rapidly and as accurately as I can the views of Thomas in the article in question. Second, I shall summarize Grisez' interpretation which is meant to supplant a traditional more or less Suarezian version of natural law and return to the more satisfying and, he feels, obscured if not forgotten Thomistic teaching on natural law. Finally, I shall offer a number of criticisms of Grisez and Finnis.

I.
SUMMA THEOLOGIAE, IaIIae, Q. 94, a. 2.

Although Thomas Aquinas is rightly looked to as a major proponent of natural law—the view that there are a number of true directives of human action every person can easily formulate for himself—it is oddly true that there is only one place in the vast body of his writings where he engages in an extended and formal discussion of law and its various kinds. Any student of Thomas will realize how unusual this is. Given the nature and occasion of his writings, Thomas was destined to discuss the same issues again and again, so much so that, at the foot of any article in the *Summa Theologiae,* there is a list of *loca parallela* to which one can repair for discussions similar to the one in the *Summa.* There are references to parallel places in the *Treatise on Law* but these are due to the ingenuity of editors rather than to the fact that Thomas is here taking up anew matters he has discussed as such elsewhere. Most notably, there is no parallel discussion to the article which is the focus of this first portion of my remarks.

The article asks: *Utrum lex naturalis contineat plura praecepta vel unum:* Is there one only precept of natural law or are there many? What does he mean by natural law? To this point we have in hand only the definition given in q. 91, a. 2: natural law is the peculiarly human way of participating in the eternal law whereby God governs creation. Every creature comes under the sway of God's governance but "Among the others the rational creature comes under Providence in a more excellent way, insofar as it shares in that Providence, providing for itself and others." The rational creature directs himself to his appropriate end and activity. Such direction is expressed in precepts[2] and the question thus comes down to: is one precept sufficient to express how we should achieve our appropriate end?

Thomas begins by likening the precepts of natural law (his use of the plural indicates how the question will be answered) to the first principles which guide theoretical discourse: both are *per se nota,* known through themselves, not derived, self-evident. A proposition is *per se nota* when no middle term is required to explain the conjunction of predicate and subject. Rather, one who knows the meaning of its terms will immediately see that the proposition is true. In the theoretical use of our mind, there is a distinction between apprehension and judgment; we must grasp the meaning of the constitutive terms of a proposition before we can constitute a proposition from them. Being is something that no one can fail to know; *illud quod primo cadit in apprehensione, est ens, cujus intellectus includitur in omnibus, quaecumque quis apprehendit.* What is known is a being, whatever else it is. On this apprehension is grounded the first indemonstrable principle: you cannot simultaneously affirm and deny the same thing.[3]

Just as being is the first thing that without qualification the mind grasps, so the good is the first thing grasped by mind in its practical function of directing to some work. An agent acts for an end which has the note of goodness. So the first principle of practical reason is going to be grounded on the notion of goodness. What is the concept of the good? The good is that which all things seek. That is what "good" is taken to mean. Something is sought insofar as it is completive or perfective of the seeker. Thus "good" does not simply designate an object of pursuit, it suggests the formality under which the object is pursued: as completive, as perfective. The first precept, the parallel in practical thought to the first principle of reasoning without qualification, the principle of contradiction, is this: The good is to be done and pursued, and evil avoided.

> *Et super hoc fundantur omnia alia praecepta legis naturae, ut scilicet omnia illa facienda vel vitanda pertineant ad praecepta legis naturae, quae ratio practica naturaliter apprehendit esse bona humana.*[4]

The precept is formed by human reason and it is meant to be directive of human action. The addressee is the human agent and the directive is: The perfection, the completion, the good in the sense of the ultimate end, is to be pursued and whatever is incompatible with that end is to be avoided.

Any other directive, any other precept which is a natural law precept, will be in effect a particularlization of this one. That is, we shall expect that there will be a multiplicity of apprehensions each expressive of some constitutive of man's end or good.

Quia vero bonum habet rationem finis, malum autem rationem contrarii, inde est quod omnia illa ad quae homo habet naturalem inclinationem, ratio naturaliter apprehendit ut bona, et per consequens ut opere prosequenda, et contraria eorum ut mala et vitanda.

The good as end or completion is the object of inclination or appetite. Man is a complex whole comprising a number of inclinations, each of which will have an appropriate good or end. If we enumerate these inclinations and notice their hierarchy we will be able to glimpse the natural law precepts which take them into account.

What is meant by the order of inclinations? This: there are some goods which men share with all creatures, others they share with only some other creatures, and some which are peculiar to men. If the human good is taken to mean the good which is peculiar and proportionate to man, it would be that which is perfective of him as the special kind of agent he is. But man is a rational agent. Therefore the good or perfection of rational activity is man's end. But what of such inclinations as that to self-preservation, common to all creatures and thus to man, and that to reproduce and form a family and raise off-spring, common to all animals and thus to men: are the ends or goods aimed at by these inclinations to form no part of the human good? Of course they are parts of man's good, but only insofar as they are humanized, that is, are pursued not just instinctively, but as the aim or goal of conscious action. As human acts, the pursuit of these ends must be rational, deliberate, responsible. Natural law precepts relating to such goods must envisage them as human goods: the precept is a directive of reason as to how we should pursue such goods. Thus goods which are not peculiar to men come to be constituents of the human good insofar as they come under the sway of the distinctive mark of human agents, reason. Sex is a *human* good not just as such, but as engaged in consciously and purposively and responsibly. That is how it becomes a *human* evil too: there is no way in which humans can engage in sexual activity other than consciously which is why the "animal" part of our nature is always a layer and never autonomous.[5]

Natural law is a dictate of reason. Precepts of natural law are rational directives aiming at the good for man. The human good, man's ultimate end, is complex, but the unifying thread is the distinctive mark of the human, i.e., reason; so too law is a work of reason. Man does not simply have an instinct for self-preservation. He recognizes self-preservation as a good and devises ways and means to secure it in shifting circumstances. Man does not merely have a sexual instinct. Recognizing the desirability of sexual companionship, reproduction, offspring, he consciously directs himself to those goods as goods without which he would not be complete.

One familiar with the opening discussions of this part of the *Summa Theologiae,* discussions concerned with the human good and man's ultimate end, will see that the several precepts of natural law are directives aiming at constituents of the human good or ultimate end. The precepts are first: Pursue your good, your ultimate end, and avoid what is destructive of it. And then there are articulations of this in precepts which express constituents of that end: Rationally pursue self-preservation; rationally pursue the good of sex, reproduction, offspring; rationally pursue the good of reason itself, truth, in all its modes, and particularly truth about the most important things.

The natural law precepts other than the first do not express means whereby the good of the first most common precept can be attained, as if they were instrumental to it. Rather they express means only in the sense of constituents of the ultimate end. Thus, it seems that the precepts of natural law are general directives toward the ultimate end, either stated most generally (the good is to be done and pursued and evil avoided), or aimed at constituents of the ultimate end. We will see later, with reference to the distinction between *comunissima, communia,* and *propria,* that there may be

need to modify this claim, but for now, by taking the obvious implication of the text, that all natural law precepts are general injunc-
tions to pursue the ultimate end or the human good, and conjoining
it with the truth that man's end is given, we can see how it can be
claimed that natural law precepts are valid everywhere and at all
times. That claim can seem controversial whenever a way of achieving or attaining the end is expressed, no matter how general the
expression.

II.
GRISEZ ON THIS ARTICLE

The essay of Germain Grisez mentioned at the outset is polemi-
cal in the sense that he is out to correct what he takes to be a fundamental misunderstanding, or fundamental misunderstandings, of
the teaching of St. Thomas with respect to the first principle of
practical reason. It is Grisez' contention that a caricature of Thomistic natural law has been accepted as good money for a long time,
that this caricature owes far more to Vasquez and Suarez than it
does to Thomas, and that this caricature is open to a number of
devastating criticisms which are ineffective against the view of
Thomas Aquinas properly understood.

From the very first paragraph of his article, we would take it
that one of the roots of the misunderstanding is connected with
confusing commands and gerundive statements, that is, treating
"Do good and avoid evil" as equivalent to "Good is to be done and
pursued and evil avoided." "Although verbally this formula is only
slightly different from that of the command . . . I shall try to show
that the two formulae differ considerably in meaning and that they
belong in different theoretical contexts."[6] Taking the first principle
to be a command, the caricature of natural law is this:

Man discovers this imperative in his conscience; it is like
an inscription written there by the hand of God. Having
become aware of this basic commandment, man consults
his nature to see what is good and what is evil. He exam-

ines an action in comparison with his essence to see whether the action fits human nature or does not fit it. If the action fits, it is seen to be good; if it does not fit, it is seen to be bad. Once we know that a certain kind of action —for instance, stealing—is bad, we have two premises, "Avoid evil" and "Stealing is evil," from whose conjunction is deduced: "Avoid stealing." All specific commandments of natural law are derived in this way.[7]

I am interested in this caricature and Grisez' treatment of it only insofar as what he says of it fills out his own understanding of what Thomas really means to say. That such a caricature is or was current, I shall not contest; nor will I say anything about its alleged Suarezian roots. These are simple negations. I am not at all implying that an examination of these historical questions would lead to criticisms of Grisez' characterization.

When one gets into Grisez' article and begins to get a glimpse of his positive interpretation, reasons why it has commended itself to many are easy to find. Although he does not stress this just as such, Grisez gives no comfort at all to those who would see in the concept of ultimate end as highest superordinating good the implication that there is some one goal or course of action that all men should pursue. Many critics of the view of ultimate end that Thomas took over from Aristotle have seen in it the absurd claim that over and above birdwatching, carpentry, and practicing law there is some specifically human task that we should all perform and which is such that to perform it well makes one a good human being. Grisez and Finnis are refreshing in their gentle insistence that the natural law view is precisely the view that there is an all but numberless variety of ways in which men can attain their completeness or perfection as men.

So, too, Grisez' interpretation puts the emphasis on the positive rather than the negative precept. To see natural law as a series of shalt nots is truly a caricature of it, for natural law precepts point to that which is fulfilling and completive of man, not simply toward things to be avoided. The latter presupposes the former and however we stand in need of moral prohibitions, any discussion of the moral life which deals almost exclusively with prohibitions can give no sense of the liberating and expansive thing the moral ideal is. Certainly such an emphasis on the negative bears little or no relation to the writings of Thomas Aquinas.

But of course I am not here simply to praise Grisez and Finnis. I have long been puzzled by the reception Grisez' article received because it seems to me to be extremely obscure at just the points where it should be clearest. There are three general headings under which I can place most of my misgivings about the Grisez interpretation: (a) the somewhat excessive distinction between fact and value (where the understanding of practical reason becomes dubious); (b) the claim that the first principle of practical reason, and perhaps the whole set of basic values, are somehow pre-moral, not-yet-ethical matters; and (c) the denial of any objective hierarchy among the basic values. I shall first of all sketch Grisez' views on these matters and, in the next section of my paper, develop my misgivings.

The Fact/Value Dichotomy

"If one supposes that principles of natural law are formed by examining kinds of action in comparison with human nature and noting their agreement or disagreement, then one must respond to the objection that it is impossible to derive normative judgments from metaphysical speculations."[8] Grisez is insistent on a distinction between the normative and factual, valuation and description, is and ought, and this insistence has, I think, a certain dated charm about it. The passage just quoted suggests that there is something illicit in the passage from such sentences as

Wheaties are good for you

to

You ought to eat Wheaties.

Finnis devotes a section of his second chapter to this matter. "Another of the three decisive issues formulated by Stone was this: 'Have the natural lawyers shown that they can derive ethical norms from facts?' And the answer can be brisk: They have not, nor do they need to, nor did classical exponents of the theory dream of attempting any such derivation.'"[9] Finnis feels this undercuts one of the most widespread misunderstandings of natural law. It is simply not true, he says, that "any form of a natural law theory of morals entails the belief that propositions about man's duties and obligations can be inferred from propositions about his nature."[10] The first principles of natural law are self-evident, underived; that is, for Finnis, the real basis for the denial that they are inferred or derived from any other propositions of whatever kind. "They are not inferred from speculative principles. They are not inferred from facts. They are not inferred from metaphysical propositions about human nature, or about the nature of good and evil, or about 'the function of a human being.' "[11] His denials become more and more sweeping.

> Principles of right and wrong, too, are derived from these first, premoral principles of practical reasonableness, and not from any facts, whether metaphysical or otherwise. When discerning what is good, to be pursued (*prosequendum*), intelligence is operating in a different way, yielding a different logic, from when it is discerning what is the case . . . but there is no good reason for asserting that the latter operations of intelligence are more rational than the former.[12]

More positively, Finnis writes

> One does not judge that "I have (or everybody has) an inclination to find out about things" and then infer that therefore knowledge is a good to be pursued. Rather, by a simple act of non-inferential understanding one grasps that the object of the inclination which one experiences is an instance of a general form of good. . . .[13]

The first underived principles of practical reasonableness, make no reference at all to human nature, but only to human good.[14] In Grisez, far more than in Finnis, this insistence leads to a somewhat unusual sense of practical reason. Grisez says that in theoretical thinking the world calls the turn, in practical thinking the mind calls the turn. Often he suggests that practical reason turns upon a malleable world which it can remake pretty much at will. One recognizes in this characterization what Aristotle and Thomas say of art far more than what they say of prudence, of the specifically moral.

The Pre-Moral Character of First Principles

If Grisez *et sequaces ejus* are insistent that moral principles, the first principles of practical reasoning, are not derived from factual truths grasped by mind speculative, they nonetheless argue for an ethical heteronomy in the following sense. The first underived self-evident principles, the precepts of natural law, are pre-moral, not moral. Moral principles are nonetheless derived from them. What this comes down to, in terms of the article in the *Summa* already cited, q. 94, a. 2, is the claim that the basic values, the goods pointed to or aimed at by the instincts, are not as such moral values. By this they do not mean, for example, that the instinctive desire for sexual congress is, when felt, neither good not bad, not yet a moral act; or that the surging up of an emotion, of anger or joy, is not as such moral or immoral. What they mean is that the comphrehensive good that is to be pursued is not a moral value. That comes down to saying that man's ultimate end is not a moral value. So too the basic values that Finnis lists, expanding a bit on Grisez, namely Life, Knowledge, Play, Aesthetic Experience, Sociability, Practical Reasonableness, and Religion are not moral values, singly, or cumulatively. "Neither this chapter nor the next [3 and 4, in which Finnis discusses basic values] makes or presupposes any moral judgments. Rather, these two chapters concern the evaluative substratum of all judgments. That is to say, they concern the acts of practical understanding in which we grasp the basic values of human existence and thus, too, the basic principles of all practical reasoning."[15]

What Finnis could mean is that the grasp of these basic values would be expressed in definitions rather than in precepts and in that sense no practical advice, moral or any other kind, is being given. Only when we judge that we should pursue the basic value or when we judge that such-and-such would be a way of attaining or participating in the basic value, stating this in a prescriptive way, only then do we enter into the domain of the moral proper. Perhaps that is what he means,[16] and then it would be like saying concept formation is not yet an activity that is true or false; truth or falsehood enter in only when judgments, employing such concepts, are made.

But if that is what Finnis means, it does not seem to be what Grisez means by speaking of these self-evident principles of natural law as pre-moral. He seems more concerned to have principles that will govern the practical activity of all men, good or bad, and which thus must split the difference between moral and immoral. If the bad man as well as the good is guided by these first principles the one will not be called good nor the other bad simply because he is guided by them.

Basic Value Egalitarianism

A moment ago I listed the Basic Values that are taken to emerge from the grasp of the goods aimed at by man's inclinations. One of the most distinctive marks of Grisez' interpretation is his claim that no one of these values is better than the others. There is no objective hierarchy among the basic values that one would have to be guided by in the formation of a life plan. Of course, in the nature of things, this man plans his life in such a way that the quest for knowledge, say, takes precedence over the other values; this man, a surgeon, puts life at the center of his life. In thus giving preference, so to say, to one basic value over others, one must not act directly against any basic value. Here we have, I think, the reason for the claim that the basic values are equally fundamental.

> More important than the precise number and description of these values is the sense in which each is basic. First, each is equally self-evidentally a form of good. Secondly, none can be analytically reduced to being merely an aspect of any of the others, or to being merely instrumental in the pursuit of any of the others. Thirdly, each one, when we focus on it, can reasonably be regarded as the most important. Hence there is no objective hierarchy among them.[17]

Finnis at any rate is aware that this tenet separates him from the text of Aquinas, to an analysis of which Grisez devoted his article.

Thomas, we recall, wrote: *Secundum igitur ordinem inclinationum naturalium, est ordo praeceptorum legis naturalis.* Finnis, taking note of this, and the way in which for Thomas the most basic inclination is one man shares with everything else, the next most basic one he shares with other animals, and so on, comments:

> But is it relevant to a meditation on the *value* of the various aspects of human well-being? Are not speculative considerations intruding into a reconstruction of principles that are practical and that, being primary, indemonstrable, and self-evident, are not derivable (nor sought by Aquinas to be derived) from any speculative considerations?[18]

Finnis concludes that Thomas here sets a questionable example and repeats that "in ethical reflection the threefold order should be set aside as an irrelevant schematization."[19] So we are back to an understanding of the speculative and practical, now so understood as to collide in important ways with Thomas's understanding.

III.
REFLECTIONS ON THE GRISEZ INTERPRETATION

A view of practical reason that regards knowledge of the world to be irrelevant to it is clearly a view different from that which we encounter in Aristotle and Aquinas. The theory of practical reasoning developed by Aquinas is a good deal more complicated than either Grisez or Finnis seem to recognize. It is well known that Thomas provides not just one but three criteria for practical reasoning, suggesting that such reasoning is more practical to the degree that it satisfies more of these criteria.[20] One of these criteria is the nature of the object—is it something that can be made or done by us—and from this point of view a quite factual statement about a house will, since a house is precisely a product of human craft, count as a piece of practical discourse; minimally practical, it is true, but one sees that it is not going to be in terms of syntax that one is going to be able to set the practical off from the theoretical. Grisez tends to want to restrict practical discourse to gerundive precepts.

Allied with this is the insistence that no transition from *is* to *ought,* from *fact* to *value* is going on in natural law. The dichotomy involved, once thought to be sharp and distinct, has come to be seen as doing duty for a number of contrasts which cannot be reduced to absolute unity. Maritain in *Neuf Lecons sur la philosophie morale* made the point that all intellectual activity is concerned with value, truth value, for instance. Indeed this is now one of the basic values Grisez and Finnis recognize and thus comes specifically under the sway of the moral. The concern not to infer from *fact* to *value,* from *is* to *ought,* may be a symptom of over-fastidiousness.

> Joe weighs two hundred and fifty pounds.
> Joe ought to go on a diet.

That transition would be said to be justified by the understood premise "It is not healthy to be overweight." And that is a value-premise. It is action guiding. But is it? We may find it odd if someone says "Who wants to be healthy?" but would we want to say some fallacy has been committed? Grisez and Finnis are clearly concerned about avoiding fallacies. But one man's fallacy may be another's common sense. Does

> Knowledge is good for man
> entail
> Men ought to pursue knowledge?

Grisez and Finnis often speak of the first proposition as a metaphysical truth having nothing to do with practical judgments. The fact is "Knowledge is good for man" is a special case of "Good is that which all men seek;" it is precisely the basic value which is the principle on which the precept "Knowledge ought to be pursued" is founded. Whatever fallacy there may be in passing from *is* to *ought,* Grisez' understanding of it threatens to undercut his own and Thomas' actual procedure.

> No philosopher, no matter what he may say, wants to regard facts about human beings as morally irrelevant. The sharp dichotomy between normative and non-normative discourse maintained by the empiricist does not obtain in

fact: there are many propositions, such that tuberculosis is a disease, or that a human child ought to be able to talk before reaching the age of five years, which do not fit comfortably on either side of the dichotomy.[21]

The claim that the first principles of practical reasoning, the self-evident principles of natural law, are pre-moral rather than precisely the principles of morality, is, I find, a strange one. It certainly sounds Pickwickian as a characterization of what is going on in the *Summa Theologiae,* IaIIae, q. 94, a. 2. Once more Finnis is clearer on this than Grisez, that is, clearer as to what motivates him in saying it.

The principles that express the general ends of human life do not acquire what would nowadays be called a "moral" force until they are brought to bear upon definite ranges of project, disposition, or action, or upon particular projects, dispositions or actions. How they are thus brought to bear *is* the problem for practical reasonableness. "Ethics" as classically conceived is simply a recollectively and/or prospectively reflective expression of this problem and of the general lines of solutions which have been thought reasonable.[22]

Finnis is being guided by what he takes to be the meaning of "moral" nowadays. The first principles of practical reasoning are not yet moral because they are too general, apparently, and Finnis thinks he finds this usage in Thomas.[23]

His reference is to the interesting text to be found at IaIIae, q. 100, a. 1 where Thomas asks if all the moral principles of the old law pertain to natural law. (Moral precepts are here distinguished from ceremonial and judicial precepts of the Old Law.) The text explicitly groups the first principles of natural law with moral precepts, so that there can be little doubt as to Thomas' own usage. But as a terminological matter it is of little importance. What Finnis wants to distinguish from what he calls moral or ethical are those precepts which direct us to pursue our ultimate end or the constituents of it.

I reply that moral precepts, distinguished from ceremonial and judicial precepts, bear on things which of themselves pertain to good morals. Since then human customs (*mores*) are said to be such by being ordered to reason, which is the distinctive principle of human acts, those customs are said to be good which agree with reason, those evil which are discordant with reason.

Now just as every judgment of speculative reason proceeds from a natural knowledge of first principles, so every judgment of practical reason proceeds from certain naturally known principles.[24]

Here Thomas refers to q. 94, a. 2. These first precepts of natural law he now calls *comunissima,* most common, and since they are precisely most common *precepts,* they cannot be simply the grasp or apprehension of basic values.[25] Nonetheless, it seems right to suggest that they are precepts which simply direct to the end, whether in general (The good is to be done and pursued, and evil avoided), or in articulating the constituents of man's good.

From which it (reason) diversely proceeds in judging of diverse things. (a) There are some things in human acts so obvious (*explicita*) that with but a little consideration they can be approved or disapproved through the common and first principle. (b) Other things indeed are such that judgment of them requires lengthy consideration of diverse circumstances, the diligent inquiry into which is not possible for everyone, but only the wise. . . .[26]

It is on the basis of these texts that I suggest that the first principles of natural law are absolute and changeless precisely because they direct to the end and do not express even at a level of high generality ways of achieving the end. The next level Thomas speaks of, a level of precepts deduced from the most common, could be thought of as directives expressing ways to achieve the end or ways to be avoided since they thwart the end. Here there could be absolutes whenever a certain mode of conduct would necessarily thwart the end, but clearly we are more likely to have precepts which are valid only for the most part. Furthermore, if "precept" in the proper sense of the word covers judgments which express means to the end and not simply end, and there is reason to think this is how Thomas understood it,[27] then one could say that the first precepts of natural law are less properly precepts, less properly moral precepts, than those expressive of means. And that would be a way of saying what Finnis and Grisez, perhaps for the same reason, want to say.

As for the denial of an objective hierarchy among basic values, one has to hold fast to the reasons for the denial—to wit, to guard against acting directly contrary to a basic value. Whether the acceptance of an objective hierarchy among basic values deprives one of a basis for forbidding acting directly against a basic value is not evident. Only if the hierarchy reduced a basic good to mere instrumental status would this follow. By the same token, recognition of an objective hierarchy among basic values in no way impedes that subjectively, that is from subject to subject, a more personal hierarchy would obtain. In any case, what must be said is that Thomas himself, as Aristotle had before him, insists on the inequality of the basic values and recognizes a hierarchy among them. That a good might be end-like yet not an ultimate end, but, subordinable to a further end, does not make it merely instrumental. Both Thomas and Aristotle take that perfection of rational activity which they call contemplation to be objectively the highest. Neither man thinks that anyone could devote himself exclusively to contemplation; the human good remains complex, irreducible to a single kind of activity. And in this perspective, the moral virtues are taken to be dispositive toward, conditions of, the contemplative use of the mind.

IV.
ENVOI

I hope these remarks about the interpretation of Grisez and Finnis will not seem churlish or petty or merely negative. If their interpretation did not have much to commend it, it would scarcely have become as influential as it is. I mentioned earlier some of its major merits, in my estimation, and I could add many more to

those. Perhaps I will not be thought too docile a disciple of Aquinas if I say that I find Grisez and Finnis at their best when they are developing Thomas' thought along its own lines and weakest when they are consciously or unconsciously deviating from it. In any case, it seems to me that natural law has been largely a matter of footnotes to the *Treatise on Law* in the *Summa Theologiae,* and that it is likely to remain this insofar as it retains strength and persuasiveness. Quite apart from its independent merits, the view of Grisez and Finnis is seen as Thomistic. This is why I concentrated on it and I mean my humble observations to be tribute rather than carping criticism. My moral is simply that one should read Grisez and Finnis in conjunction with Aquinas. A major task before us, I think, is to draw out the relations between ultimate end and the *Treatise on Law.* When this is done the main emphasis of the work of Germain Grisez will have been brought to completion.

Notes

1. John Finnis, *Natural Law and Natural Rights* (Oxford University Press, 1980). G. Grisez, "The First Principle of Practical Reason," *The Natural Law Forum* (1965), pp. 168–96. I cite the reprint in A. Kenny (ed.), *Aquinas* (London, 1970).

2. *Summa theologiae.* Thomas Aquinas. IaIIae. 92. 2c. ". . . *sicut enuntiatio est rationis dictamen per modum enuntiandi, ita etiam lex per modum praecipiendi.*"

3. One might ask why Thomas gives this expression to the first principle of all reasoning. He says it is grounded on the notion of being and not being, but then why not state the principle: it is impossible for a thing to be and not to be at the same time and in the same respect. The reason seems to be that the concept of natural law draws particular attention to the role of human reason in fashioning precepts directing action to man's end; given this, the mind's affirming and denying give rise to an expression of the first principle more obviously parallel to those of practical reason.

4. The "naturaliter" modifying practical reason's grasp of human goods refers to either or both (a) mind's apprehension of the goods in question, and (b) the immediacy of the judgment that such goods are to be pursued and their opposites avoided.

5. The dream of Kierkegaard's aesthete is to engage in sensuality in such a way as to be at once aware and unaware: to be at once a heedless innocent animal, and a conscious self-observing participant. This impossible dream is why the aesthete lives a life of despair.

6. "The First Principle of Practical Reason," as reprinted in Kenny, p. 341.

7. *Ibid.*, p. 340.

8. *Ibid.*, p. 382.

9. *Op. cit.*, Finnis, p. 33.

10. *Ibid.*, Finnis has in mind D.J. O'Conner, *Aquinas and Natural Law.*

11. *Ibid.*, p. 33.

12. *Ibid.*, p. 34.

13. *Ibid.*

14. *Ibid.*, p. 36.

15. *Ibid.*, p. 59.

16. *Ibid.*, p. 84.

17. *Ibid.*, p. 92.

18. *Ibid.*, p. 94.

19. *Ibid.*, p. 95.

20. Cf. *Summa theologiae*, Ia, q. 14, a. 16.

21. Philip Devine, *The Ethics of Homicide*, p. 43.

22. *Op. cit.*, Finnis, p. 101.

23. *Ibid.* (See also p. 30. "Even when, later, Thomas Aquinas clearly distinguished a class of practical principles which he considered self-evident to anyone with enough experience and intelligence to understand the words by which they are formulated, he emphasized that moral principles such as those in the Ten Commandments are *conclusions from* the primary self-evident principles, that reasoning to such conclusions requires good judgment, and that there are many other more complex and particular moral norms to be followed and more judgments and decisions to be made. . . ."

24. IaIIae, q. 100, a. 1.

25. *Op. cit.*, Aquinas, q. 99. a 2. ad 2m.

26. *Ibid.*, q. 100, a. 1.

27. Ibid., cf. q. 100, a. 9, ad 2m; see also q. 99, a. 1: "*praeceptum legis, cum sit obligatio, est de aliquo quod fieri debet. Quod autem aliquid debeat fieri, hoc provenit ex necessitate alicuius finis. Unde manifestum est quod de ratione praecepti est quod importet ordinem ad finem, inquantum scilicet illud praecipitur quod est necessarium vel expediens ad finem.*"

The Basic Principles of Natural Law: A Reply to Ralph McInerny

John Finnis and Germain Grisez

This article originally appeared in *American Journal of Jurisprudence* in 1981.

Ralph McInerny's "The Principles of Natural Law"[1] is generous in its estimate of the significance of our work. But we think McInerny's criticism of Grisez' article, "The First Principle of Practical Reason,"[2] and Finnis' treatise, *Natural Law and Natural Rights,*[3] involves some serious misunderstandings of our views. We suspect that some of these misunderstandings are widely shared.

There is a methodological problem which makes a commentary on McInerny's article difficult. Grisez' article is a commentary on *Summa theologiae,* I–II, Question 94, Article 2, not a general treatment of Thomas' ethics, much less a summary of Grisez' own ethics. Finnis' treatise, by contrast, states and defends his own ethical theory. It points to texts of Thomas where "they can both illuminate and be illuminated by the theory presented in [the] book";[4] but it is not a commentary, and prescinds from the question whether it is *ad mentem Divi Thomae.* McInerny's article seems to take insufficient account of the restrictions of scope and purpose of the two works he has chosen to discuss.

McInerny says that his misgivings about "the Grisez interpretation [of the teaching of St. Thomas]" can mostly be grouped under three headings.[5] So our reply also is under three headings. Under each we take space for only a few main points.

I.
"EXCESSIVE DISTINCTION BETWEEN FACT AND VALUE"[6]

At one point McInerny suggests that we share "a view of practical reason that regards knowledge of the world to be irrelevant to it."[7]

All the references McInerny offers in respect to Finnis to support this suggestion are to pages in chapter II.4 of his book. These pages are devoted to a necessary polemic against modern critics who claim that Thomas makes the logical error of trying to deduce normative propositions from theoretical propositions ("ought" from "is") and who therefore dismiss him out of hand. A Thomist must read these pages with care, particularly their statements of what Thomas' theory is *not*. To find Finnis' positive account of Thomas' theory of the relation of fact to value, the Thomist should look a bit further on in the book.[8] There Finnis explains:

> Aquinas followed Aristotle's theory of the "induction" of indemonstrable first principles by insight working on observation, memory, and experience, but extended the account to a parallel "induction" of indemonstrable first principles of practical reason (i.e., of natural law) by insight working on felt inclinations and a knowledge of possibilities: *S.T.,* I-II, q. 94, a. 2 . . .[9]

Having explained that for Thomas those first practical principles are of the form "X is a good to be pursued . . . ," Finnis gives his formal account of why such principles are principles of natural law:

> . . . thirdly, the basic forms of good are opportunities of *being;* the more fully a man participates in them the more he is what he can be. And for this state of being fully what one can be, Aristotle appropriated the word *physis,* which was translated into Latin as *natura.* . . . So Aquinas will say that these requirements are requirements not only of reason, and of goodness, but also (by entailment) of (human) nature . . .[10]

Nor does Finnis himself think "knowledge of the world to be irrelevant" to practical reason, nor even to practical reason's grasp of its basic principles. Explaining what he means by "values cannot be derived from facts," he says: ". . . my contention is that, while *awareness of certain 'factual' possibilities is a necessary condition* for the reasonable judgment that truth is a value, still that judgment itself is derived from no other judgment whatsoever."[11]

McInerny makes two points in connection with the fact-value distinction with respect to Grisez.

First, he quotes Grisez's use of the objection "that it is impossible to derive normative judgments from metaphysical speculations."[12] McInerny thinks this "suggests that there is something illicit in the passage from such sentences as

Wheaties are good for you
to
You ought to eat Wheaties."[13]

Later, McInerny says[14] both of us consider it fallacious to pass from

Knowledge is good for man
to
Men ought to pursue knowledge.

"Grisez and Finnis," McInerny says, "often speak of the first proposition as a metaphysical truth having nothing to do with practical judgments."[15] For this claim about what we "often speak of" no citation is given. None can be given, for we nowhere say any such thing.

One of the principles of *practical* thinking is that knowledge is a good to be pursued; this principle entails that knowledge ought to be pursued. But in the *practical* principle that knowledge is a good to be pursued, "good" is understood *practically* in the light of the first *practical* principle: Good is to be done and pursued. If "Knowledge is a good for man" were understood theoretically, simply as a truth of metaphysical anthropology, then it would have no more normative implication than "Knowledge is good for angels" has practical implication for us.

Nothing in our accounts of practical reason in general or of ethics in particular belittles or excludes as irrelevant to ethics a non-positivist, teleological understanding of nature and of human persons insofar as they are part of nature.[16] But if McInerny wishes to justify a conclusion such as

> Joe ought to go on a diet

he had better not be content[17] with premises such as

> Joe weighs two hundred and fifty pounds
> and
> It is not healthy to be overweight.

One must assume a more basic practical premise

> Health is a good to be pursued and protected

which itself is a specification of the very first principle of practical reason. This very first principle is *not* the truth of metaphysics or psychology, "Good is that which all men seek," as McInerny seems to think,[18] but "Good is to be done and pursued and evil is to be avoided," as Thomas unequivocally says when he treats this matter in the famous passage on which Grisez commented.

Similarly, only with the practical principle, "Health is a good to be pursued and protected," and additional factual premises can one validly pass from "Wheaties are good for you" to "You ought to eat Wheaties." We have never said that one cannot pass from metaphysical and/or factual truths *together with principles of practical reasoning* to normative conclusions. Our point rather was that there can be no valid deduction of a normative conclusion without a normative principle, and thus that *first* practical principles cannot be derived from metaphysical speculations.[19]

The second point McInerny makes about Grisez with respect to fact and value is this:

> Grisez says that in theoretical thinking the world calls the turn, in practical thinking the mind calls the turn. Often he suggests that practical reason turns upon a malleable world which it can remake pretty much at will.[20]

Again, no citation is given. Grisez nowhere says or "suggests" any such absurdity as that practical reason turns upon a malleable world which it can remake pretty much at will. In saying that "the mind calls the turn" in practical knowledge,[21] Grisez is making the same point as Thomas makes in the Prologue to his commentary on Aristotle's *Ethics:* that in contrast with the order of nature which reason finds and does not make, there are orders which reason itself makes —in the case of morally practical knowledge, in the acts of the will, and what is consequent upon them.

Grisez has taken pains elsewhere to show that there also necessarily is an order which reason does not make but only considers, an order of nature (including human nature), which is far from being "a malleable world which it [reason] can remake pretty much at will."[22] In the context of this exposition, Grisez sets out a thoroughly objectivist theory of value as *fulfillment of possibility,* in each order of reality, and emphasizes: "*What* the something is and to what order of entities it belongs must be taken for granted in distinguishing between the extent to which it already is, and the extent to which it is still short of its full possibility"[23] (and thus wanting in goodness). Thus for Grisez even in the moral world, where the mind calls the turn (reason makes, not finds, order), the subjectivism suggested by McInerny's unfortunate phrase, "can remake pretty much at will," is altogether excluded.

II.
BASIC VALUES AS PREMORAL

In discussing the premoral character of the principles of natural law, McInerny seems to conclude that he agrees with what he thinks we perhaps also want to say on this question.[24] But McInerny's view of this matter presupposes his assumption that in the absolutely first principle, "*Bonum est faciendum et prosequendum . . .* ," the word "*bonum*" refers to the *ultimate* end.[25]

Whether considered in itself or as an interpretation of Thomas, this presupposition seems to us quite untenable. Speaking of this absolutely first precept, McInerny comments:

The addressee is the human agent and the directive is: The perfection, the completion, the good in the sense of the ultimate end, is to be pursued and whatever is incompatible with that end is to be avoided.

Any other directive, any other precept which is a natural law precept, will be in effect a particularization of this one. That is, we shall expect that there will be a multiplicity of apprehensions each expressive of some constitutive of man's end or good.[26]

But note, first of all, that in Thomas' formula "Good is to be *done* and pursued," whereas in offering his interpretation, McInerny drops "to be done" and focuses on "to be pursued." This suppression of *faciendum* certainly facilitates the interpretation of *bonum* as *ultimus finis*. For either the last end is not done (though it may include doing), or, if the last end is done, it is done only when one rests in it and is no longer guiding action by reason toward it.

Second, it is by no means clear or even likely that Thomas considers all the goods to which man is naturally inclined (*omnia illa ad quae homo habet naturalem inclinationem*) to be constitutive of man's *ultimate* end. Indeed, what Aquinas does say about the ultimate end[27] seems quite unlike McInerny's view that basic human goods are "constitutive of" man's end. This view seems closer to Vatican II[28] and to some things Grisez has said[29] about the end of man than to the doctrine of Thomas.

Thirdly, Thomas holds that the absolutely first principle of practical reasoning is to its domain as the principle of noncontradiction is to the domain of thinking in general.[30] If this is so, the first principle must govern the practical reasoning of people who do evil. The Don Juan considers fornication a good to be pursued. This consideration is not simply irrational and it is action-guiding; thus, Don Juan's immoral reasoning is governed by the first principle of practical reason. But he is acting against, not toward, the ultimate end of man.

McInerny supposes that what Finnis means by saying that basic principles of natural law are premoral is different from what Grisez means, in that Grisez "seems more concerned to have principles that will govern the practical activity of all men, good or bad, and which thus must split the difference between moral and immoral."[31] But the fact is that—setting aside the last phrase, which neither of us would accept—Finnis is concerned to make the same point as Grisez, and both of us consider this to be the position of Thomas.[32] The basic principles of practical reasoning do underlie and make possible the reasoning of good people and bad people alike. The price for denying this is to say that the immoral are sheerly irrational, and thus free of moral responsibility.

However, neither of us has said that the immoral person responds to *all* the principles of practical reasoning and pursues goods consistently with all of them. The difference between moral good and moral evil arises just at this point. Practical principles do not "split the difference between moral and immoral"; rather, the less than upright conscience shapes action by some practical principles while ignoring others which also are relevant.

This important part of ethical theory (the problem of the first principle of *morality*) was not treated in the article of Grisez on which McInerny comments, for the simple reason that Thomas does not reach this problem in the passage on which Grisez was commenting.[33] When McInerny extended his critique to this problem, he ought to have attended to Grisez' treatment, in other works, of the first principle of morality.[34]

Since McInerny does not come to grips with our treatments of this problem, we say no more about them here. However, we do wish to stress that we would not call the basic human goods "premoral" in the same sense as do many contemporary moral thinkers and theologians who have adopted proportionalism.[35] Proportionalists think of the basic human goods as kinds of desirable states of affairs, measurable and commensurable, which are more or less instantiated in and by means of human acts. We think of the basic human goods as aspects of the full-being of human persons, aspects essentially immeasurable and incommensurable. For the proportionalist, the right choice is one which realizes as much premoral good and as little premoral evil as possible. For us, the right choice is one which is in accord with open-hearted love of all the basic human goods. Thus, for the proportionalist the goods are premoral in the sense that one might rightly choose to destroy, damage, or impede them. For us, the goods are premoral only in the sense that both morally good and morally bad choices are directed (although in different ways) toward one or more of them (or, at least, toward some partial aspects or appearances of one or more of them).

III.
DENIAL OF OBJECTIVE HIERARCHY AMONG THE BASIC GOODS

We have argued[36] that there is no objective hierarchy (i.e., none which would imply commensurability of value) among the basic forms of human good. McInerny says: "Finnis at any rate is aware that this tenet separates him from the text of Aquinas."[37] In fact, Finnis does not think that this tenet does separate him from the text of Thomas; Finnis says that Thomas' rationale for the "order" of the precepts of natural law "*all too easily* is interpreted as a ranking."[38] We deny what McInerny affirms, namely, that our position "collide[s] in important ways with Thomas' understanding."[39]

It is arbitrary to suppose that all order is hierarchy, and still more arbitrary to assume that the corresponding order of the precepts of natural law and of natural inclination identified by Thomas in *Summa theologiae*, I-II, q. 94, a. 2, is a hierarchy of *value*. The principle of the order identified there by Thomas is simply: what man "has in common with all substances," "has in common with all animals," and has "peculiar to himself." Why should this metaphysical principle of ordering be interpreted as a ranking of values? No doubt Aristotle has an argument that man's highest good is the good most proper to him.[40] But where does Thomas make this argument his own?[41] Would it not be disastrous for a Christian theologian, who thinks that man's supreme good is communion with God, to adopt Aristotle's line of argument, when communion with the divine persons is not proper to man, but is naturally proper only to the divine persons themselves, and is shared by their supernatural gift not only with men but also with angels?

We do not find in Thomas' text McInerny's theory that "if we enumerate [man's] inclinations and notice their hierarchy we will be able to glimpse the natural law precepts which take them into account."[42] What Thomas does say is that "all those things to which man has a natural inclination, reason naturally grasps as goods and, in consequence, as things-to-be-pursued by work, and their opposites as evils and things-to-be-avoided."[43] We do not find in Thomas what McInerny thinks he finds: that "goods which are not peculiar to men come to be constituents of the human good insofar as they come under the sway of the distinctive mark of human agent, reason."[44] Nor do we think Thomas' text supports McInerny's further interpretation: "Precepts of natural law are rational directives aiming at the good for man. The human good, man's ultimate end, is complex but the unifying thread is the distinctive mark of the human, i.e., reason."[45] The first sentence undoubtedly expresses Thomas' position, but the second does not follow from the first, and will seem thomistic only to those who read into Thomas a degree and kind of Aristotelianism we do not find in him.

Thomas is clear enough that the primary precepts of the natural law identify the goods (in the plural) for man, and that *among* these goods is the good corresponding to the natural inclination to *act* according to reason.[46] But this inclination is only one among many, and all the inclinations are for goods naturally *understandable* by reason. Where does Thomas formulate the primary precepts of natural law in McInerny's mode: "Rationally pursue self-preservation," "Rationally pursue the good of sex, reproduction, offspring," and so on? What Thomas says more naturally suggests formulations in the mode: "Life is a good to be pursued and protected" and so on.

Even if Thomas' text supported an Aristotelian hierarchy of human goods, as McInerny believes, we would reject such a hierarchy. Our reason for doing so would be not only the noncommensurability of the basic goods, which blocks proportionalist rationalizations (which McInerny takes to be our sole concern), but also the transcendence of the *good* of the first principle of practical reason. As Grisez explains in a section of his article deleted in the Kenny abridgement:

> Only by virtue of this transcendence is it possible that the end proposed by Christian faith, heavenly beatitude, which is supernatural to man, should become an objective

of genuine human action—that is, of action under the guidance of practical reason. If the first principle of practical reason restricted human good to the goods proportionate to nature, then a supernatural end for human action would be excluded. The relation of man to such an end could be established only by a leap into the transrational where human action would be impossible and where faith would replace natural law rather than supplement it.[47]

As Grisez argued in another article, contemporaneous with the one on which McInerny comments, Thomas' theory of the natural end of man remains incoherent just to the extent that he was more Aristotelian than the reality of human nature, open to divine life, allows.[48]

IV.

Because they rest on misunderstandings, McInerny's critical remarks on our work seem to us to lack cogency. These misunderstandings were compounded, we think, by McInerny's decision to criticize simultaneously our exegeses of Thomas' texts and our own independent theorizing.

We find nothing in McInerny's article which requires us to concede error in our reading of Thomas. To assume a different, "Aristotelian-Thomistic," reading of Thomas and to point out that we do not share that reading could be the point of departure for criticism of our reading. But until the alternative reading is established by arguments, its mere assertion against ours is question-begging.

McInerny's criticisms of our independent theorizing are all based upon the presupposed authority of what we have called Aristotelian-Thomism. Admirable as this philosophy is in some respects, we do not consider it as perfect as McInerny seems to think it is. Moreover, the fact that we sometimes purposely differ with Thomas himself clearly does not entail that we misinterpret him, unless one assumes that all of Thomas' positions are self-evident to those who correctly understand them.

McInerny ends his article by suggesting that a major task before us "is to draw out the relation between ultimate end and the *Treatise on Law*." Grisez' work in ethics began precisely as an attempt to carry out this task. He became convinced that Thomas' account of the ultimate end is inconsistent with his account of natural law. This conviction led him to develop his own ethical theory, which is heavily indebted to Thomas but which is autonomously grounded. We think that all who are interested in natural law would do well to shoulder the responsibility of independent philosophical work, as we and many others have done, rather than to continue to be content with neoscholastic commingling of historical interpretation and philosophical construction.

Notes

1. 25 *American Journal of Jurisprudence,* pp. 1–15; hereinafter cited as *McI.*

2. "The First Principle of Practical Reason: A Commentary on the *Summa theologiae,* 1–2, Question 94, Article 2," 10 *Natural Law Forum,* pp. 168–201, hereinafter cited as *FPPR.* McInerny's references are to an abridged version in Anthony Kenny, ed., *Aquinas: A Collection of Critical Essays* (London: 1970), pp. 340–382. But the abridgement is not, as McInerny assumes (*McI,* p. 1), a "reprint" of the original article.

3. (New York and Oxford: Oxford University Press, 1980), hereinafter cited as *NLNR.*

4. *Ibid.*

5. *McI,* p. 7.

6. *McI,* p. 7.

7. *McI,* p. 11.

8. See especially *NLNR,* pp. 78–79, which should be read with p. 45, text at n. 60.

9. *NLNR,* p. 77.

10. *NLNR,* p. 103, concluding with a reference back to pp. 35–36, where relevant texts of Thomas are quoted and analyzed.

11. *NLNR,* p. 73 (emphasis added). Finnis repeatedly discusses the relevance of knowledge of the world: pp. 17–19, 65–66, 71, and 77 (last note).

12. *McI,* p. 7, citing *FPPR,* p. 196.
13. *McI,* p. 8.
14. *McI,* p. 12.
15. *McI,* p. 12.
16. See *FPPR,* pp. 177 and 194.
17. As he seems to be: *McI,* p. 12.
18. *McI,* p. 12.
19. See *FPPR,* pp. 193–196; *NLNR,* pp. 33–34. *McI,* p. 12, accuses us of "over-fastidiousness" in our concern not to derive *ought* from *is,* and he suggests that "one man's fallacy may be another's common sense." We think that bad arguments have bad consequences; the lack of fastidiousness in much current ethics and moral theology is exacting a terrible price. Also important, careful exercise of reason according to the highest standards is to be valued for its own sake; lack of fastidiousness shows a remiss love of the basic human good of truth. As for common sense, we consider its inarticulateness about basic principles perfectly acceptable for the plain man. The philosopher, however, has the duty to try to explicate the assumptions of common sense. In the present instance, one fails philosophically if one evades the underivability of first practical principles (which Thomas says are *per se nota*—and what can this mean to McInerny?—) by falling back on (formally invalid) common sense reasoning, which always is enthemymatic.
20. *McI,* p. 9.
21. *FPPR,* p. 176. McInerny possibly is misled by his reliance on the Kenny abridgement, which so reduces Grisez' exposition of this point as to leave "the mind calls the turn" standing as an enigmatic, provocative slogan.
22. On the four orders distinguished by Thomas in the Prologue to his commentary on Aristotle's *Ethics,* and on the irreducibility of nature, see Germain Grisez, *Beyond the New Theism: A Philosophy of Religion* (Notre Dame and London: University of Notre Dame Press, 1975), pp. 230–240, 353–356, and the treatment of metaphysical relativism, pp. 205–225; see also Finnis, *NLNR,* pp. 136–139, 380, 389–391.
23. Grisez, *Beyond the New Theism,* p. 291.
24. *McI,* p. 14. We do not here undertake to criticize McInerny's conception: end : means :: first principles of natural law: moral precepts deduced from the most common principles. But we do not concede the implicit theory, which seems to us to distort and greatly oversimplify the structure of moral reality and moral reasoning. McInerny is mistaken, too, in thinking that Finnis considers first principles to be "not yet moral because they are too general" (*McI,* p. 13). Moreover, in treating Thomas' effort to elaborate moral precepts from the first practical principles, Finnis

refers (*NLNR*, pp. 30, 101, 128) to many passages other than the single text (*S.t.*, I-II, q. 100, a.1) McInerny cites (*McI*, p. 13). So far as we understand it, we do not accept McInerny's interpretation of *S.t.*, I-II, q. 100, a. 1; his translation of the passage he excerpts from the body of that article omits the word "immediately" (*statim*) which provides a pointer to the structure of Thomas' reply.

25. *McI*, pp. 3–5. On p. 13, McInerny says: "What Finnis wants to distinguish from what he calls moral or ethical are those precepts which direct us to pursue our ultimate end or the constituents of it." But what Finnis wants to distinguish from moral precepts are the precepts articulated in *S.t.*, I-II, q. 94, a. 2; and Finnis denies that these precepts are understood by Thomas (or should be understood by anyone) as directing us to our ultimate end. If Finnis thought that the first principles of practical reason direct us as McInerny thinks they do, then Finnis would have considered them to be moral precepts.

26. *McI*, p. 4.

27. *Ibid.*

28. *Gaudium et spes*, sects. 38–39. Cf., e.g., Finnis, "Catholic Faith and World Order . . . ," 64 *The Clergy Review* 309 (1979) at pp. 310, 317–318.

29. In "Man, the Natural End of," 9 *New Catholic Encyclopedia* (1967), pp. 137–138.

30. *S.t.*, I-II, q. 94, a. 2; cf. *FPPR*, pp. 170, 175–179.

31. *McI*, p. 10.

32. See *NLNR*, pp. 30, 51, with references to Thomas.

33. Finnis has argued that Thomas' account of the difference between moral thinking and merely prudential thinking is "at best, highly elliptical, scattered, and difficult to grasp, and at worst, seriously underdeveloped; and that these deficiencies occasioned the unsatisfactory responses of those who professed to follow him in the later history of philosophical theology" (*NLNR*, p. 46). Finnis therefore gives his own account of the specific difference of the moral, and of moral virtue (*NLNR*, ch. V).

34. E.g., Germain Grisez and Joseph M. Boyle, Jr., *Life and Death with Liberty and Justice: A Contribution to the Euthanasia Debate* (Notre Dame and London: University of Notre Dame Press, 1979), pp. 361–368; Germain Grisez and Russell Shaw, *Beyond the New Morality: The Responsibilities of Freedom*, 2nd ed. (Notre Dame and London: University of Notre Dame Press, 1980), pp. 80–101.

35. For our criticisms of proportionalism, see *NLNR*, pp. 112–118; Germain Grisez, "Against Consequentialism," 23 *American Journal of Jurisprudence* (1978), pp. 21–72.

36. *NLNR*, pp. 92–95; *Beyond the New Morality,* pp. 74–78.

37. *McI,* p. 10. Grisez does not discuss the question of hierarchy of values in the article on which McInerny is commenting; he explicitly prescinds (*FPPR*, pp. 180–181) from the problems of this part of the article of Thomas on which he comments. Nevertheless, McInerny criticizes what he takes to be Grisez' position without providing any reference to the places where Grisez states and defends it.

38. *NLNR,* p. 94.

39. *McI,* p. 11.

40. *Eth. Nic.* X, 7 (1178a4-5); cf. I, 7 (1097b24–1098a7).

41. The argument in *S.t.,* I-II, qq. 2–3, is considerably more complex, precisely because Thomas does hold that communion with God is the ultimate fulfillment of man.

42. *McI,* p. 4.

43. *S.t.,* I-II, q. 94, a. 2, c.; the reply ad 2 is cryptic and must be interpreted in accord with the body of this article.

44. *McI,* p. 4. McInerny adds: "Sex is a *human* good not just as such, but as engaged in consciously and purposively and responsibly." By so saying he seems to imply that the sexual capacity of human persons is per se infrahuman—an assumption which entails an indefensible dualism and which also is inconsistent with the use of *S.t.,* I-II, q. 94, a. 2, which Paul VI makes in *Humanae vitae,* sect. 10.

45. *McI,* p. 5.

46. *S.t.,* I-II, q. 94, a. 3, c.

47. *FPPR*, p. 200. That human nature grounds without limiting the possibilities open to humankind through freedom is an important truth of anthropology, unknown to Aristotle, articulated in the light of Christian faith in the supernatural vocation of humankind to fulfillment in Christ, and now universally accepted.

48. "Man, the Natural End of," pp. 134–135.

Part Three

CONTEMPORARY
REFLECTIONS
ON NATURAL LAW

The Natural Law: Recent Literature

Richard A. McCormick, S.J.

This article originally appeared in *Theological Studies,* 1967.

Theological writing continues to reveal a vigorous interest in natural law. Undoubtedly there are those who still question why the *theologian* is concerned with natural law at all. Rather recently J. Ratzinger had argued that Christian social teaching, for example, should be developed not by natural-law considerations, but by mere submission of empirical social data to the "gospel as a value-measure."[1] Through such a procedure these facts would take on their ethically normative character. It was quite possibly Ratzinger, or at least the tendency exemplified in his suggestion, that stimulated Bruno Schüller, S.J., to return to his insistence on the existence and importance of the natural law for theological methodology.[2]

Schüller approaches the natural law from two points of view. First, he shows that the natural law (which he is careful to delimit and define in a way which allows a legitimate question to be put to Scripture) is a reality recognized in Scripture. Obviously, however, this does not mean that this reality is called by name in Scripture or that it can be identified with the teaching of the Stoa as found in St. Paul. If one would want more than Schüller's own exegesis, then Schüller points to the fact that there are the likes of H. W. Schmidt, F. J. Leenhardt, J. Murray, C. K. Barrett, H. C. G. Moule, C. H. Dodd, and R. Bultmann to contend with.

Schüller's next question is: Is natural-law thinking and argumentation something Christian moral theology can dispense with? His answer is a resounding no. He repeats what he has written before, namely, that man is only capable of hearing and giving intelligent belief to the ethical message of the New Testament because prior (logically) to the revelation of God's word he already grasps and expresses himself as an ethical being. "From this experience all moral concepts and ideas receive their meaning for man." And it is precisely these moral concepts which form the only possible medium through which God can reveal the *lex Christi*. The fact that natural morality concerns him is for man his obediential potency that the law of Christ can concern him.[3] Hence theology itself can only progress in genuine understanding of the supernatural moral order when it critically reflects on that which is the necessary medium for the revelation of that order. Indeed, Schüller insists that the better theology understands the natural law, the more advantageously positioned it is to hear and understand the *lex Christi*.

Another major point made by Schüller is that natural-law reasoning is the only basis on which one can determine whether a revealed duty is transtemporal or time-conditioned. Suppose, for a moment, that the validity of a New Testament demand can only be known in faith. How could one know whether this is transtemporal in character or not? If the validity of the precept itself is guaranteed only through God's word, then also its continuing duration can only be guaranteed if this duration is an inner constitutive of the validity. But what New Testament demand carries with it a clear indication of transtemporality? However, if we understand a demand from its inner sense (natural-law reasoning), then we are positioned to discriminate between those things which oblige for all times and those which do not; for ultimately it is to one and the same reason that a demand owes its obliging force and the continuance of this obliging force.

Schüller's article is carefully wrought and deserves the serious attention of anyone trifling with the temptation to abandon the natural law as a luxury we can no longer afford.

Hans Rotter, a doctoral candidate in moral theology at Innsbruck, has pursued Schüller's line of thought in an interesting article.[4] Since revealed morality is certainly intended to represent something more in our lives than an irrational gymnastic, the commands of Christ must be able to be grasped as values, specifically as possible realizations of love. Therefore, man must find in his own experience the ability to understand these demands. This much Schüller had said.

Now if this is so, how does revealed morality differ from natural morality? Schüller had pointed out that the imperatives of the two must be *verbally* the same. Rotter suggests that natural-law morality relates to the moral message of the New Testament in the same way that implicit faith relates to explicit faith. An act of faith contains more than is expressly formulatable. Similarly, the "yes" to the imperative of conscience contains theological and eschatological depths which can only be explicitated through revelation. Rotter believes, therefore, that the New Testament's moral message is a deepening and "radicalizing" of natural law. That is, it is precisely the radicality with which Christ addresses man, the unity of individual demands in love, that surpasses what we know naturally and in an explicit way. Ultimately, then, *as far as verbal content is concerned,* revelation in the area of morality brings an explicitation of the conscience-experience in a way and a depth not otherwise possible. It is in this sense that the moral message of Christianity brings no new (i.e., foreign to conscience) content—a point Schüller had also made.

Clearly, the relationship between revelation and natural law needs much more study. But it seems that the general lines of Rotter's thought might lead one to say that the magisterium has a teaching competence where natural law is concerned precisely because the Church is commissioned to teach revelation. Or again, the magisterium does not enjoy competence to teach natural law only because that law is extrinsically necessary for the protection of the basic gospel message. Rather, at one level there is and must be an identity between natural law and revealed morality. The command of love of God and neighbor is a specification—analogously, of course—of both natural morality and revealed morality. Similarly, even more concrete norms are—again, analogously—historical specifications of both natural and revealed morality. This is not to say that the magisterium of the Church may or should descend to detailed specifications of the demands of radical love.[5] An enlightened sensitivity to changing historical and cultural factors suggests great caution here. It is only to say that here we have a point of view sharply distinguished from the separatism of those who divide morality into natural and revealed and invite the Church to concern herself all too exclusively with the latter.

But to affirm the existence of a natural moral order—that is, one grounded in the being of man as man—is to say very little about its content or the manner in which one determines this content. Most of the recent literature seems to represent an attempt to clarify these more specific points. And rightly so. One is understandably confused when one hears the "duty to respect one's neighbor" and "the prohibition of artificial insemination" both ascribed to the natural law, and without much distinction. The first is a formal, or at best a very general material, principle; the second is a rather detailed material norm. If a concept of the being of man and a moral order founded on it leads necessarily to such indiscriminate lumping of norms, then clearly it derives from a static concept of man which can never make its peace with contemporary sociology and anthropology.

Recent literature, then, represents a variety of attempts to formulate natural law in such a way that it is both founded on the being of man and yet appropriately aware of the historicity of this being. How this attempt is made differs with each author. Some emphasize especially the noetic aspects of natural law; others attempt to nuance the notion of nature. But a basic unity is discernible in the literature if one approaches it from the overriding concern mentioned above. We will mention only a few examples here.

At a three-day conference in 1965, German-speaking moral theologians discussed the meaning of natural law. Joseph Th. C. Arntz presented a carefully researched paper detailing the history of natural law within scholastic circles.[6] This interesting history reveals a snowballing process away from the balanced subjectivity of Thomas' presentation. Whereas St. Thomas understood by natural law in its strictest sense only the first practical principles (*principia naturaliter nota*),[7] subsequent theologians began to include in the notion also the conclusions derived from these principles. This is perfectly legitimate, of course; but increasingly these conclusions were thought to share the same timeless necessity as the principles and a certain immobilism set in.

In a brief essay Frederick S. Carney outlines, rather apologetically indeed, a natural-law procedure for Christian ethics.[8] He believes that the only way the serious objections against natural law can be met is by a three-fold clarification: the area of law, the meaning of nature, and the relation of human nature to law.

Where law is concerned, Carney suggests that the term "natural law" has suffered from association with physical laws (which are universal) and civil laws (which are established by the will of men). To counterbalance this, he proposes that we must be concerned with the relational aspects of the material norms of natural law—that is, with those aspects of life which are cultural and epochal. This does not mean that natural law is subjective. Contrarily, there is a criterion by means of which norms and then actions can be assessed. That criterion is preservation and fulfilment of human life in the context where it is found. But rather than emphasize law as a body of norms, Carney prefers to see it as a process of reflection upon the normal functioning of human nature.

As for nature, he proposes that we conceive this in a rather general, empty-container fashion as "the full dimensions of man's being." In filling out what this means, Carney insists that our formulas must sufficiently cover the whole range of man's existence, and therefore must adequately account for the social dimension in human existence.

Finally, the article is at pains to show that natural-law thinking as proposed does not draw normative conclusions from nonnormative premises; for man's perception of his world is not merely fact-perception, but value-perception. Carney suggestively speaks of a "thouness" in the primordial perception of reality. He refers to the "built-in presence of felt obligation that may reside in its disarmingly factual exterior."

J. Etienne, with nearly every informed modern writer, rejects a concept of nature which mirrors God as a transcendental engineer who has preplotted man's course and embedded this plan in a multitude of concrete persons.[9] Such a caricature is a result of human imagination. Rather, man's essential dignity is in his rationality. This is his prerogative and his fundamental responsibility. In the depths of his being, man becomes conscious of his rationality as his basic endowment, and therefore his basic task. It is in his life, in the "given," that man is beckoned to answer the call of the spirit.

Etienne feels that there are certain immutable traits which oblige the spirit of man to take the same paths in order to develop itself and reach greater potential. But since these constants are overlaid with personal and cultural histories, they are extremely hard to determine.

In recent months Franz Böckle has made several attempts to clarify the meaning of natural law.[10] It is Böckle's contention that the notion of nature, as grounding natural law, has confronted us in four different ways: as noetic capacity (*natura ut ratio*), as a metaphysical essence (*natura metaphysica*), as the metaphysical structure of the human act itself, and as concrete nature (especially with its biological and physiological structures). The last three of these contain obvious elements of truth, but it seems to be Böckle's contention that they provide insurmountable difficulties in grounding and explaining a natural law.

Take, for example, nature as meaning the metaphysical structure of the human act. According to this point of view, the foundation of natural law derives directly from the action itself. But the invariable structure of an action is extremely difficult to determine; for the point of departure in determining this metaphysical structure must be concrete human experience and reflexion. Such experience and reflexion, however, are time-conditioned. Actually, different acts get their proper significance only as part of a total development, of a whole life. To give a metaphysical structure to an act is to rip it from its context. Thus, marriage does not get its meaning from individual acts, but the individual act derives its significance from placement within the totality that is marriage. Böckle does not want to conclude that an intelligible structure must be denied to human acts, but only that we must be more aware of the cultural-historical setting in stating what that structure is.

Böckle then turns to what he regards as a proper understanding of natural law. Natural moral law has two senses: the strict and basic sense (primary), and the derived sense (secondary).

First, the primary sense. The unavoidable primary insights (Thomas' *naturaliter nota,* in contrast to what is discursively known) constitute the natural law in its most basic sense. However, the importance of these principles is not only or especially that they are the first normative assertions or principles of conduct. Nor must one view them as simply the unchanging source of derived conclusions. Rather, in these evident insights man experiences a transcendental "oughtness." This "oughtness" does not refer simply to the unavoidability of the principles. Before all else it speaks a transcendental claim to self-realization. In these principles man is bid to take up his existence, to commit himself freely to the project of his own formation and development. It is precisely in man's responsibility, grounded in his reason, that he shares in God's providence (eternal law), because, like God Himself, man is *sibi ipsi et aliis providens*.[11]

Therefore, the natural law is not first and foremost a formulated law at all; nor is it a handing down of general, sempiternally valid principles out of which concrete law (*Recht*) is constructed. The heart of natural law rests in this unconditioned "ought" which lies at the center of man's being.[12]

Second, the derived sense. It is here that natural law appears as formulated law. It is the sum of the universally valid formulated demands based on universal structures. What are the enduring structures pertaining to the essence of man? To discover this, Böckle appeals to a transcendental deduction, i.e., from the activity of man to those things which are necessary to its possibility. The results of this process show that the social nature of man, his spirituality, his freedom of decision, and perhaps a few more characteristics belong to the essence of man. In so far as we can draw moral demands immediately from these structures, we can speak of timelessly valid norms. "This is what Catholic theology means when it speaks of ultimately timeless and universally valid demands of natural law."[13]

It is clear that Böckle's writing derives from a strong emphasis on the noetic aspects of natural law.[14] It is out of this emphasis that he says that there are four ways of conceiving nature which come down to us in natural-law thinking. This seems inaccurate. The noetic origins of natural law are but one aspect of natural law. The metaphysical foundation is another. The structure of the concrete act is still another. No theory of natural law will be complete without all aspects, simply because all are dimensions of reality. Thus it is incorrect to set those who discuss a *natura metaphysica* (e.g., Fuchs) over against those who speak of *natura ut ratio*. Fuchs himself has written, for example: "The natural law must be considered, not as the sum of external universal laws, but as *internal* law comprising the totality of that moral norm which corresponds to the totality of man's being."[15]

Böckle's own splendid treatment of premarital coitus can serve as a good example of what I mean.[16] After an enlightening discussion of Christian morality as a radical love morality, Böckle turns to the area of sexuality and attempts to establish its significance. In particular, he rightly asserts that we must know the sense and meaning of marital intercourse if we are to understand its meaning during the premarital period. He finds three meanings in sexual intercourse. (1) It is a symbol of unity. (2) It is an expression of mutual love. (3) It is an act of mutual knowledge. Briefly, it is a sign of a total personal relationship.

With these meanings established, Böckle states that one confronts immediately a decisive supposition for the fully meaningful act of coitus: the mutual will or intent of unity.[17] It is this very intent to make a total and lasting self-gift which constitutes marriage.[18] If coitus is a sign of a mutual and total gift of the person, then the persons must actually be in this relationship. Before such a moment (i.e., before marriage) man cannot give himself unreservedly in a consciously responsible manner; for without the exchange of a full responsibility for each other, the self-gift cannot achieve its deepest and most proper sense. But Christian love demands an inner preparedness for this full meaning. Therefore, Böckle concludes, Christian love excludes premarital coitus. "Seen in this light, every premarital and extramarital coitus is and remains ultimately false and cannot be reconciled with the criterion of radical love."

Now, what has happened here? Böckle has described the meaning of coitus and upon this meaning he has built a moral norm. In doing so he has used what some authors have called the "metaphysical structure of the act"—though certainly there must be a better word for the significance of an act than that. In other words, Böckle is dealing here with natural-law reasoning. He disguises this fact by saying that it is precisely *Christian* love which demands the preparedness for full responsibility for each other. Christian love certainly makes this demand. But one would think that any genuinely human love would also demand that coitus be a marital act. Indeed, this demand can only be understood as Christian if it is first a human demand.

In the last analysis, therefore, Böckle is dealing with a legitimate specification of what it means to "take up one's existence," to "become what thou art." And he has proceeded by analysis of the structure of the act. Briefly, he has argued to a material norm in a way which, when he discusses natural law in general, he seems eager to find problematic. On Böckle's own terms, therefore, does not the natural law have to take account of all the elements he mentions if we are to get a truly complete statement of it?

George M. Regan, C.M., presents a fine summary of recent trends in natural-law thought.[19] He is particularly concerned with the meaning of human nature. Reviewing the work of Fuchs, Monden, Columba Ryan, and Charles Fay, Regan points to an increasing tendency to emphasize what he calls "concrete human nature" in elaborating natural-law theory. Abstract human nature refers to man's metaphysical being and is consequently realized in a univocal, universal, and essentially immutable way. "Concrete . . . human nature," Regan says, "refers to man's physical being as realized existentially in different historical eras and in specific situations. In this latter usage, all man's being at a given moment becomes morally relevant." It is Regan's conviction that man in his concreteness deserves more stress in moral theory. "By continuing to emphasize this more concrete understanding of man, proponents of natural law may carry greater weight in the contemporary world."[20]

This is but a sampling. If one were to back away for a moment and attempt to generalize on the direction of natural-law discussion, he might conclude that it reveals three characteristics. (1) There is an increasing tendency to approach natural law more as a thought-structure than as a normative content. The basic assertion of this thought-structure would be: man's obligation is founded on man's being. (2) This thought-structure emphasizes, above all, rational creativity in human conduct. (3) It tends to recognize formal rather than material norms as universally valid principles of natural law. This last tendency undoubtedly stems from a renewed awareness of man's historicity, and reflects a desire to relate natural law more obviously to the totality of man's being.

It is easy to agree with these emphases, if for no other reason than that they are appropriately corrective. Traditional theology, at least in its popularizations, has too often left the impression that when one deals with the natural law he is simply unpacking basic principles which, when shined up a bit, will reflect a rather comprehensive kaleidoscope of norms. There has to be a reaction to this type of thing. On the other hand, in retreating from such instant certainties and allowing full range to man's historical existence and creativity, must we not retain the courage to be concrete? Otherwise we can be left with a natural law so refined that it contemplates with equanimity the notion that "one man goes in for handball while another likes killing Jews and that is all there is to say about the matter."[21]

Notes

1. J. Ratzinger, "Naturrecht, Evangelium und Ideologie in der katholischen Soziallehre," in von Bismarck and W. Dirks, *Christlicher Glaube und Ideologie* (Stuttgart, 1964) pp. 27 ff., as cited in Schüller.

2. Bruno Schüller, S.J., "Zur theologischen Diskussion über die lex naturalis," *Theologie und Philosophie* 41 (1966) 481–503.

3. Ratzinger's attempt to bypass natural morality and to use the "gospel as value-measure" is doomed according to Schüller; for man can only be in a position to understand the gospel as a value and a value-measure because logically prior to his belief he already has an interior grasp of what an ethical value is. But this grasp is precisely the content of natural law.

4. Hans Rotter, S.J., "Naturrecht und Offenbarung," *Stimmen der Zeit* 179 (1967) 283–92.

5. On this point cf. the following for varying points of view: B. Schüller, S.J., "Die Autorität der Kirche und die Gewissensfreiheit der Gläubigen," *Der Männer-Seelsorger* 16 (1966) 130–43; F. Böckle, in *Concilium* 25, 3–6; Paul McKeever, "Theology and Natural Law," *Proceedings of the Catholic Theological Society of America* 21 (1966) 223–37.

6. Jos. Th. C. Arntz, "Die Entwicklung des naturrechtlichen Denkens innerhalb des Thomismus," in F. Böckle, *Das Naturrecht im Disput* (Düsseldorf: Patmos, 1966) pp. 87–120. The book is summarized in *Stimmen der Zeit* 179 (1967) 383–85.

7. For a recent study of natural law in Thomas, cf. Soeur Sainte-Marcelle-d'Auvergne, "De la matière du droit naturel," *Laval théologique et philosophique* 23 (1967) 116–45.

8. Frederick S. Carney, "Outline of a Natural Law Procedure for Christian Ethics," *Journal of Religion* 47 (1967) 26–38.

9. J. Etienne, "La nature est-elle un critère de moralité?" *Revue diocésaine de Namur* 20 (1966) 282–94.

10. F. Böckle. "Rückblick und Ausblick," in *Das Naturrecht im Disput*, pp. 121–50; *Grundbegriffe der Moral* (Aschaffenburg: Pattloch, 1966) pp. 47–55; *Concilium, loc. cit.*

11. 1–2, q. 91, a. 2.

12. Böckle has summarized his position elsewhere (*Concilium* 25, 4) as follows: "The best way of understanding natural law is to take it as the inner content of any concrete regulation of law and morality. This content is only visible and tangible *in a concrete and positive regulation of law and morality.*" He refers to this content as a kind of legal essence underlying any law.

13. *Grundbegriffe der Moral,* p. 50.

14. In this respect cf. also D. C. Duivesteijn, "Reflexions on Natural Law," *Clergy Review* 52 (1967) 283–94.

15. Joseph Fuchs, S.J., *Natural Law—A Theological Investigation* (New York: Sheed & Ward, 1965) p. 134.

16. Franz Böckle and Josef Köhne, *Geschlechtliche Beziehungen vor der Ehe* (Mainz: Matthias-Grunewald-Verlag, 1967) pp. 7–37.

17. Böckle uses the terms "Wille zur Bindung," "die Bereitschaft zur Hingabe der Person mit dem Willen zur Übernahme der vollen Verantwortung," and "Wille zur gegenseitigen dauerenden Hingabe und Bindung." These terms do not immediately translate into consent, but it is clear that Böckle means this.

18. At this point Böckle has an excellent exposition of the social character of marital consent and its relation to legal form. See also Jack L. Stotts, "Sexual Practices and Ethical Thought," *McCormick Quarterly* 20 (1967) 131–45.

19. George M. Regan, C.M., "Natural Law in the Church Today," *Catholic Lawyer* 13 (1967) 21–41; cf. also *Vie spirituelle, Supplément,* May, 1967, pp. 187–324.

20. Cf. Ildefons Lobo, O.S.B., "Toward a Morality Based on the Meaning of History: The Condition and Renewal of Moral Theology," in *Concilium* 25, 25–45.

21. John R. Carnes, "Whether There Is a Natural Law," *Ethics* 77 (1967) 122–29, at p. 128.

The Doctrine Lives:
The Eternal Return of Natural Law

John Courtney Murray, S.J.

This chapter originally appeared in 1960 in the book *We Hold These Truths.*

The news reported in the last chapter—that the tradition of natural law is dead—calls for some verification, before it is accepted as true. For one thing, it may be a case of mistaken identity; perhaps it was for some contrefaçon of the doctrine that the funeral rites were held. This is possible. So many misunderstandings have conspired to obscure the true identity of the doctrine that it is often mistaken for what it is not. Some of the misunderstandings are naive; others are of the learned sort. Some are the product of ignorance; others result from polemic bias.

The doctrine is accused of abstractionism, as if it disregarded experience and undertook to pull all its moral precepts like so many magician's rabbits out of the metaphysical hat of an abstract human "essence." The doctrine is also interpreted as an intuitionism, as if it maintained that all natural-law precepts were somehow "self-evident." It is also derided as a legalism, as if it proclaimed a detailed code of particularized do's and don'ts, nicely drawn up with the aid of deductive logic alone, absolutely normative in all possible circumstances, ready for automatic application, whatever the factual situation may be. The theory is also rejected for its presumed immobilism, as if its concept of an immutable human nature and an unchanging structure of human ends required it to deny the historicity of human existence and forbade it to recognize the virtualities of human freedom. It should already be clear from the earlier chapter on the origins of the public consensus that these conceptions are caricatures of the doctrine of natural law.

There is also the biologist interpretation, which imputes to natural-law theory a confusion of the "primordial," in a biological sense, with the "natural." This is a particularly gross and gratuitous misinterpretation, since nothing is clearer in natural-law theory than its identification of the "natural" with the "rational," or perhaps better, the "human." Its whole effort is to incorporate the biological values in man, notably his sexual tendencies, into the fuller human order of reason, and to deny them the status of the primordial. The primordial in man—that which is first in order—is his rational soul, the form of humanity, which informs all that is biological in him. Natural-law argument against sexual aberrations (including artificial contraception) indicts them precisely because in them man succumbs to his own biological inclinations in violation of the primordial inclinations of reason and real love.

There is also the objectivist-rationalist interpretation, which is the premise from which natural-law theory is criticized for its supposed neglect of the values of the human person and for its alleged deafness to the resonances of intersubjectivity. In point of fact, the theory never forgets that the "nature" with which it deals has no existence except in the person, who is a unique realization of the nature, situated in an order of other unique realizations, whose uniqueness, nevertheless, does not make them atomistic monads, since it is in each instance a form of participation and communication in the one common nature.

Finally, there is the charge that natural-law doctrine is not "Christian." If it be meant that the doctrine in structure and style is alien to the general Protestant moral system, in so far as there is such a thing, the charge is true enough. The last chapter will have made this clear. It would not, of course, be difficult to show that the doctrine is, in germinal fashion, scriptural. However, I shall be content here to make only four comments.

First, natural-law theory does not pretend to do more than it can, which is to give a philosophical account of the moral experience of humanity and to lay down a charter of essential humanism. It does not show the individual the way to sainthood, but only to manhood. It does not promise to transform society into the City of God on earth, but only to prescribe, for the purposes of law and social custom, that minimum of morality which must be observed by the members of a society, if the social environment is to be human and habitable. At that, for a man to be reasonably human, and for a society to be essentially civil—these are no mean achievements. The ideal of the reasonable man, who does his duty to God, to others, and to himself, is not an ignoble one. In fact, it puts such a challenge to the inertness and perversity which are part of the human stuff, that Christian doctrine from the day of St. Augustine has taught the necessity of divine grace for this integral fulfillment of the natural law.

Second, beyond the fulfillment of the ideal of the reasonable man there lies the perennial question of youth, whatever its age. It is asked in the Gospel: "What do I still lack?" (Matthew 19:21). And there remains the Gospel's austere answer, put in the form of an invitation, but not cast in the categories of ethics, which are good and evil and the obligation to choose between them. The invitation opens the perspectives of a higher choice, to "be a follower of mine." For the making of this choice there is no other motive, no other inner impulse, than the free desire to respond to the prior choice of Him whom one chooses because one has been first chosen.

Third, the mistake would be to imagine that the invitation, "Come, follow me," is a summons somehow to forsake the universe of human nature, somehow to vault above it, somehow to leave law and obligation behind, somehow to enter the half-world of an individualist subjectivist "freedom" which pretends to know no other norm save "love." In other words, the Gospel invitation, in so far as it is a summons to the moral life, is not a call to construct a "situation ethics" that knows no general principles of moral living but only particular instances of moral judgment, each one valid only for the instance; and that recognizes no order of moral law that is binding on freedom, but only a freedom that is free and moral singly in so far as it is sheer spontaneity.

Fourth, the law of nature, which prescribes humanity, still exists at the interior of the Gospel invitation, which summons to perfection. What the follower of Christ chooses to perfect is, and can only be, a humanity. And the lines of human perfection are already laid down in the structure of man's nature. Where else could they be found? The Christian call is to transcend nature, notably to transcend what is noblest in nature, the faculty of reason. But it is not a call to escape from nature, or to dismantle nature's own structure, and least of all to deny that man is intelligent, that nature is intelligible, and that nature's intelligibilities are laws for the mind that grasps them. In so far as they touch the moral life, the energies of grace, which are the action of the Holy Spirit, quicken to new and fuller life the dynamisms of nature, which are resident in reason. Were it otherwise, grace would not be supernatural but only miraculous.

I list these misunderstandings of natural law only to make the point that those who dislike the doctrine, for one reason or another, seem forever to be at work, as it were, burying the wrong corpse. For my part, I would not at all mind standing with them, tearless, at the grave of any of the shallow and distorted theories that they mistake for the doctrine of natural law. The same point will come clearer from a bit of history. At about the turn of the century it was rather generally believed in professional circles that the Scholastic idea of natural law, as an operative concept in the fields of ethics, political theory, and law and jurisprudence, was dead. In other words, it was generally assumed that the great nineteenth-century attack on natural law had been successful.

In this respect, of course, the nineteenth century exhibited those extensive powers of learned misunderstanding which it possessed to an astonishing degree. In its extraordinary ignorance of philosophical and legal history, it supposed that the "law of nature" of the Age of the Enlightenment was the *ius naturale* of an earlier and in many ways more enlightened age. It supposed therefore that in doing away with the former, it had likewise done away with the latter. This was by no means the case. The theory of the "law of nature" that was the creature of the Enlightenment was as fragile, time-conditioned, and transitory a phenomenon as the Enlightenment itself. But the ancient idea of the natural law is as inherently perennial as the *philosophia perennis* of which it is an integral part. Its reappearance after its widely attended funeral is one of the interesting intellectual phenomena of our generation.

Admittedly, the phenomenon is not yet as plain as the old hill of Houth; but it is discernible. In 1902, when Sir John Salmond published his well-known book, *Jurisprudence,* he wrote: "The idea of a law of nature or moral law (*lex naturalis, lex naturae*) . . . has played a notable part in the history of human thought in the realm of ethics, theology, politics and jurisprudence. It was long the accepted tradition of those sciences, but it has now fallen on evil days, and it can no longer be accepted as in harmony with modern thought on those matters." However, when Parker edited the ninth edition in 1927 he was impelled to add the cautious footnote: "Sir John Salmond's view that the doctrine in all its forms is now discredited cannot be considered correct." Today, thirty years later, when modern thought has caught up a bit more with the past, one might perhaps transcend the timidity of this footnote. As a matter of fact, it would seem that the ancient tradition of natural law is beginning to climb out of the footnotes of the learned books into the very text of our time, as the conviction dawns that there are resources in the idea that might possibly make the next page of the text sound less like a tale told by an idiot.

Here then might be an approach to the whole subject of natural law. It would be an historical approach, on the theme indicated by Heinrich Rommen in the title of his book, *Die ewige Wiederkehr des Naturrechts.* The idea would be to describe, first, the origins and political significance of the Western tradition of natural law; secondly, the supplanting of this tradition by a newly conceived "law of nature" that had its greatest intellectual popularity in the Age of the Enlightenment and its highest political success in the Era of Revolution; thirdly, the reaction against this law of nature, that resulted in the victory of juridical positivism (the triumph of the idea that "law is will" over the ancient idea that "law is reason"), behind whose success lay all the forces that came to power in the nineteenth century—scientific empiricism, sociologism, psychologism, historical and philosophical materialism; fourthly, today's reaction against the positivist theory, as the ideas of justice and of human rights have had a rebirth in the face of the problems raised by totalitarian government and by the multiple aspects of the social conflict and the international conflict. It is this reaction, which is in fact a progress, that has effected the latest *Wiederkehr* of the idea of natural law.

Another approach to the problem of natural law is possible—a more directly philosophical approach. The idea of natural law goes back to the remotest origins, not only of political thought, but of ethical thought—to the day when man first began to reflect on the problem, whether there be something that intrinsically distinguishes right from wrong, whether what is right ought to be, and (on the political plane) whether laws ought to be just, and whether what is just ought to be law. These problems raise the basic ethical question, whether there is a connection between "being" and "oughtness," whether the moral order is a reflex and prolongation of a metaphysical order. In consequence, they bring man to the heart of philosophy itself. In fact, every system of natural law, whether it be Aristotle's or St. Thomas's or Locke's or Pufendorf's, has its premises; it supposes an epistemology, and therefore a metaphysic (or the absence of one). On the other hand, every system of natural law has its conclusions; it issues in a political philosophy—a concept of the nature of the state, its end, scope, and functions. Consequently, to inquire what natural law is, means to inquire, on the one hand, what the human mind is and what it can know, and on the other hand, what human society is and to what ends it should work. But, as is obvious, all this is to inquire what man himself is—what this human "nature" is of which one predicates a law "natural."

Both of these approaches to the problem of natural law are evidently much too ambitious for the present purpose; I mention them only to suggest the architecture of the problem. Here I shall offer simply a comment on a conclusion suggested to the mind as it contemplates, in the light of contemporary problems, the two interpretations of the natural law that have historically put themselves forward as the basis of political philosophy. I mean the "law of nature" of the Enlightenment and the "natural law" of the *philosophia perennis,* whose origins go back to Heraclitus and to the greatest of Greek philosophers and Roman jurists, and whose developed expression is found in St. Thomas Aquinas and the later Scholastics. My suggestion is that the eighteenth-century "law of nature" (so I shall consistently call it, to distinguish it from the older "natural law") was indeed a potently revolutionary force in its own day, because of the nature of the problems of that day; today, however, its dynamism has run out, and its impotence in the face of the different problems that confront us is demonstrable.

"Today," Mr. John Bowle has suggested, "the tremendous initiative, the sprawling enterprise, of the nineteenth century may well be changing to an age of order, of consolidation."[1] Today, as perverted social patterns are attempting to impose themselves on human life, to the destruction of human freedom, our problem in the West is ourselves to create a new social pattern—a pattern of freedom, that will be truly a pattern, but that will leave to freedom all its necessary energizing dynamism. Our problem is not simply to safeguard "human rights," in the sense of fortifying each discrete individual in the possession of a heterogeneous collection of social empowerments; it is rather to erect, and secure against all assault, an *ordo juris,* an order of law that will be in consequence an order of rights and hence by definition an order of freedom. If this is so, as I think it is, the new "age of order," of just law and true freedom, must look to natural law as its basic inspiration.

THE LAW OF NATURE

Everybody knows that in the eighteenth century the "law of nature" and the "law of reason" were phrases to conjure with. With his usual engaging cynicism, that in this case does not veil the truth, the late Carl L. Becker described the phenomenon and the climate of opinion, set by Cartesian philosophy and Newtonian physics, that made it possible. To justify what one considered desirable, socially or personally, one appealed in those days to the "law of nature," as today one appeals to "democracy," always with fervor, if not always with good sense. This was true not only in France of the *philosophes,* but to a lesser degree even in America. Mr. Carl Van Doren in *The Great Rehearsal* recounts how one disturbed New Englander objected to the two-year senatorial term proposed by the Constitutional Convention, on the ground that a one-year term was a "dictate of the law of nature"; spring comes once a year, and so should a batch of new Senators.

If it is difficult for us today to share this enthusiasm for the law of nature, it is still more difficult for us to grasp the pivotal concept on which the seventeenth- and eighteenth-century theory of the law of nature depended—the concept of the "state of nature." Yet this was a concept that had all the power of a myth. It found its literary immortalizations, familiar to us all, in Defoe's *Robinson Crusoe* (1719) and Rousseau's *Émile* (1762). And its prominence in the philosophical and political literature of the time is a well-known fact.

This "state of nature" was a purely imaginary construct possible only to the eighteenth-century reason; it was an imaginary state that was nevertheless supposed theoretically to have existed. It depicted what man was and how he lived antecedently to the formation of all human communities and to the establishment of all the laws and customs of social life. The value of the concept was functional. It was a methodological postulate, an abstraction posited as the starting point for a theory of the law of nature; for in the state of nature man was ruled only by the law of nature, and consequently in this state the law of nature could be discovered in all its abstract purity. The further function of the state of nature was to explain, in conjunction with the theory of the social contract, the genesis of political society, its form, and the relative rights of government and citizen.

The state of nature was, of course, a purely formal concept; one could fill it with whatever content one wished, make it pregnant of whatever political consequences one fancied. Here, however, we may confine ourselves simply to the theory of John Locke; it had the greatest fortune both in the Anglo-Saxon and in the French political world. In Locke's system, the state of nature had the initial essential function of establishing the inalienability of the rights of man, as Locke conceived them. In the state of nature, man appears with complete suddenness as a full-grown individual, a hard little atom in the midst of atoms equally hard, all solitary and self-enclosed, each a sociological monad. The idea of man, therefore, is that of an individual who is "absolute lord of his own person and possessions, equal to the greatest and subject to nobody," as he says in his *Second Essay*. In this absolute lordship, equality, and independence consists the Lockean idea of man's "freedom," a freedom that is natural and therefore inalienable save within the limits of his own free choice. On this free individual rests a single law—the law of nature—with a single precept, that of self-preservation, the preservation of his own life, liberty, and property. This law has only one limitation—the same law as obligatory also on other individuals, who in their equally sovereign independence are likewise bound to preserve themselves. Beyond this duty of self-preservation, but subject to its primal exigencies, the individual has one further duty: "Every one, as he is bound to preserve himself, and not to quit his station wilfully, so by the like reason, when his own preservation comes not in competition, ought he as much as he can to preserve the rest of mankind."

This is the Lockean state of nature and law of nature. On it is based, by a process of pure postulation, the inalienability of the rights of the individual to life, liberty, and property, and the limitation of these rights solely by the equal rights of other individuals. The chief difficulty about this state of nature is, of course (as Locke naïvely admits), the obvious fact that it is "not to be endured." With the optimism characteristic of his age and the inconsistency characteristic of himself, Locke prattles a bit about the "innocent delights" attendant on the "liberty" of the state of nature. But it is difficult to see how a state could be delightful wherein every individual is a sort of little god almighty, whose power to preserve himself is checked only at the point where another little god almighty starts preserving *himself*. At this point, one is more sympathetic with the ruthless logic of Thomas Hobbes, who says forthrightly in his *Leviathan* that the state of nature is a "condition which we call Warre," and that the life of the omnipotent monads, among whom prevails the single law of the right of all to all things, is "solitary, poore, nasty, brutish and short." The first impulse of the law of nature, which is that of self-preservation, is, says Hobbes, that of "getting themselves out of the miserable condition of Warre." Locke puts it more politely: "Thus mankind, notwithstanding all the privileges of the state of Nature, being but in an ill condition while they remain in it, are quickly driven into society."

But how does one get these "absolute lords" into society, under government, subject to limitations on their natural omnipotence? Only by their own free act: "Men being, as has been said, by nature all free, equal, and independent, no one can be put out of this estate and subjected to the political power of another without his own consent." Society is not the product of nature but of artifice. It comes into being by the social contract, by the act of men "agreeing together mutually to enter into one community and make one body politic." Thus Locke establishes his second principle on the same grounds as the first: as the rights of man are inalienable, because man is by nature an omnipotent sociological monad, so for the same reason government must be by the consent of the governed.

Moreover, the motive of the consent, as of the "drive" that gets men into society, is self-interest, self-preservation, and particularly the preservation of what was very dear to Locke's middle-class heart, the preservation of property: "The great and chief end, therefore, of men uniting into commonwealths and putting themselves under government, is the preservation of their property, to which in the state of nature there are many things wanting." Society, paradoxically, is the product of egoism. It is an artificial contrivance to rescue the ego by restraining somewhat its egoism. The essence of social man, as of individual man, is selfishness. Finally, pursuing the same line of thought, Locke comes to his third principle, the limitation of governmental power by the "common good." This common good consists merely in the security of each individual in the possession of his property. That is the end of social life as of individual life; the social end differs from the individual end only quantitatively.

This, briefly, is Locke's theory of the law of nature, as embracing a theory of natural rights and their inalienability, of the origins of political society, and of the functions and limitations of governmental power—all based, as is clear, on an idea of man. The three characteristics of the system are obvious—its rationalism, individualism, nominalism. The law of nature, the rights of man, and the origins of society are not derived from what is "real," from the concrete totality of man's nature as it really is. They are deduced from an abstraction, a fictitious state of nature, a disembodied idea of man that is put forward as "rational" and by that sole title real, whereas it was in effect but a reflex of the socio-philosophical individualism of a superficial age.

This individualism, this atomistic social outlook, is the predominant characteristic of Locke's system. His law of nature is solely a law of individual nature, conceived after the abstract fashion of the rationalist. The premise of Locke's state of nature is a denial that sociality is inherent in the very nature of man, and the assertion that the civil state is adventitious, that man is by nature only a solitary atom, who does not seek in society the necessary condition of his natural perfectibility as man, but only a utilitarian convenience for the fuller protection of his individual self in its individuality.

Bentham's utilitarianism is, in fact, but the logical prolongation of Locke's thought. Locke's individualism completely deprives society of any organic character. Society is not organized in ascending forms of sociality that are made necessary by, and radicated in, nature itself, beginning with the family, through the occupational group, and culminating in the "perfect society," the political community as such, the *respublica.*

In Locke's theory all forms of sociality are purely contractual; they have no deeper basis in the nature of man than a shallow "reason" that judges them useful. (Even the church he will allow to be no more than a voluntary association of like-minded people—a concept congenial indeed to a certain wing of Protestantism, but one that an increasing number of Protestants today are finding it difficult to live with.) Against this evacuation of all reality from the notion of society and "social being" the Romantic movement, with its love of the "organic," was a reaction, that in time carried the world to the excesses of the totalitarianisms of race and class.

In England, of course, Locke's individualistic law of nature never had its logical social consequences. There were too many elements of the more human medieval tradition deposited in English institutions, and above all in the English common law, for the inherent consequence of Locke's theory to work itself out; I mean the dissolution of the organic character of the total political relationship and its reduction to the harsh antithesis, individual *versus* state, together with the connected idea of the juridical omnipotence of the state. However, the French enthusiasts who took up his ideas had none of the inhibitions imposed on him by his British common sense, caution, and feeling for tradition. In consequence, his law of nature, when it had passed through their politically irresponsible "reason," results in the complete social atomism of the Constitution of 1791 and the Declaration of the Rights of Man and Citizen. There it appears that there are only two "sovereignties": that of the individual over his private life and that of the state over all forms of social life. There are no autonomous social forms intermediate between the individual and the state. Not only are the traditional *états* dissolved, but it is decreed that: "There are no longer *iurandes,* nor corporations of professions, arts and crafts, nor any private humanitarian associations or private schools." (The famous *loi Chapelier* of

1793 carried this atomism to its ultimate absurdity, that produced a reaction; not even the conquering "reason" of the *philosophes* could convince a lot of sensible, provincial Frenchmen that they had only two loyalties—one to themselves as individuals and the other to the state.)

Finally, the individualism of Locke's law of nature results in a complete evacuation of the notion of the "rights" of man. It is quite evident that Locke's state of nature reveals no *ordo juris,* and no rights in any recognizably moral sense. There is simply a pattern of power relationships—the absolute lordship of one individual balanced against the equally absolute lordship of others. Significantly, Locke uses the word "power" more frequently than the word "right" in describing the state of nature. Moreover, what the social contract does, in effect, is simply to transfer this system of power relationships into the civil state, with the sole but significant difference that there is now added to it a "third power," the public power of government. In the naked essence of Locke's thought, government is the arbiter of "right," only in the sense that it is a power to check power. And its use is "right" when behind it is the consent of the community, that is, the consent of the majority, that is, again (in Locke's explanation of majority rule), "the greater force," in which is embodied "the power of the whole."

Again, Locke did not draw all the implications from his theory, but the French did. There was Montesquieu, for instance, with his doctrinaire theory that only power checks power, and that when the checks are adequate the mechanical resultant is freedom (unless, one is inclined to add, it be the situation in which the French to this day seem to delight—the paralysis of power and consequent chaos). Moreover, there was the fourth article of the Declaration of the Rights of Man, wherein the logic of Locke's theory runs out in the statement that the "limits" of individual rights "can be determined only by law," that is, by positive law. Here is the explicit denial of any *ordo juris* antecedent to the state; here is the seed of legal positivism, and the essence of Rousseau's omnipotent democracy, wherein there is complete identification of state and national community, and the consequent subjection of all forms of community life to total state control. The logical outcome of Locke's individualistic law of nature, in its French transcription, was the juridical monism of the successive French Republics. In consequence of the false antithesis, individual *versus* state, all self-governing intermediary social forms with particular ends are destroyed, in order to create "free and equal citizens," who are subject only to one law, the positive law of the state, the exclusively competent lawmaker. There is no longer any pluralism of social institutions existent and self-directing by natural or positive divine right (*e.g.,* workers' unions or the Church), antecedent to, or above the state. There is only the monistic unity of the political order, under a legislative that is juridically omnipotent, the source and origin of all right. And to enforce this political unity, by destruction of all possibly competing allegiances, there was a state-fostered political mysticism—the "civil religion" of Rousseau, which was indeed no kind of religion but simply a means to homogeneity in the state. (I have already pointed out in a previous chapter that it was against this type of liberalist individualism—as positing a social and juridical monism and a concept of the juridical omnipotence of the state, both based on the concept of the absolute autonomy of the individual human reason —that the Catholic Church directed her uncompromising attacks during the nineteenth century, under appeal to the traditional natural law.)

The third characteristic of Locke's system of natural law is its nominalism. Since he was on the one hand an empiricist in epistemology (who denied the power of intelligence to reach anything beyond the individual singular thing), and since on the other hand he wished to talk as a philosopher (using the traditional terms— man, nature, law, right, authority, society, state, etc.), Locke could not be anything but that most decadent of all philosophical things, a nominalist. All these terms to him are mere *flatus vocis,* symbols to which corresponds no metaphysical reality. For instance, society as such, or man as *ens sociale,* signifies nothing real; the terms are symbols indicating a certain amount of material utility that the individual derives from contractual forms of association with other individuals. Similarly, the law of nature is but a nominalist symbol for a collection of particular empowerments considered desirable for the preservation of "property" in the wide Lockean sense. Or again, the "common good" is nothing real in itself, a social good qualitatively distinct from individual goods, but simply a symbol for the quantitative sum of individual goods. Finally, "right" is not a term relating to a moral order deriving from the essences of things; it is simply a symbol flourished to assure the free functioning of self-interest. In the rarefied mental climate of the *philosophes,* as well as in the muzzy mysticism of Rousseau, this purely symbolic value of the phrase, "the rights of man," as a potent form of political incantation, is still more marked.

The Law of Nature as a Political Instrument

What then does one say about this individualistic law of nature in Locke's statement, and the French restatement, of it? What one says depends on whether one regards it as a piece of philosophy or as a political weapon. As a piece of philosophy—that is, as ultimately resting on an idea of man and human society—it hardly needs refutation today. As a matter of fact, the refutation of the system was supplied before the system itself was born; Aristotle himself suggested its substance, even apart from the development of Aristotelian epistemology, ethics, and political philosophy in the Scholastic tradition. However, one need not appeal to thinkers antecedent to Locke; those subsequent to him will do. Darwin, Freud, and Marx are sufficiently his judges in what concerns the pillars of his system. The genuine and true insights that lie at the root of these three latterly proposed systems have destroyed completely the Lockean idea of man, of the state of nature, and of civil society; this, notwithstanding the fact that these true insights are so denatured by their incorporation into falsely monistic systems that in their own context they are themselves false.

Darwin and the principle of continuity in nature dealt a mortal blow to the atomism of post-Reformation anthropology, with its theory of discrete individuals who "happen" suddenly and live "unattached" save in so far as with sovereign freedom they attach themselves. In evolutionary theory, man is solidary, by all that is material in him, with all life. Purified of monistic connotations, the notion is compatible with a central thesis of Christian anthropology, that asserts the law of solidarity for both flesh and spirit; but it is not compatible with Lockean individualism. Again, when Freud fulfilled his promise, "Acheronta movebo," he shattered forever the "angel-mindedness" of the Cartesian man, and the brittle rationalistic optimism founded on it with the aid of eighteenth-century mechanicism, which supposed that there were "laws of reason" in human affairs that needed only to be discovered to be acted upon, and likewise (with Rousseau) supposed that all men would, as has been said, cease to be evil, if only no one tried to compel them to be good. Finally, the Marxist intuition of the reality of the "collective" and its organic character, of the importance of material factors in society, and of the conditions of heteronomy and loss of freedom produced by the individualism of capitalist society, effectively disposed of the empty nominalism and false idealism of the "law of nature" concept of human community based solely on the social contract struck between "absolute lords."

In this day and age, therefore, one need not take with any philosophical seriousness Locke's account of human nature, or his individualistic law of nature, or his simplistic theory of the origins of society; these are all as "dated" as the clothes Locke himself wore. The same remark goes for Rousseau. How "dated" he, and the Declaration of the Rights of Man and Citizen inspired by him, actually are, may be seen, for instance, by a glance at the Italian Constitution of 1948, into whose making went the four currents of the contemporary world—the Christian Democratic, the Liberal (of the Mazzinian tradition), the Socialist, and the Communist. The Second Article will illustrate the difference of spirit: "The Republic recognizes and guarantees the inviolable rights of man, both as an individual and in the social formations in which his personality unfolds itself, and calls for the fulfilment of the duties of political, economic and social solidarity." Neither Locke nor Rousseau could have written that.

At all events, Locke's law of nature did not owe its undeniable success to its philosophical shallowness (though in a philosophically shallow age that was no disadvantage). Its philosophical weakness vanished before its strength as a political weapon in the performance of the political task that at the moment needed to be done. At bottom, the focus of Locke's thought was narrow and practical. He was not searching for a generalized theory that would make society right, but simply for a theory that would make it right for England to have resisted an autocratic king—to have cut off his head (Charles I) or at least dethroned him (James II). He wrote, as he admitted, to justify the "Glorious Revolution" of 1688, and to settle William of Orange on a throne to which his theoretical title was highly dubious. Besides this particular political aim, he had other preoccupations of a practical order that appealed to common sense. He wrote at a time when the common sense of England was weary of the socially sterile enthusiasms of the Civil Wars; when the business community of England stood looking into the long horizons of commercial prosperity opened by colonial expansion and the development of foreign trade; when mercantile influence on government in the interests of property and freedom for commercial enterprise was on the rise; when economic advantage rather than dynastic or religious rivalries was becoming the moving force in the international field. Consequently, Locke was interested in seeing government influenced by the propertied class through the principle of representation; he wanted government by the consent of the landowners and merchants (this, in effect, is what Locke's "consent of the governed" meant). He was further interested in advancing the concept that government's sole function is the guaranteeing of individual liberty (*i.e.,* property, and the freedom to increase it). In a word, his problem was to devise a law of nature that would support a political theory that would in turn support a businessman's commonwealth, a society dominated by bourgeois political influence through the medium of the "watch dog" State whose functions would be reduced to a minimum, especially in the fields of business and trade.

As an instrument for these particular political and politico-economic aims, his theory of the individualistic law of nature was admirably adapted, whatever its philosophical shortcomings. With the last of the Stuarts gone, and a new world opening up, the time was ripe for a new kind of polity; and since Locke was not its prophet but its apologist, he had honor in his own country. Whether his law of nature made philosophical sense or not, the ordinary English property owner did not trouble to ask; it delivered the goods demanded at the moment, and that was enough. I should add, too, that Locke delivered the goods—helped to create a stable and vigorous political community—largely because he restated, and did not quite succeed in denaturing, the great political truths that were the medieval heritage, but that had been obscured in the era of absolutism and the divine right of kings (which, as Kern has pointed out, was not a development but a denial of medieval ideas).

Against the principle of absolutism—the assertion of the irresponsibility of the king and the unlimited scope of his power— Locke asserted (in debased form) the central medieval tradition of the supremacy of law over government, and of government by law which is reason, not will. Against the central point of divine-right theory—that the monarch's right to rule is inalienable and independent of human agency—he asserted (on philosophically indefensible grounds) the medieval principle that sovereignty is "translated" from the people to the ruler, who is responsible to the people in its exercise and holds title to it only as long as he serves their common good. Finally, against absolute centralization of power in the monarch, he asserted (again on false premises) the medieval doctrine of the right of the people to participate in government. In other words, though Locke knew only an artificial law of nature, he asserted in effect the fundamental positions of the natural-law philosophy of the state that had been the creation of greater minds than his, operating at the center of a tradition to whose periphery he himself had moved. These truths, that were not of Locke's own devising, furnished the essential dynamism of his system. Their truth stood up, in spite of Locke's failure to understand and demonstrate it; and this truth gave them their impact on the political conscience of the time. Not even Locke's narrow individualism, his thin rationalism, and his empty nominalism could quite veil their absolute validity as imperatives of a human reason that has a greater and more universal power than was dreamt of in Locke's philosophy.

Locke had great honor also in France. The success of his theory of the law of nature, put into more doctrinaire form by French theorists, might be explained on similar lines. It was congenial to the individualistic and rationalistic mentality of that extraordinarily small group of men whose ideas succeeded in turning France upside down. They were not concerned, as Locke was, with justifying a revolution, but with making one. And they made it in the name of the law of nature. The prime value of the idea lay in its power of destruction. What these men, for a variety of reasons, wanted to do was to destroy the rigid, clumsy, anachronistic, crippling absolutism of the *ancien régime*. What they needed to lay hands on in the first instance was a corrosive, not a constructive, force. And they found it in the theory of the "rights of man," based on the individualistic law of nature.

There is no need here to go into the history of the lengthy, complicated, very bloody revolution that strove to incorporate this theory into political institutions. What I want to note is that the revolution was professedly political. It has been remarked that the political essence of the revolution was in the decision of the Third Estate on June 17, 1789, to set about the making of a constitution quite by itself, apart from the nobles and clergy, and in the subsequent resolution of the Estates General into the National Assembly. This was a political decision—the assumption by "the people" of their right to govern themselves. The problem of the moment was essentially political. And the temper of the times was largely that voiced by Rousseau when he said in his *Confessions,* describing the inspiration of his *Social Contract:* "I had come to see that in the last resort everything depends on politics, and that whatever men may do, no nation will ever be anything but what the nature of its Government may make it." The principle, like most things at the time, is on its head; its reverse is more certainly correct. However, it was the revolutionary principle. And it was allied with the further principle that government will necessarily be good, if "the people" run it; for "the people," according to Rousseau, are themselves necessarily good; it is only bad government that makes them bad. If then the "general will" of the people makes the laws, the laws will be right, because the sovereign people is always right.

Thus spake the *Éclaircissement*—as usual, mixing truth with nonsense. And also as usual, the truth derives from the Western political tradition of natural law; the nonsense, from the eighteenth-century philosophoumenon, the law of nature. The agglomeration of both (obviously, along with other causes) made the Revolution. But it was powerful enough to do so (and this is my point) for the reason that the Revolution to be made was political. The determination that existed was that of bringing to an end an era and an order of political privilege (or, in America, that of preventing the rise of such an order). The principle embedded in the political philosophy of St. Thomas Aquinas was having a rebirth under the pressure of arbitrary power on the conscience of the people: "In regard of the good ordering of rulers in a city or nation . . . the first thing [to be observed] is that all should have some share in the government . . . ." And the validity of the reason he gives, on the authority of Aristotle, was again being confirmed: "for in this way the peace of the people is preserved, and all love and cherish such an order, as it is said in the Second Book of the *Politics*" (*Summa Theologia,* I–II, q. 105, a. 1). Locke and Rousseau, in whose angular rationalistic thought there was little room for experience and psychology as sources of political philosophy, were, in fact, carried to popularity by a psychological drive of discontent born of harsh experience. In such times of discontent with the fundamental structures of society, as Laski has pointed out, the gospel of human rights always has a resurgence.

The eighteenth-century gospel, based on the individualistic law of nature, could not at the time fail to be popular. For the primary drive then was toward destruction, and the law of nature concept of human rights was an appropriate dynamism of destruction, precisely because of the philosophical nonsense it enshrined. I mean that its individualistic rationalistic nominalism, precisely because it disregarded the organic character of society, and precisely because its concept of "progress" entailed a complete denial of the past and of the continuity of human effort, was an effective solvent of the corporate institutional structure of society as it then was. It could not (in France, at least) initiate simply a movement of reform; it could only operate as an engine of destruction. In the same way, its rationalistic secularism was effective against the usurping theory of divine right on which sovereignty at the time was based. And its mobilization of the "power of the people," under the nominalist slogan of the "rights of man," was an effective counterpoise to the unendurable centralization of power in king and nobles. This theory, therefore, could ride against the evils of the time with all the force, not only of truth but of error itself. Its theoretic dogmas were, as theories, false; but, as dogmas, powerful. Its exclusive attention to the problem of politics, and its attempt to solve it by violently creating an artificial "equality of citizens" (free, supposedly, as men, because equal as citizens), could end, as it did, only in dictatorship. But at least it could accomplish the social ruin that made dictatorship inevitable. And for the moment, a work of ruin was the immediate objective; for anger was abroad as well as reason, and it was not averse to using "reason" as its instrument.

On the other hand, the theory of natural rights, based on a law of nature, had also a measure of constructive dynamism—this time, not by reason of the philosophical nonsense involved in its theoretical scaffolding, but by reason of the intuition of truth that even the scaffolding could not wholly obscure. By nature all men are, as Bergbohm despairingly said, natural-law jurists. Intuitively they reach the essential imperatives of their own nature and know them to be unthwartably imperative—however much they may subsequently deform them, and destroy their proper bases, by uninformed or prejudiced reflective thought. And just as all men by nature—by the native power of moral intelligence—know that there is a difference between the *iustum naturale* and the *iustum legale* (the one based on natural law, the other on positive law), so, too, they naturally "see" the natural-law truth that "sovereignty is from the people," however much they may then go on falsely to conceptualize this truth. Usually the suffering of injustice is needed to bring the vision, just as immunity from suffering may obscure it. It is, as Pascal said, "the passions that make us think." And in those days the theory of divine right, together with the oppressive weight of the remnants of the feudal system, generated enough passion to make men think— furiously. In their fury, they thought of the truth anciently deposited in the *lex regia* of Justinian's *Institutes,* and elaborated by the Christian intelligence since the eleventh century.

Being men of the eighteenth century, whose intelligences were by this time very superficially Christian, they did not see this truth in its proper setting, the natural law. But they at least dimly glimpsed it: "Sovereignty is from the people; therefore they are not to be ruled save by their consent, and for their common good, by a power subject to law, whose end is justice, which is an order of right." They did not, I say, know that they were looking at natural law; for the law of nature had shut off natural law from their vision. But it was, for all that, natural law that swam before them; and this obscure intuition furnished whatever positive, constructive dynamism there was behind their revolutionary, destructive efforts. So they set about their work of political liberation—the work of incorporating the doctrine of consent into the structures of government, of creating channels of consent, of establishing political institutions whereby the natural-law right of popular participation in government might be made effective. In a word, they brought into almost exclusive focus the problems of representation and suffrage, as the necessary expression of the doctrine of popular sovereignty, which was at the heart of the "principles of '89." Their dominant concern was with the external form of government.

To make a long story short, let it be said that this movement for political liberty through political equality expressed in the equal right of franchise ultimately succeeded; by the last decade of the nineteenth century "the people" were furnished with their political weapon in all the major countries of Western Europe. This was a great fundamental success indeed, though it is highly improbable that much of it was due to the law-of-nature concept of natural rights that was the theoretical justification of the original political explosion. At all events, by the end of the nineteenth century Rousseau's man, the individual atom, who had been born free and was everywhere in chains, had supposedly struck off his chains with the hammer of natural rights, based on the law of nature. The only remaining difficulty was that the unfortunate fellow found himself still in chains. And by a curious paradox, the new chains were forged by the very doctrine that was supposed to free him. The doctrine of natural rights that in the eighteenth century was the dynamism destructive of political privilege became in the nineteenth century the dynamism constructive of economic privilege. It was the bulwark of Manchesterism and the *laissez-faire* state.

No one need have been surprised at this who understood the empty nominalism of the doctrine. Its inherent ambivalence and susceptibility of opposite consequences had already been manifested. In Locke the state of nature and the individualistic law of nature had been so interpreted as to yield moderately liberalist consequences. But with Hobbes its consequences had been rigorously statist; it had been the justification of the royal absolutism of the Stuarts. The "omnipotent democracy" which Rousseau drew from the doctrine became, with Hegel, a statism that Rousseau would have repudiated. And the individualistic law of nature as evolved by Pufendorf and Thomasius was used to justify the "enlightened despotism" of the Prussian Fredericks and of the Austrian Emperor

Joseph II. The law of nature was, in effect, a veritable Pandora's box. There seemed to be a great hope at the bottom of it, but on its opening many winged evils took their flight across the face of Europe.

If one were, in fine, to sum up its political significance, one would have to say, I think, that it was able to destroy an order of political privilege and inaugurate an era of political equality; but it was not able to erect an order of social justice or inaugurate an order of human freedom. The testimony to the fact is the contemporary protest, in the name of "human rights," against the order (if one can call it an order) which is our heritage from the law of nature of the eighteenth and nineteenth centuries. The characteristics of the law of nature—its rationalism, individualism, and nominalism—made it an effective force for dissolution in its time; but today we are not looking for forces of dissolution, but for constructive forces. Similarly, its power as a solvent made it a force for liberty, in the thin and bloodless, individualist and negative nineteenth-century concept of liberty; but today we are looking for liberation and liberty in something better than this purely formal sense. We want liberty with a positive content within an order of liberty of rational design. Rousseau's "man everywhere in chains" is still too largely a fact. Our problem is still that of human freedom, or, in juridical terms, human rights. It is a problem of the definition of freedom, and then, more importantly, its institutionalization.

But the statement of the problem that we have in common with Locke and with the men of Paris and Philadelphia in 1789 has greatly changed. It is now seen to have a social dimension that no longer permits its statement in the old individualistic terms. Its multiple factors are now grasped with a realism that will not suffer its solution in the old nominalistic categories. And its background now has a new depth that the old one-dimensional, rationalistic thought never penetrated. The background is an idea of man in his nature, history, and psychology, that transcends the limited horizons of the rationalist mind. Finally, the growing conviction as to the ultimate impotence of the old attempts to solve the problem of human liberty and social order in purely secularistic, positivist terms had created a new openness to the world of metaphysical and religious values. If these alterations in the statement of the problem of freedom and human rights have in fact come about, as I think they have, they will explain the contemporary *Wiederkehr* of the ancient natural law of the Greek, Roman, and Christian traditions. Only the old idea is adequate in the face of the new problem. It alone affords the dynamic basis from which to attack the problem of freedom as posited in the "age of order" on whose threshold we stand. And it is such a basis because it is metaphysical in its foundations, because it is asserted within a religious framework, and because it is realist (not nominalist), societal (not individualist), and integrally human (not rationalist) in its outlook on man and society. In other words, the structure of the old idea of natural law follows exactly the structure of the new problem of human liberty.

NATURAL LAW IN THE NEW AGE

This is the point to which I have been coming. However, I have been so long in coming to it that there is now no time or space to develop it! I shall have to be content with some brief comments on the vital resources inherent in the idea of natural law, that indicate its new validity.

First in importance is its metaphysical character, its secure anchorage in the order of reality—the ultimate order of beings and purposes. As a metaphysical idea, the idea of natural law is timeless, and for that reason timely; for what is timeless is always timely. But it has an added timeliness. An age of order is by definition a time for metaphysical decisions. They are being made all round us. No one escapes making them; one merely escapes making this one rather than that one. Our decisions, unlike those of the eighteenth century, cannot be purely political, because our reflection on the bases of society and the problem of its freedom and its order must be much more profound. And this in turn is so because these problems stand revealed to us in their depths; one cannot any longer, like John Locke, be superficial about them. Our reflection, therefore, on the problem of freedom, human rights, and political order must inevitably carry us to a metaphysical decision in regard of the nature of man. Just as we now know that the written letter of a Bill of Rights is of little value unless there exist the institutional means whereby these rights may have, and be guaranteed, their expression in social action, so also we know—or ought to know—that it is not enough for us to be able to concoct the written letter unless we are likewise able to justify, in terms of ultimates in our own thinking about the nature of man, our assertion that the rights we list are indeed rights and therefore inviolable, and human rights and therefore inalienable. Otherwise we are writing on sand in a time of hurricanes and floods.

There are perhaps four such ultimate decisions open to our making, and each carries with it the acceptance of certain political consequences.

First, one could elect to abide by the old Liberal individualism. At bottom then one would be saying that "natural rights" are simply individual material interests (be they of individuals or social groups or nations), so furnished with an armature by positive law as to be enforceable by the power of government. In this view one would be consenting to a basically atomist concept of society, to its organization in terms of power relationships, to a concept of the state as simply an apparatus of compulsion without the moral function of realizing an order of justice; for in this view there is no order of justice antecedent to positive law or contractual agreements. In a word, one would be accepting yesterday's national and international status quo; for one would be accepting its principles.

Secondly, by an extreme reaction from individualistic Liberalism, wherein the individual as an individual is the sole bearer of rights, one could choose the Marxist concept of human rights as based solely on social function, economic productivity. One would then be saying that all rights are vested in the state, which is the sole determinant of social function. It is the state that is free, and the individual is called simply to share its freedom by pursuing its purposes, which are determined by the laws of dialectical materialism. In this view one would be consenting to the complete socialization of man (his mind and will, as well as his work), within the totalitarian state, all his energies being requisitioned for the realization of a pseudo-order of "justice," which is the triumph of collective man over nature in a classless society that will know no "exploitation of man by man." In this view, as in the foregoing one, one accepts as the ultimate reality the material fact of power—in one case the power of the individual, in the other the power of the collectivity. One bases society and the state on a metaphysic of force (if the phrase be not contradictory).

A third decision, that somehow attempts a mediation between these extreme views, is soliciting adherents today; I mean the theory that its protagonists call "modern evolutionary scientific humanism," but that I shall call "the new rationalism."

It is a rationalism, because its premise is the autonomy of man, who transcends the rest of nature and is transcended by nothing and nobody (at least nothing and nobody knowable). It is new, because (unlike the old rationalism) it maintains (with Spinoza, whom Bowle has pointed to as one of its earliest forerunners) that man is something more than reason. It identifies natural law (though the term is not frequent with it) with "the drive of the whole personality," the totality of the impulses whereby men strive to "live ever more fully." It is new, too, because it abandons the old rationalist passion for deductive argument and for the construction of total patterns, in favor of the new passion for scientific method and the casting up of provisional and partial hypotheses. Finally, it is new because it does not, like eighteenth-century rationalism, conceive nature and its laws, or the rights of man, as static, given once for all, needing only to be "discovered." It adds to the old rationalistic universe the category of time; it supplements the processes of reason with the processes of history and the consequent experience of change and evolution.

Nature, therefore, is an evolving concept, and its law is emergent. It is also wholly immanent; for the new rationalism, like the old, denies to man, his nature, or its law all transcendental reference. The new rationalistic universe, like the old, is anthropocentric; all human values (reason, justice, charity) are man-made, and in consequence all human "rights," which are the juridical expression of these values, look only to man for their creation, realization, and guarantee. Their ultimate metaphysical justification lies in the fact that they have been seen, by experience, to be the contemporaneously necessary "expression of life itself." And for "life itself" one does not seek a metaphysical justification; it is, when lived in its fullness, self-authenticating. In this system, therefore, the theological concept is "fullness of life." As this is the end for the individual (to be realized as best may be in his stage of the evolutionary process), so, too, it is the end for the state. The *ordo juris* is conceived, after the fashion of the modern schools of sociological jurisprudence or realistic jurisprudence, as a pure instrumentality whereby lawmakers and judges, recognizing the human desires that are seeking realization at a given moment in human society, endeavor to satisfy these desires with a minimum of social friction. The ideals of law or of human rights are "received" from the "wants" of the society of the time and place, and any particular *ordo juris* is throughout its whole texture experimental.

Much could be said further to explain, and then to criticize, this subtle and seductive system, so much a product of the contemporary secularist mentality (its basic premise is, of course, secularism, usually accepted from the surrounding climate, not reached as the term of a metaphysical journey—few secularists have ever purposefully journeyed to secularism). I shall say only two things.

First, the new rationalism is at bottom an ethical relativism pure and simple. Its immanentism, its allegiance to scientific method as the sole criterion of truth, its theory of values as emergent in an evolutionary process, alike forbid it the affirmation of any absolute values (that is, as long as its adherents stay within their own system, which, being men and therefore by intrinsic necessity of reason also natural-law jurists, they frequently do not, but rather go on to talk of right, justice, equity, liberty, rationality, etc., investing these concepts with an absoluteness they could not possibly have within the system). Second as an ethical relativism, the new rationalism is vulnerable to all the criticisms that historically have been advanced against that ancient mode of thought, since the time when Socrates first argued against the Sophists and their dissolution of a knowable objective world of truth and value.

Chiefly, there are two objections. The first is that the new rationalism, like all the old ones, is unreasonable—surely something of a serious objection to a philosophy. "You do not," said Socrates to the Sophists, "know yourselves—your own nature, the nature of your reason." The same ignorance, though in more learned form, recurs in the modern heirs of sophistry. Secondly, the new rationalism, like all the old ones, is ruinous of sound political philosophy. "You are," said Socrates to the Sophists, "the enemies of the *polis,* who undermine its *nomoi,* especially its supreme *nomos,* the idea of justice, for whose realization all laws exist."

This objection, of course, will be vehemently repudiated by the new rationalists. They are fond of putting their system forward as the proper ideological basis of democracy; conversely, they say that democracy is the political expression of their philosophy. Its separation of church and state is the expression of their secularist humanism. Its freedom of thought and speech are the reflection of their philosophical and ethical relativism. Its respect for human rights creates the atmosphere in which science may further the evolution of man to higher dignities and fuller life. For my part, however, I should maintain that, by a curious but inevitable paradox, the relativism of the new rationalists must find its native political expression in a new and subtle form of state absolutism. The essential dialectic has already been displayed in history. The absolute autonomy of human reason, postulated by the old rationalism, had as its counterpart the juridical omnipotence of the state. And with accidental variations the dialectic will repeat itself: the autonomy of human reason (the denial of its subjection to a higher law not of its own creation) = relativism in regard of human values = absolutism in regard of the value and functions of the state. Admittedly, the new Leviathan would not be on the Hobbesian model, but it would be for all that the "Mortal God." And the outwardly humble garments that it would wear—the forms of political democracy—would hardly hide the fact that it was in effect the *divina maiestas.* It would be a long business to explain the working of this dialectic; let me state the substance in a brief paragraph.

I take it that the political substance of democracy consists in the admission of an order of rights antecedent to the state, the political form of society. These are the rights of the person, the family, the church, the associations men freely form for economic, cultural, social, and religious ends. In the admission of this prior order of rights—inviolable as well by democratic majorities as by absolute monarchs—consists the most distinctive assertion of the service-character of the democratic state. And this service-character is still further enforced by the affirmation, implicit in the admission of the order of human rights, of another order of right also antecedent to the state and regulative of its public action as a state; I mean the order of justice. In other words, the democratic state serves both the ends of the human person (in itself and in its natural forms of social life) and also the ends of justice. As the servant of these ends, it has only a relative value. Now it is precisely this service-character of the state, its relative value, that tends to be undermined by the theories of the new rationalism—by their inherent logic and by the psychology they generate.

Psychologically, it is not without significance that evolutionary scientific humanism should be the favorite creed of our contemporary social engineers, with their instrumental theories of education, law, and government. And it seems that their inevitable temptation is to hasten the process of evolution by use of the resources of government, just as it is to advance the cause of scientific humanism by a somewhat less than human application of science. The temptation is enhanced by the circumstance of the contemporary welfare state in the midst of an urbanized and industrialized mass civilization. The "sin" then takes the initial form of a desertion of their own premises. The "socially desirable objectives" are no longer "received" from society itself (as in the theory they should be); rather they are conceived in committee and imposed on society. The humanism ceases to evolve from below, and is directed from above; it remains scientific, and becomes inhuman. This is the psychological dynamism of the system: the state tends to lose its character of servant, and assume that of master. The psychological dynamism would be less destructive were it not in the service of the logic of the system. In the logic of the system is the destruction of all barriers to the expanding competence of the state. For one thing, the new rationalism is far too pale and bloodless a creed to stand against the flushed and full-blooded power of the modern state. For another, it hardly attempts to make a stand; in fact, its ethical relativism destroys the only ground on which a stand can be made—the absoluteness of the order of human rights that stands irremovably outside the sphere of state power, and the absoluteness of the order of justice that stands imperiously above the power of the state.

These then are three possible metaphysical decisions that one can make as a prelude to the construction of the new age. None of them, I think, carries a promise that the age will be one of true order.

There remains the fourth possible decision—the option of natural law in the old traditional sense. Here the decision is genuinely metaphysical; one does not opt for a rationalization of power, but for a metaphysic of right. I say "right" advisedly, not "rights." The natural law does not in the first instance furnish a philosophy of human rights in the sense of subjective immunities and powers to demand. This philosophy is consequent on the initial furnishing of a philosophy of right, justice, law, juridical order, and social order. The reason is that natural-law thinking does not set out, as Locke did, from the abstract, isolated individual, and ask what are his inalienable rights as an individual. Rather, it regards the community as "given" equally with the person. Man is regarded as a member of an order instituted by God, and subject to the laws that make the order an order—laws that derive from the nature of man, which is as essentially social as it is individual. In the natural-law climate of opinion (very different from that set by the "law of nature"), objective law has the primacy over subjective rights. Law is not simply the protection of rights but their source, because it is the foundation of duties.

THE PREMISES OF NATURAL LAW

The whole metaphysic involved in the idea of natural law may seem alarmingly complicated; in a sense it is. Natural law supposes a realist epistemology, that asserts the real to be the measure of knowledge, and also asserts the possibility of intelligence reaching the real, *i.e.,* the nature of things—in the case, the nature of man as a unitary and constant concept beneath all individual differences. Secondly, it supposes a metaphysic of nature, especially the idea that nature is a teleological concept, that the "form" of a thing is its "final cause," the goal of its becoming; in the case, that there is a natural inclination in man to become what in nature and destination he is—to achieve the fullness of his own being. Thirdly, it supposes a natural theology, asserting that there is a God, Who is eternal Reason, *Nous,* at the summit of the order of being, Who is the author of all nature, and Who wills that the order of nature be fulfilled in all its purposes, as these are inherent in the natures found in the order. Finally, it supposes a morality, especially the principle that for man, a rational being, the order of nature is not an order of necessity, to be fulfilled blindly, but an order of reason and therefore of freedom. The order of being that confronts his intelligence is an order of "oughtness" for his will; the moral order is a prolongation of the metaphysical order into the dimensions of human freedom.

This sounds frightfully abstract; but it is simply the elaboration by the reflective intelligence of a set of data that are at bottom empirical. Consider, for instance, the contents of the consciousness of a man who is protesting against injustice, let us say, in a case where his own interests are not touched and where the injustice is wrought by technically correct legislation. The contents of his consciously protesting mind would be something like these. He is asserting that there is an idea of justice; that this idea is transcendent to the actually expressed will of the legislator; that it is rooted somehow in the nature of things; that he really *knows* this idea; that it is not made by his judgment but is the measure of his judgment; that this idea is of the kind that ought to be realized in law and action; that its violation is injury, which his mind rejects as unreason; that this unreason is an offense not only against his own intelligence but against God, Who commands justice and forbids injustice.

Actually, this man, who may be no philosopher, is thinking in the categories of natural law and in the sequence of ideas that the natural-law mentality (which is the human mentality) follows. He has an objective idea of the "just" in contrast to the "legal." His theoretical reason perceives the idea as true; his practical reason accepts the truth as good, therefore as law; his will acknowledges the law as normative of action. Moreover, this man will doubtless seek to ally others in his protest, in the conviction that they will think the same as he does. In other words, this man, whether he be protesting against the Taft-Hartley Act or the Nazi genocidal laws, is making in his own way all the metaphysical affirmations that undergird the concept of natural law. In this matter philosophical reflection does not augment the data of common sense. It merely analyzes, penetrates, and organizes them in their full abstractness; this does not, however, remove them from vital contact with their primitive source in experience.

LAW IMMANENT AND TRANSCENDENT

From the metaphysical premises of natural law follow its two characteristics. It is a law immanent in the nature of man, but transcendent in its reference. It is rational, not rationalist. It is the work of reason, but not of an absolutely autonomous reason. It is immanent in nature in the sense that it consists in the dictates of human reason that are uttered as reason confronts the fundamental moral problems of human existence. These are the problems of what I, simply because I am a man and apart from all other considerations, ought to do or avoid in the basic situations in which I, again simply because I am a man, find myself. My situation is that of a creature before God; that of a "self" possessed of freedom to realize its "self"; that of a man living among other men, possessing what is mine as the other possesses what is his. In the face of these situations, certain imperatives "emerge" (if you like) from human nature. They are the product of its inclinations, as these are recognized by reason to be conformed to my rational nature. And they are formed by reason into dictates that present themselves as demanding obedience. Appearing, as they do, as dictates, these judgments of reason are law. Appearing, as they do, in consequence of an inclination that reason recognizes as authentically human, they are "natural" law.

However, these dictates are not simply emergent in the rationalist sense. Reason does not create its own laws, any more than man creates himself. Man has the laws of his nature given to him, as nature itself is given. By nature he is the image of God, eternal Reason; and so his reason reflects a higher reason; therein consists its rightness and its power to oblige. Above the natural law immanent in man stands the eternal law immanent in God transcendent; and the two laws are in intimate correspondence, as the image is to the exemplar. The eternal law is the Uncreated Reason of God; it appoints an order of nature—an order of beings, each of which carries in its very nature also its end and purposes; and it commands that this order of nature be preserved by the steady pursuit of their ends on the part of all the natures within the order. Every created nature has this eternal law, this transcendent order of reason, imprinted on it by the very fact that it is a nature, a purposeful dynamism striving for the fullness of its own being. In the irrational creation, the immanence of the eternal law is unconscious; the law itself is a law of necessity. But in the rational creature the immanent law is knowable and known; it is a moral law that authoritatively solicits the consent of freedom. St. Thomas, then, defines the natural law as the "rational creature's participation in the eternal law." The participation consists in man's possession of reason, the godlike faculty, whereby man knows himself—his own nature and end—and directs himself freely, in something of divine fashion but under God, to the plenitude of self-realization of his rational and social being.

Evidently, the immanent aspect of natural law relieves it of all taint of tyrannical heteronomy. It is not forcibly imposed as an alien pattern; it is discovered by reason itself as reason explores nature and its order. Moreover, it is well to note that in the discovery there is a necessary and large part reserved to experience, as St. Thomas insists: "What pertains to moral science is known mostly through experience" (*Eth.*, I, 3). The natural law, Rommen points out, "is not in the least some sort of rationalistically deduced, norm-abounding code of immediately evident or logically derived rules that fits every concrete historical situation." Like the whole of the *philosophia perennis*, the doctrine of natural law is orientated toward constant contact with reality and the data of experience. The point was illustrated above, in the chapter on public consensus.

The "man" that it knows is not the Lockean individual, leaping full grown into abstract existence in a "state of nature," but the real man who grows in history, amid changing conditions of social life, acquiring wisdom by the discipline of life itself, in many respects only gradually exploring the potentialities and demands and dignities of his own nature. He knows indeed that there is an order of reason fixed and unalterable in its outlines, that is not at the mercy of his caprice or passion. But he knows, too, that the order of reason is not constructed in geometric fashion, apart from consultation of experience, and the study of "the customs of human life and .. all juridical and civil matters, such as are the laws and precepts of political life," as St. Thomas puts it. The natural-law philosopher does not indeed speak of a "natural law with a changing content," as do the Neo-Kantians, to whom natural law is a purely formal category, empty of material content until it be filled by positive law and its process of legalizing the realities of a given sociological situation. However, the natural-law philosopher does speak of a "natural law with changing and progressive applications," as the evolution of human life brings to light new necessities in human nature that are struggling for expression and form. Natural law is a force conservative of all acquired human values; it is also a dynamic of progress toward fuller human realization, personal and social. Because it is law, it touches human life with a firm grasp, to give it form; but because it is a living law, it lays upon life no "dead hand," to petrify it into formalism.

In virtue of its immanent aspect, therefore, the natural law constantly admits the possibility of "new orders," as human institutions dissolve to be replaced by others. But in virtue of its transcendent aspect, it always demands that the new orders conform to the order of reason, which is structured by absolute and unalterable first principles.

NATURAL LAW AND POLITICS

In the order of what is called *ius naturae* (natural law in the narrower sense, as regulative of social relationships), there are only two self-evident principles: the maxim, "*Suum cuique,*" and the wider principle, "Justice is to be done and injustice avoided." Reason particularizes them, with greater or less evidence, by determining what is "one's own" and what is "just" with the aid of the supreme norm of reference, the rational and social nature of man. The immediate particularizations are the precepts in the "Second Table" of the Decalogue. And the totality of such particularizations go to make up what is called the juridical order, the order of right and justice. This is the order (along with the orders of legal and distributive justice) whose guardianship and sanction is committed to the state. It is also the order that furnishes a moral basis for the positive legislation of the state, a critical norm of the justice of such legislation, and an ideal of justice for the legislator.

This carries us on to the function of natural law in political philosophy—its solution to the eternally crucial problem of the legitimacy of power, its value as a norm for, and its dictates in regard of, the structures and processes of society. The subject is much too immense. Let me say, first, that the initial claim of natural-law doctrine is to make political life part of the moral universe, instead of leaving it to wander as it too long has, like St. Augustine's sinner, *in regione dissimilitudinis.* There are doubtless a considerable number of people not of the Catholic Church who would incline to agree with Pius XII's round statement in *Summi Pontificatus* that the "prime and most profound root of all the evils with which the City is today beset" is a "heedlessness and forgetfulness of natural law." Secretary of State Marshall said practically the same thing, but in contemporary idiom, when he remarked that all our political troubles go back to a neglect or violation of human rights.

For the rest, I shall simply state the major contents of the political ideal as it emerges from natural law.

One set of principles is that which the Carlyles and others have pointed out as having ruled (amid whatever violations) the political life of the Middle Ages. First, there is the supremacy of law, and of law as reason, not will. With this is connected the idea of the ethical nature and function of the state (*regnum* or *imperium* in medieval terminology), and the educative character of its laws as directive of man to "the virtuous life" and not simply protective of particular interests. Secondly, there is the principle that the source of political authority is in the community. Political society as such is natural and necessary to man, but its form is the product of reason and free choice; no ruler has a right to govern that is inalienable and independent of human agency. Thirdly, there is the principle that the authority of the ruler is limited; its scope is only political, and the whole of human life is not absorbed in the polis. The power of the ruler is limited, as it were, from above by the law of justice, from below by systems of private right, and from the sides by the public right of the Church. Fourthly, there is the principle of the contractual nature of the relations between ruler and ruled. The latter are not simply material organized for rule by the *rex legibus solutus,* but human agents who agree to be ruled constitutionally, in accordance with law.

A second set of principles is of later development, as ideas and in their institutional form, although their roots are in the natural-law theories of the Middle Ages.

The first is the principle of subsidiarity. It asserts the organic character of the state—the right to existence and autonomous functioning of various sub-political groups, which unite in the organic unity of the state without losing their own identity or suffering infringement of their own ends or having their functions assumed by the state. These groups include the family, the local community, the professions, the occupational groups, the minority cultural or linguistic groups within the nation, etc. Here on the basis of natural law is the denial of the false French revolutionary antithesis, individual versus state, as the principle of political organization. Here too is the denial of all forms of state totalitarian monism, as well as of Liberalistic atomism that would remove all forms of social or economic life from any measure of political control. This principle is likewise the assertion of the fact that the freedom of the individual is secured at the interior of institutions intermediate between himself and the state (*e.g.,* trade unions) or beyond the state (the church).

The second principle is that of popular sharing in the formation of the collective will, as expressed in legislation or in executive policy. It is a natural-law principle inasmuch as it asserts the dignity of the human person as an active co-participant in the political decisions that concern him, and in the pursuit of the end of the state, the common good. It is also related to all the natural-law principles cited in the first group above. For instance, the idea that law is reason is fortified in legislative assemblies that discuss the reasons for laws. So, too, the other principles are fortified, as is evident.

CONCLUSION

Here then in briefest compass are some of the resources resident in natural law, that would make it the dynamic of a new "age of order." It does not indeed furnish a detailed blueprint of the order; that is not its function. Nor does it pretend to settle the enormously complicated technical problems, especially in the economic order, that confront us today. It can claim to be only a "skeleton law," to which flesh and blood must be added by that heart of the political process, the rational activity of man, aided by experience and by high professional competence. But today it is perhaps the skeleton that we mostly need, since it is precisely the structural foundations of the political, social, and economic orders that are being most anxiously questioned. In this situation the doctrine of natural law can claim to offer all that is good and valid in competing systems, at the same time that it avoids all that is weak and false in them.

Its concern for the rights of the individual human person is no less than that shown in the school of individualist Liberalism with its "law of nature" theory of rights, at the same time that its sense of the organic character of the community, as the flowering in ascending forms of sociality of the social nature of man, is far greater and more realistic. It can match Marxism in its concern for man as worker and for the just organization of economic society, at the same time that it forbids the absorption of man in matter and its determinisms. Finally, it does not bow to the new rationalism in regard of a sense of history and progress, the emerging potentialities of human nature, the value of experience in settling the forms of social life, the relative primacy in certain respects of the empirical fact over the preconceived theory; at the same time it does not succumb to the doctrinaire relativism, or to the narrowing of the object of human intelligence, that cripple at their root the high aspirations of evolutionary scientific humanism. In a word, the doctrine of natural law offers a more profound metaphysic, a more integral humanism, a fuller rationality, a more complete philosophy of man in his nature and history.

I might say, too, that it furnishes the basis for a firmer faith and a more tranquil, because more reasoned, hope in the future. If there is a law immanent in man—a dynamic, constructive force for rationality in human affairs, that works itself out, because it is a natural law, in spite of contravention by passion and evil and all the corruptions of power—one may with sober reason believe in, and hope for, a future of rational progress. And this belief and hope is strengthened when one considers that this dynamic order of reason in man, that clamors for expression with all the imperiousness of law, has its origin and sanction in an eternal order of reason whose fulfillment is the object of God's majestic will.

Notes

1. *Western Political Thought.* London: Oxford University Press, 1947.

Rethinking Natural Law

John Macquarrie

This chapter first appeared in 1970 in *Three Issues in Ethics.*

In the last chapter we reviewed some of the characteristics which seem to be pervasive contemporary images of man and which recur in different philosophies and ideologies. We found also that the characteristics discussed are compatible with the biblical under- standing of man, and even implicit in it. To take them more seri- ously would lead to new emphases and new priorities in a contempo- rary statement of Christian ethics, and these new emphases would in turn strengthen the links between Christian morals and what I have sometimes called the "general moral striving of mankind," as this manifests itself in humanism, Judaism, Marxism, and various other non-Christian life styles.

We must now explore further the common ground between Christian and non-Christian morals; and in doing this, we shall at the same time be advancing our consideration of another question announced at the beginning of the book, the question of whether, at least under present circumstances, the most appropriate way of do- ing Christian ethics is the way that sets out from the nature of man, rather than ways that begin from distinctively Christian concepts.

The next step after our discussion of contemporary human na- ture is to consider the notion of natural law. A recent important symposium, *Christian Ethics and Contemporary Philosophy,* ended with a thoughtful essay by the editor, the Bishop of Durham, on the theme: "Toward a Rehabilitation of Natural Law."[1] Although my own approach will differ from the Bishop's, I agree with him about the need for a rehabilitation of natural law, or, at least, for the recov- ery of what was of abiding value in the notion of such a law. Indeed, I believe that a viable account of natural law could make a vital contribution toward the three major problems from which we set out—the linking of Christian and non-Christian morals, the shape of a contemporary Christian ethic, and the relation between faith and morals.

But natural law—like the corresponding natural theology—is in bad repute nowadays. For a long time it has been under fire from many Protestant moralists, who prefer a christocentric approach. More recently, even some Roman Catholic moral theologians have begun to doubt whether in their tradition too much stress has been laid on natural law and too little on the New Testament. Much of the criticism of natural law has been justified. Any attempt to reformulate it in a better way will be neither an easy nor a popular undertaking. But I believe that such an attempt is urgently required.

A good starting point for our discussion is the assertion, often heard nowadays among theologians who are interested in the relation of Christianity to the secular world, that to be a Christian is simply to be a man. Presumably the expression is an echo of Bonhoeffer: "To be a Christian does not mean to be religious in a particular way, to cultivate some particular form of asceticism (as a sinner, a penitent or a saint) but to be a man."[2] "To be a Christian is to be a man"—what does this mean? Certainly, this statement when made without qualification can be misleading, and it often is. It can be understood as diluting Christianity to the point where it loses all identity; and it can also be understood in the objectionable sense of "annexing" all men to Christianity. Yet, although it can be misunderstood and oversimplified, the statement is, I believe, true in a fundamental way. So far as Christianity offers fulfillment or salvation, it offers a full humanity—or, at least, a fuller humanity.

An illustration of something like this point of view is to be found in the work of Paul Lehmann. We have already noted that, in his view of Christian ethics, the policies of the believer should be determined by "what God is doing in the world."[3] If we ask, "Well, what is God supposed to be doing in the world?" Lehmann repeatedly gives this answer: "Making and keeping human life human!" Obviously, this expression is not intended to be a mere tautology, and therefore we must assume that the word "human" is being used in a different (though related) sense on each of its two occurrences. It is in fact fairly clear that God is said to be making and keeping human life "truly human" or "authentically human" or "fully human"; and that there is therefore implied in this assertion a criterion by which a truly human or fully human life may be recognized.

Lehmann does indeed tell us what his standard of such a true humanity is—it is the "mature manhood" of the New Testament, to be tested by being set against the "measure of the stature of the fullness of Christ."[4] The "fullness of Christ" therefore is, for Lehmann, the criterion of the fullness of humanity, and so—although at first sight his idea that the business of Christian morals is to join in the work of making human life authentically human might seem to provide a liberal formula for relating the Christian ethic to general moral principles—he offers a strictly christocentric definition of authentic humanity. Furthermore, he has very few good things to say about secular moral philosophy.

However, I do not think that one must take up a christocentric position. Even if the Christian ethicist holds (as presumably he does) that authentic humanity is to be judged by the standard of Jesus Christ, there is a kind of reciprocity involved in this assertion, so that one might also say that Jesus is recognized as the Christ because he has brought to fulfillment the deepest moral aspirations of mankind. There is a hermeneutic circle here: Christ interprets for the Christian the meaning of authentic humanity or mature manhood, but he is acknowledged as the Christ or the paradigm of humanity because men have interpreted him as such in the light of an idea of authentic humanity that they already bring to him and that they have derived from their own participation in human existence. No doubt the Christian finds that his idea of authentic humanity is enlarged, corrected, and perhaps even revolutionized by the concrete humanity of Christ, yet unless he had some such idea, it is hard to see how Christ could ever become Christ for him.

At this point we may profitably turn to some of the current trends in christology. Among all theological schools there is widespread agreement in placing a new emphasis on the humanity of Christ. The attempt is made to think through from his humanity to his deity, thus following a route opposite to the traditional one, which speculated on how the divine Logos became flesh.

Two examples will provide an illustration of what we have in mind. In the background of them is an understanding of man as a being-on-his-way, similar to the idea which was sketched out in the preceding chapter. Thus Karl Rahner has argued that, from one point of view, christology can be considered as a kind of transcendent anthropology. Christhood is seen as the fulfillment of humanity, the manifestation of what a true humanity ought to be. "Only someone who forgets that the essence of man . . . is to be unbounded . . . can suppose that it is impossible for there to be a man who, precisely by being man in the fullest sense (which we never attain), is God's existence into the world."[5] Our second example is the christological study which David Jenkins undertook in his Bampton Lectures.[6] He begins by inquiring about the meaning of human personhood, and he goes on to interpret Christ as the "glory of man," a phrase suggesting a humanity brought to such a level that it becomes transparent to deity. Of course, neither Rahner nor Jenkins intends to reduce christology to anthropology. Jenkins explicitly says: "The reduction of theology to anthropology was the prelude to reducing anthropology to absurdity."[7] But both of these theologians do believe that a contemporary christology may well take its departure from what we know of the concerns and aspirations of men and show how these reach a fulfillment in Christ; and if human existence has in it the transcendence and mystery which we have seen reason to believe it has, then such a procedure will not fail to do justice to the transcendent dimension of christology. Even the "death of God" theologians recognized in Christ a kind of ultimacy which, if fully analyzed, would go beyond any "merely" anthropological view.

To put the matter in another way, Christ does not contradict but he fulfills our humanity; or, better expressed, he both contradicts it and fulfills it—he contradicts our actual condition but fulfills what we have already recognized deep within us as true human personhood.

These christological considerations are obviously of the highest relevance to our task of trying to relate Christian ethics to the moral aspirations of people who are not Christians. One can agree with Paul Lehmann that the moral criterion for the Christian is Jesus Christ; but if Jesus is recognized by Christians as the Christ because they acknowledge him, in Rahner's phrase, as "man in the fullest sense" or, in Jenkins' way of putting it, as the "glory of man," then the distinctively Christian criterion coincides with the criterion which, even if only implicitly, is already guiding the deepest moral aspirations of all men—the idea, however obscure, of an authentic or full humanity. In traditional theological language, this implicit image toward which man tends in transcending every given state of himself is the *imago Dei.*

In what sense, however, can the Christian believe that Christ does in fact fulfill the potentialities of man, so that his christhood can be considered as a kind of self-transcending humanity which is also the very image of God?[8] What kind of "fullness" or "perfection" can be attributed to him, so that he may be taken as the criterion of "mature manhood"? Of course, it must frankly be acknowledged that there are some humanists and others who find Christ much less than a paradigm for mankind. Yet even today it is remarkable how many non-Christians join with believers in acknowledging the stature of Christ. The usual complaint against Christians is not that they take Christ as the measure of human existence, but that they fail so miserably to do so! But why does the Christian make the claim he does for Christ, in his humanity?

It is quite obvious that Christ was not perfect in the sense of fulfilling all the potentialities of humanity—indeed, the very notion of this kind of perfection would seem to be self-contradictory, for no finite person could realize in himself within a limited life-span all the possibilities of human life. As far as we know, Christ was not a great painter or a great husband or a great philosopher or statesman. One of the most human of all activities is decision. Everyone, in the limited time at his disposal, has to make choices, to take up one vocation rather than another, to marry or to remain single, and so on. To decide (Latin: *de-cidere,* to cut away) is precisely a cutting away of some possibilities for the sake of the one that is chosen. Decision is to be understood as much in terms of what is cut away as in terms of what is chosen. In a finite existence, self-fulfillment is inseparable from self-denial.

Perhaps when we talk of the "fullness" of Christ, we have to look for it in this very matter of decision, so that the fullness is, paradoxically, also a self-emptying, a renunciation of other possibilities for the sake of that which has the greatest claim. We recall the parable of the merchant "who, on finding one pearl of great value, went and sold all that he had and bought it."[9] Can we say that Christ's fullness or perfection is attributed to him because he gave up all other possibilities for the sake of the most distinctively human possibility of all, and the one that has most claim upon all men, namely, self-giving love? And can we also say that because this love is the most creative thing in human life (for it brings men to freedom and personhood), then Christ manifests the "glory of man" by becoming transparent to the ultimate creative self-giving source of all, to God? And if indeed Christ is understood as the revelation of God, then this surely strengthens the argument for a basic affinity between Christian and non-Christian morals, for what is revealed or made clear in Christ is also implicit in the whole creation. In saying this, I am not "annexing" the whole creation to Christ but rather claiming that what is already present in the whole creation is gathered up in Christ. In other words, I am trying to link Christian and non-Christian moral striving not on the ground of a doctrine of redemption but on the ground of a doctrine of creation.

Christianity, I wish to assert, is not a separate moral system, and its goals and values are not fundamentally different from those that all moral striving has in view. Yet it cannot be denied that there are some ways in which the Christian ethic differs from non-Christian ethics. It seems to me that the differences have to do with the different ways in which the several groups or traditions perceive the goals that are implicit in all moral striving, and the means to these goals; or with the different ways in which they understand and engage in the moral obligations laid upon all; or with the different degrees of explicitness to which the idea of an authentic humanity has emerged in the several traditions.

Of course, there are often differences of prescription between Christian and non-Christian morals. For instance, Christianity prescribes monogamy, while some other traditions do not. But the question of judging between these prescriptions would be settled by still deeper moral convictions shared by the two or more traditions, namely, by asking which prescription best protects and enhances the true humanity of the persons concerned. A distinctive ethical tradition may help its adherents to perceive some aspects of the general moral drive with a special clarity, though equally it may dull their perception of other aspects. For instance, it could be argued that in developing its marriage institutions, the Christian tradition has been more perceptive of what makes for a true humanity than has the Islamic tradition; but one could claim on the other side that Islam has shown itself more perceptive than Christianity in fostering good racial attitudes that put human dignity before color or ethnic background. But fundamental to both traditions is respect for the human person and the desire to enhance human well-being, and this is the implied standard in any comparison of their actual prescriptions and institutions.

We are saying then that what is distinctive in the Christian ethic is not its ultimate goals or its fundamental principles, for these are shared with all serious-minded people in whatever tradition they stand. The distinctive element is the special context within which the moral life is perceived. This special context includes the normative place assigned to Jesus Christ and his teaching—not, indeed, as a paradigm for external imitation, but rather as the criterion and inspiration for a style of life. The context further includes the moral teaching of the Bible, and the ways in which this has been developed and interpreted by the great Christian moralists. There are also the practices of prayer and worship, which are formative for the community and its members. And, not least, there are the many ways in which the moral life is influenced (and, as I hope to show, supported) by Christian faith and hope.

Can we now try to spell out more definitely the nature of that common core which, as I have claimed, underlies and relates all the several moral traditions of mankind? Here we must return to the theme to which a brief allusion was made earlier—to natural law. I said that this proposal would not be very popular in some quarters, and yet, when we inquire why some Christian ethicists object so strongly to the idea of natural law, we find that they give very strange reasons. They seem to be afraid that to allow any weight to natural law would somehow infringe on the uniqueness of the Christian ethic. They seem to be afflicted with an anxiety that Christianity must somehow be distinct and perhaps even have some kind of monopoly of moral wisdom.

For instance, Paul Ramsey in one of his early books asked the question: "By what is Christian ethics to be distinguished from generally valid natural morality, if some theory of natural law becomes an authentic part and, to any degree, the primary foundation of Christian morality?"[10] This question is best answered by a counter-question: Why should we really want to distinguish Christian ethics from generally valid natural morality? I see nothing threatening in the possibility that the foundations of Christian morality may be the same as the foundations of the moralities associated with other faiths or with nonreligious beliefs. On the contrary, the more common ground Christians can find between their own ethical tradition and what Ramsey calls "generally valid natural morality," the better pleased they ought to be. For this means that there are a great many people who do not profess themselves Christians but who are nevertheless allied with Christians in their moral strivings and ideals. With them the Christian can cooperate with a good conscience—and not just as a tactical matter in some particular situation but because at bottom they share the same moral convictions.

Although Paul Lehmann identifies the end of the Christian with a true or mature humanity, he too attacks the notion of natural law and criticizes the idea of a philosophical ethic.[11] However, he does not enter into details of his objections to natural law, promising to do this in a future book. For the present, therefore, it is impossible to engage in a discussion with him on this matter.

A further objection made to the doctrine of natural law is that it does not take sin with sufficient seriousness. It assumes an innate tendency toward the good, failing to recognize the fallen condition of our human nature. I certainly have no wish to deny the fact of sin, and the question will be fully discussed later.[12] But I do not think of sin as having utterly destroyed the *imago Dei* or as having totally extinguished the drive toward authentic humanity. There is in man original righteousness as well as original sin, a tendency to fulfillment which is often impaired but never quite abolished; for if it were, the very consciousness of sin would be impossible.

Thus, although the idea of natural law is an unpopular one among many writers on Christian ethics today, their objections do not seem to be persuasive. Natural law, in some form, offers good hope of establishing a bridge between Christian ethics and general ethics. Indeed, I shall go further and claim that natural law is foundational to morality. It is the inner drive toward authentic personhood and is presupposed in all particular ethical traditions, including the Christian one.

What is natural law? The expression is ambiguous, and misleading in many ways. Nowadays it might suggest to many people the uniformities of natural phenomena, though in this sense it is more customary to talk about "laws of nature." It is very important to make plain that natural law, as an ethical concept, is quite distinct from any scientific law of nature. It is true that some moral philosophers, especially those belonging to evolutionary and naturalistic schools of thought, try to derive moral laws from biological laws. It has sometimes been argued that in the course of evolution cooperation has proved more successful than competition, and it is inferred that one should therefore be altruistic.[13] But this rests on a confusion between the idea of law as uniformity and law as a norm of conduct which can be accepted and obeyed by a responsible agent. To put the matter in another way, the confusion is between what is the case and what *ought to be* the case. One cannot proceed from statements of fact to value judgments, unless indeed one has already smuggled a value-judgment into the alleged statement of fact, as when one says that cooperation is "more successful" than competition. Theodosius Dobzhansky seems to be correct in saying that what can be established biologically is not the content of an ethic but simply "the capacity to ethicize."[14]

We must therefore turn away from biological conceptions of natural law to the strictly ethical sense of the expression. The expression "natural law" refers to a norm of responsible conduct, and suggests a kind of fundamental guideline or criterion that comes before all rules or particular formulations of law. It will be useful to pass in review some of the classic historical statements concerning this idea.

Like natural theology, natural law has its roots in the Greek rather than in the Hebrew contribution to Christian and Western reflection. Perhaps the first trace of the doctrine is to be found in a somewhat obscure saying of Anaximander in which he talks of things "paying the penalty" and "making atonement to each other" for their injustice. Commenting on this saying, Werner Jaeger remarks: "Here is no sober rehearsal of the regular sequence of cause and effect in the outer world, but a world-norm that demands complete allegiance, for it is nothing less than divine justice itself."[15] Incidentally, this comment further clarifies the distinction between "law of nature" in the scientific sense and "natural law" in the ethical sense.

Another early Greek philosopher, Heraclitus, was much more explicit on the subject of a natural law. He tells us that "all human laws are nourished by the one divine law; for this holds sway as far as it will, and suffices for all and prevails in everything." Jaeger's comments[16] are again very illuminating. He points out that Heraclitus seems to have been the first to introduce explicitly the notion of law into philosophical discourse, and, in doing so, he identified "the one divine law" with the *logos,* the primordial word or reason in accordance with which everything occurs. "This theological aspect," claims Jaeger, "makes very clear how profoundly the law of Heraclitus differs from what we mean when we speak of a 'law of nature.' A 'law of nature' is merely a general descriptive formula for referring to some specific complex of observed facts, while Heraclitus' divine law is something genuinely normative. It is the highest norm of the cosmic process, and the thing which gives that process its significance and worth." Jaeger has some further interesting remarks on the reciprocal kind of interpretation done by the Greeks, who used social and human models such as law (*nomos*) to elucidate the cosmos and then in turn sought to throw light on social structures from the order of the cosmos. Such interpretation is not, of course, "merely circular," but can provide some useful reciprocal illumination.

Moving on to Aristotle, we read: "Law is either special [*idios*] or general [*koinos*]. By 'special law' I mean that written law which regulates the life of a particular community; by 'general law,' all those unwritten principles which are supposed to be acknowledged everywhere."[17]

Some of Cicero's remarks on natural law are worth quoting. He provides a more detailed statement than does Aristotle, and especially interesting from our point of view is his theological interpretation of natural law, viewed within the context of Stoic philosophy. He writes: "There is indeed a true law, right reason, agreeing with nature, diffused among all men, unchanging, everlasting. . . . It is not allowed to alter this law or to derogate from it, nor can it be repealed. We cannot be released from this law, either by the magistrate or the people, nor is any person required to explain or interpret it. Nor is it one law at Rome and another at Athens, one law today and another hereafter; but the same law, everlasting and unchangeable, will bind all nations at all times; and there will be one common lord and ruler of all men, even God, the framer and proposer of this law."[18]

According to St. Thomas Aquinas, "Among all others, the rational creature is subject to divine providence in a more excellent way, in so far as it itself partakes of a share of providence, by being provident both for itself and others. Therefore it has a share of the eternal reason, whereby it has a natural inclination to its proper act and end; and this participation of the eternal law in the rational creature is called the 'natural law.' "[19]

One last quotation comes from Richard Hooker, in the Anglican tradition. "The general and perpetual voice of men is as the sentence of God himself. For that which all men have at all times learned, Nature herself must needs have taught; and God being the author of Nature, her voice is but his instrument. By her from him we receive whatsoever in such sort we learn. Infinite duties there are, the goodness of which is by this rule sufficiently manifested, although we had no other warrant besides to approve them. The apostle St. Paul, having speech concerning the heathen, saith of them, "They are a law unto themselves.' His meaning is, that by the force of the light of reason, wherewith God illuminateth everyone which cometh into the world, men being enabled to know truth from falsehood, and good from evil, do thereby learn in many things what the will of God is; which will, himself not revealing by any extraordinary means unto them, but they by natural discourse attaining the knowledge thereof, seem the makers of these laws which indeed are his, and they but only the finders of them out."[20]

A great many ideas are to be found in the passages quoted. The natural law is said to be unwritten; it is not invented by men but discovered by them; it is a kind of tendency rather than a code; it has a constancy or even an immutability. I certainly have no intention of attempting the defense of all the ideas contained in these quotations, even if they could be harmonized among themselves. But I do

believe that something can and must be recovered from this pervasive notion of a natural law, and that it can be very relevant to some
of our current problems. In the rest of the chapter, therefore, we
shall try to see what is possible by way of reinterpretation and
reconstruction.

The discussion will fall into two main parts. In the first, we shall
consider the theological or ontological foundations of natural law
and endeavor to interpret these in such a way that this law can
indeed be seen as a common ground for the different ethical traditions. This discussion will inevitably raise in a provisional way the
question of the relation between faith and morals, though the fuller
examination of this will be deferred to later chapters. In the second
part of the discussion, we shall consider what can be done toward
reinterpreting natural law so that it takes account of the change and
development which, as we have seen, are characteristic not only of
man's images of himself but of his very nature and of the world
around him.

1. It is acknowledged as a matter of fact that during most of the
course of human history, religion and morals have been closely associated with each other. It is true that there have sometimes been
religions with inhuman elements, practicing cruel and degrading
rites. It is true also that there have been and are many highly moral
persons who have disclaimed any religious convictions. Yet, on the
whole, we are bound to say that the bond between religion and
morals has been a close one.

How are we to understand this connection? Is it an intrinsic
one, or is it merely an external and almost accidental one? Was it,
for instance, appropriate that in the earlier stages of human development morals should be protected and inculcated by religion, but
that as man becomes increasingly adult, morals should be detached
from any connection with religion? This would parallel in the ethical field what has been true in many other fields of human activity,
in which arts and sciences that were once pursued under the aegis of
religion have become secularized and now flourish in complete
autonomy.

Some of the traditional ways of explaining the bond between
morality and religion were so inadequate and even repellent that,
rather than stay with them, one would prefer to see morality break

free from its religious associations. I refer especially to the view that religion provides the sanctions for morality and so the motivation for moral conduct, with its promise of reward for those who do good and its threat of punishment for evildoers. Such beliefs were widespread in ancient societies and persisted right down to the philosophers of recent centuries. John Locke could write: "The view of heaven and hell will cast a slight upon the short pleasures and pains of this present state, and give attractions and encouragements to virtue, which reason and interest, and the care of ourselves, cannot but allow and prefer. Upon this foundation, and upon this only, morality stands firm and may defy all competition."[21] Few people today believe in heaven and hell in the traditional sense, but they seem to be neither more nor less moral as a result. Even if there was the need for such a doctrine to buttress morality in earlier times, it would seem to have no place in the sophisticated societies of today. But more than this, I think we would say nowadays that to appeal to religion on the ground that it provides the sanctions for morality is to degrade both religion and morals. Religion is reduced to becoming a mere incentive to the moral life, while it is also suggested that men will not be moral apart from a system of ultimate rewards and punishments—surely a very cynical idea.

I believe that there is a connection between religion and morality, and that this connection is intrinsic and important. However, we must look for a way of interpreting it which will not do violence to the integrity of either religion or morality and that will not impugn the undoubtable achievements of secular morality. It can never be a question of subordinating religion to morality, or the other way around; nor can there be any question of claiming that morality is dependent on religious faith, in view of the plain fact that many nonreligious people are highly moral. Let me suggest, however, that natural law provides the link.

Though a religious faith is not to be identified with a metaphysic, it nevertheless always involves its adherents in some vision of the whole, in some fundamental convictions about "the way things are." Natural law too claims to be founded in "the way things are," in ultimate structures that are explicitly contrasted with the human conventions that find expression in our ordinary rules and customs. But natural law need not be given a theological or religious interpretation, and the conception of natural law is by no means incompatible with secular morality, and is indeed implied in some forms of it. Natural law is an ontological ground, common to the various forms of morality, receiving in some of them a religious interpretation, in others a secular. I would say that natural law (or something like it) is implicit wherever an unconditioned moral obligation is recognized. Perhaps this is implicit even in Camus, for in an absurd world it is apparently not absurd to be moral and to pursue the fulfillment of humanity.

That most people do seem to believe in something like natural law may be seen from a simple consideration. There is no human law, not even that promulgated by the highest authority, about which someone may not complain that it is unjust. There seems to be found among most people the conviction that there is a criterion, beyond the rules and conventions of human societies, by which these may be judged.

Every social group or association has some rules. These will normally be founded on the convenience of the members. If someone finds these rules unfair, and is unable to persuade the group to change them, he may have recourse to some superior set of laws to which the group itself is subject. There is always, so to speak, a higher court of appeal, a hierarchy of justice. There may be appeals through a whole series of courts, but even when the highest court of appeal has pronounced its judgment, it still makes sense for someone to say that its ruling was unjust. It is hard to see how this could be the case if justice has a purely empirical origin, explicable in terms of sociology, psychology, biology, and similar sciences.

Some jurists have held that the state is the ultimate source of law, so that what it decrees is *ipso facto* just and right—a theory, incidentally, which is no more arbitrary than the belief that what God decrees is therefore right. Such a positive theory of law, which was grounded in the state, was held in recent times by Nazi jurists in Germany. The state (or nation) was, for the Nazi, absolute. But most people would hold that there is an even more ultimate standard than the state, and that the state's laws and decrees can be unjust. According to Vernon J. Bourke, West Germany, Italy, and Japan are countries which have made considerable use of the natural law concept in reconstructing their legal and political institutions in the years following World War II.[22] It is surely significant that the three countries named were precisely lands that had for a time totalitarian rule. The concept of natural law is, among other things, a safeguard against the usurpation by the state of unlimited power.

Sophocles provided a dramatic account of the conflict between the laws of the state and the demands of "natural" justice:

> CREON: Now, tell me thou—not in many words, but briefly—knewest thou that an edict had forbidden this?
> ANTIGONE: I knew it. Could I help it? It was public.
> CREON: And thou didst indeed dare to transgress that law?
> ANTIGONE: Yes, for it was not Zeus that had published me that edict; not such are the laws set among men by the Justice who dwells with the gods. Nor deemed I that thy decrees were of such force, that a mortal could override the unwritten and unfailing statutes of heaven. For their life is not of today or yesterday, but from all time, and no man knows when they were first put forth.[23]

This scene from Greek tragedy antedates by some five hundred years a scene in the New Testament in which it is reported: "Then Peter and the other apostles answered and said: 'We must obey God rather than men.' "[24]

Of course, both of these excerpts, like the one quoted from Cicero earlier, are explicitly theological in what they say about the "higher law," and we should clearly understand that a doctrine of natural law does not necessarily commit one to a theistic belief. Governments which allow conscientious objection to military service only on *religious* grounds are acting unjustly. Indeed, one might even argue that to explain natural law or fundamental morality in terms of a divine Lawgiver is the most primitive and mythological way of expressing the idea. In the Old Testament, Moses receives the Decalogue, the basic laws of human conduct, at the hands of Yahweh. Likewise Hammurabi is depicted in Babylonian art as receiving the law from the god Marduk. In more recent times the natural law has sometimes been understood as the "will of

God." But in such cases, God has been conceived on the deistic model, as an absolute monarch in the heavens. The natural law is not the "will of God," if this is understood to mean that God's arbitrary decree determines right and wrong. Men have sometimes complained that God has been unjust to them. Their complaints may have been unfounded, but it is interesting that such complaints can even be made, for it indicates that those who make them do not identify justice simply with what God wills. Justice is such an ultimate notion that it cannot depend even on the will of God. This does not mean that it is more ultimate than God, but rather that it is not external or subsequent to God, for it belongs to his very being or nature.

The point has been put so clearly by E. L. Mascall that I can do no better than quote some sentences from him: "To the Scotists, who taught that the formal constituent of God was infinity and that will was essentially superior to intellect, it was natural to say that the moral law rested simply on the arbitrary decree of God and that actions are good because God has commanded them; to the Thomists, on the other hand, it was *being* that was fundamental, with the necessary corollary that the moral law is neither an antecedent prescription to which God is bound by some external necessity to conform, nor a set of precepts promulgated by him in an entirely arbitrary and capricious manner, but something inherently rooted in the nature of man as reflecting in himself, in however limited and finite a mode, the character of the sovereign Good from whom his being is derived. The moral law is thus in its essence neither antecedent nor consequent to God; it is simply the expression of his own self-consistency. To say, therefore, that God is bound by it is merely to say, from one particular angle, that God is God."[25]

In any case, it would be hard to imagine a more abused phrase than "the will of God." People have committed all kinds of wickedness and folly in the belief that they were carrying out the will of God. In milder but no less objectionable ways, they still pressure other people into adopting their policies by representing their own idiosyncrasies as God's will which it would be wrong to disobey—a favorite tactic in ecclesiastical debates. How right Ian Henderson was when he wrote: "To enthrone the will of God in ecclesiastical party politics is to drive out love. For the point in calling your party policy the will of God is just that it enables you to give hell to the man who opposes it. For does that not make him the enemy of God? And what a wonderful opportunity to enable you, Christian that you are, to give vent to all the lovelessness in your nature."[26] Can we be surprised if many decent secular people are suspicious of any attempt to relate morality to any transcedent reality?

Yet we have seen that most people do indeed appeal to a "natural justice" beyond any human court of appeal. The Christian theologian will no doubt seek to link this notion eventually to his concept of God, but he will do so in more sophisticated ways than by the traditional appeal to the will of God. But it is possible to hold a natural law doctrine without giving it a theological formulation, though hardly without some ontological or metaphysical formulation. For the Stoics, the natural law was understood in somewhat pantheistic terms, as the demand of the *logos* dwelling both in man and in the cosmos. Likewise, in Eastern religions, the Hindu *dharma* and the Chinese *tao* are immanent and impersonal principles, not the decrees of a transcendent deity. In modern Western philosophy, one would be more likely to found natural law on a Kantian or neo-Kantian basis of an objectively valid rational order, which grounds moral values just as it does logical values. In each case, the foundations are taken to have an ultimacy and objectivity about them. They are not just "human convention," explicable psychologically, sociologically, and anthropologically. These sciences do explain the actual empirical forms in which morality appears, but not the ultimate demand of morality. Not even the state and not human society as a whole (if this expression refers to anything) can serve as the foundation of morality, but a transhuman order so that, as Hooker expressed it, man is not so much the maker of laws as their discoverer.[27]

Though the acknowledgment of a natural law that judges every human law does not, as we have readily agreed, imply a definitely theistic understanding of the world, nevertheless it points to an ontological interpretation of morality which has at least some kinship with the religious interpretation. For, in both cases, it is supposed that moral values do belong to the very nature of things, so to speak, and are not just superimposed on an amoral reality by the human mind. But surely to recognize that morality has this ontological foundation is already to perceive it in a new depth. Without such a depth, it is hard to see how there could ever be an unconditioned obligation to which one simply could not say no without abandoning one's authentic personhood. There could be only relative obligations, imposed by the conventions of a particular society. Conversely, as has been pointed out by Fritz Buri, where there is no ontological or religious grounding of morality, there is also no sin and "one can speak only of relative but not of unconditioned evil."[28] The Nazi regime, when man (or superman) decided moral values, should remain as a terrible warning against that complete slide into relativism and subjectivism in which morality has been entirely cut adrift from an ontological basis. The notion of human responsibility and answerability, when explored in its many dimensions, implies an order which man does not create but which rather lays a demand on him.

Although therefore one must nowadays abandon such oversimplified and frequently misleading notions as that the moral law is the will of God or that religion provides sanctions for strengthening the moral law, this does not lead to abandoning all belief in an intrinsic connection between morals and religion; and one can, moreover, see a parallel to such a religious morality in a secular morality which acknowledges a natural law. In both cases, if morality is founded in "the way things are," as natural law doctrine has maintained and as religious faith has maintained, then the moral demand has about it an ultimate character that can hardly fail to let it be experienced with an enhanced seriousness.[29]

2. In the second part of our discussion, we have to take up the question of how far the traditional idea of natural law can be adapted to the thinking of an age whose concepts are dynamic rather than static. So far we have talked of "unconditioned demand" and have sought a stable foundation for morality that could safeguard us from the vagaries of a thoroughgoing relativism. But it is equally important, in the light of our earlier discussions about man, to try to reinterpret the idea of natural law in a way that allows for flexibility and growth, so that it really does protect and foster the fulfillment of human possibilities. Are we perhaps asking the impossible? Demanding elements of both constancy and stability, while also want-

ing to acknowledge the pervasiveness of change and to set everything in motion? Or is there a way of embracing both sides?

First of all, I think we should be clear about what we are looking for. We are not looking for some extended system of rules. Just as the substance of faith can never be adequately or precisely formulated in dogmatic propositions, and just as all such propositions have time-conditioned elements that need to be expressed in new and different ways in new historical situations, so the content of the moral life is never exhaustively or adequately formulated in rules and precepts.

The fact that natural law cannot be precisely formulated is already implied in some of the classic definitions and descriptions quoted above. The natural law is "unwritten" (Aristotle). In fact, the very term "law" is misleading, if it is taken to mean some kind of code. The natural law is not another code or system of laws in addition to all the actual systems, but is simply our rather inaccurate way of referring to those most general moral principles against which particular rules or codes have to be measured. It is well known that St. Thomas formulated the first precept of the natural law in extremely general terms: "Good is to be done and promoted, and evil is to be avoided."[30] At first sight, one might be tempted to ask whether this statement says anything or is just a tautology, in the sense that it simply repeats what is already contained in the notions of "good" and "evil." I think, however, we shall find there is more to it than this.

It is assumed that one can go on to elaborate other precepts of the natural law, though these would be of a general kind. Perhaps we could reckon among them the very broad prohibitions which, as we have seen,[31] Bishop Robinson accepts as possessing something approaching universal validity. But the really important point in Robinson's statement has to do not with the actual prohibitions which he lists but with the fact that the prohibited activities are all, as he says, "fundamentally destructive of human relationships."

The Decalogue, setting forth the basic demands of the moral life, might be taken as a kind of transcript of the fundamental precepts of natural law, even though the Decalogue itself is supposed to have been "revealed." But simple and basic though the Ten Commandments are, one finds even in them relative and time-conditioned elements. What, for instance, is one to say about the command concerning Sabbath observance?[32] Even with so basic a statement of the fundamental moral laws, there can be disputes as to what really belongs to natural law and what to the historical circumstances under which the statement was formulated. This reinforces our point that the natural law cannot be formulated, and that it is not so much itself a "law" as rather a touchstone for determining the justice or morality of actual laws and rules.

We may consider a more recent example. Sir David Ross lists some half-dozen *prima facie* duties, as he calls them: duties of fidelity (such as promise-keeping and truth-telling), duties of reparation, duties of gratitude, duties of justice, duties of beneficence, duties of self-improvement, and, negatively, the duty of not injuring others. These duties are called *prima facie* to allow for the situational element in morality. In an actual situation, there may be more than one claim on me, and then one has to take precedence over the other. But it is assumed that everyone is aware of the *prima facie* claims and that they are distinct from my fallible personal opinions about more peripheral ethical questions. "The main moral convictions of the plain man," writes Ross, "seem to me to be, not opinions which it is for philosophy to prove or disprove, but knowledge from the start."[33] I am inclined to agree with Ross that there is this kind of fundamental moral knowledge, given with human existence itself. Although he does not use the expression "natural law," I would think it quite appropriate. Furthermore, I would doubt whether the natural law could be particularized much beyond the half-dozen or so general duties which Ross details. And even these are *prima facie* duties, which may be superseded in an actual situation.

We have dwelt at some length on the difficulty of formulating the natural law with any precision and have seen that time-conditioned elements enter into such formulations as there are, and situational elements into its actual application. To this extent, we have already come into conflict with some of the classic descriptions of natural law, especially in their use of such words as "everlasting" and "unchangeable." But we are only at the beginning of our criticism. The notions of change and development have to be taken much more seriously than just allowing that there are changes and development in formulation. The notion of the unchangeableness of natural law was rooted in the idea of an unchanging nature, both in man and in the cosmos.

But if we acknowledge—as we already have done—that man's nature is open, and that he is always going beyond or transcending any given state of himself; and if we acknowledge further that this open nature of man is set in the midst of a cosmos which is likewise on the move and is characterized by an evolving rather than a static order; then we must say that the natural law itself, not just its formulations, is on the move and cannot have the immutability once ascribed to it. But what has perhaps more than anything else discredited the natural law concept is the tacit assumption that there was a kind of original human nature to which everything subsequent is an accretion. This is the confusion of what is natural with what is primitive. One has only to ask the question, "Is it natural to wear clothes?" to see the absurdity of trying to think of man's nature in terms of a primitive given. It is certainly futile to try to erect rules or maintain prohibitions on the basis of a "nature" that has long since been transcended. Man's very nature is to exist, that is to say, to go out of himself, and in the course of this he learns to take over from crude nature and to do in a human (and humane) way what was once accomplished by blind natural forces (both in man and outside of him) working in a rough and ready manner. An obvious example is population control, which need no longer be left to the hazards and diseases of nature without or to the tribal warfares prompted by the aggression of nature within. We have got beyond that kind of nature, and as I claimed in our discussion of man, the pill and the condom are now part of his nature.

But in admitting this, have we not cut away any ground for the other side of our argument concerning natural law? How can natural law provide a kind of criterion for evaluating particular laws? If this natural law is itself variable, can there be any reliable criterion at all? Or is everything reduced to relativism, subjectivism, and pragmatism?

I think we do still have a criterion, but its constancy is not that of a law but of a direction. So again we have to say that the word "law" is not entirely appropriate to describe the kind of thing traditionally meant by "natural law." What is meant is rather a constant tendency, an inbuilt directedness. To think of nature in dynamic terms is not to abandon all structure and reduce everything to flux. Although we talk much nowadays about change—and some people even talk about the "celebration of change"—it need hardly be said that change can be for the worse as well as for the better. The only kind of change we might want to celebrate would be change for the better. Teilhard de Chardin uses the expression "genesis" as a more precise way of saying what is meant. "In Teilhard's mind," writes Christopher Mooney. "we are not simply face to face with 'change' in the world but with 'genesis,' which is something quite different. . . . The word applies to any form of production involving successive stages oriented toward some goal."[34]

The movement that is envisaged, whether we are thinking of human nature or of cosmic nature, is a movement with direction, an ordered movement. But the movement in the cosmos is very different from the movement in man. The first kind of movement is unconscious evolution; the second has become a conscious moral striving. This corresponds to the difference between "laws of nature" and "natural law" in an ethical sense.[35] We should be quite clear that what we are talking about has nothing to do with the doctrine of an automatic progress of the human race, or with any complacent optimism. As soon as the transition is made from natural evolution to man's responsible self-development, the movement becomes subject to the risks of moral choice and to the actual reversals of sin. It is not like the unfolding of an oak from an acorn. This is something that happens, but in the case of man's development, it is a question about what *ought* to happen. At least in general terms, we know where we *ought* to be going, and we experience guilt when we go in some other direction. We know where we ought to be going because to exist as a human being is to exist with a self-understanding. This is an understanding both of who we are and of who we might become. It involves an image which summons us. To employ theological language for a moment, we might speak of the *imago Dei* both as fundamental endowment and as ultimate goal. Natural law is, as it were, the pointer within us that orients us to the goal of human existence. Actual rules, laws, and prohibitions are judged by this "unwritten law" in accordance with whether they promote or impede the movement toward fuller existence. Natural law changes, in the sense that the precepts we may derive from it change as human nature itself changes, and also in the sense that man's self-understanding changes as he sharpens his image of mature manhood. But through the changes there remains the constancy of direction.

This dynamic understanding of natural law is already implicit in St. Thomas' talk about the rational creature's having "a natural inclination to its proper act and end," while his awareness of the difference between a merely natural development in the world and man's conscious self-development is shown by his acute observation about the difference between a general providence in the world and the creature which has become itself provident.[36]

The directedness of moral striving has a constancy which prevents any lapse into sheer relativism. Even the relativisms of actual historical moral codes have often been exaggerated. Patrick Nowell-Smith claims that the more we study moral codes, the more we find that they do not differ in major principles.[37] All have the same direction, as it were. They aim at the development of a fuller, richer, more personal manhood, and to this extent they are in accord with and give expression to the natural law.

The Christian, we have seen, defines mature manhood in terms of Jesus Christ, and especially his self-giving love. But Christ himself is no static figure, nor are Christians called to imitate him as a static model. Christ is an eschatological figure, always before us; and the doctrine of his coming again "with glory" implies that there are dimensions of christhood not manifest in the historical Jesus and not yet fully grasped by the disciples. Thus discipleship does not restrict human development to some fixed pattern, but summons into freedoms, the full depth of which is unknown, except that they will always be consonant with self-giving love.

But the "natural" understanding of morality leads to conclusions not far from those of the Christian. For if man's nature is to *exist,* then he exists most fully when he *goes out* of himself. Here we strike upon the paradox of the moral life, perceived in many traditions—that the man who would "save" his life, that is to say, preserve it as a static possession, actually loses it, whereas the man who is prepared to venture out beyond himself and even to empty himself attains the truest selfhood.[38]

The discussion of this chapter, focusing on the concept of natural law, suggests that there is no conflict between the ideals of a Christian ethic and the moral ideals to be found in humanity at large. Rather, there is a fundamental similarity. Christianity does not establish a new or different morality, but it makes concrete, clarifies, and, above all, focuses on a particular person, Jesus Christ, the deepest moral convictions of men. Christ declared he was fulfilling the law, not abolishing it.[39] According to W. D. Davies, even the so-called "antitheses" in the Sermon on the Mount (those passages in which Christ explicitly contrasts his own moral teaching with that of the Mosaic law) do not annul the law but carry it to "its utmost meaning."[40] It is obvious that this view of the matter agrees very closely with the one expounded here. Christian moral teaching is an unfolding of the "natural" morality of all men.

What for want of a better name has usually been called "natural law" is still a very useful concept. We have seen that it provides a firm basis for moral cooperation and community between Christians and non-Christians. We have seen further that natural law, even if it is not explicitly interpreted in theistic terms, nevertheless allows us to see moral obligation in a new depth, as ontologically founded. It safeguards against moral subjectivism and encourages moral seriousness by locating the demand of moral obligation in the very way things are.

Notes

1. *Christian Ethics and Contemporary Philosophy,* ed. Ian T. Ramsey (London: S.C.M. Press, 1966), pp. 382–96.

2. Dietrich Bonhoeffer, *Letters and Papers from Prison,* tr. Reginald H. Fuller (New York: Macmillan, 1962), pp. 222–23.

3. See p. 40.

4. Ephesians 4:13.

5. Karl Rahner, *Theological Investigations,* Vol. I, tr. Cornelius Ernst, O.P. (London: Darton, Longman & Todd; Baltimore: Helicon Press, 1961), p. 184.

6. David Jenkins, *The Glory of Man* (London: S.C.M. Press; New York: Scribner, 1967).

7. *Ibid.,* p. 79.

8. Cf. Hebrews 1:3.

9. Matthew 13:45–46.

10. Paul Ramsey, *Basic Christian Ethics* (London: S.C.M. Press, 1953), p. 86.

11. Lehmann, *op. cit.,* p. 148.

12. See pp. 119 ff.

13. Cf. Sir Charles Sherrington, *Man on His Nature* (London: Cambridge University Press, 1940).

14. Theodosius Dobzhansky, *The Biology of Ultimate Concern* (New York: New American Library, 1967), p. 86.

15. Werner Jaeger, *The Theology of the Early Greek Philosophers,* tr. E. S. Robinson (London: Oxford University Press, 1967), p. 36.

16. *Ibid.,* pp. 115–16. Translation of Heraclitus from Jaeger.

17. *Rhetoric,* I, 10. Translation from *The Basic Works of Aristotle,* ed. Richard McKeon (New York: Random House, 1941), p. 1359.

18. Cicero, *De Republica,* III, 22–23. Translation from John Salmond, *Jurisprudence* (London: Sweet & Maxwell, 1930), p. 28.

19. *Summa Theologiae,* II/I, 91, 2. Translation from *Basic Writings of St. Thomas Aquinas,* ed. A. C. Pegis (New York: Random House, 1945), Vol. II, p. 750.

20. Richard Hooker, *Of the Laws of Ecclesiastical Polity,* I, vii, 3 (London: J. M. Dent, Everyman's Library, 1907), Vol. I, pp. 176–77.

21. John Locke, *The Reasonableness of Christianity,* ed. Ian T. Ramsey (London: A. & C. Black, 1958), p. 70.

22. Vernon J. Bourke, "Natural Law," *A Dictionary of Christian Ethics,* ed. John Macquarrie (London: S.C.M. Press; Philadelphia: Westminster Press, 1967), pp. 224–25.

23. Sophocles, *Antigone,* 450–57. Translation from *The Complete Greek Drama,* ed. Whitney J. Oates and Eugene O'Neill (New York: Random House, 1938), Vol. I, p. 434.

24. Acts 5:29.

25. E. L. Mascall, *He Who Is* (London: Darton, Longman & Todd, new edition, 1966), p. 122.

26. Ian Henderson, *Power without Glory: A Study in Ecumenical Politics* (London: Hodder & Stoughton, 1967), pp. 94–95.

27. See p. 95.

28. Buri, *op. cit.,* p. 14.

29. It may be noted that both Buri and Bultmann in their writing seem to come near to interpreting the meaning of the word "God" as that unconditioned or ultimate element which we experience in the awareness of moral obligation. This seems to reverse the traditional procedure, by deriving an understanding of God from morality rather than morality from an idea of God.

30. *Summa Theologiae,* II/I, 94, 1.

31. See p. 37.

32. Herbert Richardson has recently claimed that the Sabbath does belong to natural law, because it is related to the creation story and the "rest" of the seventh day. "This explanation of the commandment must be interpreted as implying that the Sabbath is binding not only upon Israel but also upon all other creatures. . . . it is in the same category as the commandment not to murder—it is a universal moral law." *Toward an American Theology* (New York: Harper & Row, 1967), p. 114.

33. David Ross, *The Right and the Good* (Oxford: Clarendon Press, 1930), p. 19.

34. Christopher Mooney, *Teilhard de Chardin and the Mystery of Christ* (London: Collins, 1966), p. 51.

35. See p. 92.

36. See p. 94.

37. Patrick Nowell-Smith, *Ethics* (London: Penguin Books, 1954), p. 18.

38. Cf. Mark 8:35.

39. Matthew 5:17.

40. W. D. Davies, *The Sermon on the Mount* (London and New York: Cambridge University Press, 1966), p. 29.

Natural Law in Moral Theology

Charles E. Curran

This chapter originally appeared in *Contemporary Problems in Moral Theology,* 1970.

Catholic ethical theory and its application have traditionally embraced a natural law methodology in their approach to moral questions. The manuals of moral theology, which were the textbooks of this discipline until a few years ago, and official Catholic moral teaching were based on natural law. This chapter will study the natural law methodology employed in the Catholic tradition and will primarily use as an illustration of that methodology the teaching found in the 1968 encyclical of Pope Paul VI, *Humanae Vitae,* which condemned artificial contraception in marriage. Many Catholic theologians have recently questioned both the traditional natural law methodology and the conclusions drawn from it in *Humanae Vitae* and elsewhere.[1] This chapter situates natural law in the light of my stance (developed in chapter 2 above), offers a critique of natural law in general, applies this criticism to *Humanae Vitae,* indicates how other methodologies arrive at different conclusions, and in the light of the problem of physicalism explains the reason for questioning some of the other moral teachings which have been proposed in Catholicism.

I.
NATURAL LAW IN THE TOTAL CHRISTIAN PERSPECTIVE

The encyclical *Humanae Vitae* realizes that natural law forms only a part of the total horizon of moral theology. The Apostles and their successors have been constituted "as guardians and authentic interpreters of all the moral law, not only, that is, of the law of the Gospel, but also of the natural law, which is also an expression of the will of God" (*H.V.* n. 4). The encyclical admits there is a source of ethical wisdom and knowledge for the Christian apart from the explicit revelation of the Scriptures, so that Christians and the Church do learn ethical wisdom from non-Christians and the world.

There have been many theologians especially in the more strict Protestant tradition who would tend to deny any source of ethical wisdom and knowledge which Christians share with humankind.[2] Such theologians based their position on the uniqueness and self-sufficiency of the scriptural revelation, the doctrine of justification, and an emphasis on sin as corrupting whatever exists outside the unique revelation of Jesus Christ.[3] However, contemporary Protestant theologians generally maintain the existence of some ethical wisdom apart from the explicit revelation of God in the Scriptures and in Christ Jesus, even though they may avoid the term natural law.[4] Protestant theologians in the last few decades have employed such concepts as the orders of creation (Brunner), the divine mandates (Bonhoeffer), love and justice (Reinhold Niebuhr), love transforming justice (Ramsey), common ground morality (Bennett), and other similar approaches.

The natural law theory as implied in the encyclical has the theological merit of recognizing a source of ethical wisdom for the Christian apart from the explicit revelation of God in Christ Jesus. This recognition remains a most important and lasting contribution of Catholic thought in the area of theological ethics. The difficult question for Christian theology centers on the relationship between the natural law and the distinctively Christian element in the understanding of the moral life of the Christian. The same basic question has been proposed in other terms. H. Richard Niebuhr describes five different models of the relationship between Christ and culture.[5] An older Catholic theology spoke about the relationship between nature and grace, between the natural and the supernatural. Niebuhr has described the typical Catholic solution to the question of Christ and culture in terms of "both-and"—both culture and Christ.[6] Such an approach corresponds with an unnuanced understanding of the relationship between nature and grace. The two are neither opposed nor identical; but they exist side by side. Grace adds something to nature without in any way destroying it. A simplistic view of the supernatural sees it as something added to the natural. But the natural retains its own finality and integrity as the substratum to which the supernatural is added.[7]

In such a perspective the natural tends to be seen as something absolute and sufficient in itself to which the supernatural is added. The natural law thus exists as a self-contained entity to which the law of the gospel or revelation is then added. *Humanae Vitae* seems to accept such a "both-and" understanding of the relationship between natural law and the gospel or revelation. "All the moral law" is explained as "not only, that is, of the law of the Gospel, but also of the natural law, which is also an expression of the will of God . . ." (*H.V.* n. 4). The papal letter calls for an anthropology based on "an integral vision of man and his vocation, not only of his earthly and natural, but also his supernatural and eternal, vocation" (*H.V.* n. 7). The "both-and" relationship appears again in paragraph 8 which refers to "the entire moral law, both natural and evangelical."

Not only the wording of the encyclical but the methodology presupposed in the argumentation employs a "both-and" understanding of the relationship of natural law and evangelical law. Msgr. Lambruschini, who explained the encyclical at a press conference, said that purposely no mention was made of scriptural arguments, but the entire reasoning was based on natural law.[8] Bernard Häring has criticized the encyclical because it does not even mention the admonition of St. Paul that husband and wife should "not refuse each other except by mutual consent, and then only for an agreed time, to leave yourselves free for prayer; then come together again in case Satan should take advantage of your weakness to tempt you" (1 Cor. 7:5).[9] The Pastoral Constitution on the Church in the Modern World did take heed of Paul's admonition. "But where the intimacy of married life is broken off, it is not rare for its faithfulness to be imperiled and its quality of fruitfulness ruined" (n. 51). However, the primary criticism is not the fact that there is no reference to any particular scriptural text, but the underlying understanding that the natural law is something totally integral in itself to which the evangelical or supernatural law is added.

Christian ethics cannot absolutize the realm of the natural as something completely self-contained and unaffected by any relationships to the evangelical or supernatural. Christian theology derives its perspective from the Christian faith commitment. The Christian views reality in the light of the total horizon of the Christian faith commitment—creation, sin, incarnation, redemption, and parousia. Natural law itself is thus Christocentric.[10] The doctrine of creation forms the theological basis for natural law, and Christ as logos is the one in whom all things are created and through whom all things are to be returned to the Father. Natural law theory has taken seriously the implications of the incarnation through which God has joined himself to the human, the worldly, and the historical. However, nature and creation form only a part of the total Christian view. The reality of "the natural" must always be seen in the light of sin, redemption, and the parousia. Nature and creation are relativized by the transforming Christian themes of redemption and final resurrection destiny of all creation. The natural law theory is theologically based on the Christian truths of creation and incarnation, but these aspects are not independent and unrelated to the full horizon of the Christian view of reality. The Christian situates natural law in the context of the total history of salvation which transforms and criticizes what is only "the natural." Thus in the total Christian perspective there is a place for the "natural," but the natural remains provisional and relativized by the entire history of salvation.

The full Christian view of reality also takes account of the existence of sin and its effects on human existence. However, the natural law theory as illustrated in *Humanae Vitae* does not seem to give sufficient importance to the reality and effect of human sinfulness. In section III under "Pastoral Directives" the papal letter speaks about the compassion of Christ and the Church for sinners. "But she [the Church] cannot renounce the teaching of the law which is, in reality, that law proper to a human life restored to its original truth and conducted by the Spirit of God" (*H.V.* n. 19). The implication remains that the disruptive force of sin has already been overcome by the grace of God. Such an approach has definite affinities with a simplistic view of sin as depriving the Christian of the supernatural gift of grace, but not affecting the substratum of nature. However, in the total Christian horizon the disrupting influence of sin colors all human reality.

Humanae Vitae does recognize some effects of sin in human beings. Sin affects the will, but the help of God will strengthen our good will (*H.V.* n. 20). Sin affects the instincts, but ascetical practices will enable the reason and will to achieve self-mastery (*H.V.* n. 21). Sinfulness also makes itself felt in some aspects of the social environment, "which leads to sense excitation and unbridled customs, as well as every form of pornography and licentious performances" (*H.V.* n. 22). But no mention is made of the fact that sin affects reason itself and the very nature on which natural law theory is based. Sin relativizes and affects all reality. How often has reason been used to justify human prejudice and arrogance! Natural law has been appealed to in the denials of human dignity and of religious liberty. The just war theory has been employed to justify wars in which one's own nation was involved.[11] History shows the effect of sin in the very abuses which have accompanied natural law thinking.

Recently, I have proposed the need for a theory of compromise in moral theology precisely because of the existence of sin in the world.[12] The surd brought about by human sinfulness is so oppressive that occasionally we cannot overcome it immediately. The presence of sin may force a person to do something one would not do if there were no sin present. Thus in sin-filled situations (notice all the examples of such situations in the current literature) the Christian may be forced to adopt a line of action which one would abhor if sin were not present. A theory of compromise does not give us a blank check to shirk our Christian responsibilities. However, there are situations in which the value sacrificed is not proportionate to the demand asked of the Christian. Protestant theology has often adopted a similar approach by saying that in some circumstances the Christian is forced to do something sinful. The sinner reluctantly performs the deed and asks God for mercy and forgiveness.[13] At times Protestant theology has overemphasized the reality of sin, but Catholic theology at times has not paid enough attention to the reality of sin.

The recent papal encyclical presupposes a natural law concept that fails to indicate the relative and provisional character of natural law in the total Christian perspective. Critics have rightly objected to a theory which tends to absolutize what is only relative and provisional. Take, for example, the teaching in Catholic theology on the right of private property. The modern popes have approached the question of private property in a much more absolute way than Thomas Aquinas. The differences of approach are instructive for the moral theologian. The popes, especially Leo XIII, stressed private property as the right of every individual stemming from the dignity of the human person, the person's rational nature, labor, the need to provide for self and family, and the need to overcome the uncertainties of life.[14] Thomas gave greater importance to the social function of all property and the reality of human sinfulness. Perhaps Thomas was influenced by the often-cited opinion of Isidore of Seville that according to the natural law all things should be held in common.[15] Thomas ultimately sees the sin of human beings as the reason for the existence of private property. Society would not have peace and order unless everyone possessed his or her own goods. Likewise, Thomas pointed out that earthly goods are not properly cared for if they are held in common.[16] Thomas maintained there would be no need for private property in the world of original justice.

There are other indications that private property is not as absolute a human right as proposed in some papal encyclicals. With his understanding of a more absolute right of private property, Leo XIII spoke of the obligation of the rich to share their goods with the poor as an obligation of charity and not justice.[17] However, a very respectable and long tradition in the medieval Church maintained that the rich had an obligation in justice to share their goods with the poor.[18] Even in our own day one can ask if private property is the best way to protect the dignity and freedom of the human person. The great inequalities existing in society today at the very least must modify and limit the concept of the right of private property. In our historical circumstances we are much more conscious of the social aspect of property than was Leo XIII.[19] The teaching on private property well illustrates the dangers of a natural law approach that is not relativized by the whole reality of salvation history.

The natural law theory suggested in, and employed by, the encyclical *Humanae Vitae* has the advantage of affirming the existence of a source of ethical wisdom apart from the explicit revelation of God in Christ in the Scriptures. However, such a concept of natural law tends to absolutize what the full Christian vision sees as relative and provisional in the light of the entire history of salvation. The "natural" does not and never has existed as such. All of creation must be seen and understood in the light of redemption and resurrection destiny.

II.
A CRITIQUE OF NATURAL LAW

The debate over the condemnation of artificial contraception in *Humanae Vitae* indicates a basic dissatisfaction with the natural law methodology employed in the encyclical. The encyclical uses a notion of natural law which has generally been found in the classical textbooks and manuals of moral theology, but precisely this concept of natural law is subject to severe negative criticism. This section will point out three major weaknesses in that concept of natural law: (1) a tendency to accept natural law as a monolithic philosophical system with an agreed upon body of ethical content which is the source for most, if not all, of Catholic moral teaching; (2) the danger of physicalism which identifies the human act with the physical or biological structure of the act; (3) a classicist worldview and methodology.

Not a Monolithic Philosophical System

The first defect will only be summarized here, since it is treated at greater length elsewhere. Natural law remains a very ambiguous term.[20] The first section of this study used the concept of natural as distinguished from supernatural; in addition, it has been pointed out that the word nature had over twenty different meanings in Catholic thinking before Thomas Aquinas. The word law is also ambiguous, since it tends to have a very legalistic meaning for most people today; whereas for Thomas law was an ordering of reason. Natural law ethics has often been described as a legalistic ethic, that is, an ethic based on norms and laws; but in reality for Thomas natural law is a deliberative ethic which arrives at decision not primarily by the application of laws, but by the deliberation of reason. Many thinkers in the course of history have employed the term natural law, but frequently they defined natural law in different ways. Thinkers employing different natural law approaches have arrived at different conclusions on particular moral topics. Natural law in the history of thought does not refer to a monolithic theory, but tends to be a more generic term which includes a number of different approaches to moral problems. There is no such thing as *the* natural law as a monolithic philosophical system with an agreed upon body of ethical content existing from the beginning of time.

Many erroneously believe that Catholic theology is committed to a particular natural law approach to moral problems. In practice, however, the vast majority of Catholic teaching on particular moral questions came into existence even before Thomas Aquinas enunciated his theory. Likewise, contemporary Catholic theology recognizes the need for a pluralism of philosophical approaches in the Christian's quest for a better understanding of man and his reality. There is no longer "one Catholic philosophy."

The Danger of Physicalism

Ethical theory constantly vacillates between two polarities— naturalism and idealism. Naturalism sees the human being in perfect continuity with the nature about her. Nature shapes and even determines the individual. Idealism views the human being completely apart from nature and as completely surpassing nature. Even Thomistic philosophy, the main Catholic proponent of natural law theory, knows an ambivalence between nature and reason.

The Thomistic natural law concept vacillates at times between the order of nature and the order of reason.[21] The general Thomistic thrust is towards the predominance of reason in natural law theory. However, there is in Thomas a definite tendency to identify the demands of natural law with physical and biological processes. Thomas, too, is a historical person conditioned by the circumstances and influences of his own time. These influences help explain the tendency (but not the predominant tendency) in Thomas to identify the human action with the physical and biological structure of the human act. A major influence is Ulpian, a Roman lawyer who died in 228.

Ulpian and Thomas. Ulpian defined the natural law as that which nature teaches all the animals. Ulpian distinguished the natural law from the *ius gentium.* The *ius naturale* is that which is common to all animals, whereas the *ius gentium* is that which is proper to humans.[22] Albert the Great rejected Ulpian's definition of the natural law, but Thomas accepted it, and even showed a preference for such a definition.[23] In the *Commentary on the Sentences,* for example, Thomas maintains that the most strict definition of natural law is the one proposed by Ulpian: *ius naturae est quod natura omnia animalia docuit.*[24]

In his *Commentary on the Nichomachean Ethics,* Thomas again shows a preference for Ulpian's definition. Aristotle has proposed a twofold division of *iustum naturale* and *iustum legale,* but Ulpian proposed the threefold distinction of *ius naturale, ius gentium* and *ius civile.* Thomas solves the apparent dilemma by saying that the Roman law concepts of *ius naturale* and *ius gentium* both belong under the Aristotelian category of *iustum naturale.* The human being has a double nature. The *ius naturale* rules that which is proper to both humans and the animals, such as the union of the sexes and the education of offspring; whereas the *ius gentium* governs the rational part of human beings which is proper to humans alone and embraces such things as fidelity to contracts.[25]

In the *Summa Theologiae* Thomas cites Ulpian's definition on a number of occasions.[26] In the classification of natural law again Thomas shows a preference for Ulpian's definition. Thomas accepts the division proposed by Isidore of Seville, according to which the *ius gentium* belongs to the category of human law and not the category of divine law. Thomas uses Ulpian's definition to explain Isidore's division. The natural law pertains to the divine law because it is common to humans and to all the animals.[27] In a sense, the *ius gentium* does pertain to the category of human law because humans use reason to deduce the conclusions of the *ius gentium.*

Thomas thus employs Ulpian's definition of natural law as opposed to what reason deduces (the *ius gentium*) to defend the division of law proposed by Isidore. The same question receives somewhat the same treatment later in the *Summa*.[28] The texts definitely show that Thomas knew and even accepted the definition of natural law proposed by Ulpian.

Ulpian's Concept of Natural Law. Ulpian is important for the understanding of natural law morality. The natural law for Ulpian is defined in terms of those actions which are common to humans and all the animals. There results from this the definite danger of identifying the human action with a mere animal or biological process. "Nature" and "natural" in Ulpian's meaning are distinguished from that which is specifically human and derived by reason. Traditional theology has in the past definitely employed the words "natural" and "nature" as synonymous with animal or biological processes and not as denoting human actions in accord with the rational, human nature.

Moral theology textbooks even speak of sins according to nature. The manuals generally divide the sins against the sixth commandment into two categories—the sins against nature (*peccata contra naturam*) and sins in accord with nature (*peccata secundum naturam*). "Nature" is thus used in Ulpian's sense, as that which is common to humans and all the animals. In matters of sexuality (and Ulpian himself uses the example of the sexual union as an illustration of the natural law), humans share with the animal world the fact of the sexual union whereby male seed is deposited in the vas of the female. Sins against nature, therefore, are those acts in which the animal or biological process is not observed—pollution, sodomy, bestiality, and contraception. Sins according to nature are those acts in which the proper biological process is observed but something is lacking in the sphere which belongs only to rational beings. These include fornication, adultery, incest, rape, and sacrilege.[29]

The classification of sins against chastity furnishes concrete proof that "nature" has been used in Catholic theology to refer to animal processes without any intervention of human reason. Many theologians have rightly criticized the approach to marriage and sexuality used by Catholic natural law theoreticians because such an approach concentrated primarily on the biological components of the act of intercourse. The personal aspects of the sexual union received comparatively scant attention in many of the manuals of moral theology. Ulpian's influence has made it easier for Catholic natural law thinking to identify the human act simply with the physical structure of the act.

Ulpian's Anthropology. Ulpian's understanding of the natural law logically leads to disastrous consequences in anthropology. The distinction between two parts in humans—that which is common to humans and all the animals, and that which is proper to humans—results in a two-layer version of human beings. A top layer of rationality is merely added to an already constituted bottom layer of animality. The union between the two layers is merely extrinsic—the one lies on top of the other. The animal layer retains its own finalities and tendencies, independent of the demands of rationality. Thus the individual may not interfere in the animal processes and finalities. Note that the results of such an anthropology are most evident in the area of sexuality.

A proper understanding of the human should start with that which is proper to humans. Rationality does not just lie on top of animality, but rationality characterizes and guides the whole person. Animal processes and finalities are not untouchable. Our whole vocation, we have come to see, is to bring order and intelligence into the world, and to shape animal and biological finalities toward a truly human purpose. Ulpian's concept of natural law logically falsifies the understanding of the human and tends to canonize the finalities and processes which humans share with the animal world.

A better anthropology would see the distinctive in human beings as guiding and directing the totality of one's being. For Thomas rationality constituted what is distinctive and characteristic in humans. Modern philosophers differ from Thomas on what is distinctively human. Phenomenologists tend to view the individual being as a symbolic person; while personalists look upon the human as an incarnate spirit, a "thou" in relation to other "you's." However, all would agree in rejecting an anthropology that absolutizes animal finalities and tendencies without allowing any intervention of the specifically human rational aspect of human beings.

I am not asserting that Thomas always identified human actions with animal processes or the physical structure of the act. In fact, the general outlines of the hylomorphic theory, by speaking of material and formal components of reality, try to avoid any physicalism or biologism. Nevertheless, the adoption of Ulpian's understanding of "nature" and "natural" logically leads to the identification of the human act itself with animal processes and with the mere physical structure of the act. Such a distorted view of the human act becomes especially prevalent in the area of medical morals, for in medical morality one can more easily conceive a moral human action solely in terms of the physical structure of that action.

Likewise, Ulpian's notion of nature easily leads to a morality based on the finality of a faculty independent of any considerations of the total human person or the total human community. One must, of course, avoid the opposite danger of paying no attention to the physical structure of the act or to external actions in themselves. However, Catholic theology in its natural law approach has suffered from an oversimple identification of the human action with an animal process or finality.

Marriage and Sexuality. Ulpian's understanding of natural law logically has had another deleterious effect on Catholic moral theology. Until the last decade magisterial pronouncements frequently spoke of the primary and secondary ends of marriage.[30] The latest statements of popes as well as the Pastoral Constitution on the Church in the Modern World (*Gaudium et Spes*) happily avoid this terminology.[31] However, such a distinction has obviously influenced Catholic teaching on marriage and sexuality. Many people have questioned the distinction as being contradicted by the experience of married couples.

The distinction logically follows from Ulpian's concept of the natural law and the human, although I do not claim that Ulpian is the source of such a distinction. "Primary" is that which is common to humans and all the animals. Ulpian and Thomas in citing Ulpian use the union of the sexes and the procreation and education of offspring as examples of that which is common to humans and all the animals. "Secondary" is that which is proper to humans. Since only humans and not animals have sexual intercourse as a sign and expression of love, the love union aspect of sexuality remains proper to humans and therefore secondary. The former teaching on the ends of marriage is logically connected with Ulpian's understanding of the human being and natural law. Thus the teaching of Ulpian on natural law has a logical connection with the inadequate understanding of a human action as identified with an animal process.

A More Primitive Attitude. Another historical factor based on the conditions of a primitive culture has also influenced the tendency to make the processes of nature inviolable. Stoic philosophy well illustrates a more general historical factor that tends to identify the human action with its physical or natural structure. One should avoid too many generalizations about the Stoics because Stoic philosophy included a number of different thinkers who covered a comparatively long span of years. In addition, Stoic philosophers invoked the natural law to justify practices that contemporary natural law theoreticians brand as immoral.[32] However, there is a common thrust to the ethical doctrine proposed by the Stoics.

Ethics considers human beings and their actions. We humans want to find happiness. What actions should we perform to find happiness and fulfillment? A more primitive and less technical society will come to conclusions different from those reached by a more technically and scientifically developed society. Primitive people soon realize that they find happiness in conforming to the patterns of nature.

Primitive people remain almost helpless when confronted with the forces of nature. The forces of nature are so strong that the human individual is even tempted to bow down and adore. One realizes the futility in trying to fight them. Happiness will come only by adjusting oneself to nature.

Nature divides the day into light and dark. When darkness descends, there is little or nothing that humans can do except sleep. When the hot sun is beating down near the equator, one will find happiness only by avoiding work and overexposure in the sun. In colder climates, one will be happy only when using clothing and shelter as protection against nature. If one wants to be happy, one will stay under some form of shelter and avoid the rain and snow. If there is a mountain in one's path, the wise person will walk around the mountain rather than suffer the ardors of trying to scale the peak. For people living in a primitive society (in the sense of nonscientific and nontechnical), happiness is found in conforming self to nature.

Stoic philosophy built on this understanding of life in a non-technical society. As Greeks, the Stoics believed in an intelligible world. They made the universe as a whole—the cosmos—their principle of intelligibility. Stoic philosophy held that reason governed the order of nature. Human happiness consisted in conforming to reason, that is, in conforming to the order of nature. Reason rather easily became identified with the order of nature. The primary norm of morality, therefore, was conformity to nature.[33]

We who live in a scientific and technological society will have a different view of human life and happiness. Modern people do not find happiness in conforming to nature. The whole ethos and genius of modern society is different. Contemporary humans make nature conform to them rather than vice-versa. Through electricity we can change night into day. There are very few things that moderns cannot do at night now that it is illuminated by electricity.

We contemporary people use artificial heat in the winter and air conditioning in the summer to bring nature into conformity with our needs and desires. Nature did not provide us with wings to fly; in fact, the law of gravity seems to forbid flying. However, science has produced the jet plane and the rocket, which propel us at great speeds around the globe and even into the vast universe. When a mountain looms up as an obstacle, we either level the mountain with bulldozers or tunnel under the terrain. We could never tolerate a theory which equates human happiness with conformity to nature. We interfere with the processes of nature to make nature conform to us.

But a word of caution is in order. In the last few years the ecological crisis has made us aware of the danger of not giving enough importance and value to the physical aspects of worldly existence. We are not free to interfere with nature any way we see fit. Just as it is wrong to absolutize the natural and the physical, so too it is wrong to give no meaning or importance to the natural and the physical.

These few paragraphs have not attempted to prove the influence of Stoic philosophy on St. Thomas. Rather, Stoic philosophy was used to illustrate how the conditions existing in a nontechnological society will influence the philosophical understanding of anthropology and ethics. Thomas too lived in an agrarian, nonscientific world. The nontechnological worldview would be more prone to identify the human act with the physical process of nature itself.

Reality or Facticity. A more primitive society also tends to view reality in terms of the physical and the sensible. The child, unlike the adult, sees reality primarily in terms of externals. The tendency to identify the human action with the physical structure would definitely be greater in a more primitive society. For example, the importance that Catholic theology has attached to masturbatory activity, especially the overemphasis since the sixteenth century, seems to come from viewing it purely in terms of the physiological and biological aspects of the act. Modern psychology, however, does not place that great importance on such activity.

Theologians must incorporate the findings of modern science in trying to evaluate the human act of masturbation. To view it solely in terms of the physical structure of the act distorts the total reality of this human action. Contemporary theologians cannot merely repeat what older theologians have said. Today we know much more about the reality of the human act of masturbation than, say, St. Alphonsus or any other moral theologian living before the present century.[34]

It would be erroneous to say that Catholic theology has identified the human act with the brute facticity of natural processes or just the physical structure of the act itself. In the vast majority of cases, moral theology has always distinguished between the physical structure of the action and the morality of the action. The moral act of murder differs from the physical act of killing. The physical act of taking another's property does not always involve the moral act of stealing. However, in some areas of morality (for example, contraception, sterilization, direct effect) the moral act has been considered the same as the physical structure of the act itself.

The Morality of Lying. Another area in which Catholic theologians are moving away from a description of the human act in purely physical or natural terms is lying. The contemporary theological understanding of lying serves as a salutary warning to the natural law concept found in the manuals of theology because the morality of lying cannot be determined merely by examining the faculty of speech and its finality, apart from the totality of the human person speaking and the community in which one speaks.

The manuals of moral theology traditionally define lying as *locutio contra mentem.* The faculty of speech exists to express what is in the mind. When human speech does not reflect what is in the mind there is a perversion of the faculty. The perverted faculty argument is based on the finality of the faculty of speech looked at in itself. Accordingly, a lie exists when the verbal utterance does not correspond with what is in the mind. Theologians then had to face the problem created by the fact that at times the speaker simply could not speak the truth to his hearer or questioner (for example, in the case of a committed secret). A casuistry of mental reservations arose to deal with such situations.[35]

Today most contemporary Catholic theologians accept the distinction between a lie and a falsehood. A falsehood involves an untruth in the sense that the external word contradicts what is in the mind. However, the malice of lying does not consist in the perversion of the faculty of speech or the lack of conformity between the word spoken and what is in the mind. The malice of lying consists in the harm done to society and the human community through the breakdown of mutual trust and honesty. Thus, some theologians distinguish between a lie as the denial of truth which is due to the other and falsehood which is a spoken word not in conformity with what is in the mind.

The distinction between lying and falsehood obviates the rather contrived casuistry associated with broad and strict mental reservations.[36] But what does the more contemporary understanding of lying indicate? The new definition denies the validity of the perverted faculty argument. It is not sufficient merely to examine the faculty of speech and determine morality solely from the purpose of the faculty in itself. Likewise, the malice of lying does not reside in the lack of "physical" conformity between word and thought.

To view the faculty of speech apart from the total human situation of the person in society seems to give a distorted view of lying. The faculty of speech must be seen and judged in a human context. One can interfere with the physical purpose of the faculty for a higher human need and good. Perhaps in a similar vein, the notion of "direct" in the principle of the double effect cannot be judged merely from the sole immediate effect of the physical action itself, apart from the whole human context in which the act is placed. The morality must be viewed in a total human context, and not merely judged according to the physical act itself and the natural effect of the act seen in itself apart from the whole context.

The influence of Ulpian and the view of primitive society tend to identify the total human action with the natural or biological process. A better understanding of such historically and culturally limited views should help the ethician in evaluating the theory of natural law as understood in *Humanae Vitae.* I have not proved that the human act never corresponds with the physical structure of the act. However, I think it is clear that ethicians must be very cautious that older and inadequate views of reality do not influence their contemporary moral judgments. It does seem that the definition of Ulpian and the general views of a more primitive society have a logical connection with what seem to be erroneous conclusions of the natural law theory of the manuals.

A Changed Worldview

A third major weakness with the theory of natural law presupposed in the Encyclical stems from the classicist worldview which is behind such a theory of natural law. Bernard Lonergan maintains that the classicist worldview has been replaced by a more historically conscious worldview.[37] In the same vein, John Courtney Murray claimed that the two different theories on Church and State represent two different methodologies and worldviews.[38] And today, other more radical Catholic thinkers are calling for a change from a substantive to a process metaphysics.[39] At the least, all these indications point to an admission by respected Catholic scholars that the so-called classicist worldview has ceased to exist.

The following paragraphs will briefly sketch the differences in the two approaches to viewing reality. There are many dangers inherent in doing this. There is really no such thing as *the* classical worldview or *the* historically conscious worldview—there are many different types of historical mindedness. By arguing in favor of an historically conscious worldview, I by no means intend to endorse all the theories and opinions that might be included under such a heading.

Since this section of the chapter will argue against a classical worldview, a reader might conclude that I am denying to past thinkers the possibility of any valid insights into the meaning of reality. Such a conclusion is far from true. There are even those (for example, Lonergan and Murray) who would argue that a moderate historically conscious methodology is in continuity with the best of Thomistic thought. We must never forget that some of the inadequacies in the classical worldview stem from the poor interpretation of St. Thomas by many of his so-called followers.

Two Views of Reality. The classicist worldview emphasizes the static, the immutable, the eternal, and the unchanging. The Greek column symbolizes this very well. There is no movement or dynamism about a Doric or Ionic column; the simple Greek column avoids all frills and baroque trimmings. The stately Greek column gives the impression of solidity, eternity, and immutability. Its majestic and sober lines emphasize an order and harmony which appear to last forever. This classical worldview speaks in terms of substances and essences. Time and history are "accidents" which do not really change the constitution of reality itself. Essences remain unchangeable and can only go through accidental changes in the course of time. Growth, dynamism, and progress therefore receive little attention.

The Platonic world of ideas well illustrates this classical worldview. Everything is essentially spelled out from all eternity, for the immutable essences, the universals, exist in the world of ideas. Everything in this world of ours is a participation or an accidental modification of the subsistent ideas. We come to know truth and reality by abstracting from the accidents of time and place, and arriving at immutable and unchangeable essences. Such knowledge based on immutable essences is bound to attain the ultimate in certitude.

The more historically conscious worldview emphasizes the changing, developing, evolving, and historical. Time and history are more than mere accidents that do not really change essential reality.

Individual and particular differences receive much more attention from a correspondingly more historically conscious methodology. The classical worldview is interested in the essence of human beings, which is true at all times in history and in all civilizations and circumstances. A historically minded worldview emphasizes the individual traits that characterize the individual. Moderns differ quite a bit from primitives precisely because of the historical and individual traits that an individual has acquired today.

In the more historical worldview the world is not static but evolving. Progress, growth, and change mark the world and all reality. Cold, chaste, objective order and harmony are not characteristic of this view. Blurring, motion, and subjective feeling are its corresponding features, as in the difference between modern art and classical art. Modern art emphasizes feeling and motion rather than harmony and balance. It is not as "objective" as classical art. The artists impose themselves and their emotions on the object.

Perhaps modern art is telling the theologian that the older distinction between the objective and the subjective is no longer completely adequate. Music also illustrates the change that has occurred in our understanding of the world and reality. Classical measure and rhythm are gone; free rhythm and feeling mean very much to the modern ear. What is meaningful music to the ear of the modern is only cacophony for the classicist. Changes in art and music illustrate the meaning of the different worldviews and also show graphically that the classical worldview is gone.

Two Methodologies. The two worldviews created two different theological methodologies. The classicist methodology tends to be abstract, *a priori,* and deductive. It wants to cut through the concrete circumstances to arrive at the abstract essence which is always true, and then works with these abstract and universal essences. In the area of moral theology, for example, the first principles of morality are established, and then other universal norms of conduct are deduced from these.

The more historical methodology tends to be concrete, *a posteriori,* and inductive. The historical approach does not brush by the accidental circumstances to arrive at the immutable essences. The concrete, the particular, and the individual are important for telling us something about reality itself. Principles are not deduced from other principles. Rather, the modern person observes and experiences and then tentatively proceeds to conclusions in a more inductive manner. Note that the historical consciousness as a methodology is an abstraction, but an abstraction or theory that tries to give more importance to particular, concrete, historical reality.

As we have noted above, John Courtney Murray claims that the different views on Church and State flow from the two different methodologies employed.[40] The older theory of the union of Church and State flows from a classicist methodology. It begins with the notion of a society. The definition of a society comes from an abstract and somewhat *a priori* notion of what such a society should be. The older theory then maintains that there are two perfect societies, and deduces their mutual duties and responsibilities, including their duties and obligations vis-à-vis one another. The theory concludes that the *cura religionis,* as it was then understood, belongs to the State. The State has the obligation of promoting the true faith.

What happens when the older theory runs headlong into a *de facto* situation in which the separation of Church and State is a historical fact? The older solution lies in a distinction between thesis and hypothesis, which roughly corresponds to the ideal order which should exist and the actual order which can be tolerated because of the presence of certain accidental historical circumstances. Notice the abstract and ahistorical characteristics of such a theory.

The newer theory of Church and State as proposed by Murray employs a more historically conscious methodology. Murray does not begin with an abstract definition of society and then deduce the obligations and rights of Church and State. Rather, Murray begins from a notion of the State derived from his observations of states in contemporary society. The modern State is a limited, constitutional form of government.

Its limited role contrasts with the more absolute and all-embracing role of the State in an earlier society. It does not interfere in matters that belong to the private life of individuals, such as the worship of God. Murray's theory has no need for a distinction between thesis and hypothesis, since he begins with the concrete historical reality. His conclusions then will be in harmony with the present historical situation.[41] Using a historical methodology, he can even admit that in the nineteenth century the older opinion might have been true, but in the present historical circumstances separation of Church and State is required.[42]

A classicist mentality is horrified at the thought that something could be right in one century and wrong in another. Note, however, that the historical methodology employed by Murray and Lonergan insists on a continuity in history and rejects any atomistic existentialism which sees only the uniqueness of the present situation without any connection with what has gone before or with what will follow in history.

A New Catholic Perspective. Theologians and philosophers are not alone in speaking of the changed perspective. In the documents of Vatican II the bishops do not officially adopt any worldview or methodology. But Vatican II definitely portrays reality in terms of a more historical worldview, and also employs a historically conscious methodology. The fact that the council has chosen to call itself a "pastoral" council is most significant; but "pastoral" must not be understood in opposition to "doctrinal." Rather, pastoral indicates a concern for the Christian faith not as truths to be learned but as a life to be lived.

The pastoral orientation of the council reflects a historical worldview. The bishops at the council also acknowledged that the Church has profited by the history and development of humanity. History reveals more about human beings and opens new roads to truth. The Catholic Church must constantly engage in an exchange with the contemporary world.[43]

Gaudium et Spes frequently speaks of the need to know the signs of the times. The introductory statement of this constitution asserts the need for the Church to know them and interpret them in the light of the Gospel (n. 4). The five chapters of the second section of the constitution begin with an attempt to read the signs of the times. The attention given to what was often in the past dismissed as accidental differences of time and history shows a more historical approach to reality. The constitution does not begin with abstract and universal ideas of Church, society, state, community, and common good, but rather by scrutinizing the signs of the times. *Gaudium et Spes* thus serves as an excellent illustration of the change in emphasis in Church documents from a classicist methodology to a more historically conscious approach.

The teachings on the Church as contained in the Constitution on the Church (*Lumen Gentium*) and the other documents of Vatican II also reflect a more historical approach and understanding. Previously Catholics pictured the Church as a perfect society having all the answers, and as the one bulwark of security in a changing world. However, *Lumen Gentium* speaks often and eloquently of the pilgrim Church. The charge of triumphalism rang true in the conciliar halls of Vatican II. A pilgrim Church, however, does not pretend to have all the answers.

A pilgrim Church is ever on the march towards its goal of perfect union with Christ the spouse. A pilgrim Church is constantly striving, probing, falling, rising, and trying again. A pilgrim is one who is constantly on the road and does not know there the security of one's own home. So too the pilgrim Church is a church always in need of reform (*ecclesia semper reformanda*). Change, development, growth, struggle and tension mark the Church of Christ in this world. The notion of the pilgrim Church, even in language, differs very much from the perfect society of the theological manuals.

The conciliar documents underscore the need for the Catholic Church to engage in dialogue—dialogue with other Christians, dialogue with Jews, dialogue with other non-Christians, dialogue with the world. Dialogue is not monologue. Dialogue presupposes that Catholics can learn from all these others. The call for dialogue supposes the historical and pilgrim nature of the Church, which does not possess all the answers but is open in the search for truth. The need for ongoing dialogue and ongoing search for truth contrasts sharply with the classicist view of reality and truth.

Lumen Gentium rebuilds ecclesiology on the notion of the Church as the people of God and points out the various functions and services which exist in the Church (chapter 2). Hierarchy is one form of service which exists in it. Another office is prophecy. The prophetic function exists independently of the hierarchy (n. 12). The hierarchical Church can learn, and has learned, from the prophetic voice in the Church. History reminds us that in the Church change usually occurs from underneath. Vatican Council II brought to fruition the work of the prophets in the biblical, liturgical, catechetical and ecumenical movements.

Thank God for Pope John and the bishops at Vatican II, we can say, but there never would have been a Vatican II if it were not for the prophets who went before. Many of them were rejected when they first proposed their teaching, but such has always been the lot of the prophet. The pilgrim Church, with the prophetic office, will always know the tension of trying to do the truth in love. The Church sorely needs to develop an older notion of the discernment of the Spirit, so that the individual and the total Church will be more open and ready to hear its true voice while rejecting the utterances of false prophets.[44]

The Church portrayed in Vatican II is a pilgrim Church which does not have all the answers but is constantly striving to grow in wisdom and age and grace. Thus the conciliar documents reflect a more historical view of the Church, and even employ a historically conscious methodology.

Theological Consequences

A historical worldview and a more historically conscious methodology will have important consequences when applied to the field of moral theology, for the manuals of moral theology today definitely reflect the classicist approach. In fact, there is a crisis in moral theology today precisely because such theology seems out of touch with the contemporary understanding of reality. Of course I do not claim that every modern view about reality is correct, but then not everything in the classicist worldview was correct.

Sin infects the reality we know, and the Christian thinker can never simply accept as is whatever happens to be in vogue. However, the God of creation and redemption has called us to carry on his mission in time and space. The Christian, then, is always called upon to view all things in the light of the gospel message, but whatever insights we may gain into reality and the world of creation can help us in our life.

Change and Development. The first important consequence of this new worldview and methodology affects our attitude towards change and development. The classical worldview, as we have seen, had little room for change. Only accidental changes could occur in a reality that was already constituted and known in its essence. Naturally such a view rejected any form of evolutionary theory because it was most difficult to explain evolution in such a system. On the other hand, the new worldview emphasizes the need for change. Change and growth do not affect merely the accidental constitution and knowledge of reality.

Human beings thirst for truth and constantly try to find it. The human person is never satisfied with the knowledge one has at any given moment. The contemporary person is continually probing to find out more about reality. The growth and progress of modern society demonstrate that development is absolutely necessary. The classicist methodology, on the other hand, claims a comparatively absolute and complete knowledge. Change naturally becomes a threat to the person who thinks that she or he already possesses truth. Of course, we recognize that not all change is good and salutary. There will be mistakes on the way, but the greatest error would be not to try at all.

Let us take as an example the dogmatic truth about the nature of Christ. The early christological councils proposed the formula of one person and two natures in Christ, a formula that is not present in the Scriptures. At the time there was an agonizing decision to go beyond the language of the Scriptures. But why does change have to stop in the fifth century? Might there not be an even better understanding of the natures and person of Christ today? Modern people might have different—and better—insights into the reality of Christ. Who can say that the fifth century was the final point in the development of our understanding?

When the classical worldview does speak of development, it places much emphasis on the fact that the truth always remains the same but it is expressed in different ways at different times. The same essential truth wears different clothing in different settings. However, does not the truth itself change and develop? There is more involved than just a different way of stating the same essential reality. Even in such sacrosanct dogmatic teachings there is room for real change and development.

The historical worldview realizes the constant need for growth and development, and also accepts the fact that mistakes and errors will always accompany such growth. But the attitude existing towards theology on the part of many Catholic priests in this country epitomizes the older worldview. As seminarians, they learned all the truths of the Christian faith. There was no need, in this view, to continue study after ordination, since the priest already possessed a certain knowledge of all the truths of the Christian faith.

Such an attitude also characterized the way in which theology was taught. Very little outside reading was done. The student simply memorized the notes of the professor which contained this certain knowledge. But the new methodology will bring with it a greater appreciation of the need for change and development in all aspects of the life and teaching of the Church.

Theology and Induction. Theology must adopt a more inductive methodology. Note that I am not advocating a unilaterally inductive and *a posteriori* approach for theology. However, in the past theology has attached too much importance to a deductive and somewhat *a priori* methodology. (Of course, as we shall see, with a more inductive approach moral theology can never again claim the kind of certitude it once did. At best, in some areas of conduct the ethician will be able to say that something clearly appears to be such and such at the present time.)

The classical methodology was a closed system, whereas a more historically conscious methodology proposes an open and heuristic approach. It will always remain open to new data and experience. Nothing is ever completely solved and closed, for an inductive methodology is more tentative and probing.

An inductive approach recognizes the existence of mistakes and errors, and even incorporates the necessary mechanism to overcome them. The building and manufacture of the Edsel automobile illustrates the possibility of error in a more inductive approach. Obviously, elaborate and expensive tests were run beforehand to see if there was a market for a car in the class of the projected Edsel. The decision to market the car was made on the best possible evidence. However, experience proved that the Edsel was a failure. A few years later, after similar exhaustive testing, the same company produced the Mustang, which has been a great success.

Theology, of course, is not the same as the other sciences. Progress and growth are much more evident in the area of the empirical sciences. However, the historicity of the gospel message and the historicity of human beings and the world demand a more historical approach in theology and the integration of a more inductive methodology. A more inductive approach in theology, especially in moral theology, will have to depend more on the experience of Christian people and all people of good will. The morality of particular actions cannot be judged apart from human experience. History seems to show that the changes which have occurred in Catholic morality have come about through the experience of all the people of the community. The fact that older norms did not come to grips with reality was first noticed in the experience of people.

Changes have occurred in the areas of usury, religious liberty, the right to silence, the role of love as a motive for marital relations, and other areas.[45] Certainly the rigorism of the earlier theologians on the place of procreation in marriage and marital intercourse has been modified by the experience of Christian people—for example, they held that marriage relations without the express purpose of procreation was at least venially sinful. And when the older theory of Church and State did not fit in with the historical circumstances of our day, John Courtney Murray showed that the living experience of people in the United States was more than just a toleration of an imperfect reality. In each case, experience showed the inadequacy of the older theory.

The older casuistry of mental reservation never set well with the experience of Christian people. The dissatisfaction with such casuistry played an important part in the understanding of lying now accepted by most contemporary theologians. Of course, just as theological methodology can never become totally inductive (the theologian always begins with the revelation of God in Christ), so too experience can never become the only factor in the formation of the Christian ethic. However, experience has a very important role to play. Since the experience of Christian people and all people of good will is a source of moral knowledge, an ethician cannot simply spell out in advance everything that must be done by the individual. Contemporary theology should enlarge upon and develop the concept of prudence which was an important experiential factor in the thought of Aquinas.

The Empirical Approach. Since a more historical methodology emphasizes the individual and the particular and employs a more inductive approach to knowing reality, Catholic theology will have to work much closer with the empirical and social sciences. It is these sciences that help human beings to pursue their goals and guide their development. A classicist approach which emphasized universals and essences was content with an almost exclusively deductive approach.

The Catholic Church in America today still reflects the fact that an older worldview did not appreciate or understand the need for the empirical and social sciences. The Catholic Church is probably the only very large corporation in America—I am here using "church" in the sense of a sociological entity and its administration —which does not have a research and development arm. How long could other corporations stay in existence without devoting huge sums to research and development? Heretofore, the Catholic Church has not realized the importance of change and growth.

Perhaps the crisis the Church faces today stems from a clinging to older forms of life when newer forms are required. However, without research and experimentation, who can determine which new forms are needed? The answers are not all spelled out in the nature of things.

Certitude. As we have already seen, a changed theological methodology must necessarily result in a different attitude towards certitude. The classicist methodology aimed at absolute certitude. It was more easily come by in the classical approach, for this method cut through and disregarded individual, particular differences to arrive at immutable, abstract essences. In a deductive approach the conclusion follows by a logical connection from the premise. Provided the logic is correct, the conclusion is just as certain as the premise. Since circumstances cannot change the essences or universals, one can assert that the conclusion is now and always will be absolutely certain. There is no room for any change. A deductive methodology can be much more certain than an inductive approach.

The penchant for absolute certitude characterized the philosophical system which supports the concept of natural law as found in theology manuals. Science, in this view, was defined as certain knowledge of the thing in its causes. Science, therefore, was opposed to opinion and theory. However, modern science does not aim at such certitude. Science today sees no opposition between science and the hypothetical; in fact, scientific opinion and scientific theory form an essential part of the scientific vocabulary.

Absolute certitude actually would be the great enemy of progress and growth. Once absolute certitude is reached, there is no sense in continuing research except to clear up a few peripheral matters.[46] In the Thomistic framework there was really no room for progress in scientific fields. And there was little or no room for development within the sciences, so conceived, because the first principles of the science itself were already known. The revolutionary approaches within the modern sciences show the fallacy in the Thomistic understanding of science.[47]

A more historically conscious methodology does not pretend to have or even to aim at absolute certitude. Since time, history, and individual differences are important, they cannot be dismissed as mere accidents which do not affect essential truth. This approach does not emphasize abstract essences, but concrete phenomena. Conclusions are based on the observations and experience gleaned in a more inductive approach. Such an approach can never strive for absolute certitude.

Modern science views reality in this more historical manner and consequently employs this more inductive approach. Scientific progress demands a continuing search for an even better way. An inductive methodology can never cease its working. It constantly runs new experiments and observations, for modern science aims at the best for the present time, but realizes that new progress must be made for the future.

Positive Law. A more historically conscious approach and a greater emphasis on the person attribute a much changed and reduced role to positive law. Canon law exists primarily to preserve order and harmony in the society of the people of God, and not to serve as a guide for the life of the individual Christian.[48] Nor are civil laws primarily a guide for moral conduct. Civil law as such is not primarily interested in the true, the good, and the beautiful. Civil law has the limited aim of preserving the public order.[49]

Society functions better not when law dictates to everyone what is to be done, but rather when law tries to create the climate in which individuals and smaller groups within the society can exercise their creativity and development for the good of the total community.[50] No longer is society under a master plan minutely controlled by the rules of the society. Rather, modern society's progress and growth come from the initiative of people within the society. Thus, the more historically minded worldview has a different perspective on the meaning and role of law in human life. Natural and human laws are no longer seen as detailed plans which guide and direct all human activity.

The Nature of Reality. A classicist worldview tends to see reality in terms of substances and natures which exist in themselves apart from any relations with other substances and natures. Every substance has its own nature or principle of operation. Within every acorn, for example, there is a nature which directs the acorn into becoming an oak tree. The acorn will not become a maple tree or an elm tree because it has the nature of an oak tree. The growth and "activity" of the thing is determined by the nature inscribed in it. Growth is the intrinsic unfolding of the nature within the substance.

Notice how such a view of reality affects morality. Human action depends upon the human nature. Human action is its intrinsic unfolding in the person. Nature, therefore, tells what actions are to be done and what actions are to be avoided. To determine the morality of an action, one must study its nature. The above description, although a caricature of Thomas' teaching, does represent the approach to morality of the kind of unilaterally substantialist view of reality generally assumed in the manuals.

The contemporary view sees reality more in terms of relations than of substances and natures. The individual is not thought of as a being totally constituted in the self, whose life is the unfolding of the nature already possessed. There seemingly can be no real human growth and history when future development is already determined by what is present here and now. This is the point of difference between a naturalist view and a historicist view.[51]

According to a more contemporary, relational view, reality does not consist of separate substances existing completely independent of each other. Reality can be understood only in terms of the relations that exist among the individual beings. A particular being can never be adequately considered in itself, apart from its relations with other beings and the fullness of being. An emphasis on relations rather than substances surely cannot be foreign to Catholic thinking, since theologians have spoken of the persons of the Trinity as relations.

Human experience also reminds us of the importance of relationship even in constituting ourselves as human persons. A relational understanding of reality will never see morality solely in terms of the individual substance or nature. Morality depends primarily not on the substance viewed in itself but on the individual seen in relationship to other beings. Unfortunately, the so-called traditional natural law approach frequently derives its conclusions from the nature of a faculty or the physical causality of an action seen only in itself and not in relationship with the total person and the entire community.

A brief defense of Aristotle is necessary here to avoid false impressions. Aristotle did not have a static view of reality. Nature itself was a principle of operation that tended toward a goal, but the goal was specific rather than individual. The emphasis was on the species of oak tree, that is, and not on the individual oak as such. But

Aristotle did not conceive of the human person as he did of lesser life.

As an acute observer of the human scene, he realized that most individuals do not achieve their goal of happiness and self-fulfillment. The person, he thought, does not possess an intrinsic dynamism which necessarily achieves its goal. The human being's happiness, consequently, depends not on an intrinsic tending to perfection according to the demand of nature, but rather one's happiness depends on extrinsic circumstances.

The individual person has no intrinsic orientation (a nature) necessarily bringing about personal perfection; rather, according to Aristotle, one depends more on the contingent and the accidental. The person needs freedom, health, wealth, friends, and luck to find fulfillment.[52] Notice that Aristotle himself constructed an anthropology that answers some of the strictures made against textbook natural law theories today.

The classicist worldview of the manuals tends to arrange the world in a very detailed pattern. The function of the individual is to correspond to this structure (the "natural law") as minutely outlined. One puts together the different pieces of human behavior much like one puts together the pieces of a jigsaw puzzle. The individual finds the objective pieces already existing and just fits them together. The more historical-minded worldview, on the other hand, sees the human being as creating and shaping the plan of the world. The person does not merely respect the intrinsic nature and finalities of the individual pieces of the pattern. Rather, one interferes to form new pieces and new patterns.

A different worldview, as we have seen, affects our understanding of reality. The older stressed the objectivity of reality. In this view truth consists in the mind's grasp of the reality itself. A clear distinction exists between the object and the subject. Meaning exists in the objective reality, and the subject perceives the meaning already present in reality. Modern thought and culture stress more the creative aspects (both intellectual and affective) of the subject. Modern art reveals the feelings and emotions of the subject rather than portraying an objective picture of reality. The modern cinema confronts the viewer with a very subjective view of reality that calls for imagination and perceptivity on the part of the viewer. Catholic theologians are now speaking in somewhat similar terms of a transcendental methodology in theology.

Karl Rahner has observed that natural law should be approached in this way.[53] A transcendental methodology talks about the conditions and structure in the subject necessary for it to come to know reality, for this very structure is part of the knowing process. Bernard Lonergan speaks about meaning in much the same way.[54] Human meaning can change such basic realities as community, family, state, etc. Meaning involves more than just the apprehension of the objective reality as something "out there."

A note of caution is necessary. Although Lonergan, for example, espouses a more historical consciousness and a transcendental method, at the same time he strongly proclaims a critical realism in epistemology. Lonergan definitely holds for propositions and objective truth, and truth as a correspondence. However, for Lonergan human knowing is a dynamic structure; intentionality and meaning pertain to that objectivity. He reacts against a "naive realism" or a "picture book" type of objectivity.

The problem in the past was that the objectivity of knowledge was identified with the analogy of the objectivity of the sense of sight. "Objective" is that which I see out there. Such a concept of objectivity is false because it identifies objectivity with just one of the properties of one of the operations involved in human knowing. Lonergan rejects both a naive realism and idealism.[55] It seems, however, that the objectivity talked about in manuals of moral theology is often a naive, picture-book objectivity.

The concept of natural law presupposed in Catholic theology manuals definitely reflects a classicist worldview, which sees a very precise and well-defined pattern existing for the world and human moral behavior. This ordering and pattern is called the natural law. Natural law reigns in the area of the necessary.

Within the area marked out by the pattern showing the absolute and the necessary is the contingent and the changing. Just as natural law governs the human life in the area of the principles common to all, so positive law, both civil and ecclesiastical, governs the human life in the contingent and the changing circumstances of life. The plan for the world is thus worked out in great detail in the mind of the creator, and the individual's whole purpose is to conform to the divine plan as made known in the natural and positive laws. (Despite the classical worldview of his day, in his system Thomas did leave room for the virtue of prudence and the creativity of the individual. However, the place later assigned to prudence in textbooks was drastically reduced, and thus Thomas' teaching was distorted.)

But a more historical-minded worldview does not look upon reality as a plan whose features are sketched in quite particular detail according to an unchanging pattern. Human moral life does not primarily call for conformity to such a detailed and unchanging plan. One looks upon existence as a vocation to find the meaning of human existence creatively in one's own life and experience. The meaning of human life is not already given in some pre-existing pattern or plan.

A historically conscious methodology must avoid the pitfall of a total relativism which occasionally creeps into Christianity in various forms of cultural Christianity. One needs to understand the ontological foundations of historical development; the Christian needs to understand all things in the light of the uniqueness of the once-for-all event of Christ Jesus. Both contemporary Protestant (for example, Macquarrie, Ogden) and Catholic (Rahner, Lonergan) scholars are addressing themselves to this problem.

Perhaps the characterization of the two worldviews in this chapter tends to be oversimplified. For one thing, the points of difference between them have been delineated without any attempt to show the similarities. The differences in many areas of morality—for example, the understanding and living of the evangelical norm of love and forgiveness—would be minimal. The reasoning developed in this section has prescinded, as well, from the question of growth and development in human values and morals. However, in the modern world, characterized by instant communication, rapid transportation, and changing sociological patterns, it is clear that the individual needs a more historical worldview and a more historically conscious methodology than the person who lived in a comparatively static and closed society.

III.

PHYSICALISM AND A CLASSICIST METHODOLOGY
IN THE ENCYCLICAL

The encyclical on the regulation of birth employs a natural law methodology which tends to identify the moral action with the physical and biological structure of the act. The core practical conclusion of the letter states: "We must once again declare that the direct interruption of the generative process already begun, and above all directly willed and procured abortion, even if for therapeutic reasons, are to be absolutely excluded as licit means of regulating birth" (*H.V.* n. 14). "Equally to be excluded . . . is direct sterilization. . . . Similarly excluded is every action which, either in anticipation of the conjugal act, or in its accomplishment, or in the development of its natural consequences, proposes, whether as an end or as a means, to render procreation impossible" (*H.V.* n. 14). The footnotes in this particular paragraph refer to the Roman Catechism and the utterances of more recent popes. Reference is made to the Address of Pius XII to the Italian Catholic Union of Midwives in which direct sterilization is defined as "that which aims at making procreation impossible as both means and end" (n. 13, *AAS* 43 [1951], 838). The concept of direct is thus described in terms of the physical structure and causality of the act itself.

The moral conclusion of the encyclical forbidding any interference with the conjugal act is based on the "intimate structure of the conjugal act" (*H.V.* n. 12). The "design of God" is written into the very nature of the conjugal act; the person is merely "the minister of the design established by the Creator" (*H.V.* n. 13). The encyclical acknowledges that "it is licit to take into account the natural rhythms immanent in the generative functions." Recourse to the infecund periods is licit, whereas artificial contraception "as the use of means directly contrary to fecundation is condemned as being always illicit" (*H.V.* n. 16). "In reality there are essential differences between the two cases; in the former, the married couple make legitimate use of a natural disposition; in the latter, they impede the development of natural processes" (*H.V.* n. 16). The natural law theory employed in the encyclical thus identifies the moral and human action with the physical structure of the conjugal act itself.

Humanae Vitae in its methodology well illustrates a classicist approach. The papal letter admits that "changes which have taken place are in fact noteworthy and of varied kinds" (*H.V.* n. 2). These changes give rise to new questions. However, the changing historical circumstances have not affected the answer or the method employed in arriving at concrete conclusions on implementing responsible parenthood. The primary reason for rejecting the majority report of the Papal Commission was "because certain criteria of solutions had emerged which departed from the moral teaching on marriage proposed with constant firmness by the teaching authority of the Church" (*H.V.* n. 6).

The encyclical specifically acknowledges the fact that there are new signs of the times, but one wonders if sufficient attention has really been paid to such changes. The footnotes to the encyclical are significant even if the footnote references alone do not constitute a conclusive argument. The references are only to random scriptural texts, one citation of Thomas Aquinas, and references to earlier pronouncements of the hierarchical magisterium. A more inductive approach would be inclined to give more importance and documentation to the signs of the times. The footnote references contain no indication of any type of dialogue with other Christians, non-Christians and the modern sciences. When the letter does mention social consequences of the use of contraception, no documentation is given for what appear to be unproven assumptions. Since the methodology describes the human act in physical terms, the practical moral conclusion is the absolute condemnation of means of artificial birth control. The encyclical thus betrays an epistemology that has been rejected by many Catholic theologians and philosophers today.

IV.
DIFFERENT APPROACHES WITH DIFFERENT CONCLUSIONS

Natural law theory has traditionally upheld two values that are of great importance for moral theology: (1) the existence of a source of ethical wisdom and knowledge which the Christian shares with all humanity; (2) the fact that morality cannot be merely the subjective whim of an individual or group of individuals. However, one can defend these important values for moral theology without necessarily endorsing the particular understanding of natural law presupposed in the encyclical. In the last few years Catholic thinkers have been developing and employing different philosophical approaches to an understanding of morality. One could claim that such approaches are modifications of natural law theory because they retain the two important values mentioned above. Others would prefer to abandon the term natural law since such a concept is very ambiguous. There is no monolithic philosophical system called the natural law, and also the term has been somewhat discredited because of the tendency among some to understand natural in terms of the physical structure of acts. We can briefly describe three of the alternative approaches which have been advanced in the last few years—personalism, a relational and communitarian approach, a transcendental methodology. As mentioned above, these three approaches emerge within the context of a more historically conscious worldview and understand anthropology and moral reality in a way that differs from the concept of anthropology and moral reality proposed by the classical methodology. All these approaches would deny the absolute conclusion of the papal encyclical in condemning all means of artificial birth control.

A more personalist approach has characterized much of contemporary ethics. For the Christian, the biblical revelation contributes to such an understanding of reality. A personalist approach cannot be something merely added on to another theory. A personalist perspective will definitely affect moral conclusions, especially when such conclusions have been based on the physical structure of the act itself. Personalism always sees the act in terms of the person placing the act. The Pastoral Constitution on the Church in the Modern World realized that objective standards in the matter of sexual morality are "based on the nature of the human person and his acts" (n. 51). An essay by Bernard Häring shows how a personalist perspective would not condemn artificial contraception as being always immoral.[56]

Classical ethical theory embraces two types or models of ethical method: the teleological and the deontological. H. Richard Niebuhr has added a third ethical model—the model of responsibility. The moral agent is not primarily a maker or a citizen but a responder. There are various relationships within which the responsible self exists. "The responsible self is driven as it were by the movement of the social process to respond and be accountable in nothing less than a universal community."[57] Robert Johann in developing his understanding of anthropology acknowledges a great debt to Niebuhr.[58]

In the particular question of contraception, a more relational approach would not view the person or a particular faculty as something existing in itself. Each faculty exists in relationship with the total person and other persons within a universal community. Morality cannot merely be determined by examining a particular faculty and its physical structure or a particular act in itself. The changed ethical evaluation of lying well illustrates the point. Both Johann and William H. van der Marck (who embraces a more phenomenological starting point) have employed a more relational approach to argue for the licitness of contraception in certain circumstances.[59]

A third philosophical approach espoused by a growing number of Catholic thinkers today is a theory of transcendental method. Transcendental methodology owes much to the neo-Thomist Joseph Marechal and is espoused today in different forms by Bernard Lonergan, Karl Rahner, and Emerich Coreth.[60] In general, transcendental method goes beyond the object known to the structures of the human knowing process itself. According to Lonergan, "the intrinsic objectivity of human cognitional activity is its intentionality."[61] Lonergan's ethics is an extension of his theory of knowing. Moral value is not an intrinsic property of external acts or objects; it is an aspect of certain consciously free acts in relation to my knowledge of the world. The moral subject must come to examine the structures of the knowing and deciding process.[62]

Lonergan uses as a tool the notion of horizon analysis. Basic horizon is the maximum field of vision from a determined standpoint. This basic horizon is open to development and even conversion. Lonergan posits four conversions which should transpire from the understanding of the structures of human knowing and deciding —the intellectual, the moral, the religious, and the Christian. Ethics must bring people to this Christian conversion so that they can become aware of their knowing and doing and flee from inauthenticity, unreasonableness, and the surd of sin. Thus Christian ethics is primarily concerned with the manner in which an authentic Christian person makes ethical decisions and carries them out. However, such a metaethics must then enter into the realm of the normative, all the time realizing the provisional value of its precepts which are limited by the data at hand.[63] One commentator has said of Lonergan's ethic as applied to moral theology: "The distinct contribution of the moral theologian to philosophical ethics would consist in clarifying the attitudes which are involved in man's responding in faith to the initiative of a loving God who has redeemed man in Christ."[64] Thus a transcendental method would put greater stress on the knowing and deciding structures of the authentic Christian subject. Such a theory would also tend to reject the encyclical's view of anthropology and of human generative faculties.

There has been even among Catholic theologians a sharp negative response to the practical conclusions of the papal encyclical on the regulation of birth. This essay has tried to explain the reason for the negative response. The concept of natural law employed in the encyclical tends to define the moral act merely in terms of the physical structure of the act. In contemporary theology such an understanding of natural law has been severely criticized. Newer philosophical approaches have been accepted by many Catholic thinkers. Such approaches logically lead to the conclusion that artificial contraception can be a permissible and even necessary means for the regulation of birth within the context of responsible parenthood.

V.
APPLICATION TO THE SITUATION ETHICS DEBATE

In the last few years moral theology and Christian ethics have been immersed in a controversy over situation ethics. The controversy tends to polarize opinions and fails to show the huge areas of agreement existing among Christian moralists. There are, nevertheless, many real differences in approaches and in some practical conclusions. The principal areas of practical differences between some situationists and the teaching found in the manuals of moral theology are the following: medical ethics, particularly in the area of reproduction; conflict situations solved by the principle of the indirect voluntary, especially conflicts involving life and death, e.g., killing, abortion; sexuality; euthanasia; and divorce.

These major points of disagreement have one thing in common. In these cases, the manuals of Catholic moral theology have tended to define the moral action in terms of the physical structure of the act considered in itself apart from the person placing the act and the community of persons within which she lives. A certain action defined in terms of its physical structure or consequences (e.g., euthanasia as the positive interference in the life of the person; male masturbation as the ejaculation of semen) is considered to be always wrong. I have used the term "negative, moral absolutes" to refer to such actions described in their physical structure which are always wrong from a moral viewpoint. Thus the central point of disagreement in moral theology today centers on these prohibited actions which are described primarily in terms of their physical structure.

In the area of medical ethics certain actions described in terms of the physical structure of the act are never permitted or other such actions are always required. Artificial insemination with the husband's semen is never permitted because insemination cannot occur except through the act of sexual intercourse.[65] Contraception as direct interference with the act of sexual intercourse is wrong. Direct sterilization is always wrong. Masturbation as the ejaculation of semen is always wrong even as a way of procuring semen for semen analysis.[66] Frequently in such literature the axiom is cited that the end does not justify the means. However, in all these cases the means is defined in terms of the physical structure of the act. I believe in all the areas mentioned above there are circumstances in which such actions would be morally permissible and even necessary.

Catholic moral theology decides most conflict situations by an application of the principle of the indirect voluntary. Direct killing, direct taking of one's life, direct abortion, direct sterilization are always wrong. However, the manuals of theology usually define direct in terms of the physical structure of the act itself. Direct killing according to one author "may be defined as the performance (or the omission of) an act, the primary and natural result of which is to bring about death."[67] According to the same author "direct abortion is the performance of an act, the primary and natural effect of which is to expel a nonviable fetus from its mother's womb." In these cases direct refers to the physical structure and consequences of the act itself. One exception in the manuals of theology to the solution of conflict situations in terms of the principle of the indirect voluntary is the case of unjust aggression. The physical structure of the act is not the determining factor in such a conflict situation.

In general a Christian ethicist might be somewhat suspicious of conflict situations solved in terms of the physical structure of the act itself. Such a solution seems too facile and too easily does away with the agonizing problems raised by the conflict. Likewise, such an approach has tended to minimalize what is only an indirect effect, but the Christian can never have an easy conscience about taking the life of another even if it is only an indirect effect.

The case of "assisted abortion" seems to illustrate the inherent difficulties in the manualistic concept of direct and indirect. For example, the best available medical knowledge indicates that the woman cannot bring a living child to term. If the doctor can abort the fetus now, he or she can avert very probable physical and psychological harm to the mother from the pregnancy which cannot eventually come to term. The manuals indicate that such an abortion would be direct and therefore immoral. However, in the total context of the situation, it does not seem that such an abortion would be immoral. The example of assisted abortion illustrates the impossibility of establishing an absolute moral norm based on the physical description of the action considered only in itself apart from the person placing the action and the entire community. It seems that the older notion of direct enshrines a prescientific worldview which is somewhat inadequate in our technological age. Why should the doctor sit back and wait for nature to take its course when by interfering now she can avoid great harm to the mother? In general, I do not think that conflict situations can be solved merely in terms of the physical structure and consequences of the act.

Perhaps the approach used in conflict situations of unjust aggression would serve as a better model for the solution of other conflict situations. In unjust aggression the various values at stake are weighed, and the person is permitted to kill an unjust aggressor not only to save one's life but also to protect other goods of comparable value, such as a serious threat to health, honor, chastity, or even material goods of great importance.[68] (I believe that in some cases the older theologians went too far in equating the defense of these values and the life of the aggressor.) Thus in the question of abortion there seem to be cases when it is moral to abort to save the life of the mother or to preserve other very important values. I am not proposing that the fetus is an unjust aggressor but rather that the ethical model employed in solving problems of unjust aggression avoids some of the problems created by the model of direct and indirect effects when the direct effect is determined by the physical structure of the act itself.

The present discussion about the beginning of human life centers on the criteria for identifying human life. Are the physical criteria of genetics and embryology sufficient? Or must other criteria of a more psychological and personalistic nature be employed for discerning the existence of human life? What then would be the difference between the fetus in the womb and the newborn babe who is now existing outside her mother's womb? There are many complicated problems in such a discussion. For many, the biological and genetic criteria are the only practical way of resolving the problem.[69] I am merely pointing out that the problem exists precisely because some people will not accept the biological and genetic considerations as establishing an adequate criterion for determining the beginning of human life.

Many theologians maintain the meaning of sexuality has been distorted in the Catholic theological tradition for many reasons including an overemphasis on the physical structure of sexual actuation. In the question of euthanasia, Catholic and other theistic ethicists generally approach the problem in terms of the limited dominion which the individual has over his or her own life. Today even Christians claim a greater power over their own existence both because of scientific advances and because of better understanding of participation in the Lordship of Jesus. However, in one important aspect in the area of euthanasia the question of dominion over one's life is not primary. Catholic thinking has maintained that the patient does not have to use extraordinary means to preserve life. In more positive terms, there is a right to die. Many Catholic theologians remind doctors they have no obligation to give intravenous feeding to a dying cancer patient. Likewise, a doctor may discontinue such feeding with the knowledge that the person will thus die. But the manuals of theology would condemn any positive action on the part of the doctor—e.g., injection of air into the bloodstream—under the same circumstances.[70]

At the particular time when death is fast approaching, the primary moral question does not seem to revolve explicitly around the notion of one's dominion over life. The problem centers on the difference between not giving something or the withdrawal of something necessary for life and the positive giving of something to bring about death. Is the difference between the two types of action enough to warrant the total condemnation of positively interfering? I do not think so; Catholic theologians should explore the possibility of interfering to hasten the dying process, a notion similar to the concept of assisted abortion mentioned above. But the theologian would also have to consider the possibility of a general prohibition based on the societal effects of such interference.

The problem of describing moral reality in terms of the physical description of an act viewed in itself apart from the person also manifests itself in the question of divorce. According to Catholic teaching a consummated marriage between two baptized persons is indissoluble. But consummation is defined in solely physical terms. Thus the notion of consummation as found in the present law of the Church is inadequate.[71] Moreover, divorce in general qualifies as a negative moral absolute in the sense described above. A particular action described in nonmoral terms (remarriage after a valid first marriage) is always wrong. The entire question of divorce is too complex to be considered adequately in the present context since it involves biblical, historical, conciliar, and magisterial aspects. But the concept of "the bond of marriage" adds weight to the arguments against divorce. The bond becomes objectivized as a reality existing apart from the relationship of the persons which is brought into being by their marriage vows. All Christians, I believe, should hold some element transcending the two persons and their union here and now. But can this bond always be considered totally apart from the ongoing relationship between the two who exchanged the marital promises?

Thus a quick overview shows that the critical, practical areas of discussion in contemporary moral theology and Christian ethics center on the absolute moral prohibition of certain actions which are defined primarily in terms of the physical structure of the act. Moral meaning is not necessarily identical with the physical description of an act. Modern anthropology is in a much better position than medieval anthropology to realize that fact. The underlying problem is common to every human science—the need to clearly differentiate the category of meaning as the specific data of any science involving human reality. Historians of ideas would be familiar with this problem from the nineteenth century differentiation of Dilthey between the *Geisteswissenchaften* and *Naturwissenchaften*.[72] In the Anglo-American context, Matson has recently published an informative survey of the present status of this same differentiation involving the notion of human behavior.[73]

A word of caution is in order. It appears that some proponents of situation ethics have not given enough importance to the bodily, the material, the external, and the physical aspects of reality. On the other hand, contemporary theory is less prone to accept the physical and the biological aspects of reality as morally normative. An analysis of the current scene in moral theology and Christian ethics in a broad ecumenical view indicates that the primary point of dispute centers on the existence of negative moral absolutes in which the moral action is described in physical terms. It would be unwarranted to conclude that the moral act is never identified with the physical structure and description of the act. However, one can conclude that an ethical theory which begins with the assumption that the moral act is identified with the physical structure and consequences of the act will find little acceptance by contemporary theologians.

Notes

1. E.g., *Light on the Natural Law,* ed. Illtud Evans, O.P. (Baltimore: Helicon Press, 1965); *Das Naturrecht im Disput,* ed. Franz Böckle (Dussel-

dorf: Patmos, 1966); "La Nature fondement de la morale?" *Supplément de la Vie Spirituelle* 81 (May 1967), 187–324; *Absolutes in Moral Theology?* ed. Charles E. Curran (Washington: Corpus Books, 1968).

2. Edward LeRoy Long Jr., *A Survey of Christian Ethics* (New York: Oxford University Press, 1967); Thomas G. Sanders, *Protestant Concepts of Church and State* (Garden City, N.Y.: Doubleday Anchor Books, 1965).

3. Such emphases can still be found, although not in an absolute sense, in the writings of Niels H. Söe. See Söe, "Natural Law and Social Ethics," in *Christian Social Ethics in a Changing World,* ed. John C. Bennett (New York: Association Press, 1966), pp. 289–309. The same article with a response by Paul Ramsey appeared in *Zeitschrift für Evangelische Ethik,* 12 (March 1968), 65–98.

4. John C. Bennett, "Issues for the Ecumenical Dialogue," in *Christian Social Ethics in a Changing World,* pp. 377, 378.

5. H. Richard Niebuhr, *Christ and Culture* (New York: Harper Torchbook, 1956).

6. Niebuhr actually describes the Thomistic approach as "Christ above culture." He goes on to explain that "Thomas also answers the question about Christ and culture with a 'both-and'; yet his Christ is far above culture, and he does not try to disguise the gulf that lies between them" (p. 129).

7. One cannot simplistically condemn the nature-grace and natural-supernatural distinctions. In their original historical contexts such distinctions tried with considerable success to describe and synthesize this complex reality. Although such distinctions do have some meaning today; nevertheless, many Catholic theologians realize the need to reinterpret such distinctions in the light of different metaphysical approaches. See the three articles by Bernard Lonergan, S.J., which appeared in *Theological Studies* 2 (1941), 307–324; 3 (1942), 69–88, 375–402. For an exposition of the thought of Karl Rahner on this subject, see Carl J. Peter, "The Position of Karl Rahner Regarding the Supernatural," *Proceedings of the Catholic Theological Society of America* 20 (1965), 81–94.

8. A wire release of N. C. News Service with a Vatican City dateline published in Catholic papers in this country during the week of August 4, 1968.

9. Bernard Häring, C.SS.R., "The Encyclical Crisis," *Commonweal* 88 (September 6, 1968), 588–594.

10. Joseph Fuchs, S.J., *Natural Law,* trans. Helmut Reckter, S.J., and John Dowling (New York: Sheed and Ward, 1965).

11. Christian Duquoc, O.P., *L'Eglise et le progrès* (Paris: Editions du Cerf, 1964), pp. 68–117. The author considers the past teaching in the

Church on slavery, the freedom of nations, the dignity of women, Church and State, torture, and questions of war and peace.

12. "Dialogue with Joseph Fletcher," *Homiletic and Pastoral Review,* 67 (1967), 828, 829.

13. Helmut Thielicke, *Theological Ethics I: Foundations,* ed. William Lazareth (Philadelphia: Fortress Press, 1966), 622ff.

14. Pope Leo XIII, *Rerum Novarum,* n. 7–14; Pope Pius XI, *Quadragesimo Anno,* n. 44–52.

15. Thomas explicitly cites Isidore in *I-II,* q. 94, a. 2, ob. 1. In *II-II,* q. 66, a. 2, Thomas gives the opinion proposed by Isidore without a direct reference. Thomas explains that reason has called for the right of private property not as something against natural law, but as something added to natural law.

16. The reasons adduced by Thomas in *II-II,* q. 66, a. 2, indicate that human sinfulness is a very important factor in the argument for the right of private property.

17. *Rerum Novarum,* n. 22.

18. Hermenegildus Lio, O.F.M., "Estne obligatio justitiae subvenire pauperibus?" *Apollinaris* 29 (1956), 124–231; 30 (1957), 99–201.

19. Leo XIII was conscious of the social aspect of property (*Rerum Novarum,* n. 22), but he did not emphasize it. The subsequent Popes down to Paul VI have put increasingly more emphasis on the social aspects of property. The concentration on such social aspects explains the many discussions about the notion of socialization in the encyclicals of Pope John XXIII.

20. See note 1; also my treatment of this precise question in *A New Look at Christian Morality* (Notre Dame, Ind.: Fides Publishers, 1968), pp. 74–89.

21. Jean Marie Aubert, "Le Droit Naturel: ses avatars historiques et son avenir," *Supplément de la Vie Spirituelle* 81 (1967), especially 298 ff.

22. *The Digest* or *Pandects of Justinian,* Book 1, t. 1, nn. 1–4.

23. Odon Lottin, *Le Droit Naturel chez Saint Thomas d'Aquin et ses prédécesseurs,* 2nd ed. (Bruges: Charles Beyaert, 1931), p. 62.

24. *In IV Sent.* d. 33, q. 1, a. 1, ad 4.

25. *In V Ethic.,* lect. 12.

26. *I-II,* q. 90, a. 1, ob. 3; q. 96, a. 5, ob. 3; q. 97, a. 2; *II-II,* q. 57, a. 3, ob. 1, and *in corp.*

27. *I-II,* q. 95, a. 4.

28. *II-II,* q. 57, a. 3. For a detailed analysis of Thomas's teaching that comes to the same conclusion, see Michael Bertram Crowe, "St. Thomas Aquinas and Ulpian's Natural Law," in *St. Thomas Aquinas, 1274–1974:*

Commemorative Studies, vol. 1 (Toronto, Canada: Pontifical Institute of Medieval Studies, 1974), pp. 261–282.

29. E.g., H. Noldin et al., Summa Theologiae Moralis: De Castitate, 36th ed. (Oeniponte: F. Rauch, 1958), pp. 21–43.

30. Decree of the Holy Office on the ends of marriage, April 1, 1944, AAS, 36 (1944), 103. Also various addresses of Pius XII: AAS, 33 (1941), 422; 43 (1951), 835–854.

31. Regis Araud, S.J., "Evolution de la théologie du marriage," Cahiers Laënnec, 27 (1967), 56–71; W. van der Marck, O.P., "De recente ontwikkelingen in de theologie van het huwelijk," Tijdschrift voor Theologie 7 (1967), 127–140. English summary on page 140.

32. Gerard Watson, "The Early History of Natural Law," The Irish Theological Quarterly 33 (1966), 65–74.

33. John L. Russell, S.J., "The Concept of Natural Law," The Heythrop Journal 6 (1965), 434–438; Pierre Colin, "Ambiguités du mot nature," Supplément de la Vie Spirituelle 81 (1967), 253–255.

34. Charles E. Curran, "Masturbation and Objectively Grave Matter: An Exploratory Discussion," Proceedings of the Catholic Theological Society of America 21 (1966), 95–109; also chapter 7.

35. H. Noldin et al., Summa Theologiae Moralis, vol. 2: De Praeceptis (Oeniponte: F. Rauch, 1959), pp. 553–560; E. F. Regatillo, S.J., and M. Zalba, S.J., Theologiae Moralis Summa, vol. 2 (Matriti: Biblioteca de Autores Cristianos, 1953), 1000–1018.

36. J. A. Dorszynski, Catholic Teaching about the Morality of Falsehood (Washington: Catholic University of America Press, 1949); Francis J. Connell, C.SS.R., More Answers to Today's Moral Problems, ed. Eugene J. Weitzel, C.S.V. (Washington: Catholic University of America Press, 1965), pp. 123, 124. Augustine had at one time accepted the distinction between falsehood and lying, but he later changed his opinion.

37. Bernard Lonergan, S.J., Collection (New York: Herder and Herder, 1967), pp. 252–267; Lonergan, "A Transition from a Classicist Worldview to Historical Mindedness," in Law for Liberty: The Role of Law in the Church Today, ed. James E. Biecher (Baltimore: Helicon Press, 1967). Lonergan along with other theologians such as Marechal, Rahner, and Metz maintains that although Thomas Aquinas reflected a classical worldview, the followers of Thomas distorted his teaching especially in such areas as the emphasis on a deductive methodology and a nonrelational understanding of being.

38. John Courtney Murray, S.J., "The Declaration on Religious Freedom," Concilium 15 (May 1966), 3–16.

39. Eulalio R. Baltazar, Teilhard and the Supernatural (Baltimore:

Helicon Press, 1966); Leslie Dewart, *The Future of Belief* (New York: Herder and Herder, 1966). Lonergan espouses historical mindedness but strenuously opposes the approach of Dewart. See Lonergan, "The Dehellenization of Dogma," *Theological Studies* 28 (1967), 336–351.

40. Murray, "Declaration on Religious Freedom," pp. 11–16.

41. John Courtney Murray, S.J., *The Problem of Religious Freedom* (Westminster, Md.: Newman, 1965).

42. John Courtney Murray, S.J., "Freedom, Authority, Community," *America* (December 3, 1966), 735.

43. *Gaudium et Spes* (The Pastoral Constitution on the Church in the Modern World), n. 44. For a competent one-volume translation of the documents of Vatican II, see *The Documents of Vatican II,* ed. Walter M. Abbot, S.J. (New York: America Press and Association Press, 1966).

44. Karl Rahner, S.J., *The Dynamic Element in the Church* (New York: Herder and Herder, 1964).

45. Daniel C. Maguire, "Moral Absolutes and the Magisterium," *Absolutes in Moral Theology?,* pp. 57–107.

46. Herbert Butterfield, *The Origins of Modern Science, 1300–1800* (New York: Macmillan, 1951); Lonergan, *Collection,* p. 259 ff.

47. Andreas van Melsen, "Natural Law and Evolution," *Concilium* 26 (June, 1967), 49–59.

48. *Law for Liberty: The Role of Law in the Church Today,* passim.

49. *Documents of Vatican II,* p. 686, n. 20. The footnote on the role of civil law was written by John Courtney Murray.

50. Thomas B. McDonough, "Distribution of Contraceptives by the Welfare Department: A Catholic Response," in *The Problem of Population,* vol. 2 (Notre Dame: University of Notre Dame Press, 1964), pp. 94–118.

51. Douglas Sturm, "Naturalism, Historicism, and Christian Ethics: Toward a Christian Doctrine of Natural Law," *The Journal of Religion* 44 (1964), 40–51. Note again that some Catholic thinkers see in the excessive emphasis on *res in se* apart from any relational consideration a distortion of the understanding of St. Thomas.

52. Russell, "Concept of Natural Law," pp. 434–438.

53. Karl Rahner, S.J., "Theology and Anthropology," in *The Word in History,* ed. T. Patrick Burke (New York: Sheed and Ward, 1966), pp. 1–23; Rahner, "Naturrecht," *Lexikon für Theologie und Kirche,* vol. 7, pp. 827–828.

54. Lonergan, "Dimensions of Meaning," *Collection,* pp. 252–267.

55. Lonergan, *Collection,* pp. 221–239; *Theological Studies* 28 (1967), 337–351.

56. Bernard Häring, "The Inseparability of the Unitive-Procreative

Functions of the Marital Act," *Contraception: Authority and Dissent,* ed. Charles E. Curran (New York: Herder and Herder, 1969), pp. 176–192.

57. H. Richard Niebuhr, *The Responsible Self* (New York: Harper and Row, 1963), p. 88.

58. Robert O. Johann, S.J., *Building the Human* (New York: Herder and Herder, 1968), pp. 7–10.

59. Robert O. Johann, S.J., "Responsible Parenthood: A Philosophical View," *Proceedings of the Catholic Theological Society of America* 20 (1965), 115–128; William H. van der Marck, O.P., *Toward a Christian Ethic* (Westminster, Md.: Newman Press, 1967), pp. 48–60. Note that Germain G. Grisez in his *Contraception and the Natural Law* (Milwaukee: Bruce, 1964), argues against artificial contraception although he explicitly denies the "perverted faculty" argument. However, Grisez seems to accept too uncritically his basic premise that the malice of contraception "is in the will's direct violation of the procreative good as a value in itself, as an ideal which never may be submerged."

60. For a succinct exposition of transcendental philosophy, see Kenneth Baker, S.J., *A Synopsis of the Transcendental Philosophy of Emerich Coreth and Karl Rahner* (Spokane: Gonzaga University, 1965).

61. Lonergan, *Collection,* p. 228.

62. In addition to the bibliography of Lonergan's which has already been mentioned, see Bernard J. F. Lonergan, S.J., *Insight* (New York and London: Longmans, Green, and Co., 1964); Donald H. Johnson, S.J., "Lonergan and the Redoing of Ethics," *Continuum* 5 (1967), 211–220; and John P. Boyle, "Lonergan's *Method in Theology* and Objectivity in Moral Theology," *The Thomist* 37 (1973), 589–601.

63. David W. Tracy, "Horizon Analysis and Eschatology," *Continuum* 6 (1968), 166–179.

64. Johnson, "Lonergan and the Redoing of Ethics," 219, 220.

65. Pope Pius XII, Address to the Fourth World Congress of Catholic Doctors, Rome, September 29, 1949, *A.A.S.* 41 (1949), 560; Pope Pius XII, Address to the Italian Catholic Union of Midwives, October 29, 1951, *A.A.S.* 43 (1951), 850; Pope Pius XII, Address to the Second World Congress of Fertility and Sterility, May 19, 1956, *A.A.S.* 48 (1956), 472.

66. Pope Pius XII, *A.A.S.* 48 (1956), 472; Pope Pius XII, Address to the Italian Urologists, October 8, 1953, *A.A.S.* 45 (1953), 678; Decree of the Holy Office, August 2, 1929, *A.A.S.* 21 (1929), 490.

67. John McCarthy, *Problems in Theology II: The Commandments* (Westminster, Md.: Newman Press, 1960), pp. 159, 160. The author mentions other current definitions of direct killing (e.g., an act which aims, *ex fine operis,* at the destruction of life) earlier on pp. 119–122.

68. Marcellinus Zalba, S.J., *Theologia Moralis Summa II; Theologia Moralis Specialis* (Madrid: Biblioteca de Autores Cristianos, 1953), pp. 275–279.

69. Such an approach is adopted by Paul Ramsey who claims that at least from blastocyst the fetus must be considered as a human being. For further developments in Ramsey's thought and my own critique, see Charles E. Curran, *Politics, Medicine and Christian Ethics: A Dialogue with Paul Ramsey* (Philadelphia: Fortress Press, 1973), pp. 110–131.

70. Gerald Kelly, S.J., *Medico-Moral Problems* (St. Louis: Catholic Hospital Association, 1957), pp. 128–141.

71. For a fuller critique of the notion of consummation, see Dennis Doherty, "Consummation and the Indissolubility of Marriage," *Absolutes in Moral Theology?*, pp. 211–231.

72. Wilhelm Dilthey, *Pattern and Meaning in History* (New York: Harper Torchbook, 1967).

73. Floyd W. Matson, *The Broken Image* (Garden City, N.Y.: Doubleday Anchor Books, 1966).

The Pursuit of the Natural Law

Michael B. Crowe

This article originally appeared in 1977 in *Irish Theological Quarterly*.

The natural law has always been a sign of contradiction in moral philosophy and moral theology. This is undoubtedly the contemporary experience; and, as has so frequently happened before, the struggles are interpreted as the death-throes of the concept on the one hand, or as evidence of its astonishing vitality on the other. Recent approaches to the natural law have, indeed, been more than usually dramatic and, whether one ultimately favors or rejects it, more than usually enlightening. The literature is immense; but the effort to disengage the main lines of disagreement must be made and may be expected to show, not merely where the "traditional" concept of the natural law is vulnerable, but how it needs to be modified to meet the demands of contemporary thinking. One of the latest studies of the topic begins:

> Recent theological discussions of natural law have concerned two interdependent, but separable, sets of issues. The more prominent issues have been centred around questions of the status of norms and/or absolutes. Associated with, and often confusing, these questions has been the attack on the "past, Roman Catholic, text-book approach to moral theology." The arguments surrounding this set of issues have often been muddled and hopelessly confusing attempts to come up with something called a "dynamic theory of natural law."[1]

The author goes on to argue that the issues have not been shown to be intrinsically connected and to propound the still more interesting thesis that Christian ethics does not have a stake in the natural law. Here, however, we may be content to make use of his broad division of the issues. This article will be concerned with the "attack on the past," leaving for another the question of moral absolutes.

I.
THE ATTACK ON THE NATURAL LAW

Twenty years ago the position of the natural law in Catholic thought seemed assured; complacently ensconced on the *Tractatus de legibus* it was expounded in almost identical fashion by the authors of the manuals and the text-books. That situation has given way to a widespread dissatisfaction within the Church regarding what we may for the moment call the "traditional" exposition of the natural law, and to a better-directed and more intense criticism from without, notably from Protestant writers on theological ethics. The transformation is due, in good measure, to the general hostility of contemporary philosophy toward the natural law; but it is also due to some internal flaws and contradictions in the older approach. These connected factors must be examined before the vital question can be put: what defense can today be offered for the natural moral law?

The twentieth century climate of opinion touching the natural law has been ambivalent. The nineteenth century saw the virtual eclipse of the notion—or rather the eclipse of the eighteenth century rationalist natural law, which proved quite unable to resist the criticism of the nineteenth century historical schools of jurisprudence and positivist philosophy. This dark night was hardly lightened by the stress upon natural rights, and the proliferation of declarations of the rights of man and entrenched rights in the constitutions of the age—fruits of the American and French Revolutions and the thought of John Locke and Jean-Jacques Rousseau. The first half of the twentieth century was, with the exception of milieus influenced by scholastic philosophy, still resolutely positivist. It was, in fact, the abuses of positivism that were to focus attention upon the natural law as the second half of the century dawned. The events leading up to the Second World War—and incidents in the prosecution of the war—provided the subject-matter for the indictments at the Nuren-berg War Crimes Trial. Many saw those indictments as an appeal, at least implicit, to the natural law and believed it to be a valid appeal, despite the impropriety, not to say hypocrisy, of including among the accusers those who were themselves guilty of comparable atroci-ties, and despite the difficulty of rebutting the charge that the entire exercise was simply a sophisticated example of *vae victis.*

The climate of opinion in the decade following the end of the war in 1945 was more propitious for the natural law than it has been before or since. The example of the "conversion" of Gustav Rad-bruch has often been cited. Radbruch's professedly positivist ap-proach to law, in his *Rechtsphilosophie*[2] had formed several genera-tions of German jurists, in the pre-war period and well into the Hitler era, with the result, as has been said, of delivering the German judiciary bound hand and foot into the toils of Nazism. After the war, however, Radbruch published a celebrated article in which, impressed by the enormities that had been perpetrated with the trap-pings of legality, he saw the need to qualify his former views and to move toward something like a concept of natural law.[3]

It would be much too simple a view to see in the natural law the only answer to the excesses of totalitarianism or the only defense against their repetition. It has, indeed, been argued that the doctrine of natural law has contributed to the rise of Nazism.[4] This, however, is an extreme view. There can be hardly any doubt that, in the immediate post-war period, legal positivism was considered by many to have been seriously undermined, "an hypothesis wrecked by the gruesome reality of history."[5] It was an opportunity readily taken by the already-established and greatly differing currents of thought favoring the natural law—not merely neo-scholastic but neo-Kantian, sociological and even positivist, affected in consider-able measure by the euphoria generated by the United Nations' *Universal Declaration of Human Rights* of 1948 and the progressive de-colonization of most of Africa and Asia in the 1950's.[6] The disil-lusion that has since set in provides the present-day setting in which the old objections to the natural law have taken on a new vitality and have been joined by new ones.

This is the general background against which attitudes toward the natural law in Christian theology and philosophy—the object of the present survey—must be seen. One may suitably begin with the dissatisfaction, already mentioned, of Catholic moral theologians with the natural law as it had been expounded by their predecessors.[7] Charles E. Curran, in a recent survey of Catholic moral theology classifies the reactions of the moralists in three broad categories:

> There are some who reject any change in the methodology or the practical conclusions of the manuals of moral theology. . . . Some have abandoned the concept of natural law altogether and adopted newer and different methodologies; while others, retaining the concept of natural law, have tried to show how the manuals departed from the true natural law approach of the past as seen now in better appreciation of the exact position adopted by Aquinas and not the one espoused by later scholastics.[8]

The first and diminishing category need not, perhaps, detain us; the writers in the other two categories, however, will repay study if we want to understand the case for or against the natural law in the present day world. At first sight the authors mentioned by Curran do not appear to have much more in common than their rejection of the "manualist" conception of natural law. Those who reject the natural law as the basis for ethics differ on what is to replace it; in R.O. Johann it is a "relational moral model" acknowledging a dependence on pragmatism; in J.G. Milhaven it is a "love-ethic" resembling the situationism of Joseph Fletcher; in Pierre Antoine the impossibility of developing a model of man leads to the postulation of a "morality without anthropology"; in Herbert McCabe ethics is viewed as "language and communication which sees meaning in terms of ways of entering into social life and ways of being with each other"; W. van der Marck looks for a phenomenological basis for morality; and Enda McDonagh has "outlined a moral theology built upon reflection on the experience of the moral call in the human situation." The fluidity of the topic of the natural law today is further illustrated by the bewildering kaleidoscope of opinions, identi-

fied as misconceptions needing correction, listed by those who claim
to return to the pristine notion:

> . . . abstractionism (which undertakes "to pull all its moral
> precepts like so many magician's rabbits out of the meta-
> physical hat of an abstract human essence"); intuitionism
> (which regards *all* natural imperatives as self-evident); le-
> galism (which reduces the natural law to a detailed code
> "nicely drawn up with the aid of deductive logic alone,
> absolutely normative in all possible circumstances, ready
> for automatic application"); immobilism (which denies
> the historicity of the human person); biologism (which
> confuses brute facticity with the normatively natural); ra-
> tionalism (an "alleged deafness to the resonances of
> intersubjectivity")[9]

One might indeed conclude that a concept that provokes such
varied reactions can hardly be written off without further ado. But
equally it might be said that the evidence points to an ineradicable
ambiguity and that, despite its long history, the natural law is an
idea we are better off without. Both of these conclusions seem to cut
off the debate, or at least to be premature. There is a third possibility,
which it is proposed to explore, namely that the attack upon and the
defense of the natural law have a good deal in common. If this
paradox be true, then the truth about the natural law must be sought
on that common ground.

The attack upon the natural law, with all its contemporary insights and new terminology, adds little that is specifically new to old
arguments founded upon the ambiguity of "nature" and of "law"
and upon the evident fact of moral variations. The rehabilitation of
the natural law, on the other hand, stresses the historicity of human
nature and human existence and rejects the naiveté of moral formulations in the past that failed to account for, or worse still excluded,
this dimension of the human. Let us look, in turn, at the landmarks
of this middle ground between supporters and opponents of the
natural law.

II.
THE AMBIGUITY OF "NATURE" AND OF "LAW"

It is a commonplace that the idea of "human nature" fares poorly in the philosophies of today—existentialism, logical positivism, marxism, evolutionism, scientific humanism—and the general attack need not be documented here once again.[10] It should be noticed, however, that the current defense of the natural law accepts much of this critique of "nature"—and blames eighteenth century rationalism for having imported a rigidity and an unreality into what had been a much more flexible concept in the great scholastic treatises on the natural law. This acceptance of the basic insights of contemporary thought, critical of any "unchanging, static schematizations" or any "abstract, individualistic concept of man" is neither recent nor confined to Catholic theologians defending a new kind of natural law.[11] It will be instructive to examine some of the rubrics under which this discussion of human nature is carried on.

a) "Biological" Human Nature

A widespread criticism of neo-scholastic conceptions of natural law has been that they are based on a physical or biological idea of human nature, or that they assign a biological or physical structure to certain human actions independently of the function of reason. Hans Küng in his book *Infallible?* makes the point with some trenchancy:

> They (the majority on the Papal Commission on Birth Control) found that the Encyclical's (*Humanae Vitae*) arguments based on natural law were not convincing, that its concept of what is natural is naive, is static, narrow and completely unhistorical, that it ignores man's historicity, that it dissects him in the light of an abstract conception of his nature, that the restriction of the concepts of nature and natural law to the physical and biological sphere is a regression to the long obsolete Aristotelian, Stoic and medi-

eval idea; that the distinction between natural and artificial is arbitrary (and becomes a matter for the microscope
and of milligrams).[12]

This criticism makes a number of points, the most notable, particularly as it regards the contraception controversy, being that the concept of human nature is unduly restricted to the biological dimension of man's being. And one must recall that one of the most
influential definitions of the natural law, extending from the Roman
law through medieval philosophy down almost to modern times,
was that of the jurist Ulpian—"natural law is what nature has taught
all animals."[13] Contemporary writers are not inclined to take Ulpian's definition at its face value—nor, for that mater, were the
medievals unaware of the paradox it presents—but something of its
influence can be detected in some now discredited natural law arguments, as, for instance, the one based upon the supposition that
every frustration of a natural function is wrong.

St. Thomas, like his contemporaries, was impressed by the authority of Ulpian's definition, featuring prominently in the Corpus
of Justinian. The conciliatory approach of theologians to such authorities, interpreting and explaining—even explaining away—
rather than rejecting outright, seems to explain sufficiently his use of
Ulpian. His bias is certainly toward a natural law of reason, not a
biological natural law; but there is, in the last resort, something a
little puzzling in his preference for Ulpian's definition.[14] His contemporaries and successors were faced with some of the awkward consequences of the definition—how to explain, for example, that
marriage relations are "natural" whereas fornication is "unnatural." Of obscure origins, Ulpian's definition owes its longevity in the
history of the natural law to its conspicuous adoption in the codification of Roman law under Justinian. But, even though it has hardly
been taken seriously as a definition since the seventeenth century,
this does not mean that what John Courtney Murray has described
as "the particularly gross and gratuitous misinterpretation" which
"imputes to natural law theory a confusion of the 'primordial' in a
biological sense, with the 'natural' " has been altogether aban-
doned.[15] If natural law is seen as the quest for an objective or ontological basis for morals—and the alternatives are seen to be subjec-

tivity and relativism—there will always be a danger of taking what is close to hand, namely the physical nature of man or the biological structure of certain of his acts, and making an absolute of what should be seen to be, in an important sense, relative. The contraception controversies of recent years have simply drawn attention to the danger. This ever-present danger is only avoided by appeal to some other criterion, which allows us to say which of the features of man's physical nature are important for morals and which are not, which biological structures in his actions impose an obligation and which do not. Tertullian, arguing from the premise that what God had not created must not be produced by man, concluded that purple or blue sheep were wrong! And elsewhere he condemned the use of floral garlands on the ground that what was created to be looked at and to give fragrance was being put to another and unnatural use.[16] It is easy to see the absurdity of such conclusions; but it is not so easy to provide the criterion that will enable us to distinguish between the structures that are ethically relevant and those that are not.

It may be thought that too much importance is being given to refuting a conception of natural law that has such obvious limitations. The matter, however, is not as simple as might appear. Recently a much more sophisticated notion of natural law, linking it to the "natural inclinations" in man, has attracted support—but it looks as though the arguments against the "biological" natural law militate against this too.

The question of the natural inclinations was raised by J.T. Arntz in his study of the development of natural law thinking within Thomism.[17] He distinguishes between the material and the formal aspects of the natural law in St. Thomas. The formal aspect is the rational one; St. Thomas' answer to the question: what for man are the precepts of the natural law? is that its first principles are known by reason, although non-discursively. The material aspect is given in *Summa theologiae,* 1–2,94,2—"All that toward which man has a natural inclination, reason naturally apprehends as good . . . the order of the precepts of the natural law follows that of the natural inclinations." The passage is, of course, the *locus classicus*—and it has been variously seen as epitomizing St. Thomas' thought on the natural law or as the source of all the conflicting interpretations of his thought. Arntz remarks that the passage makes more sense for the historical than for the systematic thinker. Historically, Thomas is seen to be reconciling, as was his wont, schemata of his predecessors, in this case that of Johannes Teutonicus the canonist, who brought the natural inclinations into relationship with the natural law and William of Auxerre the theologian, who insisted upon the universality of the natural law. Thomas' listing of the inclinations that man has as substance, as animal and as rational makes the most of both Teutonicus and Auxerre; and it has the additional advantage of accommodating Ulpian's definition. For the systematic thinker however, there are some unresolved difficulties. What exactly are these *inclinationes naturales?* Are they to be taken at the level of psychology? Or is there an underlying metaphysical reality? And, if so, are the inclinations themselves normative, or do they point to something else which, *solitarie sumptum* (Cajetan's phrase adopted by Arntz) may be good, but whose opposite in given circumstances may be—even must be—chosen?[18] It is, as Arntz points out, a capital question; for upon the answer to it depends the characterization of the natural law as essentially reason or essentially (biological, physical) nature. One view makes reason merely record and follow the order of nature—not at all an impossible view but one unlikely to have been St. Thomas', the alternative is to see in the natural inclinations a field into which man's reason introduces an order.[19]

In his study of the mistaken interpretations of St. Thomas[20] Arntz discovers four competing conceptions of the natural law, linking it respectively with the order of the cosmos (Ulpian), with the psycho-physical nature of man (the moralists of the late nineteenth and early twentieth centuries), with the metaphysical nature of man (Gabriel Vazquez) or with *ratio ut natura* (William of Auxerre and St. Thomas). The last he believes to be the correct view; and the misinterpretations of Thomas start with Vitoria.

Franz Böckle takes up the issue of the natural inclinations, as used by the moral theologians of this century in their arguments about the natural law and as they appear in documents of the Church magisterium. The adjectives "natural" and "unnatural" as applied to human actions refer to a biological structure, to an "inner-organic teleology" or an "immanent natural teleology" which ultimately go back to a physiological-biological understanding of human nature. Böckle recognizes the core of truth here, but insists that it cannot be the entire truth. Man's essence includes his body—man is not man without a body—and the bodily structure may not be arbitrarily treated. On the other hand this bodily structure does not of itself provide the ethical norm; that involves man's understanding of himself, in his individual and social nature.[21] It amounts to saying that there is no ethical norm, fully written out in nature and available for our inspection; for man himself has a share in the writing. This is not to say that a general pattern of man's moral conduct may not be derived from observation of "existential human ends," the "ends inherent in the tendencies and propensities of human nature."[22] But it remains true that the genuinely natural tendencies (and ends) must be identified; and some solution must be found for the cases of conflict—or apparent conflict—between natural ends.

An excellent example of the traditional treatment of the natural inclinations is found in Johannes Messner's *Social Ethics*[23]—detailed, persuasive and, one may say, optimistic.

> Man proceeds to the understanding of his own nature and its specific functions in the same way that he learns to understand the nature and functions of other things, namely, by the apprehension of the ends inherent in their tendencies and propensities.[24]

This does not require a detailed knowledge of the mode of working of all the functions in man but only of the essentials of his biological and spiritual nature. Messner's list of the existential ends of man is very comprehensive—self-preservation, bodily integrity, social respect, personal honor, self-perfection spiritually and physically, development of man's faculties, provision for one's economic welfare, including necessary property and income, enlargement of experience, knowledge and receptivity of the values of beauty, self-propagation, benevolent interest in the spiritual and material well-being of one's fellow-man, social fellowship, the establishing of peace and order, control of the forces of nature, knowledge and worship of the Creator and the ultimate fulfillment of oneself in union with Him.[25] And toward the end of the discussion there is the significant phrase: "it is well to mention that our discussion will show the impossibility of ultimate conflict between existential ends and thus between actual duties and rights."[26]

More recent writers are more aware of the difficulties in establishing the foundation of morality on the natural inclinations—more aware, perhaps, of the difficulty already seen by St. Thomas but unnoticed by some of his modern followers. Germain Grisez, for instance, having said that empirical enquiry, mainly by psychologists, has come to a remarkable consensus on what are the natural inclinations, gives the list

> which can be summarized as follows. Man's fundamental inclinations are: the tendency to preserve life, especially by food-seeking and by self-defensive behaviour; the tendency to mate and to raise his children; the tendency to seek certain experiences which are enjoyed for their own sake; the tendency to develop skills and to exercise them in play and the fine arts; the tendency to explore and question; the tendency to seek out the company of other men and to try to gain their approval; the tendency to try to establish good relationships with unknown higher powers; and the tendency to use intelligence in guiding action.[27]

The ends of these tendencies are goods and apprehended as such by the practical reason which, in its first principle underlying all human action, tells us that good must be done and evil avoided. Grisez pays a great deal of attention to the notion of practical reason—which, indeed, is an inescapable one in the present context—but one feels that, like Messner, he is optimistic about man's ability to identify the natural tendencies and about the absence of conflict (although he allows that man must choose between the goods indicated by the natural tendencies) between them.[28]

Probably the most ambitious effort to rehabilitate the natural inclinations in the context of natural law is that of Dario Composta.[29] His book is divided into three parts. The first part studies the natural inclinations from the historical point of view, in the Greeks, particularly Aristotle and the Stoics, in Christian thought from the Fathers down to the Silver Age of scholasticism, and in the natural law theorists of the seventeenth and eighteenth centuries. The second part is a psychological study of which the argument is that psychology alone cannot explain human inclinations—the fact that man's tendencies, instincts, drives, impulses escape psychological explanation is either acknowledged expressly or is deducible from the uncertainties, obscurities and contradictions in the various theories proposed. The third part of the work is a systematic study of human inclinations in relation to the natural law. Composta's basic position is that the natural law is known through the natural inclinations and is based ontologically upon them.

An important part of his case is that the only appropriate methodology for the study of the natural inclinations is philosophical. He calls it, perhaps a little unfortunately, the classical metaphysical method—for he concedes that the charge most frequently laid against this method is that it is "naturalistic and too much linked to biology."[30] He explains the method, however, as "inductive-ontological"; it is inductive in that it is based upon the concrete, existential experience of the human individual; and ontological in that the entirety of the real basis for inclinations and not, for example, part, such as consciousness, or structure or other aspects studied by methods that are psychological or purely empirical, is taken.

In the event the "classical metaphysical method" is used to face the two main problems concerning the natural inclinations, the gnoseological (how are they identified?) and the metaphysical (what is their ontological standing?). Composta's argument is wide-ranging and offers many valuable clarifications. Particularly valuable is his discussion of the three basic inclinations, as listed by Aquinas in the *Summa theologiae* 1–2, 94, 2, toward life, toward propagation and toward rationality.[31] But it cannot be said that he has solved the central issue of what, in the last resort, constitutes a natural inclination; is an inclination natural because reasonable or reasonable because natural? His concluding phrase about a reciprocal dynamic irradiation of reason and nature[32] looks very like having it both ways. To have recognized the danger of biologism is, unfortunately, no guarantee of having escaped it.

b) "Metaphysical" Human Nature

If "biological" human nature runs into difficulties as the basis for the natural law the same may be said, and with much more justice, of "metaphysical" human nature. This is a label of convenience under which may be grouped various conceptions of nature attacked in contemporary discussions of the natural law. The notorious ambiguity of the word "nature" in general and in the context of natural law forms the background to these attacks.[33] As a broad generalization it may be said that, from a variety of standpoints, contemporary writers reject the so-called "Platonic essence" thought to lie behind formulations of a natural moral law.

1) Science and Human Nature

For over a century the theory of evolution has been undermining the idea of an unchangeable human nature; and the process is accentuated in the sophisticated variation of the theory propounded by the late Julian Huxley and the many scientific humanists who follow him. In this version man now finds himself able to understand and to control the evolutionary process.[33a] The ethical question, of course, is: in what direction, to what end, shall the evolutionary process be directed? And the answer cannot be a natural law answer; for human nature itself is being re-shaped. Those who are supporters of a theory of natural law must, therefore, look farther afield for their criterion. And such may be found; but not in a concept of human nature made familiar by modern positive science. For the moment it will suffice to point out that it is not merely the theory of evolution, and its modern corollaries, that present the difficulty; modern science and technology appear to be radically opposed to anything like the traditional concept of a natural moral law.

The scientist takes the view that "human nature will continue to evolve mostly through the mass effect of applied science in transforming human subjectivity."[34] P. Heelan, from whom this sentence is taken, had begun his article by distinguishing between the two meanings of " 'nature' sedimented in common usage: one opposes it to the man-made; the other opposes it to mind or spirit, the domain of meaning, culture and values. The former meaning is Aristotelian-Christian and the latter is born of the scientific movement of the fifteenth and sixteenth centuries and issuing in the progressive mathematicizing and geometricizing of nature." The alliance of the traditional concept of natural law with the former meaning of nature puts it at a disadvantage vis-à-vis modern science. The difficulty is felt in its acuteness when one contemplates the possibilities now opened before mankind by science and technology; or, to use more moral terms, when one looks at the rate at which science-fiction becomes fact before our eyes and without, in the great majority of cases, any reference to the ethical issues that are involved. Such issues range from nuclear and other kinds of environmental pollution to interference in the human genetic process. Ultimately man is regarded as the subject, not of philosophical, but of bio-technical and anthropological study.[35] This is a factor that the moralist and the theologian cannot neglect; it lies behind a celebrated statement of Karl Rahner, which will be seen in its place with the theological developments concerning the natural law.

2) Sociology and Human Nature

"Among modern sociologists, the reputation of natural law is not high. The phrase conjures up a world of absolutisms, of theological fiat, of fuzzy, unoperational 'mystical' ideas, of thinking uninformed by history and by the variety of human situations." So Philip Selznick begins his essay on "Natural Law and Sociology"—which turns out to be a plea for cooperation, for "sociology should have a ready affinity for the philosophy of natural law."[36] The bad name the natural law has with sociologists is easily documented.[37] Erich Fechner, for instance, summarizes his case against the natural law by saying that sociology has simply removed the basis upon which it was built; as present day man can no longer bow to instinct or to the image of the gods or the heroes of the past or the universal and convincing rules of revealed religion, he must in future look, for the regulation of his life, to the model uncovered by sociological investigation.[38] The same point—that norms depend upon cultural situations—and that those situations are studied by the sociologist, is made by Franz Böckle.[39]

What is true of the sociologist is true also of the anthropologist. The anthropologist studies the moral ideas of a given culture and raises the difficulty—thought to be fatal to the idea of a natural law—of their transfer to another culture. There is here a serious difficulty; but hardly fatal to a properly-nuanced concept of the natural law. For one of the benefits of the advances in studies, such as those of the anthropologists, has been to make it very unlikely that a modern proponent of a natural moral law would fall into the mistake of taking for eternal and universal what is, in fact, temporal and culturally-conditioned. And even the specific problem of the transfer of ideas across cultural barriers is capable of solution, as may be seen, for example, in a recent discussion of ideas of E.E. Evans-Pritchard and Alasdair MacIntyre by Peter Winch.[40] And an even more optimistic view of the relationship between such studies and the natural law is argued by Philip Selznick in the article already referred to. The obstacles to the natural law on the part of sociology are seen as 1) the insistence that facts and values be not confused and 2) the moral relativism implied in sociological studies. With regard to the first of these, Selznick argues that the separation of fact and value, itself a useful principle in its place, has been taken to unreasonable lengths in excluding the study of moral ideas, such as that of a natural law. And with regard to the second, he points out that

> radical conclusions regarding human nature and moral rel-
> ativism are neither well-grounded in theory nor truly sup-
> ported by the empirical evidence. In particular, the argu-
> ment from cultural diversity is at best inconclusive.[41]

The technical arguments from sociology and anthropology may prove, after all not unanswerable. There are, however, similar arguments, more intractable because more philosophical, which may be considered under the label of convenience "phenomenology."

3) Phenomenology and Human Nature

William Luijpen's *Phenomenology of Natural Law*[42] opens with a chapter on the difficulties facing the latterday defender of the natural law, "The Ever-Recurring Dilemma." It is, however, in a later chapter, "The Thomistic Doctrine of the Natural Law," that the fullest expression of the difficulties is to be found; for, in underlining what he sees as the defects of Thomistic presentation of the natural law, Luijpen indicates the demands made by phenomenology on the elaboration of the concept. He speaks, it should be said at once, of Thomism and not of St. Thomas himself.

The criticism begins from the suggestion that the Thomistic doctrine of natural law overrates the possibility of talking about God and notably forgets God's transcendence in the detail of what is said to be His law. This raises the question about the need for God in a theory of natural law, a question that need not be examined here. One can agree with Luijpen's rejection of the *deus ex machina,* God as a way out of a philosophical impasse.[43] Luijpen's own view is that Thomistic ethics is perfectly capable of being truly philosophical even if it speaks of God, that to speak of God as the legislator of the natural law is not to renounce speculation about that law—quite the contrary. It is, however, true that some Thomists have misused terminology, that needs careful weighing:

> If we look now at the way in which Thomism bases the natural law on God, we are struck by the reckless abandon with which the necessary terms are used. According to Bender, who is a Thomist, "God has given wings to swallows." He "wills that animals eat," He has "given all kinds of things to man"; God "made birds and wanted them to fly." He has inserted the natural law into man's life because He wanted man to "have means at his disposal" to reach his ends; "in God's mind there exists a plan that expresses the order of all things to their end," and "all things tend to their own actions and ends through an imprint of God's Eternal Law." When this author wants to state clearly that God orientates actions to an end by Himself and is in no way oriented to anything else as His end, he says that God's purposive action is not "as the action of Peter who eats to remain healthy" but is "as the action of Peter who *makes* his horse eat in order that it remain healthy."

Such a way of speaking about God is naive to the point of being scandalous. If one cannot *unqualifiedly* say that God "is," then likewise one cannot blandly assert that "God directs creatures and their actions to an end to be attained" *just as* Peter directs his horse to the eating of its food.[44]

Luijpen makes no allowance for pedagogic necessities; but it must be confessed that sound doctrine easily becomes impoverished when it is filtered into text-books. His criticism here is well-based. And the difficulty runs deeper than the unfortunate terminology in which the doctrine is expressed. For the question really is whether the purpose of nature is written in nature in such a way that man can read it there.

Some, like Jean-Paul Sartre in *Existentialisme est un humanisme,* have cut this Gordian knot; if one does not accept the existence of God, the Divine artificer, the trace of whose finger may be sought in His creation, there is little more to be said on this question. But one may well accept that God does exist and is the Creator without having to sustain that the purpose of creation is written in a discernible way in creatures—and certainly not written in detail sufficient to settle the cases of moral controversy. It may, for example, be true that in many cases the purpose of nature may be read with some assurance—as the purpose of eating is to sustain life or that of sexual relations to propagate the species. But the question immediately arises as to whether there are not other purposes too— the companionship at a meal, the expression of mutual love in sexual relations; and the further question whether these purposes should not be achieved, in given circumstances, even at the expense of the former. That the question arises is clear from the most cursory acquaintance with current controversy about contraception; and the point is that it is not settled by mere inspection of "nature." Luijpen reinforces the point by reminding of the many and contradictory things advocated in the past on the basis of "nature's intentions." Slavery is a case among many. Statements in St. Thomas, and in the theologians at the time of the conquest of America by the Spaniards, make curious reading in our age of human freedoms. Another example is the justification of the existing social and economic order in the nineteenth century (the age of Marx) as the *natural* order. Or, in its time, feudalism. Or the marriage patterns, such as polygamy, opposed in the name of *natural* monogamy. To arrive at the truth in such questions requires much more than the search for something already inscribed in nature.[45]

But to return to the phenomenological objection. Luijpen argues that when a Thomist proponent of natural law appeals to "nature" and the "natural" he may well be mistaken—for the "reading" of nature is not a simple procedure—and, if mistaken, his doctrine becomes a camouflaged legal positivism. Here the divergent meanings for "nature" have full scope; not merely institutions like private property or community of possessions, but man's nakedness (for nature has not clothed him—*Summa theologiae,* 1-2, 94, 5 ad 3), the orientation of the sexual act to procreation, the "natural" authority of husband over wife . . . The list is disparate, deliberately so; and while items in it can be disputed, and Luijpen may be accused of unfairness in his presentation, there is certainly a case to be met. It is arguable that upholders of the natural law appeal to a radically unverifiable concept and that, insofar as it can be verified, it refers to time- and culture-conditioned features of human existence rather than to the timeless and unconditioned aspects it claims to represent.

Here is the kernel of the phenomenological distrust of the natural law. Natural law is vitiated by a basic failure to take account of the fact that man's nature is affected by his existence, that "history" is present in the kind of being a human is, that

> it is utterly foreign to man's real essence to represent matters as if the man who lived half a million years ago was merely a primitive edition of the cultured man of the twentieth century. Today's civilized man is the result of a long intersubjective history, of which positive anthropology and ethnology show us the origin.[46]

Precisely because this historicity of man is not taken account of, the norms of natural law are invested with characters of universality and immutability and the difficulty arising from the observable departures from these standards is ingeniously explained as defective knowledge of human nature and not as resulting from "a different mode of being of that nature and its orientations."[47] In a word, the objection to the "Thomistic" natural law is that it is "objectivist." There is an "objectivism" that needs to be asserted in order to avoid falling into arbitrariness; but excessive stress loses sight of the fact that human knowledge is a mixture of the objective and the subjective and that emphasis on the objective truth "out there" leads, in the last resort, to a Platonic doctrine of essences and, in morals— more dangerously—to impression of being in possession of absolute truth, the situation in which, in the words of Merleau-Ponty, "I piously kill my opponents."[48]

4) Theology and Human Nature

The phenomenological considerations just outlined underlie a good deal of the current theological speculation about human nature and natural law. It has more than once been observed that many of the present day difficulties in theology are fundamentally philosophical; in which context it is of interest to recall Karl Rahner's saying that the natural law calls the whole of philosophy in question.[49]

The phenomenologist point that the classical doctrine of natural law is based upon an unhistorical and indefensible conception of human nature is taken by, among others, Charles Curran. Speaking of changing theological methodology, he contrasts the "abstract, *a priori* and a historical" world-view with "the historical, the contingent, the personal and the existential" and traces the defects of the "classical" natural law to the preponderance of the former view in moral theology of the past:

> A classicist methodology tends to favor the existence of absolute, abstract, universal norms in moral theology. . . . A more historically conscious methodology will not be able to seek the absolute certitude of unchanging universal essences. A change in methodology will have to reflect the best aspects of both approaches, but the greater importance attached to a historically conscious methodology will necessarily mean less emphasis on the existence of absolute norms which are binding in all circumstances.[50]

John Macquarrie expresses the same view: "The traditional moral theology was too strongly tied to the notion of a fixed, essential human nature, set in the midst of a static hierarchically ordered universe." Moral theology and natural law must consider "the man of the modern age, caught up in rapid change" and must bow to the fact that, since man's understanding of himself is part of his existence, "the existent man himself changes too."[51] And, not to multiply authorities, the view is repeated in Wolfhart Pannenberg and others.[52]

The dissatisfaction with the "moral theology of the manuals" is, however, older than these expressions of it. Nor should it be thought that this new chapter in the history of moral theology is negative in character, based upon criticism of what has gone before. It can be said that the progressive isolation of moral theology from dogmatic and its too close alliance with canon law helped to limit its perspectives and make of it a study of sin rather than a study of virtue. It is no accident that words like "casuistry" and "legalism" have today an almost inescapably pejorative connotation. It would be too much to say that all the manuals of a generation ago were excessively preoccupied with legalities and prohibitions. But, on the whole, they cannot be said to have done justice by a noble discipline. The great scholastic moral theologians would have had little use for some of the pettifogging discussion of minutiae that passed for moral theology within living memory. There were, of course, the exceptions; the moral theologies, for instance, based upon the plan of the virtues rather than upon the schema of the Ten Commandments and the precepts of the Church. And, on the other hand, one is well aware that there must be legislation, even in morals; that Christ came, not to destroy the Decalogue but to fulfill; and that, as well as the Sermon on the Mount, there is needed, if the Church is to survive and to function as a society, a body of legislation to protect Revelation and the sacramental order. Yet, all this being understood, moral theology failed.

The failure was seen by authors like Tillman, Mersch, Leclercq and others in the 1930's and 1940's,[53] some of whom experienced the penalty of being in advance of their time (sometimes more severe than the penalty of being wrong)! The author who best succeeded in capturing this *Zeitgeist* in moral theology was Bernhard

Häring, whose *Das Gesetz Christi* (1954) has often been taken as the charter of new moral theology. It might better be described as the systematic putting to work of the *re-sourcement* that had already been going on in moral theology—the return to its sources, notably the Bible. And this has inevitably had the result of concentrating interest on the more positive and personal, concrete and historical aspects of the Christian moral teaching. In this perspective the natural law—or rather the classical interpretation of the natural law—fares poorly in spite of Scriptural references to it, including the *locus classicus* in *Romans* 2:14–15.

Here two questions properly arise. The first is concerned with the relation between natural law and the Gospel and may be examined briefly; the second, concerning the magisterium of the Church and the natural law, may be postponed.

One of the theological objections to the natural law is that, even if the concept can be made philosophically respectable, it must still fall short of what Christian morality expresses. So, for instance, F.S. Carney:

> ... the content of natural law is different from or falls short of the insights of Christian morality. It is said that, even if natural law were so conceived that its content were identical to the insights of Christian morality, action according to it would be considerably frustrated because of its failure to give adequate attention to the impairments of radical sin. It is said that action according to natural law arises from a different and less satisfactory motivation than that of appropriate Christian responsiveness of God's creating, saving and sustaining grace. It is said, finally, that natural law doctrine lacks the supporting context of the Christian church that characterizes Christian morality, especially the shared communal experience of judgment, confession, forgiveness and moral guidance.[54]

How can the natural law, by very definition a secular concept, do justice to the Christian scheme of things? When all is said and done, is the natural law not simply a watering down of the ethical teaching of the New Testament?[55] This is ground that has been fought over almost since the time when St. Paul excoriated the Romans for their sexual depravity; that they had not had the benefit of Revelation was no excuse, for they had the chidings of their conscience to guide them. The question was again posed by Gratian, in the twelfth century, in a definition of natural law that dominated the *Corpus Juris Canonici*—natural law is what is found in the Law and the Gospel.[56] It was posed, in yet another way, in the twentieth century controversy about the possibility of a Christian philosophy. Gilson has found the notion of "philosophising within Christianity" a useful schema for explaining the thought of the great schoolmen; and Maritain, in contemporary terms, argued that to neglect the supernatural is to neglect the most important dimension in human existence. Adequate philosophizing means taking account of the highest and the most important truth, available to us in Revelation; and if this does not fit the technical definition of philosophy, then so much the worse for philosophy—let's talk instead of Christian wisdom. More particularly, as regards the natural law, "pure human nature" is an abstraction of the philosophers. It never really existed—the nature of man was either elevated in original justice, or fallen by original sin and in need of redemption. In either case supernatural grace is relevant—and does it not render nature almost irrelevant?[57]

One answer to this objection is that given by Johannes Messner. He points out that "Christian moral law differs from natural moral law in that the latter is given to man through natural revelation, the former through supernatural revelation."[58] This is, of course, simply a special case of the distinction between theology and philosophy. Messner goes on to say that "In the Ten Commandments, confirmed and expounded in the teaching of Christ and the apostles, there is laid down no more than the natural law itself contains." What, then, one might ask, is the scope of Revelation?

> Supernatural revelation provides man with the full and clear understanding of his true nature, so that he may not mistake for natural in human existence what is really owing to the impairment of his nature for his whole nature. For supernatural revelation informs man unmistakably of the spiritual character of his soul, of its immortality, of his eternal destiny, of God as man's Creator and Judge, last End and highest Good.[59]

The snare of making a radical distinction between a natural law independent of revelation and a supplementary natural law for Christians is not one into which Messner falls. That it is a snare had been pointed out long ago by Jacques Leclercq[60] who spoke of distinguishing, in a particular precept, between what is natural and what comes from revelation (whether as an added force of obligation or as presenting a new situation to which a natural precept must apply). But it is not easy to say just how much is natural and how much goes beyond nature—think of the difficulty, or impossibility, of disentangling notions like the natural equality of men and the spiritual fraternity of Christians, the natural unity and indissolubility of marriage and the obligations arising out of the Christian sacrament, the rights and duties of parents in education and the supernatural obligation of handing on the Faith and so forth.

The problem remains, although it is not discussed today in quite those terms. Leclercq and Messner see very well that there cannot be any question of two human natures—one a pure human nature regulated by the natural law and the other human nature elevated by grace and illuminated by revelation. The implications of this are drawn out more fully in a writer like Josef Fuchs who sees the natural law as naturally cognoscible while having regard to a human nature that is supernaturalized. But the elements of nature and supernature require careful delineation. An obligation may be known by reference to man's nature—but we cannot tell its precise contour until we consider man's situation in a supernatural order.[61] The historicity of human existence includes, above all, the supernatural order; and the problems posed for the natural law by man's situation in grace resemble those posed by his situation in culture and in history, in space and in time. These are the problems that prompted Karl Rahner, in his brief, sometimes cryptic and highly influential note on the natural law, to recommend a transcendental method of study to do justice to the nature of man.[62] We shall return to this in the concluding section of this paper.

c) The Question of "Law"

In the past the claim of the natural law to be genuinely a law has often proved a stumbling-block; and now, it appears, unnecessarily.

Positivist legal philosophers tended to allow that moral or religious principles—or ideologies—may be relevant to law-making and law-interpretation but regarded it as provocative when such systems of ideas claimed to be "law," and superior law at that. It is nowadays abundantly clear that, no less than the word "nature," the word "law" is Janus-headed. There is no need to point the finger *des lois* gives the impression that the similarities between the Law of Gravitation and the moral law are more important than their differences;[63] it is a misunderstanding that much modern scholastic writing on the natural law found it difficult to avoid, stressing as it does the universality and uniformity of natural law. On the other hand, it is equally a misunderstanding to assert that an unjust civil law is not a law, on the ground that a law must, by definition, be just. This is to take too literally St. Thomas' famous phrase about the will of the prince, unregulated by right reason, being *magis iniquitas quam lex.*[63a] The disadvantages of having to fight a rearguard action in defense of the "legality" of natural law was long ago seen by writers like Jacques Leclercq and Odon Lottin, who can hardly be classified as other than defenders of the natural law. Leclercq suggests that St. Thomas' enthusiasm for synthesis carried him away when he put eternal law and natural law together with divine law and human law in the *Summa;* and in support he calls on Dom Lottin's observation that the Thomistic definition of law is analogical and, in order to apply to the natural law, in need of adaptation in all its elements.[64]

This battle, however, it now seems is being fought in a new way; or, rather, the natural law has found unexpected allies and the battleground has altered. It is no longer regarded as necessary to demonstrate that the natural law is law, just like civil law, and of a superior kind that must take precedence over civil law. It transpires, on the other hand, that certain concepts enshrined in civil law—"legality" or "due process" or "equality before the law"—turn out to be very like, if not actually assimilable to, a doctrine of natural law. I.T. Ramsey, in an article already referred to, leans heavily for his thesis that the natural law can be rehabilitated in Christian ethics on H.L. A. Hart's well-known "Minimum Content of Natural Law."[65] And it is, indeed, striking that Hart should make such a case. It is not, however, the only natural law gesture (if the phrase may be used) in positivist legal literature. The chapter in which Hart expounds his minimum content of natural law is entitled: "Laws and Morals," and the earlier part is concerned with natural law and legal positivism. This reminds of the great debate about the enforcement of morals in which the principal protagonists were Hart himself and Lord Devlin; Devlin's *The Enforcement of Morals* (1959) which engendered the debate may be taken as a forceful exposition of the view that the law cannot abdicate a moral responsibility. This is, however, not the place to pursue this line or to argue that there is here another example of covert natural law thinking. But it can be asserted that what Hart and Devlin have been saying, despite their differences, has been said by many others in different ways before them—and from an ostensibly positivist standpoint.

Here reference must be made once again to Philip Selznick's essay, "Natural Law and Sociology,"[66] of which it might almost be said that the theme is that

> The sublety and scope of legal ideas and the variety of legal materials should give pause to any effort to define law within some simple formula. The attempt to find such a formula often leads to a disregard for more elusive parts of the law and excessive attention to specific rules.[67]

Selznick's handling of terms like "the rule of law," the "legal order," "legality," "judicial creativity" and "justice" itself (all of which, he points out, are value-terms and insufficiently investigated by sociology) is instructive. One might compare the approach with that of Aquinas to notions like those of "rationality" or "the common good" in connection with law. The point is that these concepts, doctrines or principles (however one may like to describe them) support the view that the legal order has "an implicit internal morality."[68] This, admittedly, begins discussion rather than ends it—for it must be possible to distinguish between good and bad law and to distinguish between the bad law that is merely bad policy and the bad law that violates, or only incompletely realizes, the ideals of legality. In a word—and here Selznick quotes Morris Cohen—it must be possible to appeal from the law that is to the law that ought to be, from positive law to the principles of justice.[69]

This is the area in which the natural law can play its part; and it is here incidentally that the relevance of sociology to the natural law is seen. If the proper aim of the legal order and the special contribution of legal scholarship are "progressively to reduce the degree of arbitrariness in the positive law," then the method of natural law "because it offers a rule, a guide to inquiry" is welcome. It is worth remarking that the placing of limits upon the arbitrary exercise of political or legislative power may well be said to have been the historical function of the doctrine of a natural law and, in fact, the thread of continuity linking its various forms in successive historical epochs.[70] And it should scarcely be necessary to add that the natural law Selznick has in mind is not a rigid pre-fabricated natural law but a flexible one. He affects the celebrated phrase of Rudolf Stammler —a natural law with "variable content"[71]—and indicates that in the natural law there is a "dialectic of continuity and change." The fact that the natural law varies is not tantamount to saying that it is arbitrary; natural law may presume changing legal norms, but this does not involve the abandonment of "the quest for universals or the assertion of them when they are warranted."[72] In a word, one must remember that, as the inquiry proceeds, it is always possible that the basic premises will be revised, and that, as society changes, new rules and doctrines are needed in order to give effect to natural law principles by adapting them to new demands, new circumstances, new opportunities. The net result is a conclusion, which can come as no surprise after the considerations seen in the earlier part of this paper concerning "human nature":

> These perspectives demand that we detach natural law from illusions of eternal stability.[73]

III.
A REHABILITATED NATURAL LAW?

It was suggested earlier in this paper that a common ground might be discovered between supporters and opponents of the natural law in our time. Some of that ground has been explored in what has gone before, mostly from the point of view of those who reject what they believe to be an outmoded concept of the natural law. It will be useful now, briefly and by way of conclusion, to look at some of the more positive efforts of contemporary theology to rehabilitate the natural law. In effect this means looking at the kind of answer that can be made to the most pervasive objection noted to the "traditional" natural law, the objection, to put it in a phrase, that it lacks historicity.

There is no doubt that many of the traditional expositions of the natural law—the "manualist" natural law—proceeded as if human nature had no history and were a non-temporal and imperceptible thing.[74] This, in a way, was its strength—its resistance to changes depending upon time and space seemed to guarantee a universality and an immutability that enabled it to sit in judgment on the temporal and the spatial in human conduct. But this no longer carries conviction. So many currents of contemporary thought, existentialism, personalist philosophies, phenomenology, agreeing in hardly anything else, proffer the insight that human existence is so conditioned by temporality and culture that moral theology can no longer isolate itself. The best complexion that can be placed on the older accounts of the natural law is that the emphasis was wrong, too much upon the qualities of universality and immutability believed to be necessary, and too little upon the subjectivity involved. The danger inherent in this one-sided emphasis was remarked upon in somewhat sybilline fashion by Karl Rahner, in the celebrated half-page article on the natural law in *Lexikon für Theologie und Kirche* already referred to.[75] F. Böckle makes the same point, stressing that nothing is more damaging to the proper founding of the natural law than falsely absolutizing of what is, in fact, relative to history and to culture.[76]

Historicity, then, is inescapably part and parcel of any conception of a natural law that is to have any chance of acceptance today. It has not been an easy lesson for theology to learn—but it is being learned, as seen from the variety of authors cited in the earlier part of this study.[77] One may take as an example the article by Johannes Gründel in *Sacramentum Mundi*.[78] In that article, Johannes Gründel remarks that natural law is usually elaborated with the help of and within the scope of the tract on law in the *Summa theologiae* of St. Thomas (1–2, 90–108)—but often with an unawareness of the subtlety and flexibility with which Thomas handles his concepts.

The static conception of human nature that emerged was all too vulnerable to the criticisms of our time. A closer reading of Aquinas would have helped; or indeed of the Scriptures, which give little encouragement to thinking in terms of an abstract nature of man. Man is a social being; and as social is involved in historical development; his actions cannot be judged by reference to an abstract metaphysical nature. Man's nature is part of the development—it is changing and man himself is in some way author of the change—which increases, not diminishes, man's responsibility. There is here, according to Rahner, need for a new "transcendental" method for the study of human nature and natural law.[79] And if it be asked how standards or criteria of behavior may be established on the basis of a changing nature, the answer must be that the recognition of the changing character of man's existence and the developments of human nature brings also the realization that there is the human subject of those changes.

This is not a quibble; here contemporary expositions, like that of Gründel, believe that they touch on the most profound truth in this matter. The moral theologian cannot neglect the historical changes in man and society, cannot dismiss them as accidental, because it is precisely these changes and possibilities of change that exhibit man's shaping as a human person. The development is not completed; nor can it be predicted which data will be of importance tomorrow for their effect upon the future development of human existence. And, finally, the knowledge of the natural law is itself an historical process.[80]

If this seems excessively radical, to be, in effect, the abandonment of any recognizable natural law, the impression will be corrected by a study of Gründel's approach to the vexed question of moral variations. This problem is not a discovery of our age—although historical, anthropological and cultural studies have given it a new urgency. St. Thomas, for example, was aware of the difficulty presented by moral variations—the different codes and different moral convictions depending upon time and place and circumstance—to a law making claims to universality and immutability. His explanations may be placed under three main headings: 1) the influence of the passions; 2) the unequal development of human reason; and 3) the diversity of background, situation and circumstance.[81] Modern upholders of the natural law, like Gründel, are saying the same thing, but with more insistence and in more sophisticated terminology. It is insisted, to begin with, that more precision is available—and demanded—in the expression of moral precepts. The auxiliary studies of anthropology and sociology help us to avoid the trap of an over-hasty identification of precepts as timeless and unchanging when, in fact, they are time-conditioned and culture-bound. One would be far more circumspect today than in the past in asserting, for instance, that private property is a matter of the natural law, or that to take interest on money is unnatural or that woman comes under the natural dominion of man.

Again, today's writer on the natural law is much more alive to the effects of changed situations on morals—the different function of money, for example, in a modern industrial and in a medieval rural economy; or the reality of warfare before and since the advent of nuclear weaponry, or before and since the (still rudimentary) organization of international authority; or capital punishment or the indissolubility of marriage against backgrounds of social complexity formerly unknown. But most importantly of all, there is the change in man himself. This consideration excites most suspicion—because it has been used to undermine the doctrine of a natural law. But it should be recalled that St. Thomas taught that human nature is changeable—*natura humana mutabilis est*—without, however, having to spell out this mutability in the detail required today.[82]

What remains, then, of the unalterable natural law? One can say that the moral law is unalterably the law of man's (changing) nature. Or if this appears too paradoxical, one may say with Bruno Schüller, that the only absolute is the connection between obligation and being, between *Sollen* and *Sein;* the correlation between man's duty and what man is does not decide the issue whether man's nature changes. This latter question is not one for ethics or moral theology at all, but for metaphysical anthropology.[83]

If it looks, then, as if many modern theologians and moralists are adopting a standpoint intermediate between absolutism and relativism, this does not spell the end of the natural law. It spells the end of a natural law based upon an eternal and unalterable human nature; but that natural law can no more resist the contemporary critique than the eighteenth century rationalist natural law could survive the onslaughts of the historical schools of the nineteenth century. The result is the great advantage of our being able to seek the true lineaments of the natural law—this is the positive sense of the "pursuit" of the natural law in the title of this article. It would be a great pity if the pursuit were to be confined to the negative operation of banishing an untenable concept of natural law or removing the assumptions, themselves incapable of being sustained, which supported it.

Notes

1. S. Hauerwas, "Natural Law, Tragedy and Theological Ethics" in *American Journal of Jurisprudence,* 20 (1975), p. 1. Cf. I.T. Ramsey, "Towards a Rehabilitation of Natural Law" in *Christian Ethics and Contemporary Philosophy,* London, 1966, pp. 382–396, especially pp. 383–385.

2. The 3rd 1932 edition, translated by K. Wilk as *Legal Philosophy,* is in *20th Century Legal Philosophies,* vol. IV, Harvard, 1950, pp. 47–224; the 4th German edition appeared in Stuttgart, 1950 and the 5th (edited by E. Wolf after the author's death) in 1956, also at Stuttgart.

3. "Die Erneuerung des Rechts" in *Die Wandlung,* 2 (1947), pp. 8–16, reprinted in W. Maihofer (ed.) *Naturrecht oder Rechtspositivismus,* Darmstadt, 1972, pp. 1–10; cf. L.R. Ward, "Natural Law in Contemporary Legal Philosophy" in *Proceedings of the American Catholic Philosophical Association,* 1959, p. 141 R.D. Lumb, "Law, Reason and Will" in *Philosophical Studies,* 10 (1960), pp. 186–189.

4. So, for example, L.C. Midgley, *Beyond Human Nature: The Contemporary Debate over Moral Natural Law,* Brigham Young University Press, 1968, pp. 53–63.

5. W. Luijpen, *Phenomenology of Natural Law,* Pittsburgh, 1967, p. 27.

6. G.E. Langmeijer, "Philosophie du droit" in *Philosophy in the Mid-Century* (ed. R. Klibansky), Firenze, 1958, Vol. II, p. 247. The neo-scholastics will be referred to in what follows. The leading neo-Kantians in this matter are Hans Kelsen (b. 1881), Rudolf Stammler (1856–1938) and Giorgio Del Vecchio (1878–1970); of these the most "objective" is Del Vecchio; it is debatable whether Kelsen's *reine Rechtslehre* and Stammler's *Naturrecht mit wechselndem Inhalt* really amount to assertions of natural

law. The "sociological" natural law may be represented by Roscoe Pound (1870–1964) and the positivist leaning toward natural law by H.L.A. Hart's "minimum content" theory of natural law in his *The Concept of Law,* Oxford, 1961, ch. 9. On the climate of the post-war decades see D. Composta, *Natura e ragione,* Zurich, 1971, p. 9.

7. Cf. E. McDonagh, "Moral Theology and the Need for Renewal" in *Moral Theology Renewed,* Dublin, 1965, pp. 13–30; id., *Invitation and Response,* Dublin, 1972, p. vii: "The developments which have taken place over the past fifteen years in the discipline known as 'moral theology' within the Roman Catholic Church are at least so far-reaching as to make the manuals in near-universal use even ten years ago almost entirely irrelevant now."

8. "Catholic Moral Theology Today" in *New Perspectives in Moral Theology,* Notre Dame, 1974, p. 6. This essay appeared in slightly different form as "Moral Theology: The Present State of the Discipline" in *Theological Studies,* 34 (1973).

9. R. McCormick, "Human Significance and Christian Significance" in G.H. Outka and P. Ramsey (ed.) *Norm and Context in Christian Ethics,* London, 1969, p. 239. McCormick refers to J.C. Murray's *We Hold These Truths: Catholic Reflections on the American Proposition,* New York, 1960, pp. 295–296 and to Murray's remark (op. cit., p. 298)—"I list these misunderstandings of natural law only to make the point that those who dislike the doctrine, for one reason or another, seem forever to be at work, as it were, burying the wrong corpse. For my part, I would not at all mind standing with them, tearless, at the grave of any of the shallow and distorted theories that they mistake for the doctrine of natural law."

10. M.B. Crowe, "Natural Law Theory Today" in *The Future of Ethics and Moral Theology,* Chicago, 1968, pp. 78–81.

11. W. Pannenberg, "Toward a Theology of Law" in *Anglican Theological Review,* 55 (1973), pp. 395–420, at. pp. 398, 399; cf. L.C. Midgley, op. cit., Part III, "Protestant and Catholic Views on Natural Law Compared," pp. 53–77. Midgley traces a development of Maritain's views in this matter; and Maritain was influenced by Yves Simon. See Simon's posthumous work (ed. V. Kuic), *The Tradition of Natural Law: A Philosopher's Reflections,* New York, 1965.

12. H. Kung, *Infallible? An Inquiry,* New York, 1971, p. 35.

13. Ulpianus, *Liber I Institutionum; Codex Iuris Civilis,* Inst. I, 1; Dig., I, 1, 3: "Jus naturale est quod natura omnia animalia docuit."

14. C.E. Curran, *New Perspectives in Moral Theology,* Notre Dame, 1974, p. 7, criticizes J.M. Aubert's interpretation of St. Thomas as one-sided "for he fails to appreciate that Thomas did employ Ulpian's understanding

of natural law as that which is common to man and all the animals." This does justice neither to Aquinas nor to Aubert. Cf M.B. Crowe, "St. Thomas and Ulpian's Natural Law" in *St. Thomas Aquinas Commemorative Studies,* Toronto, 1974, Vol. I, pp. 261–282.

15. *We Hold These Truths,* New York, 1960, p. 296. E. McDonagh, in outlining the dangers inherent in describing morality in ontological terms, refers to the misunderstanding of "extending the being too far, to include, for example, biological elements in an undifferentiated way" (*Invitation and Response,* Dublin, 1972, p. 25).

16. A. Laun, *Die Naturrechtliche Begrundung der Ethik in der neueren katholischen Moraltheologie,* Wien, 1973, pp. 69–70; cf. Ph. Delhaye, *Permanence du droit naturel,* Louvain-Lille-Montreal, 1960, p. 123.

17. "Die Entwicklung des Naturrechtlichen Denkens innerhalb des Thomismus" in F. Böckle (ed.) *Das Naturrecht im Disput,* Dusseldorf, 1966, pp. 87–120.

18. Art. cit., pp. 97–100, "Die Rolle der inclinationes naturales"; cf. Cajetan, *Comm. in 1-2ae. q.39. a.1.*

19. It should be pointed out that 1–2, 94, 2 is not the only discussion of the natural inclinations in St. Thomas. Cf. *In 2 Sent.,* d. 42, q. 2, a. 5; *Summa contra gentiles,* III, c. 129; *In 5 Eth.,* lect. 12 (ed. Spiazzi, n. 1019); and especially *In 6 Eth.,* lect. 2 (ed. Spiazzi, n. 1131) where the difficulty of the relationship between reason and the inclinations is roundly faced.

20. Art. cit., pp. 100–120, "Die Fehlwege in der spateren Interpretation des hl. Thomas."

21. In *Das Naturrecht im Disput,* pp. 121–150, "Ruckblick und Ausblick."

22. Art. cit., pp. 139–140—"Der Mensch ist Mensch nur im Leib. Darum darf er auch die leiblichen Strukturen nicht ungestraft willkurlich missachten. Aber diesen Strukturen *an sich* kommt keine ethische Normkraft zu. Sittliche Norm ist in jedem Fall nur das Verstandnis dieser Wirklichkeit und ihre Sinngebung durch den Menschen"; cf. W. Pannenberg, "Toward a Theology of Law" in *Anglican Theological Review,* p. 408; W. Luijpen, *Phenomenology of Natural Law,* Pittsburgh, 1967, pp. 98–100.

23. Translation of his *Naturrecht,* St. Louis-London, 1949, pp. 19–27.

24. Op. cit., p. 19.

25. Op. cit., p. 21.

26. Op. cit., p. 26.

27. *Contraception and the Natural Law,* Milwaukee, 1965, p. 64.

28. See also G. Grisez, "The First Principle of Practical Reason: A commentary on the *Summa theologiae,* 1–2, question 94, article 2" in *Natural Law Forum* 10 (1965), pp. 168–196 and reprinted in abridged form in A.

328 / Michael B. Crowe

Kenny (ed.) *Aquinas: A Collection of Critical Essays,* London, 1969, pp. 340–382. The relation between the first principle of the practical reason and other principles is discussed by E. D'Arcy, *Conscience and its Right to Freedom,* London-New York, 1961, pp. 49–71.

29. *Natura e ragione: studio sulle inclinazioni naturali in rapporto al diritto naturale,* Zurich, 1971.

30. Op. cit., pp. 191–199.

31. Op. cit., pp. 218–243.

32. Op. cit., p. 244—"Una conclusione ovvia emerge dal nostro discorso: il diritto naturale e una irradiazione dinamica della natura sulla ragione e, viceversa, una irradiazione illuminante della ragione sulla natura." Cf. F. Hammer, "Bemerkungen zur Sexualanthropologie des Thomas von Aquin" in *Zeitschrift fur katholische Theologie,* 98 (1976), pp. 1–8, especially p. 8 for an interesting reflection on St Thomas' text on the specifically human inclinations "quorum proprium est excogitare aliquid ut bonum et conveniens, praeter id quod natura requirit" (1–2, 30, 3). On the logical problem of the natural inclinations see P.J. McGrath, "Natural Law and Moral Argument" in J.P. Mackey (ed.) *Morals, Law & Authority,* Dublin, 1969, pp. 67–68.

33. Cf. A. Lalande, *Vocalbuaire technique et critique de la philosophie,* 8me ed., Paris, 1960, pp. 667–673; J.C. Piquet, *Le vocabulaire intellectuel,* Paris, 1957, p. 67; P. Foulquie et R. Saint-Jean, *Dictionnaire de la langue philosophique,* Paris, 1962, s.v. "nature"; R. Paniker, *El concepto de naturaleza: analisis Permanence du droit naturel,* Louvain, 1960, pp. 9–21; E. Wolf, *Das Problem der Naturrechtslehre,* Karlsruhe, 1955; M.B. Crowe, "Human Nature—Immutable or Mutable?" in *Irish Theological Quarterly,* 30 (1963), pp. 204–231 at pp. 205–206; F. Böckle, *Das Naturrecht im Disput,* "Ruckblick und Ausblick," Dusseldorf, 1966, pp. 121–150; N. Bobbio "Quelques arguments contre le droit naturel" in *Le droit naturel, Annales de philosophie politique,* 3, Paris, 1959, pp. 180–181.

33a. See for example J. Huxley, *Evolution in Action,* London, 1953, pp. 141–161.

34. P. Heelan, "Nature and its Transformations" in *Theological Studies,* 33 (1972), p. 502.

35. Cf. N. Hurley, "The Natural Law and Man's Open-ended Nature" in *New Catholic World,* 216 (1973), Nov.–Dec., pp. 259–263; also A.G.M. Van Melsen, "Natur und Moral" in F. Böckle (ed.) *Das Naturrecht im Disput,* pp. 77–78; also K.M. Weber, "Ethische Probleme der Biotechnik und Anthropotechnik" in *Artzt und Christ,* 2 (1965), p. 231 and L. Strauss, *Natural Right and History* quoted by D. Composta, *Natura e ragione,* pp. 10–11.

36. In J. Cogley and others, *Natural Law and Modern Society,* Cleveland, New York, 1983.

37. Cf. A. Laun, *Die naturrechtliche Begrundung der Ethnik in der neueren katholischen Moraltheologie,* Wien, 1973, p. 22, citing G. Meyer, R. Hofman and J.G. Ziegler; D. Composta, *Natura e ragione,* Zurich, 1971, pp. 11–13 casts a very wide net to include F.X. Kaufmann, J. Dabin, N. Bobbio, G. Fasso, P. Piovani, J.G. Arntz and even Jacques Leclercq.

38. E. Fechner, "Die Bedeutung der Gesellschaftswissenschaft fur die Grundfrage des Rechts" in W. Maihofer (ed.) *Naturrecht oder Rechtspositivismus,* Darmstadt, 1972, pp. 257–280.

39. In *Das Naturrecht im Disput,* Dusseldorf, 1966, p. 10.

40. P. Winch, *Ethics and Action,* London, 1972, pp. 8–49 "Understanding a Primitive Society"; pp. 50–72, "Nature and Convention"; pp. 73–89, "Human Nature."

41. Art. cit., p. 168. Cf. M. Ginsberg, *On the Diversity of Morals,* London, 1962, p. 97, "There is no necessary connection between the diversity of morals and the relativity of ethics."

42. Pittsburgh, 1967.

43. Op. cit., p. 92 "Erich Fechner . . . rejects the Thomistic theory of the natural law because a philosopher, he thinks, should not cover up the fact that he is caught in a philosophical *cul de sac* by seeking a theological exit."

44. Op. cit., p. 97.

45. There is no difficulty in adding to Luijpen's list of contradictory, and often absurd moral judgments said to be dictated by nature. Cf A. Ross, *On Law and Justice,* London, 1958, p. 247; N. Bobbio, "Quelques arguments contre le droit naturel" in *Annales de Philosophie politique* 3 (1959), Paris, pp. 181–183. Luijpen takes some of his examples from A.M. Knoll, *Katholische Kirche und scholastisches Naturrecht,* Wien, 1962 of which he says: "Full of rancour as it is, a work of August Knoll presents us with an imposing and well-documented list of examples which one cannot simply disregard as irrelevant" (p. 94). See also A. Laun, *Die naturrechtliche Begrundung der Ethnik in der neueren katholischen Moraltheologie,* Wien, 1973, p. 22, note 28 for the condemnations of vaccination and street-lighting as unnatural!

46. Op. cit., p. 101.

47. Op. cit., p. 102.

48. Op. cit., pp. 103–111; M. Merleau-Ponty, *Sens et non-sens,* Paris, 1948, p. 189.

49. "Mit Recht bemerkt Rahner, dass das Naturrecht die ganze Philosophie ins Spiel bringt"—A. Laun, op. cit., p. 22 citing K. Rahner, "Bemer-

kungen uber das Naturgesetz und seine Erkennbarkeit" in *Orientierung* 19 (1955), p. 239.

50. "Absolute Norms in Moral Theology" in G.H. Outka and P. Ramsey, *Norm and Context in Christian Ethics,* London, 1968, pp. 139–173; cf. pp. 168–169.

51. *Three Issues in Ethics,* New York, 1970, pp. 42–45.

52. "Toward a Theology of Law" in *Anglican Theological Review,* 55 (1973), pp. 395–420; cf. p. 407—"A theology of law . . . cannot proceed by deducing the fundamental contents of law from certain principles, not even from specifically theological principles. . . . A theology of law is in its proper province only when the foundations of law appear within the horizon of history . . . only the narration of human history expresses the closest approximation of what man is *in concreto.*" Cf. N.H.G. Robinson, *The Groundwork of Christian Ethics,* London, 1971, Appendix B, especially pp. 302–307.

53. See the short bibliography in E. McDonagh, "Moral Theology, the Need for Renewal" in *Moral Theology Renewed,* Dublin, 1965, p. 20. Jacques Leclercq's *L'Enseignement de la morale chretienne,* Paris, 1952, bore the Imprimatur of the Rector of the University of Louvain. Its temporary withdrawal from commerce was never satisfactorily explained. It would nowadays be considered quite unrevolutionary, even innocuous.

54. "Outline of a Natural Law Procedure for Christian Ethics" in *Journal of Religion* 47 (1967), pp. 26–38, at p. 27; cf. the objections of Reinhold Niebuhr, cited in L.C. Midgley, *Beyond Human Nature,* 1968, p. 67.

55. Cf. B. Schopf, "Das Naturrecht in der katholischen Moraltheologie" in *Naturordnung* (1961), p. 99.

56. *Decretum Gratiani* I, 1—"Jus naturale est quod in lege et evangelio continetur."

57. This is the objection brought by N. Monzel against J. Messner; cf. J. Fuchs, *Natural Law—A Theological Approach,* Dublin, 1965, pp. 181–193, originally published as "Christliche Gesellschaftslehre" in *Stimmen der Zeit,* 164 (1959), pp. 161–170.

58. *Social Ethics: Natural Law in the Modern World,* St Louis-London, 1949, pp. 84–87, "Christian Moral Law."

59. Op. cit., p. 84.

60. *Lecons de droit naturel,* 2me ed. Namur-Louvain, 1933, t. I, pp. 72–84, "Droit naturel et droit chretien."

61. *Natural Law—a Theological Approach,* Dublin, 1965, pp. 52–58, "The Philosophical Concept of Nature"; see the same author's *Theologia moralis generalis,* Roma, 1960, Pars Prima, pp. 66–68.

62. *Lexikon fur Theologie und Kirche,* Band 7, Freiburg, 1962, col. 827–828.

63. Montesquieu, *De l'esprit des lois,* Partie I, livre I, ch. 1; J.S. Mill, "Nature" in *Three Essays on Religion,* 3rd ed. London, 1923; H.L.A. Hart, *The Concept of Law,* Oxford, 1961, pp. 182–183; F.S. Carney, "Outline of a Natural Law Procedure for Christian Ethics" in *Journal of Religion,* 47 (1967), p. 28.

63. 1–2, 90, 1 ad 3; see the commentary in S. Cotta, *II concetto di legge nella Summa theologiae di S Tommaso d'Aquino,* Torino, 1955, pp. 22–27.

64. J. Leclercq, *La philosophie morale de saint Thomas d'Aquin devant la pensee contemporaine,* Louvain, 1955, pp. 386–388; O. Lottin, *Principes de morale,* t. II, Louvain, 1947, pp. 102–103—"Que conclure? Puisque nous n'avons de Dieu qu'une connaissance analogique, disons d'abord que la définition thomiste de la loi ne s'applique qu'analogiquement a la loi eternelle. Puisque, pour etre appliquee a la loi naturelle, la définition thomiste a du etre adaptee en chacun de ses elements, concluons ensuite et d'une maniere plus generale que la définition thomiste n'est pas une notion univoque, s'appliquant absolument dans le meme sens aux diverses especes de lois."

65. "Towards a Rehabilitation of Natural Law" in *Christian Ethics and Contemporary Philosophy,* London, 1966, pp. 382–396; H.L.A. Hart, *The Concept of Law,* Oxford, 1961, pp. 189–195. Cf. A.P. d'Entreves, "A Core of Good Sense: Reflections on Hart's Theory of Natural Law" in *Natural Law,* 2nd (revised) ed., 1970, pp. 185–203.

66. In J. Cogley et al., *Natural Law and Modern Society,* Cleveland, New York, 1962, pp. 154–193.

67. Art. cit., pp. 175–176.

68. Selznick quotes the phrase with approval from Lon Fuller, "Positivism and Fidelity to Law—a Reply to Professor Hart" in *Harvard Law Review,* 71 (1958), p. 645.

69. Art cit. p. 178—"This is sometimes put as an appeal from 'laws' to 'the law' and there is merit in that approach. But it has the disadvantages of suggesting that 'the law' is something disembodied and unspecifiable, when in fact all we mean is that general principles of legality are counterposed to more specific legal materials." The suggestion is attributed to Roscoe Pound. See also Pound's "The Revival of Natural Law" in *Notre Dame Lawyer,* 17 (1942), pp. 287–372.

70. This is the theme of A.P. d'Entreves' *Natural Law,* London, 2nd (revised) edition, 1970.

71. P. Selznick, art. cit., p. 184.

72. Ibid.

73. Art. cit., p. 185.

74. Cf. C.E. Curran, *New Perspectives in Moral Theology,* Notre Dame, 1974, pp. 5–22.

75. Bd. 7, Herder, Freiburg, 1962, col. 827–828.

76. *Das Naturrecht im Disput,* Dusseldorf, 1966, p. 14—"falsche Verabsolutierungen."

77. Cf. W. Pannenberg, "Toward a Theology of Law" in *Anglican Theological Review,* 55 (1973), p. 397—"Contemporary theology has not yet accepted the comprehensive significance of the historical character of all human reality, despite the fact that it was disclosed by the biblical understanding of God."

78. Bd. III, Herder, Freiburg, 1969, col. 707–719.

79. K. Rahner, "Heutige Aufgaben hinsichtlich des Naturrechts" in *Lexikon fur Theologie und Kirche,* Bd. 7, 1962, col. 827—"Das wirkliche bleibende, sein sollende Wesen des Menschen kann darum nur in einer transzendentalen Erkenntnis als solches erfasst und von dem bloss universal Faktischen an ihm unterscheiden werden. Es ware weiter genauer zu unterscheiden zwischen einer bloss physisch-physiologischen Struktur des faktischen Menschen und einer als sein sollend transzcendental nachweisbaren Struktur im menschlichen Seinsgefuge. Von da aus musste genauer durchdacht werden, wie weit eine solche transzcendentale Wesenserkenntnis des Menschen reicht und ob von da aus jene Konkretheit der sittlichen Normen erreicht werden kann, die die Schul-tradition als noch unter das Naturrecht fallend betrachtet, oder ob solche mehr konkreten Normen in einier mehr sekundaren und abgeleiteten Weise (wie?) an das 'transzcendentale' Naturrecht gebunden werden konnen. Solche Uberlegungen sind heute darum vor allem wichtig, weil der Mensch von heute den (nicht schlechthin falschen, aber unangemessenen) Eindruck hat, er sei gerade das Wesen, das 'sich selber macht,' also seine 'Natur' verandern konne."

80. K. Rahner, loc cit.—"Die Erkenntnis dieser Natur ist selbst ein geschichtliche Prozess. . ."

81. See for instance S. Deploige, *Le conflit de la morale et de la sociologie,* 4me ed., Paris, 1927, pp. 291–292.

82. J. Grundel, in *Sacramentum Mundi,* Bd. II, Herder, Freiburg, 1969, s.v. "Naturrecht" 711–713, 'Geschichtlichkeit"; M.B. Crowe, "Human Nature—Immutable or Mutable?" in *Irish Theological Quarterly,* 30 (1963), 204–231.

83. B. Schuller, "Wie weit kann die Moraltheologie das Naturrecht entbehren?" in *Lebendiges Zeugnis* 1/2 (1965), cited in F. Böckle, *Das Naturrecht im Disput,* p. 128.

The Natural Law
and Objective Morality:
A Thomistic Perspective

William E. May

This chapter first appeared in *Principles of Catholic Moral Life,* 1980.

The teaching of Thomas Aquinas on the natural law has been the subject of extensive research. Many excellent books and articles are available to help anyone who is interested to investigate this topic in depth.[1] Why, then, one more essay devoted to this question?

In reply I can say, first, that the thought of St. Thomas on this subject is so rich that it merits renewed study. Even more important, however, in my judgment is the help that a study of Aquinas will bring to assessing critically recent developments in Roman Catholic moral theology. Thus before having recourse to the thought of St. Thomas, it will be worthwhile to review briefly these developments so that we can come to Aquinas with specific questions in mind.

Some Recent Developments in Roman Catholic Moral Theology

Today a significant number of Roman Catholic moral theologians find it necessary to dissent from authoritative teachings of the Roman Catholic Church on moral questions. The magisterium of the Church teaches that some specifiable sorts of human acts are wicked and contrary to the principles of the natural law. Among these are abortion, infanticide, euthanasia, willful self-destruction or suicide, genocide, the devastation of entire cities with their inhabitants, contraceptive intercourse, fornication, adultery, and sodomy.[2] A great many contemporary Roman Catholic moral theologians believe that contraceptive intercourse can be morally good,[3] even for unmarried persons;[4] several have explicitly affirmed the possibility that abortion, fornication, adultery, and sodomy can at times be virtuous;[5] and a few have written that infanticide,[6] euthanasia, and suicide[7] can at times be morally good choices. No contemporary Catholic moral theologian has as yet, to my knowledge, explicitly affirmed that genocide or the devastation of entire cities with their inhabitants might, under certain circumstances, be a morally good act. Still, as we will see, even these sorts of human acts cannot be excluded *in principle* by the kind of natural-law thinking advanced by some of these theologians.

The theologians supporting these positions claim that the natural-law thinking embodied in recent magisterial documents such as the encyclicals of Pius XII, Paul VI's *Humanae Vitae,* and the *Vatican Declaration on Certain Questions of Sexual Ethics* is ahistorical and physicalistic. Thus Charles E. Curran, commenting on the *Vatican Declaration,* says that the moral methodology found in it describes the fundamental principles of the moral order as "eternal, objective, and universal,"[8] and by so doing does not give "enough importance" "to developing historical and cultural realities."[9] Thus, too, Daniel C. Maguire can write, in an essay advocating the view that it can be morally good for a human person to intervene creatively and choose the time of his own demise rather than "await in awe the dispositions of organic tissue," as follows:

> Birth control was, for a very long time, impeded by the physicalistic ethic that left moral man at the mercy of his biology. He had no choice but to conform to the rhythms of his physical nature and to accept its determinations obediently. Only gradually did technological man discover that he was morally free to intervene creatively and to achieve birth control by choice.[10]

In place of this physicalistic, ahistorical natural law, these theologians propose a different model of the natural law. This has recently been developed at some length in a work by Timothy E. O'Connell that has won the praise of Curran, John F. Dedek, Josef Fuchs, and Agnes Cunningham as a significant articulation of the best in contemporary Roman Catholic moral thought.[11] A presentation of its leading ideas will therefore give us an understanding of the natural-law theory shared to a considerable degree by those Catholic moralists who find the teachings of the magisterium flawed by physicalism and an ahistorical perspective.[12]

O'Connell notes that "the traditional moral maxim, do good and avoid evil, may have some colloquial significance, but as a precise description of the living of our lives it is simply and inevitably impossible."[13] Because of our finitude and the limitations imposed upon us by the sociotemporal world in which we live, "our best hope is to do as much good as possible and as little evil as necessary."[14] The natural law proposed by O'Connell—and in advancing it, he draws together in a synthetic manner the thought of such writers as Josef Fuchs, Bruno Schüller, Louis Janssens, and Richard A. McCormick[15]—is described by him as "real, experiential, consequential, and proportional."[16] The characteristics of consequentialism and proportionalism are critically important, because in the final analysis, as O'Connell observes, "specific actions are to be evaluated from a moral point of view by considering their actual effects, or consequences."[17] In developing this insight of contemporary theologians into the nature of the natural law, O'Connell says that we discover the right thing to do "by balancing the various 'goods' and 'bads' that are part of the situation and by trying to achieve the greatest proportion of goods to bads."[18] In keeping with this consequentialist and proportionalistic natural law, O'Connell holds that the principle of double effect as traditionally understood must be rejected. It must be rejected because it held that one could not rightfully choose to do a deed having evil effects if those evil effects were directly intended or willed. But the direct intention of evil[19] is not, according to the consequential-proportional natural law of O'Connell and other modern theologians, morally significant, since it is precisely the consequences of an act that make it to be *morally* good,[20] however much "premoral" evil must be intended. Thus O'Connell argues that the maxim, " 'The end does not justify the means' must be rejected if by 'end' one means the consequences of one's act, for it is these consequences precisely that justify the means."[21]

This theory of the natural law rejects the view that there can be any specifiable sorts of human acts that are *always* wrong.[22] Thus the acts of deliberately willed abortion, directly intended infanticide, and even genocide and the deliberate devastation of entire cities with their inhabitants are, *in theory* at least, morally justifiable. They are *morally* wicked, as Richard A. McCormick explains, in the absence of a proportionate good, but they become morally good, despite the massive "premoral" evil they entail, in the presence of a proportionate good.[23] Since it is, however, hardly possible that there can ever be any good proportionate enough to justify the choice to destroy an entire race (genocide) or to perform acts entailing similar "premoral" evil, there are some sorts of acts that can be regarded practically as "disproportionate" to any realizable good.[24] Therefore, these moralists concede that there are some specifiable sorts of moral precepts or norms that are "virtually" exceptionless or "practically" absolute.[25] However, and this is very important, these moralists do not believe that these norms are truly unexceptional. In their theory one cannot claim, for instance, that it is *always* wrong to destroy an entire city with its inhabitants because this act could become morally good were its execution necessary to achieve a proportionate good.

In advancing this model of natural law, contemporary Roman Catholic moral theologians manifest an ambiguity to St. Thomas, or rather claim that his thought on natural law is ambiguous. On the one hand, some complain that his understanding of natural law is too physicalistic. Curran, for example, asserts that St. Thomas, by accommodating within his thought Ulpian's definition of natural law as "that which nature has taught all animals," definitely tends "to identify the demands of natural law with physical and biological processes."[26] Similarly O'Connell holds that St. Thomas includes "the demand to conform to animal facticity under the rubric of natural law."[27] Both writers regard this as a serious defect in St. Thomas's thought; it is precisely the flaw that makes many magisterial teachings untenable.

On the other hand, several of these theologians appeal to St. Thomas to support their positions. Thus Curran also writes that

"Thomas' own understanding of the natural law does not seem to justify the insistence on universally valid, absolute norms of human behavior."[28] To support this claim Curran cites the teaching of St. Thomas that the more remote or particular precepts of natural law are valid "for the most part," but can be deficient in "particular instances."[29] Daniel Maguire does likewise. In arguing against a "taboo" mentality that would claim that there are unexceptional rules designating in advance of actual performance whether specific human acts are right or wrong, Maguire appeals both to this teaching of St. Thomas on the deficiency of the more remote precepts of natural law and to his teaching that "human actions are good or bad according to their circumstances."[30] Finally, Maguire, Franz Scholz and others[31] claim that St. Thomas's interpretation of certain events in the Old Testament (e.g., Abraham's willingness to sacrifice his son Isaac) can best be understood as acknowledging that we can directly intend evil for the sake of a proportionate good.[32]

With this background of contemporary Roman Catholic moral theology in mind, I shall examine the teaching of St. Thomas on natural law and objective morality. Three central issues will merit consideration: (1) the meaning of natural law for St. Thomas and the significance of Ulpian's definition; (2) the development of our knowledge of natural law; and (3) "exceptions" to natural-law precepts.

THE MEANING OF NATURAL LAW IN ST. THOMAS

St. Thomas dealt with the subject of natural law formally and at some length in his *Summa Theologiae,* and references to natural law and to such allied notions as conscience, synderesis, providence, and divine law are found throughout his works, from his early *Scriptum super IV libros Sententiarum* onwards.[33]

In the *Summa Theologiae* Thomas prefaces his discussion of natural law with a consideration of law in general and of God's eternal law, and it is important for us, if we are to understand his notion of natural law, to understand the meaning that he gives to law in general and to the eternal law.

Law in General

Thomas considers law as an extrinsic principle of human actions, as distinguished from virtue, which is an intrinsic principle. Initially he describes it as a "rule or measure of actions whereby one is induced to act or is restrained from acting." It then follows that law pertains to reason because "reason, which is the first principle of human acts, is the rule and measure of human acts."[34] Law as such is thus, for Thomas, something brought into being by reason; it is an *ordinatio rationis.* That law as such belongs to reason and is indeed constituted by or brought into existence by an act of reason is made quite clear by Thomas in his reply to some objections. One objection had claimed that law cannot pertain to reason because St. Paul had spoken of a "law" that he discovered in his members (Rom. 7:23). In replying to this, Thomas observes that a law can be said to be "in something" in two ways:

> In one way [law is said to be in something] as in that which rules and measures. And because this is proper to reason, it follows that in this way law exists in reason exclusively.

He continues by saying that law can be said to exist in something in another way as in that which is ruled and measured:

> And it is in this way that law is in all those things that are inclined toward something in virtue of some law; thus any inclination arising from some law can be called a law not *essentially,* but as it were in a participative sense.[35]

Another objection had contended that law cannot belong to reason inasmuch as it can be neither the power of reason itself, nor one of its habits or facilities, nor one of its acts. In replying to this, Aquinas states that the practical reason, or intelligence as ordered to action, in deliberating about what is to be done brings into being "universal propositions directed to action." These universal propositions of the practical reason play a role in deliberative inquiry about what is to be done comparable to that played by the universal propositions of the speculative reason relative to the conclusions that it establishes. "Universal propositions of this kind," Aquinas writes, "of the practical reason as bearing on what is to be done possess the meaning of law."[36] From this it is clear that for St. Thomas *law as such not only pertains to reason but consists of propositions or precepts that are brought into existence by reason as "practical," that is, as directed to action, to deliberation about the deeds that can be done by self-determining agents.* Here Aquinas clearly indicates that these actions can be judged "good" or "bad" in terms of propositions or precepts brought into existence by "practical reason."

Eternal Law

In considering the eternal law, St. Thomas first notes that the entire community of the universe is governed by God's mind. The eternal law is the *"ratio"* or "ruling idea of things that exists in God as the ruler of the universe."[37] Eternal law directs the entire created universe and the activity of all created things. The eternal law is, therefore, the *"ratio* or exemplar of divine wisdom insofar as it is directive of all acts and movements."[38] Eternal law has as its end the good of the whole created universe, and it is promulgated to those subject to it by the act of creation.[39]

Natural Law

Thomas teaches that all creatures are subject to and thus participate in this eternal law of God. But the manner of their participation differs because of their different modes of being.[40] Nonintelligent, nonrational beings participate passively in the eternal law because from it they receive an "impression" by virtue of which they "have tendencies to their proper acts and ends."[41] The eternal law and, thus, *law,* is found in them in a purely passively participated manner; *it exists in them as in beings that are regulated and measured by law.*[42] Intelligent, rational creatures, on the other hand, participate in the eternal law in a more noble manner because they are capable of providing for themselves and for others. Their active, intelligent participation in the eternal law, making it possible for this law to be found in them as in beings who rule and measure what is to be done, is precisely what is meant by natural law.[43]

It is very important, if we are to understand properly the teaching of St. Thomas, to bear in mind that natural law, as the actively intelligent participation by the rational creature in the eternal law, exists in the rational creature not as in that which is ruled and measured by law but as in that which rules and measures. The natural law of St. Thomas meets his own criterion for the meaning of law in its proper, formal sense. By this Thomas means that natural law, like all law in the proper sense and like the eternal law of God, is a work of reason. Natural law as it exists in the rational creature is distinct from the eternal law that exists in God the superintelligent Creator, but it is not separate from this eternal law. It is this eternal law itself mediated to or shared by the rational creature.[44] It marks both the nobility of the rational creature as the being created in the image of God and the great love that God has for the rational creature, whom he wills to share actively in his own provident wisdom.

St. Thomas makes this quite clear when he rejects the views, held by many of his medieval predecessors, that natural law is a power or a habit, in particular the habit of synderesis or of first principles of the moral order.[45] St. Thomas grants that the natural law may, in a secondary or derivative sense, be regarded as a habit insofar as the judgments of practical reason that together go to constitute it may be habitually kept in mind, but in the proper sense of the term natural law is *not* a habit, nor is it a power. Rather it is a reality brought into existence (*constitutum*) through reason; it is a work of human intelligence as ordered to action (*ratio practica*), just as a proposition or judgment of the speculative intellect is an achievement of human intelligence as ordered to knowing for the sake of knowing. The natural law, therefore, is something that we ourselves bring into existence through our own intelligent activity—it is *quod quis agit*—not something enabling us to bring things into existence through our practically oriented intelligent activity—*quo quis agit*.[46]

As such and properly, then, natural law is for St. Thomas an achievement of practical reason. It consists of a body of propositions or precepts—true judgments—made by the human intelligence as ordered to action and as ruling and measuring action, that is, as determining whether a proposed act is morally good or morally wicked.[47] As law, natural law is not in St. Thomas's judgment innate. What is innate is the God-given ability of the rational creature to come to know the body of true practical judgments, that is, judgments having to do with the moral meaning of the actions that the human person can freely choose to do. These judgments together go to make up or constitute natural law.

Also innate are "natural inclinations" orienting the human person to basic or fundamental goods perfective of his or her being. According to St. Thomas, "natural inclinations" or tendencies are those inclinations possessed by all beings in their own distinctive way whereby they are directed toward the realization of the end for which they were created.[48] The natural inclinations of a being orient it to the end(s), that is, good(s) for which it was made.[49] Rational creatures—human beings—like all beings, have natural inclinations, and these inclinations have a role to play in the way that human persons come to know the natural law. We shall soon look into this matter, but prior to doing so it is pertinent to examine briefly St. Thomas's accommodation into his teaching of Ulpian's famous definition of natural law as that which nature has taught all animals.

Ulpian's Definition and Natural Law

It will be recalled that some contemporary Catholic moral theologians, for example, Curran and O'Connell, lament St. Thomas's use of Ulpian's definition. According to them, his doing so clearly shows a physicalistic understanding of natural law, a requirement to submit passively to brute facticity. The preceding analysis of St. Thomas's teaching on natural law should be sufficient to falsify this contention. St. Thomas insists throughout his writings that law, properly and formally speaking, is something that belongs to reason. It is *aliquid rationis,* an *ordinatio rationis.* Law as such, and this includes natural law, can be predicated properly and formally *only* of reason, either divine reason or created reason. It may, however, be predicated in a derivative, secondary sense of what is ruled and measured and is therefore subject to law and to the rule of reason.[50]

St. Thomas certainly did make use of Ulpian's definition, both in his early *Scriptum super IV Libros Sententiarum* of Peter Lombard and in such later writings as the *Summa Theologiae.* Moreover, Thomistic scholars disagree over the significance to be given to his use of Ulpian. The great historian of twelfth- and thirteenth-century moral theology, Dom Odon Lottin, while insisting (*pace* Curran and O'Connell) that St. Thomas, in making room within his thought for Ulpian's definition, "in no way intended to withdraw from reason the mastery that it exercises over all the tendencies of man,"[51] nonetheless believes that at the heart of Aquinas's notion of natural law lies a "secret sympathy" for Ulpian's definition,[52] and he also believes that "the truly personal thought of St. Thomas" on the natural law is found in his early *Commentary on Lombard's Sentences* rather than in the *Summa Theologiae.*[53] Some observations on Lottin's position will be given at the end of this section; it is necessary now to look at St. Thomas's use of Ulpian's definition.

St. Thomas provides his most extensive analysis of natural law in his Lombard *Commentary* in connection with his discussion of a problem that had plagued his predecessors in their attempts to relate natural law to Scripture. How could the polygyny of the Old Testament patriarchs be reconciled with natural law?[54] This issue itself is not our concern here but rather St. Thomas's thought on natural law.

In his analysis St. Thomas insists on humanity's difference from other animals. Since they lack intelligence, brute animals are impelled by a force of nature to perform actions proper to them; they are incapable of regulating their actions by any kind of judgment properly so-called, by law in its proper sense. There is, St. Thomas says, in brute animals a natural *aestimatio* leading them to perform actions appropriate to them, but no rational principle of activity. Rational animals, on the contrary, can know the end and relationship of means to end. They can therefore direct their own actions and govern themselves. In this early work St. Thomas teaches that the natural law exists in the rational creature as a "natural concept" whereby the human person "is directed to acting suitably with respect to actions proper to him, whether these belong to his generic nature, such as generating life, eating, and so forth, or whether they belong to his specific nature as man, such as thinking and things of this kind."[55]

What is most instructive about this passage is that in it St. Thomas explicitly holds that natural law is related to human intelligence, not to brute animality. The thought expressed here and elsewhere in this early writing[56] is thus of a piece with the thought of St. Thomas on natural law that we have already examined: Natural law is proper to rational creatures alone.

In the course of his discussion of the polygyny of the fathers, St. Thomas makes it quite obvious that he judges polygyny to be *contrary* to natural law, although in a way not so contrary to natural law as polyandry is.[57] One of the objections to this teaching had urged that a plurality of wives is in no way opposed to natural law because natural law, as Ulpian said, is "that which nature has taught all animals," and it is obvious that in the animal kingdom it is by no means unnatural for one male animal to mate with several females. It is in replying to this objection that St. Thomas takes up the celebrated definition of Ulpian, along with the definitions of Cicero and Gratian.[58] St. Thomas says that natural law can refer to something that is natural by *reason of its principle or source.* This is the way Cicero understood it, because he said that it was something not generated by opinion but rather by a kind of innate power (*ius naturae est quod non opinio genuit, sed quaedam vis inseruit*). He then notes that the principle from which natural law springs may be extrinsic to the being ruled by the natural law, and in this sense St. Thomas understands the definition given by Gratian that the natural law is everything that is contained in law and gospel (*ius naturale est quod in lege et in Evangelio continetur*). Finally, he says that natural law may be understood not as referring to what is natural by reason of its principle or source but by reason of "nature," that is, *by reason of the subject matter with which the natural law is concerned (tertio dicitur ius naturale non solum a principio, sed a natura, quia de naturalibus est).* If natural law is taken in this sense, it is opposed to reason or set off vis-à-vis reason. Consequently:

> . . . understood in this very limited sense, those things that belong *only* to men, although they are commanded by reason, are *not* said to be of the natural law; rather only those things that natural reason commands about matters common to man and other animals belong to the natural law in this sense.[59]

It is very important to understand St. Thomas here. He is surely *not* saying that the natural law, properly and formally as law, is something infrarational, an instinct that humanity shares with other animals, brute animal facticity. For he has stressed in the body of the article that natural law as such pertains only to human beings. In brutes there is no natural law, only a natural *aestimatio,* a power or force of nature impelling them to act in ways appropriate to achieve their ends. Thus in this celebrated passage St. Thomas is by no means repudiating what he had to say in the body of the article (or what he shall subsequently affirm in later writings) about the intrinsic rational character of natural law. He accepts Ulpian's definition of the natural law *only in the sense that it refers to the* subject matter with which natural law is concerned. The natural tendencies or inclinations that human beings share with other animals are fit matter to be brought under the rule of law, that is, under natural law as an achievement of human intelligence. This is evident from the text in question, for St. Thomas explicitly states that the natural law, understood even in this limited sense,[60] has to do with those things that "*natural reason commands* with respect to matters common to man and other animals" (*illa tantum quae naturalis ratio dictat de his quae sunt homini aliisque communia*).[61]

St. Thomas also makes room for Ulpian's definition in his later works, in the *Summa Theologiae*[62] and in his Commentary on the *Nicomachean Ethics.*[63] But in all these places the room given by St. Thomas to Ulpian's definition of natural law as the law that nature has taught all animals is quite intelligible and in accord with his own teaching on the natural law. Natural law as defined by Ulpian never has the meaning of the *ordinatio rationis* or *dictamen rationis,* the achievement of practical reason, that St. Thomas considers to be the essential element of law and of natural law in the formal sense.[64] Ulpian's definition can never be used in reference to natural law as that which is in something *sicut in mensurante et regulante*. It uniformly refers to natural law only in an accommodated sense, as found in something only "participatively, as it were" (*quasi participative*).[65] In brief, Ulpian's definition of natural law has pertinence to the tendencies or inclinations that human beings possess by virtue of being, in truth, animals, albeit animals of a special kind—tendencies that can be grasped by practical reason along with the real goods toward which they incline the human person. Once these tendencies and the goods correlative to them are understood by practical reason, the human person can make the judgment (articulate the proposition) that these are goods to be pursued and done. It is only when such propositions are articulated by practical reason that natural law in its formal sense is operative.[66]

From all this it is clear that Ulpian's definition did have an influence on St. Thomas. But it is in my judgment necessary to dissent from Lottin's contention that his more personal thought on natural law is present in the Lombard *Commentary* and that St. Thomas had a secret sympathy for Ulpian's definition, as though he preferred it to other definitions of natural law. Aquinas is quite clear throughout his writings, and particularly insistent in the *Summa Theologiae,* that natural law is formally and properly something that belongs to human practical reason. Thus with D. O'Donoghue and others I believe that Lottin's interpretation of St. Thomas's use of Ulpian is misleading.[67]

THE DEVELOPMENT OF OUR KNOWLEDGE OF NATURAL LAW

Formally and properly natural law is an achievement of human practical reason, consisting of a set or body of principles or precepts about what is and what is not to be done. Since St. Thomas rejects any kind of innate knowledge,[68] it is evident that he considers our knowledge of natural law and its precepts to be something that we acquire in life and that he recognizes a development in our knowledge of natural law both as individual persons and as members of the human community. The purpose of this section of this essay is to give the basic outlines of St. Thomas's thought on this subject.

The Role of Natural Inclinations and First Principles of Natural Law

Reference has already been made to innate natural inclinations. These are *not* to be identified with natural law, because natural law is an achievement of human reason, not something given. Nor are these natural inclinations innately known, as should be obvious from St. Thomas's position on innate knowledge. Still they function as dynamic sources of our cognitive struggle to come to know what we are to do if we are to be the beings we are meant to be, if we are to act rightly. Correlative to these inclinations[69] are fundamental or basic goods of the human person—goods we need if we are to be fully ourselves, if we are to be the beings God wills us to be. These goods likewise are not innately known, but St. Thomas affirms that we "naturally apprehend" the goods to which our natural inclinations direct us.[70] By this he means that there is no need for discursive, syllogistic reasoning in order for us to know these goods. To know them we need experience of life, but given this experience, we know these goods spontaneously, and in knowing them we make true practical judgments about what we are to do and not to do. These judgments of the practical reason are self-evidently true[71] and are articulated in propositions or precepts that serve as starting points or principles for intelligent deliberation about human action.

Among our natural inclinations are our inclination, as intelligent beings, toward being and truth and the fullness of being and of truth, and our inclination, as beings with an intelligent appetite or will, toward the good. Thus the absolutely primordial principle of natural law, brought into existence by the activity of practical reason, is that *good is to be done and pursued and evil is to be avoided.*[72] This is absolutely primordial because it is the basis for any kind of freely chosen intelligent human act and likewise the basis for any further *ordinatio* or command of practical reason. This precept needs no proof nor can it have any. Its truth is evident immediately to the human mind on understanding what "good" means.

Here it is very important to note that for St. Thomas, the very first principle of natural law is a proposition of practical reason ordering us to pursue and do good and avoid evil. The good that we are to do and pursue through our free and intelligent activity is by no means limited by him to the moral good; it includes the full range of good, embracing everything that is judged truly to be a good of the human person. Naturally, moral good is within the scope of the good that we are to do and pursue and moral evil within the scope of the evil we are to avoid. The important thing for us to realize is that St. Thomas teaches that the very first principle of natural law requires that the whole range of human good is to be done and pursued and that all human evil is to be avoided.[73] His thought on this subject is, therefore, quite different from that of the contemporary theologians whose opinions were surveyed at the beginning of this essay. They drive a wedge between the moral good and what is variously termed "premoral," "nonmoral," or "ontic" good and hold that we can rightly intend deliberately "premoral" evil for the sake of proportionately greater "premoral" good. They hold that we are to do evil for the sake of a greater good.

That St. Thomas includes the full range of good achievable through human action within the scope of this primary precept of natural law is made abundantly clear from the fact that he teaches that there are in fact several "first" principles of natural law, and there are several "first" principles precisely because the good that we are to do and pursue includes the full range of good to which we are naturally inclined. The principle that good is to be done and pursued and evil is to be avoided is absolutely first, because it is implicit in all the other primary or first precepts of the natural law, so that a denial of them would entail the absurdity of denying it.[74] But the other primary precepts are not deduced from the precept that good is to be done and pursued and evil is to be avoided in any rationalistic manner. They too are self-evidently true and need no proof.

In other words, when St. Thomas says that there are several first or primary principles or precepts of natural law, he means that we can know, in a nondiscursive way, not only that good is to be done and pursued and that evil is to be avoided but also that there are generic kinds of goods that we ought to pursue in our lives through freely chosen and intelligent deeds, and that the evils destructive of these goods are to be avoided. He affirms this because there does exist within the human person a set of ordered natural inclinations directing us to all the goods corresponding to real but diverse dimensions or levels of our being. Because we are beings who subsist in ourselves—substantial beings—continuation in being is a good that we naturally seek, and thus life itself is a basic human good worthy of human choice and pursuit. Because we are living animals, bodied beings, who can share our lives with a new generation, procreation and human sexuality are goods that need to be pursued intelligently and protected. Because we are animals of a very special kind, human animals, with the inclinations or tendencies of intelligent and self-determining beings, we are inclined to live in communities and together with others to pursue the goods of truth and justice, friendship and peace, and we thirst for union with God. We are naturally inclined to these goods because we are the kind of beings we are, and these goods, consciously known, form the basis for true propositions of practical reason.

Note that all these primary or basic precepts of natural law are directive principles of human activity. They inwardly shape human choice and action so that without them it is impossible to act humanly at all, no matter whether the act chosen is *morally* good or not. These precepts are generic in nature and point us in a direction. They do not give us *a priori* knowledge of which specific human acts are good or bad, nor from them can we deduce rationalistically, precinding from experience, specific rules of conduct. They are directives or starting points for intelligent human activity.

Secondary and More Remote Precepts of Natural Law

St. Thomas teaches that more specific judgments or precepts about what is good or bad do belong to the natural law and are related to these basic, primary nondiscursively known precepts. He holds that more specific precepts of natural law can be "derived" from these more common precepts in two general ways. One is "after the manner of conclusions from the common principles of natural law" (*a principiis communibus legis naturae per modum conclusionum*); the other is "after the manner of a determination" (*per modum determinationis*) of what natural law means in more particular human situations. He gives, as an example of a precept derived in the first way from the more common precepts of natural law, the precept that *one ought not to kill,* holding that it is, as it were, a conclusion drawn from the more fundamental precept that *evil ought not to be done to anyone.* As an illustration of a determination of natural law, he suggests that the *way* an evildoer is to be punished is something to be settled by particular human societies, and settled, of course, in a just way, in accordance with a more basic precept that *one who sins or does evil ought to be punished.* St. Thomas says that precepts or judgments of the first kind, although belonging in one way to human positive law, nonetheless belong to natural law because they carry its force. Precepts of the second type are more properly the work of human positive law, but still, in order for such determinations to be just, they need to be in accord with the more common and fundamental precepts of natural law.[75]

When St. Thomas says that more specific natural law precepts—sometimes called secondary precepts—are derived from the more common or primary precepts, he in no way means that these precepts are known in a rationalistic, *a priori* manner. As R. A. Armstrong observes in an important study of natural law in Aquinas, the more specific natural-law precepts are "more deeply involved with the varying circumstances and details which surround any and every moral act."[76] Knowledge of these circumstances and details can only be achieved through experience and the discovery, by human intelligence, of the reality or truth-making factors that give to human acts their intelligibility or meaning. Judgments made on the basis of this knowledge require a "consideration" or "reflection," and some of these judgments can be made more easily than others. There is in other words, a gradual progression from the more general, direction-giving principles of natural law to its more specific directives of action or rules of action.

Here a key text to understand the thought of St. Thomas is that in which he argues that *all* moral precepts belong to natural law but do so in different ways. Aquinas writes:

> Every judgement of practical reason proceeds from certain
> principles that are known naturally . . . and from these it is

possible to make progress in diverse ways in making judgments about different things that are to be done. For there are some things that are so explicit in human acts that at once, with only a little consideration, they can be given approval or disproval in terms of those common and first principles (*quaedam . . . possunt approbari vel reprobari per illa communia et prima principia*). But there are other things for whose judgment a good deal of consideration of the diverse circumstances is required; and to consider them diligently is simply not the task of just anyone but of the wise . . . thus these things belong to natural law but nonetheless they require the discipline whereby those of less capacity (*minores*) are instructed by the wise.[77]

As this text shows, St. Thomas teaches that more specific precepts of natural law become known only by an intelligent "consideration" of human experience. Some more specific precepts (for instance, the precepts found in the Decalog) can become known after only a little consideration because they are closely connected with the primary precepts. Others can be known only with considerable difficulty and after much reflection simply because the relevant moral considerations or factors contributing to the moral meaning of the acts to be judged are much more difficult to discover, so that only the "wise," that is, persons who have the virtue of prudence,[78] are capable of making good moral judgments with regard to them.

Natural law, for St. Thomas, is an achievement of practical reason endeavoring to bring intelligent order into actions that human persons can freely choose. It is the participation of the human person in the eternal law of God, and it is a participation that deepens and develops both in the individual person and in the human community. It begins in precepts made "naturally," nondiscursively—precepts that give direction to human action while leaving undetermined the meaning of specific sorts of human acts; it proceeds to make more and more specific judgments concerned with more and more specific sorts or kinds of human acts and the conditions in which human beings act. Secondary precepts and those even more remote (from primary) precepts dependent upon both primary and secondary precepts are more specific than the basic or primary and generic precepts of natural law. They provide directives for human action by prescribing or proscribing specifiable sorts of human deeds. This leads us to a consideration of the question of "exceptions" to natural-law precepts.

"EXCEPTIONS" TO NATURAL-LAW PRECEPTS

St. Thomas teaches that natural law is absolutely unalterable so far as its primary precepts are concerned. But he says that its secondary precepts, which are like particular conclusions from the primary precepts, although unchangeable "in the majority of cases," can nonetheless experience change "on some particular and rare occasions."[79]

How is his teaching here to be understood? Earlier in this essay I noted that some contemporary Roman Catholic moral theologians appeal to this and similar passages in St. Thomas to support their claim that there are no moral absolutes in the sense of universal negative prohibitions, such as the prohibition taught by the magisterium of the Church against directly intended abortion. The thought of St. Thomas, as I intend to show here, provides no support for this claim.

The Difference Between Speculative and Practical Knowledge

St. Thomas certainly recognizes that it is unrealistic and hence foolish to expect the same kind of precision in moral judgments that is possible in speculative matters. Speculative knowledge is concerned with what actually exists, not with what-is-to-be-done through human actions; therefore there is a necessity in speculative judgments lacking in practical judgments. He puts it this way: "Speculative or theoretic reason is occupied with natural truths that cannot be other than they are, and so without mistake it discovers truth in the premises from which it starts." Practical reason, on the other hand, is concerned with "contingent matters with which human acts deal, and although there is some necessity in common precepts, the more we get down to particular cases the more we can be mistaken." Because of this difference in the subject matter of the conclusions of speculative and practical reason St. Thomas says that "in matters of action truth or practical rectitude is not the same for everyone with respect to specifics but only with respect to common principles."[80] He illustrates this point by observing that we can conclude (by using as our starting point for deliberative or practical inquiry the precept that we ought to act intelligently) that we should return to their rightful owners goods that we hold in trust. Nonetheless, this very good and true conclusion of practical reason is not universally applicable and admits of exceptions. For instance, it would be irrational and therefore contrary to a basic natural-law precept to act automatically in accord with this conclusion were the rightful owner to demand return of his property in order to use it for a wicked purpose such as attacking the common good.[81]

Contingencies and the Specification of Human Acts

St. Thomas's teaching on this matter is eminently intelligible and in accord with his whole thought on the morality of human acts and the meaning of natural law and its precepts. Still we must understand his thought properly. To do so, it is necessary to recall that the reality ruled and measured by natural-law precepts is the reality of freely chosen human acts. Natural-law precepts are, as St. Thomas says, "universal propositions of practical reason."[82] The human acts ruled and measured by these precepts are particulars, and these particular human acts must also be known if we are to determine whether or not they conform to natural-law precepts. Particular, individual human acts can, of course, be known to be *instances of specific sorts or kinds* of human action, and St. Thomas makes it abundantly clear that there are certain specifiable sorts or kinds of human acts that are morally wicked and therefore unworthy of human choice and contrary to precepts of natural law.[83] Among the sorts of human acts that are always morally wicked are stealing,[84] lying,[85] fornicating,[86] commiting adultery,[87] and intending to kill a fellow human being on one's own authority.[88] This list is illustrative, not taxative.

However, and this is the important consideration, St. Thomas teaches that the determination of the moral species of a human act differs from the determination of the species of a natural object or physical action because of the contingent nature of a human act. A natural object or physical action, which is the subject matter of speculative inquiry, is determined in its species by a naturally given form. A human act, which is the subject matter to be known in practical deliberative inquiry, is not determined to be an instance of a specific class by reason of any natural form but rather by a form that is determined by practical reason itself.[89] But in order for practical reason to make this determination, it must take into account the various contingencies or circumstances in which the act is done.

A human act, St. Thomas teaches, is determined to be the sort or kind of act that it is by reason of its object,[90] which is entitatively one and the same with the proximate end[91] that the moral agent must intend.[92] Nonetheless, and this is the precise point that St. Thomas makes, and which Maguire misunderstands, in the question in which he asks whether any circumstance or contingency can determine the moral goodness or wickedness of an act, a contingency can inwardly change the moral object that the agent must intend as the proximate end of his act. In other words, a circumstance that enters into the very condition of the objective act and thus specifies it can be morally determinative.[93] Thus the contingency that the rightful owner may seek his or her property for an evil purpose or may seek it while drunk can make all the difference in the world in determining whether one ought to act in accord with the remote precept of natural law that *one ought to restore goods held in trust to their rightful owners.* This contingency, which was not included in the articulation of the precept—and, St. Thomas says, it would be impossible to include every morally relevant contingency in the articulation of such precepts—changes the species of the human act that is to be done. It changes it from one ruled and measured by this precept to one that is *not* ruled and measured by it. This particular remote precept of natural law is "defective" to the extent that it does not nor cannot include within its articulation those contingencies that can inwardly change the moral species of the act toward which it directs us.

These observations should be of help to us in assessing the claims of some contemporary Roman Catholic theologians that St. Thomas's teaching on the natural law affords no reason for holding that there are moral absolutes. Since he does unequivocally teach that there are such absolutes, as has already been indicated, his teaching on the matter of "exceptions" to remote conclusions of natural law needs to be understood properly and not misused to support the view that on occasion acts such as adultery, fornication, the directly intended destruction of fetal life, etc. can be morally good.

Finally, it is necessary to say something about the claim made by some authors, for example, John Dedek, Daniel Maguire, Franz Scholz, and Richard A. McCormick, that the best way to understand St. Thomas's teaching on certain Old Testament events, such as Abraham's willingness to sacrifice his son Isaac, is to say that he subscribes to the view that we can directly intend a "premoral" evil for the sake of a higher good (itself premoral). In other words, these authors invoke the teaching of St. Thomas in interpreting certain Old Testament events as authoritative support of their view that it can sometimes be morally good to intend evil directly so that good may come about.[94]

God and Natural-Law Precepts

I submit that this is a wholly inaccurate and misleading interpretation of relevant Thomistic texts and the thought of St. Thomas. Aquinas did, of course, teach that Abraham did not act wrongly in choosing to sacrifice his son Isaac at the command of God.[95] He does not, however, argue that Abraham was intending to do an evil for the sake of some proportionate or higher good. Rather he teaches that the act Abraham intended was not, in truth, an act of homicide because of the very relevant contingency that God, the Lord of life, had intervened and by so doing had inwardly changed the species of the act in question so that it was not an act of homicide but one of obedience and hence of virtue.[96] Here it is important to realize that for St. Thomas evil is the deprivation of a *due* good.[97] Life is a basic, fundamental good of human persons, a good to be respected and indeed reverenced in them by their fellow beings, because it is a good gift from God. But God, in the thought of St. Thomas, owes no one anything. Life is a free gift from him, one that he can also take away.[98] Thus Abraham's choice to obey God was not a choice entailing the direct intent of what was known by him to be evil.

In other words, in offering an interpretation of the Genesis account of Abraham's willingness to sacrifice Isaac in obedience to a divine command, St. Thomas teaches that the act in question is one that is not contrary to the natural-law precept enjoining us not to slay the innocent *precisely because* the act in question is not an act of homicide. His whole point is that God, as supreme Lord of creation and author of the moral order, can inwardly change the moral species of the act (and thus the object of the act and the proximate end intended by the agent) through his free and intelligent activity so that the "form" of the act discovered by practical reason is different from the "form" of act prohibited by precepts of natural law.[99] In the very same question of the *Summa Theologiae* in which he discusses this problem, St. Thomas insists that the moral precepts of the Decalog, which follow with necessity and with only a modicum of consideration from the primary precepts of natural law,[100] are absolutely indispensable, even to God.[101] Moreover, St. Thomas makes it abundantly clear that God, and God alone, can act in such a way that an act lethal to an innocent human person can be inwardly changed in its species so that it is not in truth an act, morally, of homicide but one of obedience.[102] It is, therefore, in my opinion a serious misuse of St. Thomas's teaching on this matter to infer that it supports the position that one can rightly intend evil directly for the sake of a good end. That position—that one can directly intend evil for a good end—is explicitly repudiated by St. Thomas[103] and no wonder, for it is a direct violation of the very first precept of natural law, which directs that *good is to be done and pursued and evil is to be avoided.* Far from regarding this as an unrealizable "maxim," as O'Connell and those whose views O'Connell so ably summarizes believe, St. Thomas considers this an absolutely universal and binding precept in terms of which all others are to be understood.

CONCLUSION

This analysis of St. Thomas's teaching on natural law and objective morality has, I hope, been of some help in assessing the meaning of our moral lives and in providing a basis for critically appraising recent developments in Roman Catholic moral theology. The natural law of St. Thomas is by no means a static conformity to physical or biological laws. It is, rather, a dynamic and ever growing participation of the human subject, whose personal life is profoundly influenced by the communities in which he or she lives, in the eternal law of God. It is a work of intelligence, an intelligence that respects the self-determining freedom of the human person, but an intelligence that nonetheless recognizes that evil is not to be done for the sake of good. It is the work of an intelligence that is capable of determining objectively the meaning of moral or human acts, and of persons who are summoned to a life of unspeakable bliss with God. We answer the summons to that life by our willingness to do good and by our unwillingness to choose to do what we come to know as evil.

In conclusion, I would like to note that advocates of dissent from magisterial teaching will find little support in St. Thomas. He is a humble advocate of papal authority, and affirms quite clearly that the teaching of the Roman Pontiff is to be accepted over that of any theologian, however learned.[104]

Notes

1. The following studies are helpful for understanding St. Thomas's teaching on natural law: R. A. Armstrong, *Primary and Secondary Precepts in Thomistic Natural Law Teaching* (The Hague: Martinus Nijhoff, 1965); M. B. Crowe, *The Changing Profile of the Natural Law* (The Hague: Martinus Nijhoff, 1977), pp. 136–91; Walter Farrell, *The Natural Moral Law According to S. Thomas and Suarez* (Dichtling: St. Dominic's Press, 1930); Germain G. Grisez, "The First Principle of Practical Reason: A Commentary on the *Summa Theologiae* 1–2, Q. 94, A. 2," *Natural Law Forum* 10

(1965) pp. 168–96, reprinted with abridgments in *Aquinas: Critical Essays,* ed. A. Kenny (New York: Anchor, 1976). Dom Odon Lottin, *Le droit naturel chez Saint Thomas d'Aquin et ses predécésseurs* (Bruges: Beyaert, 1931); Lottin, "La valeur des formules de saint Thomas d'Aquin concernant la loi naturelle," *Mélanges Joseph Maréchal* 2 (Bruxelles: L'Edition universelle, 1950), pp. 346–77; William E. May, "The Meaning and Nature of the Natural Law in Thomas Aquinas," *American Journal of Jurisprudence* 22 (1977) 168–89; D. O'Donoghue, "The Thomist Concept of Natural Law," *Irish Theological Quarterly* 22 (1955) 89–109; Paul Overbeke, "La loi naturelle et le droit naturel selon S. Thomas," *Revue Thomiste* 57 (1957) 53–78, 450–95.

2. For abortion, infanticide, euthanasia, genocide, willful self-destruction, and the devastation of entire cities with their inhabitants, see Vatican Council II, *Gaudium et Spes* 27, 51, 79, 80. For abortion, see also Pius XII, "Address to the Italian Doctors," November 12, 1944 in *Discorsi e Radiomessaggi* ⅞ (1945): 191; John XXIII, *Mater et Magistra,* 194; Paul VI, Allocution, "Salutiamo con paterne effusione," December 9, 1972, *AAS* 64 (1972): 1777; Sacred Congregation for the Doctrine of the Faith, *Declaration on Procured Abortion,* November 18, 1974.

For contraception, see, for instance, Paul VI, *Humanae Vitae* (1968).

For fornication, adultery, and sodomy, see Sacred Congregation for the Doctrine of the Faith, *Declaration on Certain Questions of Sexual Ethics (Persona Humana),* December 29, 1975 (Washington, D.C.: United States Catholic Conference, 1976).

3. A sampling of contemporary Roman Catholic authors who take this position can be found in *Contraception: Authority and Dissent,* Charles E. Curran, ed., (New York: Herder and Herder, 1969) and in *The Catholic Case for Contraception,* Daniel Callahan, ed. (New York: Macmillan, 1969). This view is also represented in a work commissioned by the Catholic Theological Society of America, Anthony Kosnik et al., *Human Sexuality: New Directions in American Catholic Thought* (New York: Paulist Press, 1977).

4. This, for instance, is the position taken by Philip S. Keane, *Sexual Morality: A Catholic Perspective* (New York: Paulist Press, 1977), p. 109.

5. On abortion, see, for example, Daniel Callahan, *Abortion: Law, Choice, and Morality* (New York: Macmillan, 1970); Daniel C. Maguire, *Death by Choice* (Garden City, N.Y.: Doubleday & Company, 1974), pp. 199–202, and also *The Moral Choice* (Garden City, N.Y.: Doubleday & Company, 1978), p. 448; John F. Dedek, *Contemporary Medical Ethics* (New York: Sheed and Ward, 1975), pp. 109–36; Richard A. McCormick,

"Abortion: A Changing Morality and Policy?" *Hospital Progress* 60, no. 2 (February 1979): 36–44. It should be noted that none of these authors would hold that abortion on demand is morally good. Yet they all agree that directly intended abortion can be, in some instances, the morally justifiable choice.

On fornication and adultery, see Michael Valente, *Sex: The Radical View of a Catholic Theologian* (New York: Bruce, 1970); Kosnik et al., pp. 151–65.

On sodomy, see John McNeill, *The Church and the Homosexual* (Kansas City: Sheed, Andrews and McMeel, 1976); Charles E. Curran, "Dialogue with the Homophile Movement," in his *Catholic Moral Theology in Dialogue* (Notre Dame, Ind.: Fides, 1972); Kosnik et al., pp. 208–15. McNeill holds that sodomitic acts between adult, homosexually constituted persons in a relatively stable relationship are completely good, with no trace of evil. Curran believes that a degree of evil is present insofar as heterosexuality remains the ideal, but he sees sodomitic behavior as morally justifiable. Kosnik et al. are somewhat undecided whether to follow McNeill or Curran, but they agree that homosexual behavior is not necessarily immoral.

6. On infanticide, see Maguire, *Death by Choice,* pp. 7 and 12–13. On p. 7 Maguire cites Millard S. Everett to the effect that "no child should be admitted into the society of the living" who suffers "any physical or mental defect that would prevent marriage or would make others tolerate his company from a sense of mercy." As Paul Ramsey points out, Maguire "indicates no disagreement with such criteria." Paul Ramsey, *Ethics at the Edges of Life* (New Haven: Yale University Press, 1978), p. 206, n. 30.

In addition to Maguire, Albert Jonsen, a former Jesuit, finds it possible to defend infanticide as morally permissible in some instances. See *Ethics of Newborn Intensive Care,* Albert Jonsen and Michael J. Garland, eds., (Berkeley, Calif.: Institute of Governmental Studies, University of California, 1976), and an article co-authored by Jonsen, "Critical Issues in Newborn Intensive Care: A Conference Report and Policy Proposal," *Pediatrics* 55, no. 6 (June 1975): 756–68.

7. On euthanasia and willful self-destruction, see various writings by Maguire. In addition to his *Death by Choice* (see note 5) Maguire has defended mercy killing and deliberate suicide in "The Freedom to Die," originally published in the August 11, 1972 issue of *Commonweal* and reprinted in *New Theology 10,* edited by Martin Marty and Dean Peerman (New York: Macmillan, 1973), pp. 186–99, and in "A Catholic View of Mercy Killing," in *Beneficient Euthanasia,* Marvin Kohl, ed. (Buffalo: Prometheus Books, 1975), pp. 34–43.

8. It is very necessary, I believe, to note that the passage in the *Vatican Declaration* to which Curran objects so strongly is in fact an internal citation by that document of Vatican Council II, *Dignitatis Humanae*, 2, 3. Ironically Curran continues in his essay to contrast the approach to moral questions taken by the *Declaration* to what one finds in the documents of Vatican II!

9. Charles E. Curran, "Sexual Ethics: A Critique," in his *Issues in Sexual and Medical Ethics* (Notre Dame, Ind.: University of Notre Dame Press, 1978), pp. 38–39.

10. Maguire, "The Freedom to Die," in *New Theology 10*, p. 189.

11. Timothy E. O'Connell, *Principles for a Catholic Morality* (New York: Seabury Press, 1978). Curran's praise is contained in the Foreword that he contributed to the book. The encomia of Dedek, Cunningham, and Fuchs are printed on the book jacket.

12. I say "to considerable degree" because the theologians who basically agree to the positions developed by O'Connell differ among themselves in many ways.

13. O'Connell, p. 152. Although O'Connell's work is heavily in debt to the work of Richard A. McCormick, I believe that McCormick may have significantly modified his position. In "A Commentary on the Commentaries," an essay that he contributed to *Doing Evil to Achieve Good*, Richard McCormick and Paul Ramsey, eds. (Chicago: Loyola University Press, 1978), McCormick now frankly admits that it is impossible to weigh the human goods and to balance off good effects and evil effects (see in particular pp. 229 ff.). It would thus appear that McCormick now would repudiate the way O'Connell expresses matters as utilitarian.

14. O'Connell. The sentence is thrice repeated on pp. 152–53.

15. The pertinent literature here is extensive. McCormick has surveyed it quite thoroughly both in his *Ambiguity in Moral Choice* (Milwaukee: Marquette University Theology Department, 1973), in his "Notes on Moral Theology," for *Theological Studies* 33 (1972): 68–86; 36 (1975) 85–100; 38 (1977) 70–84; and 40 (1979) 59–80, and in the essay noted above in note 13. These works should be consulted for bibliographies. I have addressed this movement and the literature involved in several places. See, for instance, my *Becoming Human: An Invitation to Christian Ethics* (Dayton: Pflaum, 1974), chap. 4; "Modern Catholic Ethics: The New Situationism," *Faith and Reason* 4 (Fall 1978): 21–38; and "The Moral Meaning of Human Acts," *Homiletic and Pastoral Review* 79, no. 1 (October 1978): 10–21. Perhaps the most compelling essays criticizing the movement reflected in this literature are those of Paul Ramsey, "Incommensurability and Indeterminacy in Moral Choice," in *Doing Evil to Achieve Good*, pp. 69–144,

and of Germain G. Grisez, "Against Consequentialism," *American Journal of Jurisprudence* 23 (1978): 21–72. Recently McCormick and Curran edited an anthology entitled *Readings in Moral Theology, No. 1: Moral Norms and the Catholic Tradition* (New York: Paulist Press, 1979). The anthology reprints important essays by Fuchs, Schüller, Janssens, and other contemporary Catholic theologians in which the consequentialist approach is set forth. Included are only two essays opposing this trend, namely, those of John R. Connery S.J. and Paul Quay S.J. It is my opinion that McCormick and Curran chose *not* to include the strongest articles opposing this trend, namely, articles by Paul Ramsey, Germain Grisez, and others.

    16. O'Connell, p. 148.

    17. Ibid., p. 147.

    18. Ibid., p. 153.

    19. Here it is necessary to observe that these contemporary writers sharply distinguish between "moral" evil and what they variously term as "premoral," "nonmoral," "ontic" evil. See the literature referred to in note 15 for the development of this distinction.

    20. McCormick provides a Latin equivalent of this proposition when he holds that it is morally proper to intend directly a "premoral" evil *in ordine ad finem proportionatum.* See McCormick, "Notes on Moral Theology," *Theological Studies* 33 (1972): 74–75.

    21. O'Connell, p. 172.

    22. Those who support this view agree that it would always be wrong directly to intend what they call *moral* evil, e.g., the sin of another person. They also hold that it would always be wrong to intend to *murder* someone. But they maintain that *murder* is a moral term, not a purely descriptive term, and that it means an "unjust" killing deliberately and intentionally of another. Their point is that it is impossible to use nonmoral terms to describe an act that would *always* be morally wicked. When I suggested that it would always be wrong to use public funds to pay one's mistress or that it would always be wrong to torture a person (cf. "The Moral Meaning of Human Acts," p. 13), McCormick responded that the words *mistress* and *torture* are not descriptive terms but morally evaluative terms ("Notes on Moral Theology," *Theological Studies* 40 (1979): 78–79). It is instructive that he ignored another example given, namely, that "it is always wrong to have coition with a brute animal." I hold that *mistress* and *torture* are not morally evaluative but simply descriptive, and I find it illuminating that McCormick chose to ignore the other example. It is absurd to consider *coition with a cow* as a *moral* phase; it is descriptive.

    23. McCormick, *Ambiguity in Moral Choice,* p. 53: ". . . it is the presence or absence of a proportionate reason (good) which determines

whether my action—be it direct or indirect psychologically or causally—involves me in turning against a basic good in a way which is morally reprehensible."

24. In "A Commentary on the Commentaries," McCormick seems to me to be coming to the position that there are some sorts or kinds of deeds, such as devastating entire cities with their populations, that are as it were intrinsically *disproportionate*, a shift in his position to some extent. See pp. 250–51. Nonetheless, in this essay McCormick still insists on the teleological, i.e., consequential, nature of all concrete moral norms and must admit that, in principle at any rate, even the devastation of an entire city with its inhabitants could be morally good.

25. On this point, see McCormick, "Notes on Moral Theology," *Theological Studies* 32 (1972): 68–86, particularly at pp. 77 ff. In his *The Moral Choice*, Maguire speaks of concrete norms, such as a norm not to rape, as having "unimaginable exceptions," p. 162. By this he means that the justification of a rape of a mentally retarded girl, for instance, is almost unimaginable. Nonetheless, on his own principles it could be morally good. Perhaps there is a lack of imagination in Maguire, for it is not too difficult to conclude that many people might well imagine instances in which this sort of deed might be quite justifiable.

26. Curran, "Natural Law and Contemporary Moral Theology," in his *Contemporary Problems in Moral Theology* (Notre Dame, Ind.: Fides, 1970), p. 106. See also his "Absolute Norms in Moral Theology," in his *A New Look at Christian Morality* (Notre Dame, Ind.: Fides, 1968), pp. 75–89.

27. O'Connell, p. 138.

28. Curran, "Absolute Norms in Moral Theology," p. 83.

29. Ibid., pp. 82–83, citing *Summa Theologiae* 1-2, 94, 4.

30. Maguire, *The Moral Choice*, pp. 117–18, citing *Summa Theologiae* 1-2, 18, 3, *sed contra.*

31. Ibid., pp. 250–52. See also F. Scholz, "Durch ethische Grenzsituationen aufgeworfene Normenproblemen," *Theologischpraktische Quartalschrift* 123 (1975): 341–55; McCormick, "Notes on Moral Theology," *Theological Studies* 40 (1979): 79–80; John Giles Milhaven, "Moral Absolutes and Thomas Aquinas," in *Absolutes in Moral Theology?*, Charles E. Curran, ed. (Washington: Corpus, 1968), pp. 154–85. Of these articles Milhaven's is quite important and in many ways very helpful. Milhaven acknowledges quite frankly that St. Thomas definitely does teach that there are moral absolutes in the sense of universal negative prohibitions (cf. pp. 158, 169). Still his argument, and that of the other authors cited in this note, is that Aquinas was inconsistent in doing so and that the logic of his thought

concerning the justifiability of the deeds attributed to the Old Testament patriarchs commits him to the position that a proportionately good end can justify intending evil.

N.B. The article by F. Scholz referred to above has now been translated and printed in McCormick and Curran's anthology mentioned in note 15 above, *Readings in Moral Theology, No. 1: Moral Norms and the Catholic Tradition.*

32. The texts from St. Thomas pertinent to this matter are well presented in Milhaven's article.

33. For the historical development of St. Thomas's thought on natural law see Crowe and Lottin. Lottin and Crowe, in an earlier article ("St. Thomas and the Natural Law," *Irish Ecclesiastical Record* 76 (1951): 293–305) follow the chronology of Aquinas's works proposed by Grabmann and Mandonnet, and consequently consider the discussion of natural law in the *Commentary on the Nicomachean Ethics* (written, according to Grabmann, c. 1261–64 and, according to Mandonnet, c. 1266) chronologically prior to the presentation in the *Prima Secundae* of the *Summa Theologiae.* In his *Changing Profile of the Natural Law,* Crowe adopts the more accurate chronology proposed by R. A. Gauthier ("La date du commentaire de saint Thomas sur l'éthique à nicomaque," *Recherches de théologie ancienne et médiévale* 18 (1951): 66–105 and *Sententia Libri Ethicorum (Sancti Thomae de Aquino Opera Omnia* t. xlvii, Romae, 1969) praefatio, p. 201), who suggests the years 1271–72 for the composition of the *Commentary on the Nicomachean Ethics,* making it either contemporary with or perhaps a little after the composition of the *Primae Secundae.*

34. *Summa Theologiae* 1–2, 90, 1.

35. Ibid., ad 1.

36. Ibid., ad 2.

37. Ibid., 1–2, 91, 1. On the innovative character of St. Thomas's discussion of eternal law and the relationship between the eternal law and natural law, see Crowe, "St. Thomas and the Natural Law," pp. 302–3; Lottin, "Les Premiers Exposés scholastiques sur la loi éternelle," *Ephemerides Theologicae Lovanienses* (1937): 287–301; Walter Farrell, *The Natural Moral Law,* pp. 25–33.

38. *Summa Theologiae* 1–2, 93, 1.

39. Ibid., 91, 1, ad 1 and ad 2; 93, 1, ad 2.

40. This is an instance of a universal metaphysical principle of St. Thomas: *Quidquid recipitur ad modum recipientis recipitur.*

41. *Summa Theologiae* 1–2, 91, 2.

42. Ibid., 91, 2, and ad 3.

43. Ibid., 91, 2. On this matter it is worth noting what O'Donoghue

has to say. He observes: ". . . there are two ways of understanding rational participation. We might see it as *receptive* participation: created reason is receptive of Eternal Law just as irrational nature is . . . though in a higher way. . . . Or we might see rational participation as *legislative,* as participation in the very activity of legislating. . . . That we must understand rational participation in the second sense, seeing human reason as regulative rather than regulated, is clear from the fact that St. Thomas identifies the Natural Law with the 'propositions' or 'precepts' of natural reason. The matter is put beyond doubt by the discussion in Q. 93, a. 6, where a sharp distinction is drawn between participation in Eternal Law by way of *inclinatio naturalis ad id quod est consonum legi aeternae* and *ipsa naturalis cognitio boni.* . . . That which differentiates Natural Law from natural inclination, and makes it law in the proper sense, is the fact that it is the work of reason, expression rather than impression. It comes from God, as all human things . . but the mind receives it, not as itself an object which is revealed by it, but as becoming a source of light, discerning and declaring the truth for human activity (cf. 1–2, 91, 2)." In O'Donoghue, pp. 93–94.

44. On this it is instructive to consult Appendices 2 and 3 (pp. 162–71) by Thomas Gilby, the editor and translator of vol. 28 of the new Dominican Translation of the *Summa Theologiae* (New York: McGraw-Hill, 1966).

45. On the views of Thomas's predecessors see Lottin, and Crowe, *The Changing Profile of the Natural Law,* pp. 111–35.

46. *Summa Theologiae* 1–2, 94, 1.

47. Here it important to stress the role that practical reason plays for St. Thomas and the significance of the difference between speculative and practical reason. On this point, see Germain G. Grisez, *Contraception and the Natural Law* (Milwaukee: Bruce Publishing Company, 1964), chap. 3, and the literature cited there.

48. *Summa Theologiae* 1–2, 91, 2; 94, 2.

49. See ibid. 1–2, 8, 1; *De Veritate* 25, 1. See Armstrong, pp. 32–33, 46–48.

50. *Summa Theologiae* 1–2, 90, 1, ad 1 and ad 2.

51. Lottin, *Le droit naturel chez Saint Thomas. . . ,* p. 62: "Saint Thomas n'entend toutefois aucunement par là retirer à la raison la maitrise sur toutes les tendances de l'homme et il accepte tout ce qu'Albert le Grand avait dit à ce sujet."

52. Ibid., p. 66: "Mais cette habilitè même trahit le fond de la pensée de saint Thomas, je veux dire: ses sympathies sécrètes pour les formules du droit romain."

53. Lottin, "La valeur des formules de saint Thomas d'Aquin con-

cernant la loi naturelle," pp. 368–69; cf. pp. 375–76. In *Le droit naturel* Lottin says: "La définition la plus stricte du droit naturel est donc celle d'Ulpianus, le juriste romain: *'ius naturae est quod natura omnia animalia docuit.'* " (p. 62).

54. *In IV Sententiarum* d. 33, q. 1, a. 1.

55. Ibid.: "Lex ergo naturalis nihil est aliud quam conceptio homini naturaliter indita, qua dirigitur ad convenienter agendum in actionibus propriis, sive competunt ei ex natura generis, ut generare, comedere, et huiusmodi; sive ex natura speciei, ut rationari, et similia."

56. See *In 1 Sententiarum* d. 39, q. 2, a. 2.

57. In the body of the article of *In IV Sententiarum* d. 33, q. 1, a. 1, St. Thomas asserts that polygyny is indeed against the natural law in the sense that it at least impedes partially the marital good of fidelity and the peace and harmony that ought to reign in the family. He notes that it totally destroys the good of the sacrament of marriage, but he concedes that it is not totally destructive of the good of procreation and in this sense is not contrary to natural law in the same way that polyandry is, inasmuch as polyandry is destructive of the good of procreation.

58. In the text of his article St. Thomas erroneously attributes to Isidore the definition of the natural law given by Gratian, namely, as *that which is contained in the law and the gospel.* Cicero had defined it as *that which is not generated by opinion but by a certain innately given power.*

59. *In IV Sententiarum* d. 33, q. 1, a. 1: "ius naturale multipliciter accipitur. Primo enim ius aliquod dicitur naturale ex principio, quia a natura est inditum; et sic definit Tullius . . . dicens: Ius naturae est quod non opinio genuit, sed quaedam innata vis inseruit. Et quia etiam in rebus naturalibus dicuntur aliqui motus naturales, non quia sint ex principio intrinseco, sed quia sunt a principio superiori movente . . . ideo ea quae sunt de iure divino dicuntur esse de iure naturali, cum sint ex impressione et infusione superioris principii, scilicet Dei; et sic accipitur ab Isidoro . . . qui dicit, quod ius naturale est quod in lege et in Evangelio continetur. Tertio dicitur ius naturale non solum a principio, sed a natura, quia de naturalibus est. Et quia natura contra rationem dicitur, a qua homo est homo; ideo strictissimo modo accipiendo ius naturale, illa quae ad homines tantum pertinent, etsi sint de dictamine rationis naturalis, non dicuntur esse de iure naturali; sed illa tantum quae naturalis ratio dictat de his quae sunt homini aliisque communia; et sic datur dicta definitio, scilicet, Ius naturale est quod natura omnia animalia docuit."

60. I believe that it is proper to translate, "strictissimo modo accipiendo . . . illa tantum [esse de iure naturali] quae naturalis ratio dictat de his quae sunt homini aliisque communia" as follows: "in a *very restricted*

and limited sense . . . those things [are of natural law] which natural reason commands about matters that are common to men and other animals." This ought not to be translated as "in the most strict and precise sense," for in the most precise and formal sense this is *not* the meaning of natural law. For *strictissimus* as having the meaning of "most limited and restricted," see Roy J. Deferrari et al., *A Lexicon of St. Thomas Aquinas based on the Summa Theologica and Selected Passages of His Other Works* (Washington, D.C.: Catholic University of America Press, 1949) 5:1055, where this precise text (cited as *Summa Theologica* III, Supplement, 65, 1) is used to illustrate the meaning of "most rigid in interpretation." On this whole subject see my essay, "The Meaning and Nature of the Natural Law in Thomas Aquinas."

61. See text cited in note 59, particularly *in fine.*

62. In the *Summa Theologiae* St. Thomas refers (at least by implication) to the definition of Ulpian in 1-2, 94, 2; 95, 4, ad 1.

63. *In V Ethicorum,* lect. 12, n. 1019.

64. *Summa Theologiae* 1-2, 90, 1; 90, 1, ad 1 and ad 2; 91, 2.

65. Ibid., 1-2, 90, 1, ad 1; 91, 2, ad 3.

66. On this see Germain Grisez, "A Commentary on the First Principle of Natural Law . . ."

67. O'Donoghue, p. 91. In my judgment, Aquinas retained Ulpian's definition, in a limited way, in his thought precisely because he held that the inclinations we share with other animals are truly substantive human inclinations, not a part of a nature subhuman in character. The goods to which they direct us are, moreover, truly substantive goods of the human person, goods that are to be loved and pursued through human action. For further development of this matter see my "The Meaning and Nature of the Natural Law in Thomas Aquinas," pp. 180–81.

68. *Summa Theologiae* 1, 85, 1.

69. Perhaps these inclinations can be even more fittingly called "needs" of the human person. On this matter see Mortimer Adler, *The Time of Our Lives: The Ethics of Common Sense* (New York: Holt, Rinehart and Winston, 1970), pp. 84–97. See also my "Natural Law, Conscience, and Developmental Psychology," *Communio* 2 (1975): 3–31.

70. *Summa Theologiae* 1-2, 94, 2.

71. On this subject see Armstrong, pp. 24–55.

72. *Summa Theologiae* 1-2, 94, 2. This text is so central that it should be cited at length. After first drawing an analogy between practical and speculative inquiry in which he affirms that we need principles or starting points for both, St. Thomas writes: "Sicut autem ens est primum quod cadit in apprehensione simpliciter, ita bonum est primum quod cadit

in apprehensione practicae rationis, quae ordinatur ad opus: omne enim agens agit propter finem, qui habet rationem boni. Et ideo primum principium in ratione practica est quod fundatur supra rationem boni, quae est, *Bonum est quod omnia appetunt.* Hoc est ergo primum praeceptum legis, quod bonum est faciendum et prosequendum, et malum vitandum. Et super hoc fundantur omnia alia praecepta legis naturae: ut scilicet omnia illa facienda vel vitanda pertineant ad praecepta legis naturae, quae ratio practica naturaliter apprehendit esse bona humana." Note that here St. Thomas insists that the good that is to be done includes everything that practical reason naturally grasps as humanly good. He does not restrict the good that is to be done or the evil that is to be avoided to moral good or evil.

73. This is clear from the text cited in the previous note. On this subject one of the finest commentaries is provided by Grisez in the article to which reference has already been made.

74. This aspect of St. Thomas's thought is well expressed by Armstrong, pp. 38–41 and by Eric D'Arcy, *Conscience and Its Right to Freedom* (New York: Sheed and Ward, 1965), pp. 56–64.

75. *Summa Theologiae* 1-2, 95, 2.

76. Armstrong, p. 93.

77. *Summa Theologiae* 1-2, 100, 1.

78. On the meaning of prudence in St. Thomas, see ibid., 2-2, questions 47–51.

79. Ibid., 1-2, 94, 5.

80. Ibid., 94, 4.

81. Ibid.

82. Ibid., 90, 1, ad 2.

83. St. Thomas is no legalist in the sense that he teaches that something is wrong because it is forbidden or good because it is commanded. Rather his notion of law is grounded on intelligence, ultimately the intelligence of God and proximately the intelligence or practical reason of God's rational creature. His point is that because something really is good it is in accord both with God's eternal law and the rational creature's active participation in it and that because something is really evil and opposed to the *bona humana* (cf. *Summa Theologiae* 1-2, 94, 2, text cited in note 72), it is contrary to both eternal law and natural law.

84. Cf., e.g., *Summa Theologiae* 2-2, 66, 5 and 6. In 66, 7 Thomas teaches that in cases of necessity a person has the right to the superfluous goods of another so that their appropriation is *not* theft. The moral object of the act has been inwardly changed.

85. Cf., e.g., ibid., 2-2, 110, 1 and 2.

86. Cf., e.g., ibid., 2-2, 154, 2.

87. Cf., e.g., ibid., 2-2, 154, 8.

88. Cf., e.g., ibid., 2-2, 64, 7. The entire point of this important article is to highlight the centrality of intent in moral action. St. Thomas expressly teaches here that it is wicked for a private person, in defending his or her own life against attack, to intend directly the death of the assailant. This article contains the essential elements of what later became known as the "principle of double effect." For more detailed analyses of this text and its significance in assessing the thought of St. Thomas, see Joseph T. Mangan, "An Historical Analysis of the Principle of Double Effect," *Theological Studies* 10 (1949): 41–49; Germain G. Grisez, "Toward a Consistent Natural Law Ethics of Killing," *American Journal of Jurisprudence* 15 (1970): 64–96. The centrality of intent for St. Thomas in this text is badly misunderstood by Louis Janssens in an influential article "Ontic Evil and Moral Evil"; *Louvain Studies* 4 (1974): 114–56. Janssen's essay is now found in *Readings in Moral Theology, No. 1* (see note 15 above).

89. *Summa Theologiae* 1-2, 18, 5.

90. Ibid., 18, 2 (on the specification of the human act by its object) and 18, 4 (on the specification of the human act by its end). An excellent exegesis of these and parallel passages is provided by Augustine Joseph Brennan C.SS.R., *Moral Action in Aristotle and Aquinas* (Canberra, Canberra, Province of the Redemptorist Fathers, n.d.), pp. 47–50, 64–72. See also Theo G. Belmans, "La spécification de l'agir humain par son object chez Saint Thomas d'Aquin (Art. II)," *Divinitas* 23 (1979): 7–61.

91. It is important to note the difference between the proximate end of the human act, one that must be intentionally present to and willed by the agent, and the remote end. For instance, the proximate end of the act of stealing, an end that this act itself realizes and an end objectively one and the same with the act of stealing, is the usurping of goods that rightfully belong to another. One might do this deed for some ulterior or remote end, say, almsgiving, but the act would remain an act of theft and would therefore be contrary to natural-law precepts. The centrality of the distinction between proximate and remote ends is luminously explained by St. Thomas in *Summa Theologiae* 1-2, 1, 3, and ad 3. His whole point is that human acts are morally specified by the proximate end intended by the agent and realized objectively in and through the deed. The contemporary Roman Catholic theologians who propose a consequentialistic natural law (*do evil for the sake of a greater good*) attempt to justify acts by the remote or ulterior ends to which they are ordered.

92. On this point, cf. Brennan, pp. 22–26 and the texts of St. Thomas cited there.

93. *Summa Theologiae* 1-2, 18, 10.

94. For Maguire, Scholz, and McCormick, see note 31. Dedek has appealed to the same teaching of St. Thomas for the same purpose in his article "Intrinsically Evil Acts in St. Thomas," scheduled for publication in *The Thomist.* It is instructive to observe that in this article Dedek never alludes to or attempts to incorporate the teaching of St. Thomas on the objective determinants of the morality of human acts (*Summa Theologiae* 1-2, pp. 18–21) in seeking to analyze his teaching on the behavior of Abraham, Hosea, and the Israelites in "taking" the goods of the Egyptians.

95. The pertinent texts from St. Thomas on this matter are provided by Milhaven. Among the principal Thomistic texts are *Summa Theologiae* 1-2, 100, 8, ad 3; 2-2, 104, ad 2; *De Malo* 3, 1, ad 17; 15, 1, ad 8; *In I Sententiarum* d. 47, q. 1, a. 4 and ad 2.

96. *Summa Theologiae* 1-2, 100, 8, ad 3. In his Lombard Commentary, *In I Sententiarium* d. 47, q. 1, a. 4, and ad 2, St. Thomas even holds that God's action here is "quasi-miraculous."

97. *Summa Theologiae* 1, 48, 3.

98. For St. Thomas "the aliveness of living things is their very being (*esse*)" (*Summa Contra Gentes* 1, 98), and *esse* is the gift of God's free act of creation (*Summa Theologiae* 1, 45, 5).

99. Ibid., 1-2, 100, 8 and ad 3.

100. Ibid., 1-2, 100, 1.

101. Ibid., 100, 8.

102. Ibid., ad 3.

103. Among the texts in which St. Thomas expressly rejects the view that one can do evil to attain good are: *Summa Theologiae* 2-2, 64, 6 and 7; 154, 2; *De Malo* 15, 1, ad 3.

104. *Quodlibetal Questions* 9, 8 c, in *Quaestiones Quodlibetales,* Raymond Spiazzi, ed. (Romae: Marietti, 1949): "we must rather abide by the Pope's judgment than by the opinion of any of the theologians." Cf. *Summa Theologiae* 2-2, 1, 10; 11, 2, ad 3.

Natural Law Today

Richard M. Gula, S.S.

This chapter first appeared in *Reason Informed by Faith*, 1989.

Since the tension between the "order of nature" and the "order of reason" approaches to natural law has been so paramount in subsequent Catholic theology, we need to give more attention to the meaning and implications of each and show examples of their use in official Catholic teaching.[1]

NATURAL LAW IN MAGISTERIAL DOCUMENTS

The manner of deriving a moral position on the basis of the "order of nature" over the "order of reason" and pronouncing specific moral judgments on acts in themselves has found its way into the documents of the magisterium on sexual and medical moral matters pertaining to reproduction. For example, Pius XI in *Casti Connubii* (1930) says this:

> But no reason, however grave, may be put forward by which anything intrinsically against nature may become comfortable to nature and morally good. Since, therefore, the conjugal act is destined primarily by nature for the begetting of children, those who in exercising it deliberately frustrate its natural power and purpose sin against nature and commit a deed which is shameful and intrinsically vicious.[2]

This same understanding of natural law appears again in Pius XII's *Address to Midwives* in 1951:

Nature places at man's disposal the whole chain of the causes which give rise to new human life; it is man's part to release the living force, and to nature pertains the development of that force, leading to its completion. . . . Thus the part played by nature and the part played by man are precisely determined.[3]

Paul VI carried this understanding of natural law forward in *Humanae Vitae* in 1968 by maintaining:

Nonetheless the Church, calling men back to the observance of the norms of the natural law, as interpreted by the constant doctrine, teaches that each and every marriage act (*quilibet matrimonii usus*) must remain open to the transmission of life. . . .

To make use of the gift of conjugal love while respecting the laws of the generative process means to acknowledge oneself not to be the arbiter of the sources of human life, but rather the minister of the design established by the Creator. In fact, just as man does not have unlimited dominion over his body in general, so also, with particular reason, he has no such dominion over his generative faculties as such, because of their intrinsic ordination toward raising up life, of which God is the principle.[4]

Paul VI also reflects St. Thomas in making the order of nature superior to the order of reason in sexual matters by claiming:

The church is the first to praise and recommend the intervention of intelligence in a function which so closely associates the rational creature with his Creator; but she affirms that this must be done with respect for the order established by God.[5]

In 1975 the Sacred Congregation issued *Persona Humana,* the Declaration on Certain Questions Concerning Sexual Ethics, which repeats the perspective of *Humanae Vitae,* as can be seen from this excerpt:

> The main reason [that masturbation is an intrinsically and seriously disordered act] is that, whatever the motive for acting in this way, the deliberate use of the sexual faculty outside normal conjugal relations essentially contradicts the finality of the faculty.[6]

The same understanding of natural law is used again by the Congregation in its 1986 letter to bishops, "The Pastoral Care of Homosexual Persons." It points out that homosexual acts are deprived of their essential finality and are intrinsically disordered (n. 3). While this letter does appeal to personalism by claiming to base its teaching on the reality of the human person in one's spiritual and physical dimensions (n. 2), the personalist perspective is not carried through consistently. The method of the document is ultimately based on the essential nature of the sexual faculty which is taken to be the same as the whole personality.

Similarly, the 1987 document on bioethics, "Instruction on Respect for Human Life in its Origin and on the Dignity of Procreation," of the same Congregation is mixed in its natural law perspective. Even though it uses more personalistic terms and admits in the Introduction to a preference for the rational and not the biological emphasis of natural law, it falls back on natural law physicalism in treating some specific issues. For example, in the Introduction we read:

> Therefore this law [the natural moral law] cannot be thought of as simply a set of norms on the biological level; rather it must be defined as the rational order whereby man is called by the Creator to direct and regulate his life and actions and in particular to make use of his own body. . . .

> [Artificial interventions regarding procreation and the origin of life] must be given a moral evaluation in reference to

the dignity of the human person, who is called to realize his vocation from God to the gift of love and the gift of life.[7]

Yet behind these personalistic terms and openness to the rational order lie the framework and conclusions of physicalism regarding the morality of reproductive interventions. For example,

> Homologous artificial insemination within marriage cannot be admitted except for those cases in which the technical means is not a substitute for the conjugal act but serves to facilitate and to help so that the act attains its natural purpose.[8]

Physicalism, however, does light up some truth. Part of being human is to have a body whose structure and functions cannot be arbitrarily treated. So the strength of the physicalist approach to natural law is that it clearly recognizes the "giveness" of human nature. Human effort must indeed cooperate with the fixed character of human existence in promoting the well-being of human life. The weakness of this approach, however, is to mistake the "givens" of human nature as the whole of human nature, or to take the fixed character of human existence as being closed and beyond the control of human creative development. The danger of physicalism is to derive moral imperatives from bodily structure and functions and to exclude the totality of the person and his or her relational context in making a moral assessment.

Karl Rahner has captured well the tension between the giveness of nature and human creative capacities in this statement:

> For contemporary man, nature is no longer the lofty viceroy of God, one which lies beyond man's control, but instead has become the material which he needs so as to experience himself in his *own role of free creator* and so as to build *his* own world for himself according to his own laws. Of course, it is true that this material of human creativeness has laws proper to itself which will weigh heavily on man. It is true that this human creativeness consequently subjects itself, whether it likes it or not, to what is

alien and given to it; it is not pure creativeness as we acknowledge it of God; it does not come completely from within and it is not simply a law unto itself; it does not evoke matter and form out of nothing, and hence this creativeness of man, which has to deal with the laws of matter, is naturally also in every case a growth in obedience and "servitude" in the face of an alien law . . . but it is creation in knowing, willing and mastering sense, a creativeness which forces nature into its own service.[9]

The physicalist approach to natural law has been criticized on many counts.[10] Typical of the critical reactions to this approach to natural law and the conclusions it yields is this one by the Georgetown philosopher, Louis Dupre, made during the birth control debates of the 1960s:

> Such a way of reasoning about nature contains, I feel, two basic flaws. It confuses man's biological structure with his human nature. And it takes human nature as a static, unchangeable thing, rather than as a principle of development. Man's biological life and its intrinsic laws are but one aspect of human existence.[11]

Charles E. Curran has been consistent in his criticism of the physicalist approach to natural law. His criticisms run along several lines. He finds physicalism to reflect the naive realism of the classicist worldview. This means that physicalism is based on an essentialist definition of human nature which has no room for change; it views nature as a finished product so that change and historical process are incidental; also, it depends on a moral order that is fixed and undeveloping. Physicalism gives exaggerated importance to the human physical and biological nature in determining morality and puts these on a par with the whole personality. It also separates the action from the totality of the person and the full moral context. Physicalism claims too many negative moral absolutes based on the action taken in itself, and it does not make room for historical development and the creative intervention of reason to humanize the given patterns of nature.[12]

Catholic theology today is trying to revise the physicalist approach to natural law which dominated the manuals and the magisterial decrees on sexual ethics and medical moral matters pertaining to reproduction. Many theologians today are saying that natural law is not necessarily tied to physicalism and the classicist worldview; it belongs also in a worldview that takes experience, history, change, and development seriously. Contemporary theology's use of natural law is more historically conscious and taps into the second strain of interpretation of natural law, the order of reason.

The trend in Roman Catholic moral theology today is to develop more and more the rational aspect of the natural law tradition. In this use, reason, and not the physical structure of human faculties or actions taken by themselves, becomes the standard of natural law. Building on Thomistic foundations, this approach understands reason (*recta ratio*) in the broad sense of the dynamic tendency in the human person to come to truth, to grasp the whole of reality as it is. A morality that has reason as its basic standard, then, is a morality based on reality. The work of reason is to discover moral value in the experience of the reality of being human. This seems to be the fundamental direction which recent trends in interpreting the natural law are taking. Much more attention is being given today to the total complexity of reality experienced in its historically particular ways.[13]

In a natural law approach which emphasizes the rational aspects, the human person is not subject to the God-given order of nature in the same way the animals are. The human person does not have to conform to natural patterns as a matter of fate. Rather, nature provides the possibilities and potentialities which the human person can use to make human life truly human. The given physical and biological orders do not dictate moral obligations; rather, they provide the data and the possibilities for the human person to use in order to achieve human goals.

The natural order remains an important factor to consider if the human person is to base moral norms on reality. But the natural order is not to be taken as the moral order. The human person can creatively intervene to direct the natural order in a way that is properly proportionate to full human development. The "nature" which reason explores is no longer separated from the total complexity of personal, human life taken in all its relationships.[14]

This understanding of natural law has important implications for morality. Natural law morality is objective morality insofar as it is based, not on selfish interest, but on a critical effort to grasp the whole of human reality in all its relationships. Insofar as reality continues to change, moral positions must be open to revision. Inasmuch as we can grasp only a part of the whole at any one time, specific moral conclusions based on natural law will necessarily be limited and tentative. These conclusions are reliable insofar as they reflect as accurate a grasp of human reality as is possible at one time. But such conclusions must necessarily be open to revision since more of the meaning of being human is yet to be discovered.

While right reason is the full exercise of our capacity to grasp the whole of reality, the full exercise of reason is limited by individual capacities, emotional involvements which bias the interpretation of data, and cultural conditions which influence one's perspective on reality (cf. I–II, q. 94, a. 6). All of these factors necessarily place limitations on moral judgments, contribute to moral differences, and lead to more modest claims of certitude than did the order of nature approach to natural law.

The order of reason approach to natural law is used in magisterial documents on social ethics.[15] Even though the great social encyclicals *Rerum Novarum, Quadragesimo Anno,* and *Pacem in Terris* reflect something of a static social order, they do move away from the order of nature interpretation of natural law evident in decrees on sexual and medical moral matters to an interpretation of natural law which is based on the prudential use of reason. Consider this brief excerpt from *Pacem in Terris* (1963) as a point of illustration for this shift:

> But the Creator of the world has imprinted in man's heart an order which his conscience reveals to him and enjoins him to obey: *This shows that the obligations of the law are written in their hearts: their conscience utters its own testimony. . . .* But fickleness of opinion often produces this error, that many think that the relationships between men

and states can be governed by the same laws as the forces and irrational elements of the universe, whereas the laws governing them are of quite a different kind and are to be sought elsewhere, namely, where the Father of all things wrote them, that is, in the nature of man.[16]

In that encyclical John XXIII could address all persons of good will, not just Catholics specifically or Christians in general, because he emphasized that reason can discover the demands of human dignity placed in creatures by the creator.

Paul VI reflects a dynamic view of natural law in his great social encyclical *Populorum Progressio* (1967). He appeals to the creative intervention of the human person and the community to direct natural processes toward fulfillment:

In the design of God, every man is called upon to develop and fulfill himself, for every life is a vocation. At birth, everyone is granted, in germ, a set of aptitudes and qualities for him to bring to fruition. Their coming to maturity, which will be the result of education received from the environment and personal efforts, will allow each man to direct himself toward the destiny intended for him by his Creator. Endowed with intelligence and freedom, he is responsible for his fulfillment as he is for his salvation. He is aided, or sometimes impeded, by those who educate him and those with whom he lives, but each one remains, whatever be these influences affecting him, the principal agent of his own success or failure. By the unaided effort of his own intelligence and his will, each man can grow in humanity, can enhance his personal worth, can become more a person.[17]

In his apostolic letter of 1971, *Octogesima Adveniens* (more popularly known as "A Call to Action"), Paul VI also expressed a dynamic view of natural law. It is based on the order of reason which grounds morality in reality and yields tentative moral positions open to development.

In the face of such widely varying situations it is difficult for us to utter a unified message and to put forward a solution which has universal validity. Such is not our ambition, nor is it our mission. It is up to the Christian communities to analyze with objectivity the situation which is proper to their own country, to shed on it the light of the Gospel's unalterable words, and to draw principles of reflection, norms of judgment and directives for action from the social teaching of the Church.[18]

A comparison of documents representing the order of nature approach to natural law with those representing the order of reason approach shows the two different methods which have been operating in Catholic moral theology side by side to give us our moral norms and moral positions.[19] The clear distinctions and definitions which were possible by using the order of nature approach in sexual and medical moral matters are not present in the areas of social ethics. On the basis of the order of nature criteria, Catholic sexual ethics and medical ethics pertaining to reproduction have achieved a degree of certainty, precision, and consistency of moral judgment which we do not find in the documents on social ethics. The order of reason approach to understanding natural law does not yield the clear unambiguous positions which the order of nature approach does.

The church's epistemological claims in regard to natural law in social matters are more modest, more cautious, and more nuanced than those in sexual ethics and medical moral reproductive matters. In social ethics, the church readily accepts the inevitability of conflict on the philosophical level as well as in social life. The above excerpt from *Octogesima Adveniens* acknowledges this and the American bishops openly acknowledge inevitable diversity in their recent pastoral letters on war and peace and the economy. In *The Challenge of Peace* (1983) we read:

When making applications of these principles we realize— and we wish readers to recognize—that prudential judgments are involved based on specific circumstances which

can change or which can be interpreted differently by people of good will.

... On complex social questions, the Church expects a certain diversity of views even though all hold the same universal moral principles.[20]

From such a perspective, the church accepts conclusions of the application of general principles which are limited, tentative, and open
to revision—all of which are characteristic of the order of reason
strain in the tradition of natural law.

A review of what we have seen thus far will prepare us for a
synthetic view of the profile of natural law in contemporary Catholic moral theology. For this review, see the accompanying chart
which contrasts the salient features of both approaches to the natural law. The examples under the order of nature approach actually
show a mix in their use of natural law. However, the order of nature
interpretation of natural law does dominate to control the moral
method and conclusions of these documents.

SYNTHETIC DESCRIPTION OF NATURAL LAW

In light of the tradition of natural law just considered, we can
bring together a synthetic description of natural law which high-
lights its salient features.

The Meaning of "Natural"

As it is used in natural law theory, "natural" is not opposed to
"artificial," nor does it refer to the well-defined given structures and
functions of the body or of any created reality. To equate "natural"
with well-defined patterns in creation leads to a natural fundamentalism and yields a "blueprint" of "maker's instructions" theory of
the natural moral law. Such an approach has no room for the distinctively human, creative aspects of moral knowledge and freedom. Moral knowledge would be simply the matter of discovering

the given patterns in the world, and freedom would be reduced to a matter of abiding by or violating what is given.

Rather, the notion "natural" in natural moral law theory is more accurately construed as shorthand for the total complexity of human reality taken in all its relationships and with all its potential. What pertains to "nature" is accessible to all and provides the potential with which human creativity must deal in order to achieve human wholeness. Since "nature" is constantly changing, it continues to make new demands on us. As a result, change, revision, and development would be constitutive of the natural moral law.

The force of "natural," then, is not to oppose what is artificial or to point to a fixed pattern in the world. Rather, it is to ground morality in reality lest moral obligations become the product of self-interest groups or subjective whim. "Natural" is what is in reality providing the potential which would make it possible for each person to come to wholeness in community with others seeking wholeness.

The Meaning of "Law"

The notion of "law" in natural moral law theory is "law" only in a secondary sense. It is "law" in the sense of disclosing moral obligation. But it does not have the meaning of a codified system of rights or regulations prescribed by a legislator, such as the Bill of Rights or the Nuremberg Code. Nor does it have the sense of a scientific law of uniform behavior, such as the law of gravity or the law of thermodynamics. While uniformity is indeed an important aspect of law in the regulation of elements and organisms, human moral behavior is not regulated in the same way as animate or inanimate objects are. Human moral behavior respects the creative human capacity for knowledge and freedom.

The force of "law" in natural moral law theory is the force of reason in the Thomistic sense of *recta ratio*—the inclination to grasp the whole of reality and come to moral truth. "Law" then means that reason is the basic standard by which we discern moral obligation in the total complex of human relationships. As we discover more and more what contributes to human well-being and

TWO STRAINS OF INTERPRETATION
OF NATURAL LAW
AND IMPLICATIONS FOR MORAL NORMS

FEATURES	"THE ORDER OF NATURE"	"THE ORDER OF REASON"
1. Designation of Moral Norms	"According to Nature"	"According to (right) Reason"
2. Source of Moral Norms	"Written in Nature" God is the author of nature. God-given structures take priority over anything derived from human reflection.	"Human Experience" taken in all its complexity and in its relationships Norms express the prudent use of reason in the human, rational effort to grasp moral obligation grounded in human experience.
3. Knowledge of Moral Norms	Observe the way nature works.	Rational grasp of human experience. Reason is expressed through whatever means would help us grasp the meaning of being human in all its fullness.

FEATURES	"THE ORDER OF NATURE"	"THE ORDER OF REASON"
4. Violation	Any interference with the order designed by God is gravely serious. No "light matter" here.	Acting against what you know to be a true expression of what most fulfills human potential as this can be known through reason's reflection on human experience.
5. Examples	*Casti Connubii* (1930) Pius XII's *Address to Midwives* (1951) *Humanae Vitae* (1968) *Persona Humana* (1975) *Letter on the Pastoral Care of Homosexual Persons* (1986) *Instruction on Bioethics* (1987)	*Rerum Novarum* (1891) *Quadragesimo Anno* (1931) *Pacem in Terris* (1963) *Gaudium et Spes* (1965) *Populorum Progressio* (1967) *Octogesima Adveniens* (1971) *The Challenge of Peace* (1983) *Economic Justice for All* (1986)

personal wholeness in community, we can formulate with confidence these discoveries of value into guiding norms, such as respect human life, treat others as you would wish to be treated. Insofar as these norms reflect truly human values, they can be invoked as guiding principles for all peoples.

From these understandings of "natural" and "law" we can put together a synthetic definition which reflects the core of the Catholic natural law tradition: natural law is reason reflecting on human experience discovering moral value.

The Function and Value of Natural Law

Natural law functions in the Catholic moral tradition more as an approach to discovering moral value than as a body of established content. As an approach to moral value, it yields three basic convictions which are hallmarks of Catholic morality.[21]

1. Natural law claims the existence of an objective moral order.
This claim follows from the conviction that morality is grounded in reality. On this basis Catholic morality claims some actions as right and some as wrong since moral obligation is not something which can be made up at will, nor is it dependent on a single individual's or group's interest. This conviction places natural law morality in strict opposition to the extreme forms of situation ethics which emphasize the uniqueness of each moment of moral choice and an unpredictably changing moral order. It also puts natural law morality in strict opposition to voluntarism (or legal positivism) which makes the will of the legislator the determiner of the morally right or wrong.

2. Natural law morality is accessible to anyone independently of one's religious commitment.
This conviction claims that our knowledge of moral value and moral obligation is available to anyone who is able to do the critical work of reflecting on human experience with an interest in discovering moral truth. It enables the Catholic tradition to argue for the rightness of particular actions without recourse to religious insight

or motivation. As such, this puts Catholic natural law morality in strict opposition to a divine command theory of ethics, such as that of Karl Barth, which requires access to divine revelation to know what is morally required. It enables Catholic morality to engage in ecumenical dialogue on moral issues not only with other Christian traditions, but also with non-Christian religions as well as with non-religious persons.

The claim that the natural law is accessible to everyone does not mean that everyone actually knows what is morally required or is equally committed to it. This does not change the fact that morality has an objective ground. It may, however, render a person less culpable of immorality. For example, not every murder is committed by a morally culpable person, but that does not lessen the immorality of murder. This conviction is the basis in natural law for the requirement of a keen pastoral sensitivity when dealing with others who may not be culpable in some moral matters. The traditional Catholic distinction between the objectively immoral action and the subjectively non-culpable person derives from this conviction.

3. The knowledge of moral value can be universalized.

The Catholic moral tradition has addressed its teaching to all people of good will in the belief that it is teaching the truth about being human generally. To discover an objective moral value which renders some actions right and some wrong is to discover something which would apply wherever that value is at stake or those particular actions are done.

These are three hallmarks of Catholic morality rooted in its natural law tradition and still viable today. From these we can move on to sketch the characteristic features of a contemporary profile of natural law which represents the dominant tendency of a significant number of contemporary Catholic theologians.

CONTEMPORARY PROFILE OF NATURAL LAW

While no totally systematic treatment of a revised theory of natural law has yet been made, at least certain key features which would make up the profile of such a theory have emerged. Timothy E. O'Connell has outlined them well as real, experiential, historical, and proportional.[22] I will summarize his presentation here and add the component of "personal" which, though implicit and running through all his other features, he does not identify specifically.

Real

Natural law asserts that morality is based on reality. Realism stands, on the one hand, in opposition to legal positivism which makes something right merely because it is commanded. On the other hand, realism stands against a morality based on personal whim whereby one can arbitrarily decide what is right and wrong. The dimension of realism in a natural law theory means that the moral life, ultimately, is not merely a matter of obedience to positive law, nor is it a matter of doing whatever you want. The moral life is a matter of doing the good. The moral person and the moral community must discover what is morally good by critically reflecting on the total complexity of human reality in all its relationships. The more we discover what it means to be human the more we may have to revise our previously accepted conclusions in morality. Our views of what is moral may change as our knowledge of what it means to be authentically human develops. This is the fundamental direction of a contemporary natural law approach to morality. A moral position based on natural law, then, would be an expression of what the moral community discovers in its experience to be most contributing to the full actualization of human potential to attain human wholeness.[23]

Experiential

If morality is based on reality, we come to know morality through experience. The experience of what helps or hinders human well-being precedes and directs the course of a moral argument. For example, we see what lying does to people before we put together arguments about what makes lying wrong. This suggests an inductive method for moral theology and an appeal to empirical evidence in our process of deriving moral norms and carrying on moral evaluations.[24] We discover moral value through our experience of living in relationship with self, others, God, and the world. A moral position of the community ought to reflect its collective experience of what it means to live this relational life. The inherited formulations of a moral position are tested by continued experiences of what builds up and promotes the dignity of human life. All this means that our moral theology must pay close attention to human experience, past and present, in telling us what it means to be human.

Consequential

Closely related to the experiential is the consequential. With the feature of "consequential" we are entering an arena of much controversy, especially because "consequences" are often interpreted too narrowly to mean the short-run, immediate consequences.[25] Consequences are an important part of moral meaning, but consequences *alone* do not tell us what is right or wrong. The totality of moral reality includes more than consequences. Yet consequences are important if we are going to pay attention to the accumulation of human experience. The moral community's ongoing experience of what helps and hinders the well-being of human life gives rise to a moral position. These positions are retained within the community as a way of passing on to the next generation the accumulated wisdom of the moral community's experience of moral value.[26]

Historical

One of the most frequent criticisms made of traditional natural law theory, especially of the order of nature strain of interpretation, is that it fails to account for the possibility of change and development. Its static view of the moral order produced universal and immutable positions. In contrast, the historically conscious worldview of contemporary theology has as a central characteristic the reality of change and development. Contemporary theology asks whether we can continue to presume that moral conclusions drawn on the basis of historically conditioned experience and a limited perspective can be equally valid for all times, places, and peoples. Whereas traditional moral theology grounded natural law norms in the abstract, ahistorical, metaphysical nature of the human person which it held to be unchanging through the ages, contemporary natural law theory grounds its position in the human person concretely realized in various stages and situations of history. But nothing is more damaging to natural law than to absolutize what is, in fact, relative to history and to culture. Contemporary theology recognizes that it cannot ignore the unfinished, evolutionary character of human nature and the human world. Historical changes cannot be dismissed as accidental to what it means to be human. The evidence of experience and the verification by data of the historical sciences are too strong to support such a position.

The influence of historical consciousness on morality today is great. Moral teaching today must be able to take into account our fundamental capacity for change and development. What has built up human well-being in the past may, or may not, continue to do so in the present or future.[27] This historical component of natural law leaves room for change and development. A moral position developed from this approach will reflect the tentativeness of historical consciousness and the provisional character of moral knowledge.[28]

Proportional

O'Connell's last component is introduced to help us answer the practical moral question, "What ought we to do?" At the most fundamental level, we ought to do what is genuinely good, what is most loving, what truly contributes to the well-being of persons and community. Yet we know that we are limited in so many ways—such as our personal capacities and skills, our time, and our freedom. The good we do comes mixed with some bad. Our moral efforts are directed toward trying to achieve the greatest proportion of good to evil. The component of proportionality in natural law tells us that we are doing the morally right thing when we achieve the greatest possible proportion of good over evil.[29] This, in fact, gets to the heart of the Christian virtue of prudence as it comes to us through St. Thomas (I–II, q. 61, a. 2). It tells us that moral persons must be able to guide us in our prudential judgments, i.e., in our judgments of proportionality.

Personal

Gaudium et Spes (1965) is a landmark document for the shift from "nature" to "person" in an official Church document.[30] This historically conscious, empirically oriented, personally focused document of the Second Vatican Council introduced new considerations into natural law by the attention it calls not to human nature as such, but to the human person. Part I of that document lays the groundwork for this shift, and Part II addresses specific problems in light of a personalistic perspective. We have already explored the implications of the shift from nature to person under the analysis of Louis Janssens' version of the personalistic criterion of "the human person adequately considered." Again in brief summary, they are: (1) to be a moral subject, i.e., to act with knowledge and in freedom; (2) to be an embodied subject; (3) to be an historical subject with continuing new possibilities; (4) to be an embodied subject who is part of the material world; (5) to be related to others; (6) to be in a social group with structures and institutions worthy of persons; (7) to be called to know and worship God; (8) to be unique yet fundamentally equal (cf. Chapter 5).

A person-based morality avoids the fragmenting of human nature into distinct faculties each having its own inherent purpose and morality independently of other aspects of the person and of the totality of the person's relationships. The shift from "nature" to "person" acknowledges not only what all persons have in common, but also their differences as unique individuals with a distinct origin, history, cultural environment, and personal vocation from God. The focus on the person in natural law theory can move us closer to realizing that our vocation as persons is to image the divine community of persons.

These in brief are the salient features of a contemporary profile of natural law. It is rooted in the order of reason strain of the natural law tradition, and it is consistent with the historically conscious worldview of contemporary theology. This approach to natural law calls for an inductive method of moral argument which takes historical human experience seriously. It is sensitive to the ambiguity of moral experience and to the limitations of formulating absolute, universal, concrete moral norms. The use of natural law in Catholic morality today is becoming more open to the great complexity and ambiguity of human, personal reality. Its conclusions, while as accurate as the evidence will allow, are accurate enough to be reliable but must necessarily be tentative and open to revision.

With this overview of the tradition and use of natural law in Catholic moral theology, we are ready to explore in the following chapters the particular applications of natural law in the form of human, positive law, and moral norms.

Notes

1. For a comparison of the natural law approaches in sexual and social ethical documents, see Christopher Mooney, "Natural Law: A Case Study," in *Public Virtue: Law and the Social Character of Religion* (Notre Dame: University of Notre Dame Press, 1986), pp. 140–150. See also Charles E. Curran, "Catholic Social and Sexual Teaching: A Methodological Comparison," *Theology Today* 44 (January 1988): 425–440.

2. Unless otherwise indicated, all excerpts from official ecclesiastical documents in this section are taken from the handy resource book, *Official Catholic Teachings: Love and Sexuality,* ed. Odile M. Liebard (Wilmington, N.C.: McGrath Publishing Company, 1978). This quote is on p. 41.

3. *Ibid.,* p. 102.

4. *Ibid.,* pp. 336–337.

5. *Ibid.,* p. 339.

6. *Ibid.,* p. 436.

7. Congregation for the Doctrine of the Faith, "Instruction on Respect for Human Life in its Origins and on the Dignity of Procreation," St. Paul Editions (Boston: Daughters of St. Paul, 1987), pp. 8–9.

8. *Ibid.,* p. 31.

9. "The Man of Today and Religion," *Theological Investigations,*

Vol. 6, translated by Karl-H. and Boniface Kruger (New York: Seabury Press, 1974), p. 8.

10. See, for example, the excellent article by Edward A. Malloy, "Natural Law Theory and Catholic Moral Theology," *American Ecclesiastical Review* 169 (September 1975): 456–469, especially pp. 457–461.

11. Dupre, *Contraception and Catholics: A New Appraisal* (Baltimore: Helicon Press, 1964), pp. 43–44.

12. See Curran's "Absolute Norms in Moral Theology," *Norm and Context in Christian Ethics,* edited by Gene Outka and Paul Ramsey (New York: Charles Scribner's Sons, 1968), pp. 139–173; also "Absolute Norms and Medical Ethics," in Curran's edited collection *Absolutes in Moral Theology?* (Washington: Corpus Books, 1968), pp. 108–153; and his "Natural Law," in *Directions,* pp. 119–172.

13. Summaries of trends in natural law thinking can be found in Richard A. McCormick, "Moral Notes," *Theological Studies* 28 (December 1967): 760–769; also, George M. Regan, *New Trends in Moral Theology* (New York: Newman Press, 1971) pp. 115–144. For a Protestant view of trends in Catholic natural law thinking, see James M. Gustafson, *Protestant and Roman Catholic Ethics: Prospects for Rapproachement* (Chicago: University of Chicago Press, 1978), pp. 80–94. For some creative articles on natural law, see those by Curran in the note above; also Bernard Häring, "Dynamism and Continuity in a Personalistic Approach to Natural Law," *Norm and Context,* Outka and Ramsey, eds., pp. 199–218; Michael B. Crowe, "Natural Law Theory Today," *The Future of Ethics and Moral Theology,* Richard A. McCormick, *et al.* (Chicago: Argus Communications Co., 1968), pp. 78–105.

14. This is a point clearly made by Josef Fuchs; see especially "Human, Humanist and Christian Morality," *Human Values and Christian Morality* (London: Gill and Macmillan Ltd., 1970), pp. 140–147, especially at p. 143.

15. For a study of natural law in the social encyclicals, see Charles E. Curran, "Dialogue with Social Ethics: Roman Catholic Ethics—Past, Present, Future," *Catholic Moral Theology in Dialogue* (Notre Dame: Fides Publishers, 1972), pp. 111–149.

16. Unless otherwise indicated, the excerpts from ecclesiastical documents on social ethics are taken from the convenient resource, *Official Church Teaching: Social Justice,* ed. Vincent P. Mainelli (Wilmington, N.C.: McGrath Publishing Co., 1978). For this first excerpt, see p. 64. For an interpretation of "imprinted in man's heart" that follows the order of reason approach to natural law, see Fuchs, "Human, Humanist and Christian Morality," *Human Values,* pp. 144–147.

17. Mainelli, ed., *Social Justice*, p. 210.

18. *Ibid.*, p. 255. This excerpt also shows the elements of a moral method for reflecting on a social issue: namely, situational analysis, religious convictions, and moral norms. Not included is a consideration of the "agent," which is often hard to identify in a social issue.

19. Such a comparison is astutely made by Charles E. Curran in "Catholic Social and Sexual Teaching: A Methodological Comparison," *Theology Today* 44 (January 1988): 425–440.

20. *The Challenge of Peace* (Washington: USCC, 1983), paragraphs 10–12, pp. 4–5. The bishops make a similar claim in their letter, *Economic Justice for All* (1986), paragraphs 20–22.

21. What follows is a summary of the key themes of the section "Basic Catholic Principles" concerning moral objectivity in Philip S. Keane, "The Objective Moral Order: Reflections on Recent Research," *Theological Studies* 43 (June 1982): 260–262.

22. O'Connell, *Principles for a Catholic Morality* (New York: Seabury Press, 1978), pp. 144–154.

23. Daniel C. Maguire confirms "realism" in his approach to morality. See *The Moral Choice* (Garden City: Doubleday & Co., 1978), p. 220.

24. This has been a consistent theme of John G. Milhaven. See his "Toward an Epistemology of Ethics," *Theological Studies* 27 (June 1966): 228–241; also, "Objective Moral Evaluation of Consequences," *Theological Studies* 32 (September 1971): 407–430; and "The Voice of Lay Experience in Christian Ethics," *CTSA Proceedings* 33 (1978): 35–53. See also Maguire, *The Moral Choice*, pp. 221–222. Robert H. Springer is another Catholic theologian who has appealed to the empirical grounding for morality in his "Conscience, Behavioral Science and Absolutes," in Charles E. Curran, ed., *Absolutes in Moral Theology?* pp. 19–56. Charles E. Curran has written a valuable article identifying some of the difficulties involved in moral theology's efforts to dialogue with empirical science. See his essay "Dialogue with Science: Scientific Data, Scientific Possibilities and the Moral Judgment," *Catholic Moral Theology in Dialogue*, pp. 65–110.

25. Richard A. McCormick, "Moral Notes," *Theological Studies* 36 (March 1975): 93–100, reviews pertinent literature on the interpretation of "consequences."

26. The issue of how to regard consequences is receiving a great deal of attention in the moral literature. In addition to McCormick's "Notes" above, see the balanced treatment of Maguire, *The Moral Choice*, pp. 150–170. For two essays negatively critical of consequences, see John R. Connery, "Morality of Consequences: A Critical Appraisal," *Readings in Moral Theology No. 1: Moral Norms and Catholic Tradition*, edited by Charles E.

Curran and Richard A. McCormick (Ramsey: Paulist Press, 1979), pp. 244–266. In the same collection, see also Paul M. Quay, "Morality by Calculation of Values," pp. 267–293.

27. John Noonan's work, *Contraception* (Cambridge: Harvard University Press, 1965), shows how historical factors influence the weight given to competing values in different historical periods. Natural law theory that is historically conscious will be cautious about issuing single, unambiguous answers for all times.

28. This has been a consistent theme of Charles E. Curran in his analysis of natural law. See for example his "Natural Law" in *Directions in Fundamental Moral Theology* (Notre Dame: University of Notre Dame Press, 1985), pp. 119–172.

29. The idea of proportionality has been receiving a great deal of attention in recent years. For some seminal works on this notion in the collection edited by Curran and McCormick, *Readings in Moral Theology No. 1,* see Peter Knauer, "The Hermeneutic Function of the Principle of Double Effect," pp. 1–39; Louis Janssens, "Ontic Evil and Moral Evil," pp. 40–93; Richard A. McCormick, "Reflections on the Literature," pp. 294–340. Also see the collection of essays responding to Richard A. McCormick's major contribution to this discussion, *Ambiguity in Moral Choice,* which is the first chapter in the collection, *Doing Evil to Achieve Good,* edited by Richard A. McCormick and Paul Ramsey (Chicago: Loyola University Press, 1978).

30. David F. Kelly has traced the methodological development of Catholic teaching on medical ethics in America from natural law physicalism (1900–1940) to empirical personalism (1965 and beyond). "Empirical personalism" is a shorthand formula for the contemporary understanding of natural law. Kelly shows it emerges with the impetus of the shift made at the Second Vatican Council. See his *The Emergence of Roman Catholic Medical Ethics in North America* (New York: Edwin Mellen Press, 1979), pp. 416–436 and 449–454.

Nature as the Basis of Morality

Franz Böckle

This article first appeared in *Personalist Morals*, 1988

The question of the approach of mankind toward nature is the same as that of the *relationship between nature and praxis*. Ever since the teleology of nature has been disputed by the natural sciences, the concept of nature in modern practical philosophy has been problematic.[1] Nature is now understood, on the one hand, as a necessary structure, which emerges all the more clearly the more the cultural superstructure is stripped away. It therefore becomes important for nature to be liberated and for all human activity to be consistently understood as natural. Alternatively, nature can be viewed as mankind's pure and hypothetical original condition, preceding human history. Extricating ourselves from nature becomes a process of liberation, and history itself becomes the place where this liberation occurs. Both these reductions of the concept of nature have one thing in common—nature and history are seen to be incommensurable. "Naturalism and historicism are but two sides of the same coin."[2]

The concept of nature is determined by our prior understanding of human praxis. It can therefore be varied arbitrarily. There is, however, a fundamental relationship between nature and praxis that is, to a certain extent, irreversible. According to its most universal tendency, nature is the reality that is not set free from praxis, but necessarily presupposes it. By nature, human beings are predisposed to transcend nature. Human actions are not simply natural events: thus, they can only be justified as acts and not simply as natural events. How, then, should the activity whereby mankind transcends nature be defined and what is the significance of nature in that activity? This question has become the focus of discussion in recent years, as an investigation of the philosophical works of Karol Woj- tyła might illustrate.

I.
THE CONCEPT OF "NATURE" IN THE TRADITION OF MORAL THEOLOGY

By the 5th century B.C. at the latest, the Greek word φύσις was used to "refer terminologically to everything which we human be- ings have not made and for which we are not responsible, everything which exists and occurs without human agency and its conse- quences."[3] *Nature* here is in correlative *contrast to human praxis,* i.e., to the "human sphere of life, where this is shaped by laws and convention (νόμος), tradition and customs (ἔθος), by statute (θέσις) and craft (τέχνη)."[4] Ethical theory is concerned with the proper relationship between the reality of nature already present, on the one hand, and the world of norms fashioned by human beings, on the other. Ethics, of course, focuses directly on the praxis of life. However, no moral or legal order can endure if the link with reality is lacking. There is fundamental agreement on this. What remains controversial is the *way* in which extant reality has a bearing on the moral and legal orders. The answer has always been dependent on how the reality of nature was interpreted.

The beginnings of philosophy are characterized by releasing mankind's moral ties with a nature mythologically suffused with the arbitrariness of the gods. At the same time, the representatives of Ionian natural philosophy saw nature as normative in what is cer- tainly a new way: as a cosmos based on ordered rules, it is to be seen as a rationally comprehensible, alternative model to the norms of myth. After an era of critical examination by the Sophists, and against the background of Platonian and Aristotelian interpretation, the Stoics incorporated substantial elements of natural philosophy in their teaching. After the collapse of the city states, "in the Stoic view the *world* as cosmos is one single rational organism, one single polis on a grand scale. The divine universe . . . becomes, for the

Stoic, that home which one's own polis can no longer provide."[5] Admittedly, this basic principle of Stoic thinking underwent considerable change. It moved away from a natural order envisaged as a union with God towards a split involving the recognition by the intellect of what God intended in the natural order. Thus, the rational insight of the wise person (φρόνεσις) is decisive for moral cognition. The moral law of nature

> no longer lies in the universe outside mankind, man's insight itself is now the law that sets the norm: in order properly to achieve what is natural, man must follow his understanding. A concept of natural law which was originally taken from metaphysics and natural philosophy has changed into a psychological and anthropological concept. Only the thought can be spoken which says that man must always follow the voice of God as He speaks to man in his intellect.[6]

This development and expression of neo-Platonian and Stoic thinking exerted an enduring influence on moral theological tradition. This influence affects both the substantiation of the natural moral law by participation in divine reason (1) and the substantiation of the indispensible content of a naturally moral order (2).

1. The Natural Moral Law as Participation by Practical Reason in Divine Reason

The natural moral law, in its primary and true meaning in Thomas Aquinas, does not refer to a natural moral code, to a collection of extant norms, nor even to the sum total of all those precepts and prohibitions which can be justified rationally. In Thomas Aquinas' own words, the natural moral law is "participation (by a rational being) in eternal reason, whereby the being possesses a natural inclination to the actions and the objective which are appropriate to his existence." (S.Th. I.II., q. 91, a. 2). This means that the natural moral law is obviously an internal law; in modern terms we would speak of a structural law of practical reason. Insights of practical reason differ from theoretical insight in being cognitional in their mode of acknowledgment. Practical reason carries out such acknowledgment according to a supreme rule "which gives all judgments used for direct actions the form: viz. that what is seen to be good is to be done and what is seen to be bad is to be eschewed."[7] For Thomas Aquinas, this rule is the primary principle of practical reason, analogous to the principle of contradiction as the primary principle of theoretical reason. This principle is sustained by the original conscience, syndereisis, which shapes the character of practical reason. Insofar as practical reason cannot evade the recognition of unlimited good, Thomas Aquinas calls syndereisis a natural disposition.

"Natural," therefore, is here used in the sense of originally present with practical reason. The practical principle, the supreme rule itself, however, is not innate, being—like any rule—constituted by reason (*constitutum a ratione,* q. 94, a. 1). A person attains the primary principle by the *activity* of reason. In activating practical reason the principle achieves awareness, thereby gaining direct insight. It is precisely in this process of constituting the rule as well as in the rule itself thus constituted that Thomas finds the elements of the definition of the law "in its true meaning" preserved for the natural moral law.[8] It is a law which is recognized in praxis. By establishing its laws for itself in this way, human reason participates in divine reason. "For the nomothetical character of the natural law, what is important is not the *ratio* in God, but the *ratio* of man. Man is suddenly the subject of the law: he himself has the *providentia* for himself. God *and* human *ratio* appear *at the same time* as the subject of the 'provision of reason'."[9]

Nevertheless, as a supreme rule the principle (*bonum faciendum*) is not a rule which exerts direct control over human actions. It does not lay down what is right or wrong in detailed judgments. It subjects the concrete judgments on actions to the control of unlimited good (the goal of human actions which is appropriate to the nature of the person) and only gives them the mode of obligating truth on the basis of this goal. What is revealed in this interplay of the planning and scrutiny of practical reason is the structure of moral reason in general. And the natural moral law is accordingly nothing more than the intrinsic, structural law of reason controlling human actions, whereby reason subordinates its self-determination and self-assessment to the demands of unlimited good. In this self-determination by reason and free will subject to the demands of good lies the *imago Dei* of the person and thus the basis of dignity.

2. Norms of a Naturally Moral Order

The nomothetical activity of reason is not exhausted in the self-commitment to absolute good by reason which controls human actions in acknowledging cognition of the supreme rule. The regulative activity of practical reason cannot deny recognition to further general principles either. In q. 94, a. 2, Thomas Aquinas also speaks of further precepts of the natural moral law, the binding character of which, however, rests in the primary principle. All that practical reason includes, in a natural way, as a human value falls within the jurisdiction of the supreme rule. In reply to the question, what are the relevant values for human beings in the openness of their existential potentiality, he joins the theologians of his time in pointing to what he calls "natural inclinations" (*inclinationes naturales*). These include the instinct of *self-preservation* shared by all life, the inclination toward *preservation of the species* common to all sentient beings, and the orientation toward *rational self-development,* which is only present in human beings.

The significance of these natural inclinations in Thomas Aquinas' system has been variously interpreted over the past 25 years. Discussion centers particularly on the concept of the "goods" present in man and signaled by the natural inclinations. Is Thomas Aquinas referring here to a metaphysical, ontological order or is he simply perceiving "existential purposes," which need to be observed in any rational order of social existence? We cannot discuss this question in the space available here. There are, however, good reasons for thinking.

that from a *philosophical* point of view for Thomas, there is no derivational incline leading from metaphysics to ethics. Ethics begins by ascertaining man's original tendencies

and characterizing their goals as "good"; it does not begin
with the metaphysical character of reality or even that of
mankind. Their formulation will thus consist in creating
generally comprehensible rules which enable each person,
individually and jointly with all others, to attain these desirable goals, thereby making it possible to fulfil their existential potentiality, while taking into account the conditions, situations and circumstances.[10]

In the natural inclinations, the reflecting person is opened towards fundamental, essential purposes, which have to be observed
in the actions which are governed by the law of reason. Thus the
instinct of self-preservation demonstrates the value of life and of all
that is necessary to sustain life. Or the natural instinct to preserve
the species leads one to realize the importance of sexuality or of
bringing up children. Life, the existence of two sexes, the ability to
produce and bring up children, all this and others are "goods" which
in the responsible moral action of persons are given. Thomas
Aquinas does not maintain that all human beings are conscious of
this: he is, however, convinced that reflection reveals these insights
in their most general form (as *prima principia*) as evident. But what
reason thus sees as good in a natural way must also be converted into
actions, i.e., the fulfillment of goals signaled by the natural inclinations proves obligatory. Yet Thomas Aquinas does not infer the
existence of an order of obligation on the basis of an ontological
order; instead, the dimensions of human self-preservation and self-
development are subordinated to the moral law of reason. He
ascribes this law of reason itself, in what is basically a theological
argument, to the participation of the rational being in divine reason.

Thus, the natural moral law does not consist in a natural order
from which norms can be read off. Rather, it is that intrinsic law
which lays claim to human persons as moral beings so that they may
shape themselves and the world, and which allows them to become
aware, by simple reflection, of the most important of the goals (fundamental legal values) that are inalienably entrusted to their responsibility. This cognition of fundamental legal values does not, however, imply anything about how these are to be realized or preserved.
The actual shape which the legal and moral order takes is left to the

interpreting and determining process of investigation and thought. At the same time, it cannot be denied that even Thomas Aquinas and the scholastic tradition which followed him were fond of falling back on the *rectitudo naturalis* in the moral assessment of concrete actions.

Thus Thomas states that in rationally regulating the physical and sensory sphere (*circa corporalia et sensibilia*) it is very important to "ensure that each part of a person and each of the person's actions should attain the goal envisaged" (SCG III, 122). Or in reply to the question whether every lie is a sin, he answers unmistakably in the affirmative, pointing out: "Since, therefore, words by their nature are signs of one's thoughts, it is unnatural and unseemly to express in a word something which one does not have in one's mind" (II II q. 110, a. 3). For this reason, lying is by its very nature bad.

In the course of history, a strong tendency became evident to extend the range of validity of the natural moral law to encompass this *rectitudo naturalis* of individual actions. In the late scholastic period in Spain, for example, this resulted from the legitimate need to establish, for the colonial peoples, a universal legal and moral law which is as concrete as possible. According to Suarez (1548–1619), the judgment of reason shows the intrinsic goodness or badness of human actions, pointing *"consequenter"* to the will of God, who commands or prohibits accordingly.[11] Thus the moral law of nature lies in *naturalis ratio* as the faculty of judgment about what is appropriate or inappropriate to nature.[12] At the same time, obligation derives from the will of God, not from either the rational judgment or the intrinsic order of the act. The purely rational judgment about the goodness or badness of an action would, in itself, not be binding if the will of God were not contained in this judgment. Although the philosophical teachings on natural law of Hugo Grotius (1583–1645), Samuel Pufendorf (1632–1694), Christian Thomasius (1655–1728), and the Leibnitz-Wolffian scholastic philosophy of the eighteenth century were not based on the objective judgment of actions, in their tendency to derive rights, which are as concrete as possible, from a social nature of human beings which is understood as an ideal, they do, however, share common ground with the Spaniards.

It was inevitable that with the extension of the natural moral law to concrete norms of action, the universality of its validity would become increasingly questionable. In legal history, Hans Welzel blames this extension for the rapid "collapse of natural 'law',"[13] in the process of which the material problems were left for the representatives of German idealism to solve. In the sphere of the scholastic doctrine of natural law, what we initially experience is, however, a process of reinforcement in the sense of essentialism. It is only in more recent developments, particularly in the revival of the doctrine of natural law in the post-war period, that there is a clearly defined tendency

> to escape that rigidity which sets in as soon as rationalist boldness stipulates what must *semper et pro semper* legally happen. The prevailing opinion is inclined to concentrate natural law in the narrowest and strictest sense of the term . . . to a sum of basic principles which appear as axioms, and the principles and basic relationships of the legal order which can definitely be inferred by "simple rational activity."[14]

"To each his own," "Treaties must be honored," etc., are examples of such principles. It is plain to see that what is meant by these in the final analysis are those fundamental values which experience shows are important for our social existence. By experience and reflection, the most important legal values can be shown to be necessary. Similarly, it can be demonstrated that there are inalienable, basic attitudes (the basic values: liberty, justice, and solidarity). As early as the 1960's, representatives of legal philosophy[15] rightly pointed out that the fight against legal positivism could only be won by proving a "natural" doctrine of legal values based in experience, not by a natural legal doctrine. In the meantime, the demonstration for universal human rights has taken up this appeal.

II.
PERSON AND NATURE IN SEXUAL ETHICS

1. The Anthropological Approach of Karol Wojtyła

The philosophical foundation of the concept of the person developed by K. Wojtyła in the Introduction to "Person and Action"[16] is rooted in a methodological conception which starts out from the experience of one source of knowledge, more precisely, from the (self-) experience of the acting person. Experience, in this context, is not used in its empirical sense, but in the phenomenological sense of a direct experiencing of the object (the correlation of act and acting person), of a cognitive act encompassing both the senses and the intellect.[17] The phenomenological approach to experience is, however, only intended as an instrument of a phase of the analysis, which must be followed by induction (as a means of "inter-subjectivization") and reduction (as a consistent penetration of revelation of the object). Thus one moves from "experiencing" to "understanding" and "discovery," i.e., to comprehension of the "actual existing reality"[18] which underlies experience. In this context, the relationship between person ("the being ego") and action ("the acting ego") is expressed by the axiom *operari sequitur esse* (action follows being).

Within the framework of his attempt at a phenomenology of action, K. Wojtyła primarily sees in this axiom a "gnoseological dependence" (the possibility of gaining access to a person via his actions), which, however, follows in turn from the assumption of a converse causal dependence of action on being. In other words, the axiom *operari sequitur esse* is reversible: "Since, therefore, the 'operari' derives from the 'esse,' it is . . . the true path to knowledge of the 'esse'." "In this way, from human 'operari,' we not only gain the cognition that man is the 'subject' of his actions."[19] This path leading to the truth via the person, who involves the self as a subject and realizes the self as an "object" and at the same time is obliged to see the other in the same personality, is tremendously productive for ethics. This is particularly true of sexual ethics. *Sexuality* should by no means be regarded from the biological aspect alone. It concerns the innermost core of the human person as such. This holistic view of human sexuality and capacity for love is the fundamental characteristic of the sexual morality propagated by Pope John Paul II. Love requires the whole person and involves the whole person. Love always implies the involvement of one person with another for the sake of that person. Libidinous treatment of the subject as an object is not love. The person concerned may indeed derive pleasure from the fact that he or she is coveted, that he or she does not merely arouse detached affection. But love is more than this; it goes beyond desire, it does not regard the other person as the object or instrument of a person's own ego. The ego opens itself to the *thou,* so as to affirm it and become involved in its discovery of itself. Personal love is not a using, an *uti,* it is a joint experiencing, a *frui.* Sexuality is only "consummated in a truly human fashion" if it is integrated in love of this kind. "Total physical self-giving would be a lie if it were not the sign and fruit of total personal self-giving in which the whole person, including the temporal dimension is present."[20]

However, the limits of the method of realistic phenomenology become apparent when it embarks upon an ontologically comprehensive definition of the person and human realization. This is where the method must be subjected to critical scrutiny. I wish to make four critical remarks.

a) The epistemological status of what is termed "reduction," which is the decisively intermediate stage for insight into a comprehensive personal conception of being human, is left unclarified. The phenomenological proof of ontological structures, and thus of the link between the philosophy of consciousness and the philosophy of entity, is not convincing. *On the one hand,* reduction provides access to the subjectivity of the person. It is supposed to supply the link between the evidence drawn from experience of the dynamic unity of the subject and cognition of the ontic unity of the person with his or her structural "authenticnesses."[21] The notional link between ontology and phenomenology is made possible by the *potentia-actus* scheme: the foundational potentialities present in the structure of the person correspond to the actualization of the person in action.[22] Therefore, by making visible the dynamics of the *actus personae* in its dialectic of transitivity and intransitivity, intrasitivity and anthropology, the analysis of consciousness completes the picture of the human person, thereby making an important contribution to the view of person in the tradition of the philosophy of entity.[23]

On the other hand, in contrast to phenomenology, it is precisely the necessity for the contribution of the philosophy of entity which is stressed, since this alone can guarantee a sound, realistic, dynamic concept of the person (influenced by perfectioristic principles). As a result, even in connection with the analysis of the subconscious (at the somatic level, though also at the emotional level) the structural priority of potentiality over consciousness is made into a requirement, with the consequence that "an analysis of the human being, of the acting person, if it were to be grounded on consciousness alone, would from the first be doomed to inadequacy."[24] This means, however, that the independent contribution of phenomenology is, so to speak, only a special case of its primary function, viz., of serving as a method of providing evidence for the ontological anthropology which is presupposed. This implies that the hoped-for compatibility of the philosophy of entity and the philosophy of consciousness is endangered. For the concept of reality presupposed here is difficult to reconcile with the insight of these philosophies, which is fundamental to modern thinking, that cognition is never absolute and can only be present in the subject in its historical refraction.

b) What has been said above is also true of a "realistic phenomenology" of morality. For K. Wojtyła, "realism" in this sphere means that the person does not (as Scheler assumes) represent a unity of value-experience based on consciousness. Rather, he sees it as a primarily dynamic unity rooted in the real connection of the person with action by means of the principle of causality (correlation of suppositum and ego). The causality of the person and, closely connected with this, the relationship with values, duty, and the moral value of action (as a real personal value) are results of a comprehensive analysis of experience purified of emotionalistic and idealistic premises. If, however, even the autoteleology of the human person in one's actions and the entire associated complex of the dynamics of striving for self-realization and self-perfection in those actions (the perfectioristic aspect of "becoming" of the person) can only, in the last resort, be comprehended by ontological categories, the analysis of consciousness in order to supply evidence for normative ethics likewise has only a secondary function as evidence of an extant order of obligation (*Sollensordnung*).

However, as long as the method of a link between subjectivity and objectivity (which is what realistic phenomenology involves) is not sufficiently clarified and proven for anthropology, the consequences for ethics must also be examined as to their range of applicability and usefulness. This is true both for the personalistic norm and for the relationship between a fundamental personal norm and its categorical content. In K. Wojtyła's ethical thinking, the personalistic norm has the rank of a supreme principle, being the standard by which the moral value of each action must be gauged. As the various formulations in *Love and Responsibility* suggest, the personalistic norm in its deep structure can be understood first and foremost as a value-judgment emphasizing the high value of the person as such, to which only the affirmation of the person in love represents an appropriate "response." The source of obligation for the person as a subject, which lies directly in experience, is located in the objective "truth about the value" of the person as an object. The personalistic norm—primarily a supreme value-judgment, which accordingly prescribes a specific, basic attitude (we might call it motivation) for every act (positive: to accept the person; negative: to use the person not only as a means)—almost attains the degree of universality of "bonum faciendum, malum vitandum." It thus does not lend itself, either, to a simple deduction of norms. Bruno Schüller has convincingly shown that although the personal dignity of human beings is a necessary element in the substantiation for norms, it is by no means sufficient in itself.[25]

True, the observance of personal dignity represents the criterion for what is morally good in an action. It does not, however, provide the sole criterion for its correctness. Ascertaining personal dignity gives no clue to how it is to be transformed into concrete norms, since the affirmation of the person (as *bonum honestum*) in concrete actions, though rooted in the basic attitude of benevolence, must concern itself with the question "What is good for the person?" and realize itself in the choice of a *bonum utile* which is in the interests of the person. "The person can, namely, even if it transcends the values which are subordinate to the physical, operative norms, only be effectively affirmed by their true realization."[26] Methodologically this implies that a starting-point based on a sound conception of the person is an important and inalienable element in ethical evidence, which, however, necessarily requires to be supplemented by a method of substantiating norms as soon as it deals with concrete ethical questions.

c) Until the method of realistic phenomenology is adequately clarified regarding its epistemological status, the integration of person and nature will not be sufficiently assured from an ethical point of view either. This deficiency is all the more regrettable, since the personalistic approach of the moral philosopher K. Wojtyła and present Pope John Paul II has proved to be exceedingly productive. If in sexual morality it really is a double norm, which calls for the observance of the finality of the act as well as of the personalistic norm,[27] the problem is precisely that according to the statements in "Love and Responsibility" the link between the *per se* of the finality of the conjugal act and the *per se* of free mutual love is merely made "per accidens."[28] The resultant danger of the ethical argument becoming split in two directions can only be effectively countered if human sexuality is previously integrated into a holistic love of person, in which love not only has "procreative value" *per accidens,* but *per se* possesses an expressive quality for personal relationships.

d) An even more problematic point is the assessment of morally correct actions by realistic phenomenology in the sphere of the medical ethos, i.e., within the context of medical therapy. One example of this is the doctrinal decision[29] by the Congregation of the Doctrine of the Faith on homologous i.e., only between husband and wife, extra-corporal fertilization. There can be no serious doubts about the therapeutic character of homologous fertilization. It is a case of the correction of a natural defect by means of substitution. It is the substitution that is unique and new in this treatment. The doctor does not intervene with corrective measures in the woman's organism, rather he is carrying out a dispositive act leading to the conception of a new person by bringing together the gametes. This difference between the more traditional methods of treating sterility and substitution therapy is certainly of considerable importance from an ethical point of view. By his or her actions the doctor not only enters into a relation with the woman (or the man), but also directly with the *child.* From this ensues a new and not insignificant responsibility of the doctor for the child conceived as a result of his or her intervention. This is the decisive factor which led the West German Medical Council, in its guidelines, to reject extra-corporal fertilization outside marriage. The Congregation, however, rejects the method as such. It maintains that fertilization carried out outside the bodily contact of the married couple remains "devoid of the significances and values expressed in the language of the body and the union of the human persons" (p. 28). The child must be the "fruit of the love of its parents. It cannot be desired and conceived as a product of the intervention of medical technology" (*ibid*). *In vitro* conception, it adds, is the "result of a technical act which primarily determines fertilization" (p. 30).

This argumentation basically amounts to the assertion that medical assistance in bringing together the gametes is a violation of the dignity of the parents or of the child thus conceived. This urgently requires consistent proof if it is to be used to justify an unconditional prohibition. The Instruction lists as reasons several indications, which, however, principally take for granted what they are in fact supposed to justify. For example, it is claimed that a homologous *in vitro* fertilization is "a morally inadmissible technique" even if "every compromising link with the practice of abortion, the destruction of embryos and masturbation were absent," adding in justification, "because it deprives human procreation of its inherent and natural dignity" (p. 30). This is, first of all, an assertion which needs to be proved. "Human procreation" apparently refers to the whole procedure whereby a human *act* (the sexual act) is linked to such an extent with a biological *process* (fertilization) that the act is no more than dispositive for the process of bringing together and combining the gametes.

Since the concept of "dignity" primarily leads one to think of the dignity of the human person and a corresponding act, we shall have to consider the implementation of the conjugal act as far as the question of the dignity of procreation is concerned. If this is carried out with mutual consideration and—as we are assuming here—as the "cause" and with the aim of having a child of one's own, the dignity of the act cannot be objectively denied. What it lacks is not "natural dignity" but the "natural opportunity" leading up to actual procreation. The gametes cannot combine in the woman's body; therefore they are provided with the opportunity for union outside the body. Sexual union in the service of procreation can achieve its aim and purpose completely. The child is—as the Instruction requires—"the product of a mutual gift" (p. 28). In what, then, does the violation of the dignity of procreation lie? In the fact that the child is "desired as the product of intervention by medical technology?" (p. 28). Can we speak properly here of a "product" of technology? Any serious observer will see that what is happening here is not the mere product of human interference; what we are dealing with is not an artificially produced person, it is a child who has evolved out of the gametes of its parents. The doctor is not "making" a human being! Nor should this be insinuated in any serious discussion. This is a technical aid which enables the gametes to combine. But this is precisely what occurs in *homologous insemination,* which is expressly permitted, provided it is applied in order to "assist the normally consummated act to achieve its objective" (p. 31, citing Pius XII, 1949).

There is even less difference which is relevant to the dignity of persons from the method of introducing ova and sperm into the woman's Fallopian tubes, which the Instruction allegedly does not condemn either. In all three methods we have a comparable means of assisting the gametes to combine with one another, thereby "assist[ing] the normally consummated act to achieve its objective." The difference lies solely in the *place* where the gametes are allowed to combine. The Fallopian tube seems more "dignified" than the test-tube. It is indisputable that the Fallopian tube is the natural place of fertilization. If this is not possible without the assistance of medical technology, then the doctor selecting the method to be used does so according to the chances of success and minimization of injury which are of decisive importance. The question of the "naturalness of the place" must remain secondary. Seen thus—and in my opinion this is the only appropriate view of the situation—there is *per se* no morally relevant difference between the two methods discussed, in order to "assist the normally consummated act to achieve its objective." Where a married couple, because of a sterility which cannot be overcome by any other means, can be enabled to have a child by extra-corporal fertilization, I fail to see why the mere intervention in the natural process of procreation should be an immoral act! The possibilities of abuse and dangers must, of course, be excluded. But the possibility of abuse does not mean that correct use should be prohibited. And here we are solely concerned with the question of the moral evaluation of the therapy as such. As I see it, realistic phenomenology in the last analysis appears to neutralize the relationship of person and nature, giving nature priority. By contrast, we wish to give priority to the person.

2. The Relationship of Person and Nature Viewed from the Priority of the Personal

a) Personal entity is an entity of human existence and vice versa. The person is, therefore, not an immaterial entity without essence, since one always "exists" in and through one nature. This implies an inseparability of person and nature, or of "essence" and "existence," which excludes an opposition of both without neutralizing their differences.

b) For the correspondential relationship of person and nature the decisive factor is: Should we interpret the extant entity from the aspect of the personal or the personal from the aspect of the extant entity? If an ontology turns directly to all-encompassing reality (*das Seiende*), it runs the risk of understanding this reality via the material object. As a result, the person is also made to conform to the material object and its structure or is comprehended as a thing whose nature is perfect, the basic nature of the person thereby being misunderstood. By contrast, if an ontology is based on the person, in which the relationship to the entity as such becomes apparent as a result of reflection, the material object can also be explained and elucidated in the light of personal structure. Only in this way can a holistic interpretation of what is human and personal occur in the ethical dimension as a holistic interpretation of the nature with which we are confronted.[30]

c) Ethics, no less than any form of comprehension, is thus referred to the field of structures and, as such, has to grasp the sphere of the implementation of concrete nature. This sphere can primarily be visualized as a boundary. The boundary indicates, first of all, that the sphere of an action is established by a nature which in itself possesses a definite, fixed structure, and which opens up certain possibilities: i.e., nature forms the boundary of all kinds of actions which can only occur within nature. The person does not, therefore, exist without its own nature, i.e., it pre-possesses a sphere which sets limits on its freedom but also gives it its potentialities.

Empirical and, even more so, historical boundaries are not as fixed as a material boundary. They are not immutable, and can be changed by human actions. The concept of the boundary overlaps with the concept of challenge, i.e. nature is not simply something already present *per se,* it is something assigned to us to shape in our own pattern. This means that nature is not a stable entity, compact and self-contained, which is being arbitrarily changed; it is only thus that it becomes visible that nature is the emergence of human person in actuality. By one's thoughts and actions, person must give shape to "nature"; this is why the concept of challenge overlaps with the concept of scheme (*Entwurf*). The human person must ascertain and shape his or her place in a moral decision based on freedom, and he or she must do this from the holistic profusion of human reality. The concept of scheme indicates that there are meanings of acts which cannot be comprehended and described at all as direct responses to direct challenges. Without this holistic self-realization and openness, the field of moral existence cannot be completely defined. No human sphere, no human stratum can be comprehended or shaped in a moral way other than in a human fashion.

d) From the structures of interdependence linking person and nature, the following consequences can be drawn for the moral guidance of human sexuality.

—Preservation of the species and life-long partnership require personal synthesis for the guidance of human sexuality. That sexuality should be consummated in sexual love and that it should also serve the preservation of the species is undisputed. But sexual love as a personal, holistic relationship of two people cannot be specified by a relationship whose object lies outside these two people. The personal partnership cannot be a means to something else; this would be a denial of the intrinsic value of the person: procreation (nature) would then be placed higher, ontologically, than love (person).

—As personal love, human sexuality must first of all have its ontological determination in itself. Certainly, true love is orientated towards fertility, and this is due to its inner nature. But it is not possible to state that this orientation is directed towards specific results, i.e., the procreation of children, as a specifically ontological constituent. In an accessorial sense we can probably speak of the child as being the aim of conjugal love.

—An exclusion of fertility from love on principle debases love, forcing it into sterile isolation; exclusion from an individual sexual act, by contrast, can be justified from the point of view of the moral goals of the whole person. *Humanae Vitae* can also be interpreted this way, in our view. However, the encyclical also believes that this exclusion must not occur by intervention in the biological process in accordance with the meaning of the act as indicated in biological laws, that it must instead be effected by periodic abstinence. That implies, however, that the pattern of a person's sexual behavior is being primarily interpreted from the biological aspect and is being made dependent on this. This corresponds to an ontology of reality being made subordinate to the material object. For a long time this was the dominant pattern in the intellectual history of the West, from the Greeks onward. However, if any philosophy ought to challenge this it is Christianity, replacing it with an ontology of freedom subordinate to the person. Such a view will judge the form of the sexual relationship, inclusive of its technical cultivation, entirely according to the law of personal love. This considerate personal love, which seeks the other person for his or her personal value, will not demand any less self-discipline for one's own desires, but it will not tie this discipline to a biological rhythm, subordinating it instead to the one law, which states that the other person must never become a means to an end. Love such as this is receptive to intellectual and physical fruitfulness. It ought, however, to be clear that the controversy about the methodological question in *Humanae Vitae,* in the last analysis, is rooted in a philosophical attitude of mind, not in a basic aspect of Christian existence.

Notes

1. Robert Spaemann, "Natur," *HPhG* IV, 956–969, p. 963.
2. *Ibid.,* p. 964.
3. Maximilian Forschner, "Natur als sittliche Norm in der griechischen Antike," *Der Mensch und die Natur* (eds. W. Eckermann and J. Kuropka; Vechta: 1986) p. 9.
4. *Ibid.*
5. M. Forschner, "Natur," p. 22.
6. The German edition of Thomas Aquinas (= DThA), v. 13, Commentary by Otto Hermann Pesch (Heidelberg: Kerle, 1977) pp. 569f.
7. Ludger Honnefelder, "Gewissen und personale Identität," *Gewissensbildung heute* (ed. Arbeitskreis kath. Schulen in freier Trägerschaft in der Bundesrepublik Deutschland und in Berlin West Bonn: Kaiserstr. 163, 1986) 24–38, p. 27.
8. "sicut in regulante et mensurante," p. 91, a. 2.
9. *DThA,* v. 13, p. 554.
10. O.H. Pesch, "Commentary on 94, 2," *DThA,* v. 13, pp. 577ff.
11. Cf. Franciscus Suarez, *De Legibus,* Lib. II, cap, 6, n. 8: "Ergo ratio naturalis quae indicat quid sit per se malum vel bonum homini, consequenter indicat esse secundum divinam voluntatem ut unum fiat, et aliud vitetur."
12. *Ibid.,* Lib. II, cap, 5, n. 9: ". . . est vis quaedam illius naturae, quam habet ad discernendum inter operationes convenientes et disconvenientes illi naturae, quam rationem appelamus."
13. Hans Welzel, *Naturrecht und materiale Gerechtigkeit, Jurisprudenz in Einzeldarstellung,* 4 (4th ed.; Göttingen: Vandenhoek und Ruprecht, 1962) pp. 162f.
14. Hans Dieter Schelauske, *Naturrechtsdiskussion in Deutschland. Ein Überlick über zwei Jahrzehnte: 1945–1965* (Köln: Bachem, 1968), p. 352.

15. Arthur Kaufmann, "Die ontologische Struktur des Rechts," *Die Ontologische Begründung des Rechts, Wege der Forschung,* 22 (ed. A. Kaufmann; Darmstadt: Wissenschaftliche Buchgesellschaft, 1965) 470–508.

16. Karol Wojtyła, *The Acting Person, Analecta Husserliana: The Year Book of Phenomenological research,* 10 (transl. Andrzej Potocki; Dordrecht: Reidel, 1979).

17. See John Paul II, *Dem Leben in Liebe dienen, Apostolisches Schreiben über die Aufgaben in der Welt von heute* (Freiburg i. Br.: 1982) pp. 16 ff.

18. *Ibid.,* pp. 24–26.

19. K. Wojtyła, "Person: Subjekt und Gemeinschaft," K. Wojtyła, Andrzej Szostek, and Tadeusz Styczen, *Der Streit um den Menschen. Personaler Anspruch des Sittlichen* (Kevelaer: Butzon und Bercker, 1979), p. 20; cf. *The Acting Person,* p. 73.

20. "Familiaris Consortio," nr. 11.

21. K. Wojtyła, *The Acting Person,* pp. 179; cf. also S. Dinan, "The Phenomenological Anthropology of K. Wojtyła," *The New Scholasticism* 55 (1981) 317–330.

22. K. Wojtyła has expressed this very clearly in the following sentences: "Human actions thus provide us with a specific insight into the structure of the person . . . this structure presents itself as a set of conditions necessary for the occurrence of what is directly given in experience" ("The Structure of Self-Determination as the Core of the Theory of the Person," *Tommaso d'Aquino nel suo settimo centenario. Atti del congresso internazionale, Roma-Napoli 17/24 Aprile 1974,* v. 7 (Naples: 1978) 37–44, p. 42. Cf. also, *The Acting Person,* p. 20f; also, the remark by G. Küng, "Der Mensch als handelnde Person. Zum philosophischen Werk des neuen Papstes," *Universitas* 34 (1979) 157–162, p. 159: ". . . die allgemeine Einstellung, das Bemühen um den phänomenologischen Aufweis ontologischer Strukturen ist typisch Ingardenisch."

23. K. Wojtyła, *The Acting Person,* p. 56ff.

24. *Ibid.,* p. 91f.

25. Bruno Schüller, "Die Personwürde des Menschen als Beweisgrund in der normativen Ethik," *Theologie und Philosophie* 53 (1978) 538–555.

26. Andrzej Szostek, "Zur gegenwärtigen Diskussion über den Utilitarismus," *Person im Kontext des Sittlichen* (eds. Joachim Piegsa and Hans Zeiments; Düsseldorf: Patmos, 1979) 82–95, esp. p. 94.

27. See the passage quoted by the editors of *Liebe und Verantwortung* (= *Love and Responsibility;* Munich: 1979) p. 264, n. 16, where K. Wojtyła himself speaks of two norms, of which the norm of the natural order is

"more elementary and more fundamental" (*elementarer und grundlegender*), whereas the norm derived from the dignity of man only plays "a consummatory role" (*eine vervollkommnende Rolle*).

28. See *Love and Responsibility*, p. 46.

29. "Instruktion über die Achtung vor dem beginnenden menschlichen Leben und die Würde der Fortpflanzung. Antworten auf einige aktuelle Fragen," *Verlautbarungen des Apostolischen Stuhls*, 74 (Bonn: 1987). The Instruction was also published in an official English version, "Instruction on Respect for Human Life in its Origin and on the Dignity of Procreation. Replies to Certain Questions of the Day" (Vatican: Polyglot, 1987). Page references provided in the text are taken from the English version.

30. Johannes Baptist Lotz, "Person und Ontologie," *Scholastik* 38 (1963) 335–360.

Nature and Supernature

John Mahoney, S.J.

This chapter originally appeared in *The Making of Moral Theology*, 1987.

The first two chapters of this study on the making of moral theology have drawn attention to the influence of the major Church institution of confession and to the legacy of the most dominating of Church thinkers in the development of the subject through the centuries. Another major source of development in any subject is the power of ideas—the control exercised on men's minds by major concepts. Of the ideas which have powerfully shaped moral theology in its long making none have achieved more prominence, or perhaps notoriety, than those of "nature" and of "the supernatural." The idea that human nature is to be considered a source of moral knowledge and a basis of moral obligation has been increasingly contested within recent years. And perhaps no other aspect of moral theology is today more elusive, and to many more puzzling, than the whole subject of revelation and grace and the sphere of what is termed the supernatural. The purpose of this chapter is to trace the developments of thought resulting in these two central and contrasting elements, nature and supernature, and to offer some reflections on that development. Since supernatural has the literal meaning of "above the natural," we may best begin by considering how the ideas of nature, and natural law, have come to occupy so central a place in moral theology.

We have already seen how the early Christian writers and thinkers were prepared to adopt and adapt from the Graeco-Roman culture of their day elements of ethical thought and conventions which appeared to them consonant with living and commending the teaching of Jesus. Of these elements none was more appealing to early Christianity than the glimpses caught by pagan thinkers of an inherently rational structure to reality, as best exemplified in the Stoic teaching on universal order and reason.

NATURE, REASON, AND MORALITY

In accepting, and indeed appropriating, Stoic teaching on the moral life as an exercise of man's reason in subordination to a higher principle of reason which pervades all of reality, early Christian thinkers were to adopt a principle of divine cosmic and human order, or *ordo,* which, with contributions from the Book of Wisdom, has been a major intellectual feature of the history of Christian moral thinking.[1] The Athenian convert, Athenagoras, was to explain in his *Apology,* written about 177, that "man himself, so far as he that made him is concerned, is well ordered, both by his original nature, which has one common characteristic for all, and by the constitution of his body, which does not transgress the law imposed upon it."[2] "We are in all things always alike and the same, submitting ourselves to reason, and not ruling over it."[3] In the contemporary treatise *On the Resurrection of the Dead* we are informed that, since everything in nature has an end peculiar to itself, as we know from common sense and observation, there must likewise be a peculiar end for men "whose actions are regulated by the innate law and reason, and who live an intelligent life and observe justice."[4]

> The final cause of an intelligent life and rational judgment is to be occupied uninterruptedly with those objects to which the natural reason is chiefly and primarily adapted, and to delight unceasingly in the contemplation of Him Who Is, and of His decrees, notwithstanding that the majority of men, because they are affected too passionately and too violently by things below, pass through life without attaining this object.[5]

The Palestinian theologian, Justin, who was martyred about the year 165, explains of the Christian God that "in the beginning he made the human race with the power of thought and of choosing the truth and of doing right, so that all men are without excuse before

God [cf. Rom. 1:20]; for they have been born rational and contemplative."[6] God, he explains in his celebrated *Dialogue with Trypho the Jew,*

> sets before every race of mankind that which is always and universally just, as well as all righteousness; and every race knows that adultery, and fornication, and homicide, and such like, are sinful; and though they all commit such practices, yet they do not escape from the knowledge that they act unrighteously when they do so, with the exception of those who are possessed with an unclean spirit, and who have been debased by education, by wicked customs, and by sinful institutions, and who have lost, or rather quenched and put under, their natural ideas.[7]

One can see in the writings of Tertullian a similar acceptance of the Stoic ethical resources of nature and reason. Romans should not believe the calumnies directed against Christians unless they would behave in a similar manner themselves, for they are fellow human beings.[8] It is to Tertullian, of course, that we owe the historic exclamation which concludes his questionable argument from pagans' spontaneous and everyday invocation of one "god" that in everyone the soul is "Christian in its very nature."[9] It is by this one great God that "we find this whole fabric of the universe to be once for all disposed, equipped, ordered as it stands, and supplied with the complete guidance of reason."[10]

Augustine too could find much in common with non-Christian ethical teaching. In what was to become a key-passage for the Middle Ages he explains how Christians can and should use what is true and useful in the profane sciences. As the Hebrews were commanded by God to despoil the Egyptians of their gold and silver, so "certain most useful moral precepts" are to be found among the Gentiles as minerals of divine providence to be found everywhere which the Christians should take from them for the just purpose of preaching the Gospel.[11] The Stoic influence, however, is most clear in Augustine in his systematic exploitation of the concept of order in the whole of God's creation. Underlying everything is an eternal law of God, "the divine reason or the will of God commanding the natural order to be respected and forbidding its disruption."[12] "The idea of the eternal law, which is impressed on us, is the idea by which it is just that everything be perfectly ordered;"[13] order, for Augustine, being defined as the disposing of equal and unequal things each in its right place. Hence it follows, according to his famous definition, that "peace" is that "tranquility which is to be found in the right ordering of everything."[14]

All the things which God has created are good, and so the rational soul acts well with reference to them if it maintains order, and if by distinguishing, choosing, and assessing, it subordinates the lesser things to the greater, the bodily to the spiritual, the lower to the higher, and the temporal to the eternal.[15] Within man also "when reason controls the movements of the soul, man is said to be ordered. For it is not a right order, or even to be called order at all, when the better is subject to the worse."[16] A popular version of Augustine's ethics, then, might well be a place for everything and everything in its place, a view which he finds aptly illustrated in the physical universe and in the natural properties of bodies. For him "in every soul, as in every body, there is a weight drawing it constantly, moving it always to find its natural place of rest; and this weight we call love."[17] This observation by Gilson on what is perhaps Augustine's most famous metaphor of love in terms of gravity is well borne out in *The City of God:*

> If we were stones, waves, wind or flame, or anything of that kind, lacking sense and life, we would still show something like a desire for our own place and order. For the specific gravity of a body is, in a manner, its love, whether a body tends downwards by reason of its heaviness or strives upwards because of its lightness. A material body is borne along by its weight in a particular direction, as a soul is by its love.[18]

The ordering brought about by love is, for Augustine, spelled out in the two commands of love of God and love of neighbor.[19] And the internal order required of the good loving man can be well expressed in the four controlling virtues of prudence, justice, temperance, and fortitude, which Ambrose and Augustine adopted from Stoicism. Temperance "bridles the lusts of the flesh to prevent their gaining the consent of the mind." Prudence helps us avoid mistakes in our choices between good and evil. "The function of justice is to assign to each his due; and hence there is established in man himself a certain just order of nature, by which the soul is subordinated to God, and the body to the soul, and thus both body and soul are subordinated to God." Fortitude bears all ills with patient endurance.[20] In a splendid and almost mystical meditation on the divine ordering of all things Augustine observes that God "created all things in supreme wisdom and ordered them in perfect justice."[21] And so pervasive is this concept of *ordo* in the thought of Augustine that Roland-Gosselin could conclude, "the idea of order, law, truth, justice, which is nothing but the idea of reason, is very dear to Saint Augustine. It means that any disorder, whether physical, rational, or moral, is and can only be a partial disorder which is always compensated in such a way that the universal order is never compromised or even disturbed. . . . It is a Stoic concept, but purified of all pantheism and fatalism."[22] Thus, for man, the moral challenge is to locate one's self and all one's actions reasonably, harmoniously, and justly in one's proper place in the divine scheme of things.

To this Christian reflection on the best of pagan ethics, notably in Stoicism, was added its later absorption of key ideas from Roman law, and particularly of the *ius naturale,* or "the just by nature" of the Roman jurists, which as the expression of universal reason was considered to be the basis of the *ius gentium,* the law of peoples, constructed by Rome as an instrument of its colonial and imperial government.[23] Thus, the seventeenth-century archbishop of Seville, the learned Isidore, whose famous and fanciful work on *Etymology* had an intriguing effect on the Scholastic age, explained that, unlike human positive legislation, the *ius naturale* is the law observed everywhere by the prompting of nature, such as that ordaining the marriage of man and woman, the procreation and rearing of children, common ownership and freedom, self-defense, and the like.[24] The Church's canonists developed and perpetuated the idea of natural law as of divine origin and as the basis for all justice, described by Rufinus as "the divine power which nature implants in man, impelling him to do good and avoid evil."[25]

AQUINAS AND 'THE LAW OF NATURE'

It was in the Dominican friar, the Italian Thomas of Aquino, that in the thirteenth century moral theology was to find its first fully and systematically articulated expression of natural law theory. It is this which has remained the classical exposition embraced by moral theology and the Church since his day, and which has also had the deleterious effect of portraying Aquinas as pre-eminently, even exclusively, a moral philosopher to the loss of his far more important contributions as a moral theologian.[26] In the *Summa* of theology, that great Gothic cathedral of human thought which Aquinas explained in his introduction was intended for beginners in theology, he shows how in man's return to the God who is his origin and his destiny he is aided by God's instructing him by law and helping him by grace.[27] The essence of law is to be a rational rule and measure of actions, directing them in an orderly manner to their purpose or end; and this enables Aquinas to offer his famous definition of any law as an order, or arrangement, of reason for the common good.[28] Within this generic concept and definition of law Aquinas's great philosophical advance was to distinguish the eternal law clearly from what Augustine had called its "impression" on us, and to explore that impression as the raw material in man's constitution for the moral "law of nature." All creatures have "impressed" in their very being inherent tendencies which reflect the ordering and orientation which God their creator wishes for them. Man as a rational being sharing in God's providential activity is aware of what God has impressed in his nature and he is capable of freely accepting and embracing the order of his being and his place in the divine scheme of things. This knowing and free acceptance of his nature as created and destined by God is man's observance of the law of his nature, or of the "natural law."[29]

In a major passage Aquinas explores and applies the implications for man of the nature God has given him. The first thing which strikes us about anything is that it is a thing, a being. And the first thing which occurs to our minds as obvious is the principle that we cannot assert that something is a being and at the same time deny it. There is a similar first principle in the area of action, based now not on being and not-being but on good and not-good. Since there is always a purpose to what we do, the first thing we always look for is whether an action we contemplate fits in with our basic human desires, that is, whether or not it is good. In other words, the first thing which occurs to our minds as obvious is the principle that what is good should be brought about and what is evil, or not-good, should be avoided.

We naturally see as good whatever we are naturally inclined to, and the precepts of natural law express in terms of our various inclinations this first moral principle to pursue good and avoid evil.

> There is therefore an order of precepts of natural law corresponding to the order of natural inclinations. First, there is an inclination in man towards the good corresponding to what he has in common with all individual beings, the desire to continue in existence in accordance with their nature. In accordance with this inclination those matters which conserve man's life or are contrary to it are governed by natural law. Secondly, there is in man an inclination to some more specific objects in accordance with the nature which he has in common with the other animals. According to this, those matters are said to be of natural law "which nature has taught all animals," such as the union of male and female, the bringing up of children, and the like. Thirdly, there is in man an inclination to good according to the nature of reason which is peculiar to him. He has a natural inclination to know the truth about God, and to live in society. Accordingly those matters which concern this inclination are matter for natural law, such as that a man avoid ignorance, that he not offend others with whom he should have converse, and other matters relating to this.[30]

Aquinas, then, takes it as axiomatic that we should do what is good and not do what is bad, and he defines good in terms of those fundamental satisfactions to which every human being is essentially and naturally orientated. The general conclusions which he derives from his way of thinking in the light of each fundamental tendency, whether it be towards individual survival, or survival of the species, or in pursuit of truth and of social harmony, then have to be applied in increasing detail, and so he can build up a whole logical scheme of moral reasoning as these tendencies are considered and their realization explored in more and more specific instances. In this way, he points out, one can in theory descend by a series of logical steps from the most general precepts of the law of man's nature to the most particular applications, and the more circumstantial one's conclusions become, the less certain and predictable they are.

> In speculative matters [for example, geometry] there is for everyone the same truth in principles as there is in conclusions, although the truth is not known by everyone in the conclusions but only in the principles which are called [by Boethius] "the general concepts." In matters of action, however, there is not the same truth or practical rightness for everyone with regard to particulars as there is with regard to what is general. . . .[31]

On the whole it has been the fate of Aquinas' natural law teaching in moral theology that the logical appeal and coherence of his system has been stressed, while the provisionality and contingency of conclusions as they come closer to individual situations, features which he himself carefully built into his theory, have been either neglected or ignored.

In the centuries following Aquinas his teaching on natural law was to become an authoritative and central feature of moral theology and the outstanding example of its respect for, and expectations from, the power of human reasoning in the moral sphere. One line of divergence in the period immediately after him, through nominalism and Occamism and their stress on the absolute power and freedom of God, as we shall have occasion to consider later, was to introduce a note of provisionality to the point of scepticism and moral agnosticism into the whole system.[32] Another line of development, with which we are not concerned in this study, was pursued through the works of Grotius and Pufendorf, and arose from exploring the implications for natural law not so much of God's absolute power but of the speculative possibility of there not being a God. It was this line of thought which was to result in what Oskar Köhler describes as "the detheologization of natural law" to become "at once the foundation of the tolerant state as well as its becoming an absolute concept as the *primum principium* of political and social life."[33] The mainstream of Thomistic natural law theory, however, is to be found proceeding powerfully through the great Spanish Dominican and Jesuit scholars of the fifteenth and sixteenth centuries —Vitoria, Suarez, and Vasquez—as well as through the Italian Bellarmine, particularly with the universal adoption in the Universities of the *Summa Theologiae* of Aquinas as a universal textbook and a text to be explained, expanded, and applied by the leading theologians of the Church to contemporary issues.

Thus developed, the doctrine of natural law became an increasingly useful resource in official Church teaching on moral matters. The 1864 *Syllabus* in which Pope Pius IX collected and classified eighty of the errors which he had so far had occasion to condemn (and in which he was aided by the future Pope Leo XIII) asserted the need for civil law to conform to the law of nature, and vindicated the indissolubility of marriage as based on natural law.[34] He had also, as early as the first encyclical letter of his pontificate in 1846, made the first papal reference to Communism in describing it as "a doctrine particularly at variance with natural law,"[35] a view on which Pius XI was to elaborate in 1937.[36] But it was with the pontificate of Pope Leo XIII that the doctrine of natural law was to flourish, partly as the result of another Scholastic and Thomistic revival which he strongly and authoritatively encouraged, and partly in its being considered a particularly apt instrument in the development of the Church's social and political teaching in a world which might listen to reason even if it would not heed the revealed word of God. So, against full-blooded socialism, the right of property and ownership was based on human nature and on "the most holy law of nature."[37] Duelling was strictly forbidden by natural law, and the secrecy and disruptive potential of freemasonry were things which nature would not permit.[38] Nature was the basis of the social needs of man,[39] as also of clarifying the relationships between Church and State.[40] The superiority of divine and natural law was asserted over the claims of human legislation, "for it is just as wrong to command as it is to do whatever violates the law of nature or the will of God."[41] And the Pope who in 1879 was putting forward the 'golden wisdom' of

Thomas Aquinas as the basis of neo-scholasticism was nine years later to deliver a teaching on the eternal law and on natural law which was clearly based on the doctrine of Aquinas:

> To see why man needs a law we should consider his power of choice and the need for our wills not to be at odds with right reasoning. The natural law is written and engraved in the minds of individuals because it is human reasoning itself ordering us to act rightly and forbidding us to sin. But that prescription of human reason can have the force of law only if it is the voice and interpreter of a higher reason to which our mind and freedom should be subject. So the law of nature is the eternal law, to be found in rational beings and inclining them to their due act and end, and that in turn is the eternal reason of God the creator who governs the whole universe.[42]

The application of natural law thinking by Leo XIII in his teaching on working class conditions and the rights of workers was to be echoed in later social encyclicals of further Popes;[43] and at the outbreak of the Second World War Pope Pius XII devoted the first encyclical of his pontificate to the subject of natural law, expressing the conviction that the ills of modern society arose from the rejection, in private and public life, and in international relations, of a universal norm of morality, the natural law itself.[44]

> This natural law has for its foundation God the all-powerful creator and father of all, the supreme and most perfect lawmaker, and the most wise and just judge of human behavior. When the eternal Deity is rejected, then the principle of all morality collapses, and silence or feebleness fall upon the voice of nature which teaches the unlearned and even the primitive what is right and wrong, permitted or not permitted, and warns them that some day they will give account before the Supreme Judge of what they have done well and done badly.[45]

Pope Pius XII and his successors were to continue to see "right reason" and the moral precepts generated by human nature as a major resource for all men in every area of behavior, including, of course, the ethics of human reproduction. Pius XII had condemned contraception as contrary to natural law, a teaching repeated by Paul VI in *Humanae Vitae* and renewed by Pope John Paul II in 1981, particularly in the latter's reference to the moral order as revealing and setting forth the plan of God the Creator as a response to "the deepest demands of the human being created by God."[46] Pius XII in particular deployed natural law argumentation also to condemn sterilization, as Pius XI had done,[47] and artificial insemination, as Leo XIII had done as early as 1897,[48] as well as the further medical advances of *in vitro* fertilization.[49]

The whole development of Catholic natural law theory has not gone unchallenged, especially in recent years, and this particular application of the persistent confidence of the Church's moral tradition in the power of human reasoning to identify moral claims through a consideration of man's nature raises a host of questions relating not just to the application of this law of nature in particular areas of human behavior, but also to the more fundamental issues of the presuppositions and methodology of natural law theory in general. Some of these issues will fall to be considered later in this work, but for the present we may turn to some connected questions which have been of equally fundamental importance in the making of moral theology, and in particular to the subject of the supernatural.

THE STORM OVER THE SUPERNATURAL: JANSENISM

Granted that through the use of "right reason" and recourse to the moral law of man's nature one can come to a correct appreciation of the morality or immorality of different human actions, does it follow that one who thus acts in accordance with reason and natural law will thereby be pleasing to God? The answer to this apparently simple question was for centuries to exercise and often to perplex theologians, and to engage moral theology, and the Church, in probably the greatest running battle in the history of theology— the long crisis of Jansenism.

What had enabled Aquinas to exploit the statement of Augustine that God's eternal law is "impressed" on his creatures, and to explore the constitution and the moral implications of that impression on man, was his full-blooded acceptance of Aristotelian metaphysics. Profoundly imbued and stimulated by the thirteenth century's discovery of the full works of Aristotle, Thomas brought to his examination of human nature a speculative, metaphysical, and not quite unhistorical method of analysis, quite diverse from the Neoplatonist and intensely experiential approach of Augustine. As Gilson explains of Augustine,

> His doctrine is the metaphysics of his own conversion and remains preeminently the metaphysics of conversion. . . . He had had actual experience of the radical insufficiency of nature and this is the reason for his constant concern to keep within their actual limits the capacity of essences and the efficacy of their operations. . . . [P]articularly attentive to the actual insufficiency of nature to satisfy the desire for things divine which God has placed within it . . . he underscores its congenital and acquired deficiencies.[50]

Thus it is that "whereas the nature probed by St. Thomas Aquinas is a metaphysically indestructible essence whose intrinsic necessity resists even the corruption of original sin and surrenders to it only the graces removed by it and the powers weakened or vitiated by it, Augustine uses the word "nature" to describe the actual state caused by sin and what there is left in that state to justify man's hope of finding a way out of it."[51]

Even Augustine, however, could not find himself totally negative in his estimation of man's nature as it existed after Adam's sin of pride and the fall of humankind. He acknowledges that although man's condition was now justifiably wretched, yet God in his goodness "has filled even this misery with innumerable blessings," including the fact that "there is still the spark, as it were, of that reason in virtue of which he was made in the image of God: that spark has not been utterly put out."[52] And in his great survey of human history he was to concede that one reason for the past endurance and extent of the Roman Empire was the presence and influence of men of good moral character.[53] Individuals such as Cato were "good men in their way," and if not saints they were at least "less depraved" than others.[54] Nevertheless, he points out, "when such men do anything good, their sole motive is the hope of receiving glory from their fellow men. . . . By such immaculate conduct they labored toward honors, power and glory, by what they took to be the true way." And—like the Pharisees—they received their reward in full, from men.[55] "These were the two motives which took the Romans to their wonderful achievements: liberty, and the passion for the praise of men."[56] The Stoics had been correct in showing how the Epicureans had vitiated all seemingly moral behavior by making the pursuit of pleasure the dominant motive and reward; and the same, although perhaps to a lesser degree, must apply to the motive and reward of human glory, "which may not be a female voluptuary, but is puffed up with empty conceit."[57]

On one occasion Augustine seems to entertain a less disparaging judgement on the glory that was Rome when he observes that, although he has sufficiently explained why God should have assisted the Romans "who are good according to the standards of the earthly city" to attain the glory of their Empire, "it may be that there is another more hidden cause on account of the diverse merits of mankind, which are better known to God than to us."[58] But his almost invariable way of accounting for the Roman virtues is to distinguish sharply between true or genuine virtue and its counterfeits. "It is the conviction of all those who are truly religious, that no one can have true virtue without true piety, that is, without the true worship of the true God; and that the virtue which is employed in the service of human glory is not true virtue."[59] His standard of true virtue is exacting. "Virtue is truly virtue when it refers all the good things of which it makes good use, all its achievements in making good use of good things and evil things, and when it refers itself also, to that end where our peace shall be so perfect and so great as to admit of neither improvement nor increase."[60] Without such overall "ordering" of one's activities explicitly toward the Christian God all human enterprises lose the name of virtue. "In serving God the soul rightly commands the body, and in the soul itself the reason which is subject to its Lord God rightly commands the lusts and the other perverted elements. That being so, when a man does not serve God, what amount of justice are we to suppose to exist in his being?"[61]

Appearances, then, can be deceptive. "Not infrequently, to be sure, the obvious vices are overcome by vices so masked that they are reputed virtues; and the king of these is pride, an exalted self-satisfaction which brings a disastrous fall."[62] This mask of human pride and self-satisfaction also conceals an interior emptiness in such men, an absence of God at work.

> Thus the virtues which the mind imagines it possesses, by means of which it rules the body and the vicious elements, are themselves vices rather than virtues, if the mind does not bring them into relation with God in order to achieve anything whatsoever and to maintain that achievement. For although the virtues are reckoned by some people to be genuine and honourable when they are related only to themselves and are sought for no other end, even then they are puffed up and proud, and so to be accounted vices rather than virtues. For just as it is not something derived from the physical body itself that gives life to that body, but something above it, so it is not something that comes from man, but something above man, that makes his life blessed.[63]

On these and similar passages in Augustine two observations may be made. The first is that he ascribes a worthlessness to what is considered human virtue either because it is a sham, bleeding internally from self-satisfaction, or more systematically because he has so defined virtue as to exclude what other men would call virtue. The virtues of the philosophers, "the morality of the earth-born society," he would call good, but "a good of little importance," precisely and simply because "a brief and true definition of virtue is "rightly ordered love.' " Herein lies the significance of the request in the *Canticle* of the Bride of Christ, the City of God, to "set love in order in me." And this is for Augustine the key to all true and genuine morality. "This is true of everything created; though it is good, it can be loved in the right way or the wrong way—in the right way, that is, when the proper order is kept, in the wrong way when that order is upset."[64] If, then, due and proper love of God does not permeate the whole of man's behavior and the moral virtues, as it should, why bother to consider them important, or call them virtues?

If it were simply a matter of choosing how virtue is to be defined, little would appear to follow from Augustine's refusal to ascribe the term to non-Christian conduct. But there is a more important observation to be made of his theological attitude and his unwillingness to concede any ultimately real importance to human achievement. "Those who are endowed with true piety and who lead a good life . . . attribute to the grace of God whatever virtues they may be able to display in this present life, because God has given those virtues to them in response to their wish, their faith, and their petition."[65] *Da quod iubes, et iube quod vis!* What makes all the difference for Augustine between virtue and vice, as we have seen above, is that "just as it is not something derived from the physical body itself that gives life to that body, but something above it, so it is not something that comes from man, but *something above man*, that makes his life blessed."[66] In this appeal to "something above man" we can discern an intimation of the whole developing theology not of nature but of supernature, which was to result, in the Scholastic age and beyond, in a vast superstructure of "created grace" apparently overlaid on the natural network of human living and human relationships. It was not enough to love God and one's neighbor; it had to be done with "supernatural" love. Since the Fall of man and the ruination of his nature, "none of the perfections God maintains therein has now the slightest value as regards salvation. The rare and precarious virtues which remain can regain their initial supernatural value only if God grants it to them by means of a special assistance adapted to the needs of fallen nature, namely by grace."[67]

This Augustinian appeal to the need for a supernatural resource in order to engage in truly virtuous behavior was later to be found in Aquinas transposed into an Aristotelian key, in his teaching on charity as the "form" of the moral virtues.[68] J. P. Kenny observes of the term "supernatural" that in its Neoplatonist origin and its introduction into Western thought in the ninth century through translations of the Pseudo-Dionysius it was used to refer to a superior being, and that its full possibilities for theology were to be developed only in the thirteenth century by Aquinas, in his applying the term not just to superior beings but to effects brought about in natural beings which were well beyond their ordinary and native capacities. And this

Aquinas was the more able to do by his developing from Aristotle, and for the first time in theology, a firm, stable understanding of what is to be understood by natures and their essential properties.[69] Once that basic substratum was clearly identified, the universe of the supernatural could be confidently explored. And one consequence of this for moral theology was to lay all the stress on supernatural moral activity as alone sufficient for salvation, to the detriment of merely human, natural, and terrestrial moral behavior. Morality became a two-tier activity in requiring supernatural motivation and even "infused" moral virtues which alone could count with God.[70] The Christian sat upstairs on the Clapham omnibus.

The Scholastic elaboration of the supernatural in the light of man's natural resources, particularly when contrasted with the Augustinian view of the ruinous state of human nature after the Fall, led to the greatest storm ever to rock moral theology, that to which the name Jansenism is globally applied. At its center was the posthumous work of Jansen to which we have already referred, the massive intellectual construction of a lifetime which has been given the tragic epitaph by de Lubac of being based on a fatal misunderstanding of one distinction in Augustine's teaching on grace.[71] The storm clouds had been gathering, however, long before the death of Jansen in 1638, in the sixteenth and seventeenth century controversies over the relationship between man's free act of his will and God's action on him through grace—the famous *De Auxiliis* controversy between Dominican and Jesuit theologians on the Augustinian "helps" given by God to man to enable him to act well. The Spanish Dominican theologian, Dominic Bañez, propounded the theory which he claimed to be that of Aquinas, that God moves, or almost prods, man into successful action by his grace—the theory of "physical pre-motion." But the Spanish Jesuit, Francis Molina, judging such a theory as destructive of human freedom in its attempt to secure divine initiative, depicted God rather as foreseeing the action which man would freely choose to do and in the light of that knowledge giving man the grace to do it. Thus was born the theory of "middle knowledge," or God's *scientia media,* by which he knows not only what actually is the case and what will be the case, but also what would be the case; that is, not only actuals and futures but also "futuribles." This difference in ways of analysing the mechanics of

God's actions aroused a quite astonishing controversy and enduring animosity, or *odium theologicum,* between the sons of St. Dominic and the sons of St. Ignatius and their students and sympathizers, and led to the dispute eventually being called to Rome for papal arbitration, the only official outcome being that neither side was condemned but that in 1611 silence was authoritatively imposed on all the protagonists.[72]

Such silence was too much to hope for, of course, and the faculty of the University of Louvain, strongly Augustinian and anti-Jesuit, continued to combat Molinism, the aim which motivated the young Cornelius Jansen to begin his monumental study of Augustine. Jansen's predecessor as professor of theology at Louvain, Baius, whom we have already met contending that God does sometimes ask the impossible of man, had already run into trouble with other European universities for his views on grace and on human nature, and Rome was eventually drawn to condemn a series of propositions alleged to be found in his various works, including a statement that "all the deeds of unbelievers are sins, and the virtues of the philosophers are vices."[73] Behind this and other assertions of du Bay one can discern a view on the "basic depravity of man's fallen nature and his impotence of himself to will anything but sin."[74] And it was this theological anthropology which Jansen was to buttress and build into a complete system through his quarryings in Augustine. The disedifying spectacle of the Louvain theologians condemning the Jesuits as Pelagians for vaunting man's moral freedom, and being in turn condemned of Calvinism, with attempts to prevent Jansen's work being published, culminated in 1653 in papal condemnation of five propositions ascribed to Jansen—an action which only exacerbated the hostilities by adding to controversy over what Augustine had meant further dispute over what Jansen himself had meant.[75]

Jansenism, however, was much more than an academic theological quarrel. As de Lubac observes, it refers also to "the vast religious and moral movement to which his name is attached."[76] For the quality of religion in early seventeenth-century France was profoundly depressing. Jedin paints a sombre picture of a clergy almost totally uneducated, both in general and professionally, and of decadence in religious orders, which all gave sad proof that the Church reforms envisaged and demanded by the Council of Trent were largely dead letters.[77] It was from such a background that there arose various reform figures and movements: Bérulle and the founding of the French Oratory; Jean-Jacques Olier and his Compagnie de Saint-Sulpice; Monsieur Vincent de Paul; and the Basque Jean Duvergier de Hauranne, Abbé de Saint-Cyran, to whom, according to de Lubac, Jansenism owed its success and its greatness, and without whom it would have been merely another academic aberration.[78] Saint-Cyran was a convinced Augustinian, and with Bérulle he "sought to derive from Augustine a method that would make souls realize their total dependence on God and their personal wretchedness."[79] Among the means chosen to instill this realization, in a throwback to the penitential practice of the early Church, Saint-Cyran introduced the practice of deferring absolution from sins and reception of Holy Communion for several weeks, so that true repentance could be proved by good behavior, a devout practice adopted with enthusiasm by Mère Angélique Arnaud and her Paris community of Cistertian nuns at Port-Royal.[80]

The Jansenist movement, then, in the words of Cragg, aimed at a purification of the French Church.[81] As such it inevitably fell foul of the political aims of the all-powerful Cardinal Richelieu and the French Court of Louis XIV. Disapproval from Rome, and resistance to such disapproval, also inevitably revived the tension between the claims of the Gallican Church to independence in matters of jurisdiction and discipline from the centralizing bids of Rome beyond the Alps. And the anti-papal and reforming spirit of Augustinian Jansenism also picked out as one of its most dangerous and most insidious foes what it viewed as among the major causes of the decline of true religion, the laxity of morals, and the overweening claims of the papacy: the powerful and papalist Society of Jesus, which had from the first attacked the teaching on grace from Louvain and which had unsuccessfully intrigued to prevent publication of Jansen's *Augustinus.* It was a disciple of Saint-Cyran—the brother of Mère Angélique of Port-Royal and the author of a popular work entitled *On Frequent Communion* (which advocated infrequent reception)—the Sorbonne professor Antoine Arnaud, who led the major spirited attack in his *The Moral Theology of the Jesuits.* And this detailed and painstakingly documented disclosure of the laxism of Jesuit theories of morality was to be put to more eloquent and biting use two years later by another friend of the community of Port-Royal, the young convert mathematician, Blaise Pascal, in his imaginary and anonymous newsletters to a friend in the country. Later in this study we shall have occasion to discuss the moral reasoning castigated in the *Provincial Letters,* our concern for the present being to consider the mentality, and the anthropology, underlying them and the whole Jansenist movement, of which Voltaire wrote, "I know of no sect more barbarous and more dangerous than the Jansenists. They are worse than the Scottish Presbyterians."[82]

Not, of course, that the free-thinking Voltaire was any friend of his former schoolmasters, the Jesuits, whom he regarded as "enemies of the human race, driven out of three countries, and regarded with horror by the whole earth."[83] But his comparison of Jansenism with Scottish Presbyterianism may be seen as an indication of the profound affinities with Calvinism of which the Jansenists were continually accused by Jesuits and others in their extreme Augustinian pessimism about the state of fallen man and the selective and impenetrable workings of God's grace.[84] In strict Jansenism, fallen man is completely at the mercy of his desires, whether for evil or for good. Of himself he can delight only in evil, in love of himself and of creatures, and his will is invincibly drawn in that direction. Should God decide to number him, however, among the few He will save, then grace will so flood his will as to conquer and overcome all other delights and draw him irresistibly in love to God and to his will.[85] The effect of such beliefs was, as Mère Angélique was to write, to annihilate man before God,[86] and, as Matteucci observes in describing the rigorist and repressive nature of Jansenist piety, to present Jesus as a severe and inscrutable redeemer and themselves as an elite ranged against the humanistic spirit of the times which seemed to glorify man at God's expense.[87] Among the many and increasingly exasperated Church condemnations of Jansenism we may note its rejection of the extreme views that Christ had not died for all men but only for those who are finally saved and that, as we have already seen, even to the just some of God's commands are impossible since grace is not granted to make them possible.[88] In a later attempt to quell the persistent movement Rome's Holy Office issued in 1690 a condemnation of thirty-one "errors of the Jansenists" which in-

cluded their views that "even if there were invincible ignorance of
the natural law anyone acting against it in the state of fallen nature
would still be guilty of formal sin"; that "every deliberate human
action is either love of God, and therefore charity of the Father, or
love of the world, and therefore concupiscence of the flesh, and as
such evil"; that "an unbeliever necessarily sins in everything he
does"; that "whatever is not of Christian supernatural faith operative through love is a sin"; and, for good measure, that "where anyone finds a teaching clearly based in Augustine he can absolutely
hold and teach it, all papal Bulls to the contrary notwithstanding"![89]

In thus responding to what it judged the excessive supernaturalism of Jansenism, the Church's moral tradition was at pains not
to exceed the balance which it considered had been achieved by the
Council of Trent, drawing upon the fifth century Council of Arles,
that although the fall of Adam had weakened and distorted man's
freedom of choice it had not extinguished it.[90] It was true that Trent
had taught that unbelievers were excluded from the kingdom of
God.[91] Nevertheless, it also anathematized anyone who would say
"that all the works done by anyone before justification, and whatever their reason, are sins and deserve God's hatred."[92] This balance
the Church was to continue to aim at in the eighteenth century in
condemning views of Pasquase Quesnel, who succeeded Arnaud as
leader of the Jansenists, and in condemning similar views enunciated in 1794 at the Jansenist-inspired Synod of Pistoia.[93] Not, of
course, that the Church was entirely optimistic about the natural
resources of fallen human nature. It was persuaded that fallen man's
ability to do good naturally, or at least not to sin in every one of his
actions, was a very precarious one, almost more theoretical than
actual, and one which he could not maintain for any extended period of his life. And in this it based itself not only on the experience
even of the justified but also on the Pauline interpretation of world
history without Christ, in God's solemn triple abandonment of dis-
believers to their own unnatural devices (cf. Rom. 1:24–31).[94]

GOOD PAGANS OR ANONYMOUS CHRISTIANS?

In the storm over the supernatural two of the questions at issue
were whether, once man knew what he ought to do he was naturally

capable of actually doing it without supernatural aid from God, and whether he was able to do it in the manner in which God wished it done. Generally speaking, it may be said that medieval theology, based on Augustine, was to develop in answer to the former question a theory of "healing" grace which would restore the full "natural" resources of man who had on the road to Jericho been not only robbed of his riches but also physically harmed. But in order for man further to act in the way in which God wished, out of a "supernatural" love, it would be necessary for God graciously to replace the riches with which he had originally freely endowed the victim of sin, by the gift of "elevating" grace enabling him to raise his sights to God and to rise above his nature and so act well for love of Him. In this way Christ, the Good Samaritan, came to the aid of man who had been, as the axiom expressed it, both "despoiled of his riches and injured in his nature."[95] Post-Tridentine theology was to explore both the wounds of fallen nature and the gratuitous quality of the supernatural gifts of God by speculating on the possibility of a human nature which was neither elevated in Adam, nor fallen through sin, nor redeemed in Christ, a state of "pure nature" and of its potentialities and its conjectured natural destiny. It was from this concept of pure nature that there was to arise controversy over whether man so constituted would have a "natural" desire for the Beatific Vision, ultimately sharing fully in the divine life in a way which was somehow "owed" to him by God who had created in him this natural desire.[96]

In all these speculations and complicated constructs, theology, and the Church in its teaching on nature and supernature, were aiming above all to preserve intact what they considered two fundamental truths: that God's grace is freely given and can in no sense be considered something which he owes to man, or to which man has a right based on any incompleteness or exigency arising from the nature which God created;[97] and that man himself, even after sin, is somehow capable of actively cooperating and responding to God's overtures of grace.[98] More recently, however, such scholastic and neo-scholastic analyses of various types of grace and of the intricate mechanics of grace have come to appear remote, if not obsolete, particularly in their application to the possibility of fallen man's ability to behave in a way which is "naturally" good without being "supernaturally" good. Juan Alfaro observes that "the supernaturality" of grace does not express what grace is in itself . . . but it does signify the absolute freedom of God and of his giving of himself to man."[99] As for "nature," that, as Alfaro also points out, is "a theological concept" in relation to grace, but as Karl Rahner has argued, it is a "vestigial concept," or a remainder "arrived at by abstraction from divinizing grace in man."[100] This idea of "nature" as an abstraction, or as what remains when one considers it in isolation from God's grace, indicates that such an idea or concept has never in fact actually been realized in human history.

Rahner, who has been the principal and most influential exponent of such developments from post-Tridentine and neo-scholastic theology, writes of the traditional theological distinction between nature and grace, "in this most widespread view of it, grace is a superstructure above man's conscious spiritual and moral life, although it is, of course, also an acknowledged object of his faith and recognized as the highest, the divine, life in him which alone has power to bring him salvation."[101] "In short, the relationship between nature and grace is thought of as two layers laid very carefully one on top of the other so that they interpenetrate as little as possible."[102] But, he maintains, "it is perfectly acceptable to hold that man's whole spiritual life is permanently penetrated by grace. Just because grace is *free and unmerited* this does not mean that it is rare (theology has been led astray for too long already by the tacit assumption that grace would no longer be grace if God became too free with it). Our whole spiritual life takes place within God's will for our salvation."[103] He writes of "grace which enfolds man, the sinner and the unbeliever too, as his very sphere of existence which he can never escape from," and concludes that "actual human nature is *never* "pure" nature, but nature in a supernatural order."[104]

Within this scheme of what Rahner calls the "supernatural existential," what then becomes of "nature?" Not only is it a *Restbegriff,* or what is left when one withdraws from consideration all reference to grace and the supernatural, but it is well nigh impossible in practice to filter out in one's consideration of human experience the supernatural ingredients in order to collect a "pure" deposit of the natural.

Certainly the philosopher has his own well-grounded concept of the nature of man: the irreducible substance of human being, established by recourse to human experience independently of verbal revelation. This concept may largely coincide with the theological concept of man's nature, in so far as without Revelation the greater part of what goes beyond this "theological" nature is not experienced, and at any rate is not recognized *as* supernatural without the help of Revelation to interpret it. But in principle the content of this philosophical concept of man need not simply coincide with the content of the theological concept of man's "pure" nature. It can in concrete fact contain more (i.e., something already supernatural, though not as such). When therefore one undertakes to state with precision what exact content is intended by such a concept of a pure nature, in particular as regards God and his moral law, the difficulties, indeed the impossibility, of a neat horizontal once again become apparent for us, as the history of theology shows only too clearly.[105]

To the phenomenon of "good" pagans Augustine had responded, as we have seen, mainly by impugning their motives for acting, so that their virtues were at best only counterfeits of the true virtue which must be motivated and "ordered" by explicit love for the true Christian God. And this could only be done with help "from above" on pain of their "virtuous" conduct being virtuous at best only within the mundane terms of the earthly city or, as later theology was to re-express it, being virtuous only in "natural" terms. The line which more recent speculation has followed is to decline to take such a systematically derogatory attitude toward ordinary human behavior, and to argue a case for its being fully acceptable to God as at least "implicitly" motivated and directed by genuine love which cannot be dissected with such ease as previous theologians have considered. In other words, if it is true that only with the help of God's grace can individuals consistently observe the moral law then two possible conclusions follow. The first, which appealed to Augustine and has been the tendency in the Church's moral teaching for centuries, is that, despite any appearances of isolated virtues to the contrary, the behavior of unbelievers is frequently sinful. The other is, by contrast, a more generous willingness to accept the genuine worth of the behavior of unbelievers and to conclude that they are regularly the cooperative recipients of God's grace.

This theological *volte-face* cannot, of course, be an isolated move and it inevitably raises the question of consequent fundamental shifts in other areas of theology, notably those of the function for moral behaviour of what Rahner calls "verbal Revelation" and of the role of the Church as the, or an, instrument of salvation, as we shall consider in more detail later. Within the doctrine of grace, however, the fundamental issue which a rehabilitation in Christian eyes of the moral behavior of "good pagans" raises is how it can come about that they are the willing recipients of the grace of Christ whom they either do not know or have, for one reason or another, rejected but in whose name alone man can be saved. Somehow or other, by a mysterious and hidden dispensation of God, the grace of Christ is available outside the category of faith and visible adherence to his Church. And so the problem of the good pagan became the hypothesis of the "anonymous Christian," whose practical conclusions at any rate, whatever may be thought of the sometimes intricate theology underlying it, were adopted by the Second Vatican Council.[106]

The idea of anonymous Christianity is today invariably linked with the name of Karl Rahner as its chief exponent, and it is a logical development of his thinking on the supernatural existential.

> No matter what a man states in his conceptual, theoretical, and religious reflection, anyone who does not say in his *heart,* "there is no God" (like the "fool" in the psalm) but testifies to him by the radical acceptance of his [own] being, is a believer. But if in this way he believes in deed and in truth in the holy mystery of God, if he does not suppress this truth but leaves it free play, then the grace of this truth by which he allows himself to be led is always already the grace of the Father in his Son. And anyone who has let himself be taken hold of by this grace can be called with every right an "anonymous Christian."[107]

[T]his self-communication by God offered to all and fulfilled in the highest way in Christ . . . constitutes the goal of
all creation and—since God's word and will *effect* what
they say— . . . stamps and determines man's nature and
lends it a character which we may call a "supernatural
existential." . . . [T]his means that the express revelation of
the word in Christ is not something which comes to us
from without as entirely strange, but only the explicitation
of what we already are by grace and what we experience at
least incoherently in the limitlessness of our transcendence.[108]

From such reflections Rahner is able to conclude,

if one believes seriously in the universal salvific purpose of
God towards all men in Christ, it need not and cannot
really be doubted that gratuitous influences of properly
Christian supernatural grace are conceivable in the life of
all men (provided they are first of all regarded as individuals) and that these influences can be presumed to be accepted in spite of the sinful state of men and in spite of
their apparent estrangement from God.[109]

For the Augustinian explanation that in the good behavior of
the unbeliever his virtuous conduct is only apparent and superficial,
Rahner would substitute the explanation that it is his unbelief which
is only apparent, and that the efficacy in history of God's will that all
men should be saved can be presumed to prevail over the belief that
all men have sinned. What this comes to mean in practice, with
regard to the expressly Christian revelation, is that man "already
accepts this revelation whenever he really accepts *himself completely,* for it already speaks *in* him. Prior to the explicitness of official ecclesiastical faith this acceptance can be present in an implicit
form whereby a person undertakes and lives the duty of each day in
the quiet sincerity of patience, in devotion to his material duties and
the demands made upon him by the persons under his care."[110]

The possibility of a Christianity which is "anonymous," particularly as elaborated in Heideggerian terms by Rahner, is one which

arouses a variety of reactions. Some would view in it a patronizing attitude toward the "best" of non-Christian moral thinking, past and present. Others might incline to see in it, with its foundation in the refusal to distinguish clearly in human experience between the natural and the supernatural, a threat to the autonomy of moral philosophy. Others might again see it as a covert recruitment drive for Christians from among those who had been previously viewed as rather puzzling good pagans. And yet, modern theologians have by no means been the first to adumbrate a theology of the influence of Christ, and not just of a unitarian God, at work in the thinking and lives of unbelievers. As early as the second century the attitude of some Christians to what they considered the best of pagan thought, including moral thinking, was not just hospitable, as we have seen. It also took on a proprietorial dimension by Christians laying claim to what was good in such thought. Sometimes this is naïvely expressed in terms of laying a prior claim to such thinking as originating with Moses and the Prophets, from whom Plato and other philosophers among the pagans historically derived their doctrines.[111] At other times the acceptability of some pagan ethics would find a more theological explanation in the idea of the Stoic *logos,* or reason permeating all reality, being identified as the creative Johannine *Logos,* or Word of God, whose seed was scattered and sown throughout creation in the minds of men. This doctrine of the *Logos spermatikos* we find developed strikingly in Justin, who refers to "seeds of truth among all men," and who explains how Christ is "the Word of whom every race of men were partakers; and those who lived according to reason, [or the Word,] are Christians, even though they have been thought atheists; as, among the Greeks, Socrates and Heraclitus, and men like them; and among the barbarians, Abraham, and Ananias, and Azarias, and Misael, and Elias, and many others. . . ."[112] The seed was not always permitted to grow undisturbed, and the devils are always at pains to distort the truth, to blind men and to persecute all who thus "live a reasonable and earnest life." Their hostile activity is even more strongly directed against those "who live not according to a part only of the word diffused [among men], but by the knowledge and contemplation of the whole Word, which is Christ."[113] No doubt, those who have known only a part of the word have often contradicted themselves, but "whatever things were rightly said among all men, are the property of us Christians."[114] Nor is it just a matter of the apprehension of truth, in a speculative manner. "Those who did that which is universally, naturally, and eternally good are pleasing to God."[115]

REASON AND REVELATION

Another fundamental question which can be asked in the light of moral theology's espousal of natural law theory and the Church's persistent confidence in the power of man's rationality to apprehend what he ought to do and ought not to do is, what then is the point or the purpose for morality of Revelation or, for that matter, of religion? Ronald Knox, in his summary of *The Belief of Catholics,* was quite forthright in his reply. "Neither Catholicism nor any other form of Christianity pretends to have a special morality of its own; religion is meant to enforce, not to supersede, the natural code of morals."[116] Today the idea of religion "enforcing" anything has an unpleasant ring of compulsion and sanction, but if Knox is to be understood as meaning that religion *reinforces* knowledge of the natural code of morals then he is closer to the Church's tradition. And yet there has also persisted a view that the matter is not so easily settled, that just as in the area of moral performance there are twin sources of action, the natural and the supernatural, so in the sphere of moral knowledge man has two resources of information, his natural reason and supernatural Revelation.

Pelagius and his followers were prepared to concede the benefit to man of a grace which would illuminate his mind, and in this at least they seem to have been at one with Augustine. The latter's theology of original sin had included in its dire effects not only disorder in the will but also a darkening of the mind, resulting in "that terrifying abyss of ignorance, as it may be called, which is the source of all error, in whose gloomy depths all the sons of Adam are engulfed, so that man cannot be rescued from it without toil, sorrow and fear."[117] We have seen, however, that Augustine was to number among the blessings which he could still count after the Fall a spark, or glimmer, of reason which had not been totally extinguished by sin.[118] Scholastic theology was to maintain this tradition of a darkening, although not a complete extinction, of man's capacity for moral knowledge, and found in this the rationale for a divine verbal revelation of such knowledge. As Aquinas explained, after the Fall, "as time went on, sin too began to take more hold on man, to such an extent that, with his reason darkened by sin, the precepts of the law of nature were not enough for living rightly, and they had to be determined in the written law."[119] Over and above natural law and human law, however, Aquinas also saw a need for a "divine law," that is, the moral contents of the Old and New Testaments, as arising from four considerations. Two of these concern the inadequacy or incompleteness of human law, either to forbid all evil behavior, which might have undesirable social consequences, or to cope with interior acts.[120] The other two considerations relate to man's supernatural end and to the uncertainty of human judgment. Law directs man to actions corresponding to his final end, and since man is ordered toward the end of eternal beatitude, which exceeds the proportion of his natural human ability, he needs a comparable law from God directing him to this end. Moreover, because of the uncertainty of human judgement, especially concerning contingent and particular matters, a variety of judgements is to be found about human actions which also gives rise to different and conflicting human laws. And so that man can know without any doubt what he should do and not do, he needed to be directed in his own acts by a divine law which cannot be mistaken.[121]

We have already seen Aquinas express confidence in man's reason being able to come to some knowledge of God's eternal law based on the identification of, and respect for, fundamental tendencies which exist in human nature as created by God. We have also seen him identify the good which man is morally obliged to pursue defined in terms of the fulfilment of those tendencies.[122] In this way he was able to formulate a series of moral precepts of natural law: some very general in content, which he calls "primary precepts"; and others increasingly specific in their content and conclusion, which he calls "secondary precepts." Students of St Thomas seem agreed that there is a vagueness in his works about which precepts of natural law were considered primary by him, and which secondary,[123] and it is arguable that for him the primary precepts are very general and non-specific, lying within the area between the first axiomatic principle that good is to be done and evil avoided and such precepts as those of the Decalogue. As he explains, "some matters are derived from the general principles of the law of nature by way of conclusions, as the injunction 'not to kill' can be derived as a sort of conclusion from 'Do evil to no one.' "[124] And he was of the view that the primary principles of the law of man's nature are known to all men, whereas when one begins to become more specific in drawing conclusions from such first principles difficulty can arise from two complicating factors. One of these is the complexity of moral situations, so that as a matter of fact general natural law conclusions do not cover every eventuality.[125] The other is more to do with man's capacity for moral argumentation as it becomes more specific and complicated. In some instances incapacity in individuals is simply a matter of limited natural endowments, but in many other instances the incapacity arises from a variety of moral factors.

> There are some very common, or general, precepts of natural law which are known to all, and other secondary and more particular precepts derived from them. The former general precepts can never as such be entirely expelled from men's hearts, but their application to a particular situation can be, if reason is prevented by desire or some other emotion from making the application. Secondary precepts can be driven from men's hearts, either through wrong convictions (as can happen even in speculative matters), or through bad customs or habits, as some thought robbery not a sin, or even vices against nature, as Paul states (Rom. 1:24–7).[126]

The participation by man in God's eternal law through knowledge, then, can be corrupted and depraved in such a way that the natural knowledge of good is darkened by passions and the habits of sin.[127] For Aquinas, then, not all the conclusions of natural law are universally known, and the more one descends from the general to the particular, the more possible it is for reason to be unduly influenced by the emotions, or by customs, or by fallen nature. "Caesar tells us that the Germans once thought there was nothing wrong with robbery, even although it is expressly against the law of nature."[128]

Aquinas remained, however, convinced that morality is essentially rational conduct, and as such it must be accessible, at least in principle, to human reason and wisdom. In his systematic discussion of the Old Testament as part of divine law he explains that, since all morality must be consonant with reason, then "all moral precepts belong to the law of nature,"[129] and the Ten Commandments are conclusions which "a little thought" can derive from "the two first general precepts of the law of nature," love of God and love of neighbor.[130] But the Commandments in their turn can be viewed also as principles which by dint of more subtle and wise consideration yield further reasonable conclusions.[131] Moreover, the precepts of the New Law are substantially the same as those of the Old,[132] and in fact the New Law added very little to the precepts of the law of nature.[133] For even the counsels commended by Jesus (the "evangelical" counsels of poverty, chastity, obedience) can be seen to be reasonable means for some people to achieve their end better and more readily by liberating themselves from the good things of this world, whether it be wealth, or the pleasures of the body, or independence.[134]

In the teaching of Aquinas, then, the purpose of Revelation, so far as morality is concerned, appears to be essentially remedial, not absolutely necessary for man but in practice almost indispensable. In the opening sentence of his *Summa* of Theology, discussing the purpose of God's revelation, he explains that in general man's need for a Revelation about God in order to attain salvation covers not only matters which exceed his natural comprehension but also those which can be investigated by human reason, since this can be carried out "only by a few people, requires a lot of time and is subject to many errors."[135] This being so, the Christian revelation contains in its moral teaching no substantial element over and above what is accessible to human reason without such revelation.

Such was to continue to be the Church's doctrine on man's natural knowledge of the requirements of morality, and the tradition was firmly stated in the nineteenth century particularly in papal and conciliar teaching which, in the views of Flick and Alszeghy, "completed the teaching already formed on fallen man's freedom of will with similar teaching on the powers and weaknesses of the intellect in the present state of man."[136] The occasion for such statements was the movements of rationalism and fideism which largely occupied the Church in that century. Pope Pius IX, the Pope of the First Vatican Council, had some years previously taken exception to the writings of the Munich Professor Frohschammer on the capacity of philosophy and human reason to dispense with Revelation,[137] and the Council was to echo the papal (and Thomist) teaching by asserting that, on the one hand, Revelation was an absolute necessity in disclosing to man the supernatural end destined for him by God, and on the other hand that although not absolutely necessary on other matters it enabled "those matters relating to God which are not in themselves inaccessible to human reason, to be known by all, even in the present condition of the human race, readily, with firm certitude and without any admixture of error."[138] Following Vatican I, Pope Pius XI was to allow that in the area of morality "there are many matters which are not in themselves inaccessible to human reason," but he also warned that the attractions of pleasure and the difficulties of married life can easily deceive people left to themselves and lead to rationalization.[139] The age of Leo XIII, as we have earlier shown, saw a systematic and neo-scholastic expansion in the application of natural law theory,[140] but the cautionary note was once again stressed in 1950 by Pope Pius XII, despite his own confident appeals to human reason and natural law. In his encyclical, *Humani Generis,* which was aimed to quell the post-war "new theology" apparently undermining the whole tradition of the supernatural, but which events may have shown to be more of a panegyric preached over the grave of neo-scholasticism, he admitted that human reason really can by its own natural powers and light come to a true and certain knowledge of God "and of the natural law imprinted in our minds by the Creator." But he went on to stress that there are many obstacles to prevent this from happening, since such knowledge carries implications for a personal commitment and for self-denial. The intellect is hampered by emotions and imaginings as well as by the lower desires resulting from original sin.

> The result is that in such matters men willingly persuade themselves that what they do not want to be true is really false or at least doubtful. For this reason divine "revelation" must be said to be morally necessary, so that those

matters of religion and morality which are not in themselves inaccessible to reason can be known by all, even in
the present condition of the human race, readily, with firm
certitude and without any admixture of error.[141]

THE SCOPE OF REVELATION

In so stressing the "moral," or practical, need for Revelation
only as a remedy to overcome the human failings which can impede
the natural exercise of ordinary human reason, Pope Pius XII was
only continuing the steady moral tradition going back through his
predecessors to Aquinas, and indeed to Augustine. Revelation as
such has nothing in matters of moral behavior to add to the best of
human thinking, but such human moral thinking is by no means
always or invariably at its best. It is interesting to note, however, the
reluctance with which many Catholics greet this conclusion and the
ways in which they struggle against it, unwilling to accept that, so far
as content is concerned, there is nothing specifically distinctive
about Christian ethics as compared, for instance, with the best of
humanist ethics. At times there appears a persistent seeking for a
Christian "plus factor," a miracle ingredient which will make the
significant difference between the two, and there is almost a sense of
being cheated or defrauded when this is not forthcoming or is
denied.

It may be that such reaction arises from a confusion between
religion and morality, akin to some public support for religious
schools or education which will teach children how to behave properly, a function for religion which is also mirrored in the minds of
some school, and post school, children by their resistance and re-
sentment toward a religion portrayed almost entirely in terms of
moral duties and Church regulations. Such an approach to religion
is, of course, profoundly unchristian, ignoring the fact that, for the
Christian, morality is above all a free response in love to the invitation of a loving and liberating God, and that what is primary in
religion is God's actions, not ours, and, basic to Christianity, God's
actions in spite of ours.

It may also be, however, that the sense of something missing if

Christian and "human" morality are simply equated is pointing towards the need for an enriched view of morality rather than towards an impoverished view of religion. It might be expressive of a fundamental dissatisfaction with the traditional distinction between nature and supernature as this has been elaborated in the Church's moral teaching, and as it is reflected in moral matters in the distinction between reason and Revelation. To act according to reason and to act according to nature are frequently regarded as synonymous, although it is sometimes suggested that in the thought of Aquinas they betoken two differing and unreconciled approaches to human morality. Latent in this suggestion is the idea that acting reasonably may give more room for moral maneuver in such disputed areas as contraception than acting according to the profound built-in inclinations of human nature.[142] Such a line of argument, however, does not take sufficiently into account that for man to act according to reason is acting according to his nature as a rational being, and that to act unreasonably would for him be to act unnaturally. Nor does it make clear what constitutes reasonable action, which has to do with the manner in which man reaches his moral conclusions but of itself says nothing concerning the subject-matter about which he should act reasonably. In other words, man's nature includes reason but is more than reason. It has other elements of givenness about which man is to act reasonably but which are not identical with reason, such elements as the volitional, emotional, corporeal, and social aspects of his humanity.

Traditionally, then, to act according to nature has been considered as delivering the content of moral behavior, and when Revelation has been more than simply remedial in supplying for the actual deficiencies in man's reasonable activity it has been regarded as indicating a supernatural quality conferred by God on that activity rather than as adding anything to the content or the conclusions of morality. The supernatural element has not effected any change in the program of natural behavior, but has transformed its quality through making it the carrier of charity, almost as if the Christian were living and acting simultaneously at two different levels. In this scheme of things and way of viewing morality the "nature" according to which all men must act has continued to be the metaphysical essence as analyzed speculatively by Aquinas. It is true that he distinguished different states of human nature before and after sin, but nature itself he considered to remain essentially the same and unchanged.[143] If, however, as Rahner contends, man is living in a supernatural existential, and "nature" as such is a *Restbegriff,* an incomplete or remainder concept with something missing, then as such a concept it is scarcely an adequate basis for producing the program of human morality to which all men are, as a matter of fact, invited by God. There cannot be any question of regarding natural law, or what Aquinas preferred to call the law of nature, as a covert or implicit extension of the purely abstract possibility of "pure" nature. In other words, there is a mysterious or "supernatural" element to nature itself as it historically exists, to which moral theology with its long indebtedness to Stoic and Aristotelian ways of thinking has not given its attention. One charge made today against the application of natural law theory, in some of its details at least, is that it works with a concept of nature which has been philosophically defective in being too unhistorical, as we shall see later, and in being considered in isolation from the social and technological developments which have come into prominence over the years.[144] To this, it appears, should be added the further possibility that the concept of nature, and the conclusions derived from it, have been theologically defective in not taking sufficiently into account the continuity and the actual—as opposed to the conceptual—indivisibility of God's onward purpose for man in Christ.

The Second Council of Arles, in 473, referred to the "law of nature" as "the first grace of God,"[145] with an apparent sense of such continuity and cumulative divine purpose. And it may be significant for moral theology that Pope Paul VI made reference to "principles of a moral teaching on marriage which relies on natural law illuminated and *enriched by divine revelation.*"[146] Enrichment is surely more than correction or than mere remedial potential. But Pope Paul's point is not that what the moral tradition, following Aquinas, held about the equivalence of biblical moral teaching and the natural law is inadequate. It is that a "natural" view of man as a source for moral reasoning is inadequate and does not correspond to the reality that "man is made a new creature who can respond in love and genuine freedom to the plan of his Creator and Savior."[147] The continuity and the interpretation in history of God's work as both Creator and Savior have the effect, if not of blurring, at least of rendering academic the conceptual distinction between nature and supernature. As Pope Paul concluded, the Church "can only teach the law which is appropriate to a human life which has been restored to its genuine truth and is led by God's Spirit."[148]

It may also be a growing dissatisfaction with the traditional concept of "nature" which has contributed in recent years to the focus of moral attention moving from "human nature" to "human person" or "human dignity." Thus, the Second Vatican Council was certainly not unaware of the whole moral tradition centered on the law of nature when it nevertheless considered basing objective moral standards on "the dignity of the human person," and finally decided to propose the need for such standards as based on "the nature of the [human] person and his acts."[149] It is also worthy of note that the Council's Decree on Religious Freedom, which Pope Paul VI described as "one of the major texts of the Council,"[150] opened with the statement, "A sense of the dignity of the human person has been impressing itself more and more deeply on the consciousness of contemporary man."[151] John Courtney Murray, the American Jesuit whose labors and writings had done much to forward in the Church the subject of religious freedom, considered this decree "the most controversial document of the whole Council" and pardonably described the debate on the subject as "the greatest argument on religious freedom in all history." The hidden agenda, he explained, was not the issue of religious freedom, but that of the development of doctrine in the Church leading to the conciliar teaching. "The course of the development between the *Syllabus of Errors* (1864) and . . . [this decree] . . . still remains to be explained by theologians. But the Council formally sanctioned the validity of the development itself; and this was a doctrinal event of high importance for theological thought in many other areas."[152]

One such area, as we shall consider later, has to do with the role of the Church in the salvation of individuals.[153] But the founding of the right to religious freedom on the dignity of the individual human person can be seen as further indication of the move from human nature to the human person and his dignity as a basis for moral reasoning. In the circumstances it is significant that the criterion of person rather than nature can be seen flourishing in the thought of

Pope John Paul II, notably in the first encyclical of his pontificate, and in his Apostolic Exhortation on the Christian Family, in which, with reference to the subject of contraception, he invites theologians to shed more light on "the biblical foundations, the ethical grounds and the personalistic reasons behind this doctrine."[154] It is equally significant that in his encyclical *Redemptor Hominis* the Pope stresses that the object of divine Revelation includes man himself, not now just one "supernatural" dimension of human nature, but the unitary object of God's love and God's single design and destiny.[155]

The implications of this shift in focus and terminology for moral theology are still unfolding. It may be suggested that what it betokens is the establishment of a single perspective of God's creative and salvific enterprise concerning humankind, and a concentration on individuality and personal destiny, rather than, as formerly, a stress on nature as such and on a uniformly and systematically applied distinction between nature and supernature. If God is historically calling all men and women to ultimate life with him, the invitation has been delivered, and ultimately only God can really say which men have definitely refused the invitation, which have not yet opened it, and which are at present reading it. As even Augustine acknowledged, "it may be that there is another more hidden cause on account of the diverse merits of mankind, which are better known to God than to us."[156] It may also be that the shift of attention which sees divine Revelation as including the mystery of man himself in God's designs of love puts in question the enterprise to identify what is the specific factor in "Christian ethics," or at least replaces the supposition that there is a "plus factor" in Christian ethics with the realization that there is a factor missing in any attempt to identify purely natural ethics. As Rahner expresses it, "Who is to say that the voice heard in earthly philosophy, even non-Christian and pre-Christian philosophy, is the voice of nature alone (and perhaps of nature's guilt) and not also the groaning of the creature, who is already moved in secret by the Holy Spirit of grace, and longs without realizing it for the glory of the children of God?"[157] It may turn out, in other words, that philosophical ethics are really anonymous Christian ethics.

Finally, it may also be that such a unitary approach to the moral enterprise and program for man will give rather more weight to the Church's claim to competence over the whole field of morality. If, in the past, the basic argument for this universal competence has been that both divine and natural law issue from one and the same God, for the future, even if these can or should be conceived distinctly, they must be seen as God's and the Church's attention focusing on what Pope John Paul II has expressed as man, not in the abstract but in his historical entirety.[158]

Notes

1. Cf. Wis. 8: 1, "She reaches mightily from one end of the earth to the other, and she orders all things well."

2. A *Plea for the Christians,* ch. 25 (trans. Pratten), in *The Writings of Justin Martyr and Athenagoras* (Edinburgh, 1867), p. 408; Migne, *PG* 6, 949.

3. Ibid., ch. 35 (p. 419); *PG* 6, 969.

4. *On the Resurrection of the Dead,* ch. 24 (ibid., p. 455); *PG* 6, 1021.

5. Ibid., ch. 25 (p. 456); *PG* 6, 1021–4.

6. *First Apology,* ch. 28 (trans. Dods), in *The Writings of Justin Martyr and Athenagoras,* p. 31; *PG* 6, 372. It is to Justin that Christian theology is primarily indebted for the Stoic idea of natural law (φύσεως νόμος) (Spanneut, op. cit. p. 253). For him, in fact, "the Stoics are first-rate on ethics," H. Chadwick, *Early Christian Thought and the Classical Tradition* (Oxford, 1966), p. 11. On the Stoic theme of λόγος (trans. "reason") and of λόγος σπερματικός in Justin, cf. L. W. Barnard, *Justin Martyr: His Life and Thought* (Cambridge, 1967), pp. 96–9; Chadwick, op. cit., p. 16; *infra,* pp. 102, 344.

7. *Dialogue,* ch. 93 (*The Writings,* p. 217); *PG* 6, 697.

8. "Homo est enim et christianus, et quod et tu," *Apol.* 8; *PL* 1, 313.

9. "O testimonium animae naturaliter christianae," *Apol.* 17; *PL* 1, 377.

10. *Apol.* 11; *PL* 1, 333–4.

11. *de doc. chr.,* 2, 40, 60; *PL* 34, 63. Cf. Gilson, op. cit., pp. 125–6.

12. "Ergo peccatum est, factum vel dictum vel concupitum aliquid contra aeternam legem. Lex vero aeterna est, ratio divina vel voluntas Dei, ordinem naturalem conservari iubens, perturbari vetans. Quisnam igitur sit in homine naturalis ordo, quaerendum est. . . . Proinde, sicut anima corpori, ita ipsius animae ratio caeteris eius partibus, quas habent et bestiae, naturae lege praeponitur: inque ipsa ratione, quae partim contemplativa est, partim activa, procul dubio contemplatio praecellit," *Contra Faustum,* 22, 27; *PL* 42, 418.

13. "Ut igitur breviter aeternae legis notionem, quae impressa nobis est, quantum valeo verbis explicem, ea est qua iustum est ut omnia sint ordinatissima," *De lib. arb.,* 1, 6; *PL* 32, 1229.

14. "Pax omnium rerum tranquillitas ordinis. Ordo est parium dispariumque rerum sua cuique loca tribuens dispositio," *De civ. Dei,* XIX, 13, 1; *PL* 41, 640.

15. "Sicut enim bona sunt omnia quae creavit Deus, ab ipsa rationali creatura usque ad infimum corpus: ita bene agit in his anima rationalis, si ordinem servet, et distinguendo, eligendo, pendendo subdat minora maioribus, corporalia spiritualibus, inferiora superioribus, temporalia sempiternis; ne superiorum neglectu et appetitu inferiorum (quoniam hinc et ipsa fit deterior) et se et corpus suum mittat in peius, sed potius ordinata caritate se et corpus suum convertat in melius," *Epist.* CXL, 2, 4; *PL* 33, 540.

16. "Hisce igitur motibus animae cum ratio dominatur, ordinatus homo dicendus est. Non enim ordo rectus, aut ordo appellandus est omnino, ubi deterioribus meliora subiiciuntur," *De lib. arb.,* 1, 8, 18; *PL* 32, 1231.

17. Gilson, op. cit., p. 134.

18. *The City of God,* 11, 28 (trans. Bettenson, pp. 462–3); *PL* 41, 341–2. Cf. *Conf.,* XIII, 9, 10 (*PL* 32, 849): "pondus meum amor meus; eo feror quocumque feror."

19. *De civ. dei,* XIX, 14; *PL* 41, 642–3.

20. Ibid.; *PL* 41, 628–9.

21. "Deus ergo naturarum omnium sapientissimus conditor et iustissimus ordinator," ibid., cap. 13; *PL* 41, 641. Thus Gilson can explain that, for Augustine in considering evil actions, "the malice of the act is never due to the goodness of its object but to the perversion of our love for this good. In such cases, our error is not in loving what is good, but in violating order by not preferring what is better," op. cit., p. 136.

22. B. Roland-Gosselin (ed.) *Œuvres de s. Augustin,* i (Paris, 1949), p. 524. Cf. pp. 525–6.

23. Cf. B. F. Brown, "Natural Law," *NCE*, x, 252. On the Latin development of *ius naturale, ius gentium,* and *lex naturalis,* cf. J.-M. Aubert, *Le Droit romain dans l'oeuvre de saint Thomas* (Paris, 1955), pp. 91–105; O. Lottin, *Principes de morale,* t. ii (Louvain, 1947), pp. 33–6. (For a fuller treatment by Lottin, cf. his *Le Droit naturel chez s. Thomas et ses prédécesseurs* (Bruges, 1931).) Aquinas views *ius naturale* as underlying *ius gentium,* in contrast with *ius civile, STh* Ia 2ae, q. 95, a. 4 et ad 1.

24. "Jus, aut naturale est, aut civile, aut gentium. Jus naturale est commune omnium nationum, et quod ubique instinctu naturae, non constitutione aliqua habeatur, ut: viri et feminae coniunctio, liberorum susceptio et educatio, communis omnium possessio, et omnium una libertas, acquisitio eorum quae caelo, terra marique capiuntur. Item depositae rei vel commodatae restitutio, violentiae per vim repulsio. Nam hoc, aut si quid simile est, nunquam iniustum, sed naturale, aequumque habeatur," *Etymologiae,* Lib. 5, cap. 4 (*PL* 82, 199).

25. Quoted *NCE,* ibid. Rufinus was the first systematic commentator on the *Decree* of Gratian.

26. Cf. Mahoney, *Seeking the Spirit* (London, 1981), pp. 114–15. On the central role in Aquinas' moral theology of the Spirit and of the wisdom (not prudence) which the Spirit imparts, cf. ibid. On Aquinas' teaching on natural law it is useful to bear in mind the observation of Thomas Gilby, OP, in Aquinas' *Summa Theologiae,* vol. xxviii (London, 1966), p. 170, that "the terms *"jus"* and *"lex"* are more or less interchangeable in the *Summa.*"

27. *STh* Ia 2ae, q. 90, proem.

28. "Et sic ex quatuor praedictis potest colligi definitio legis, quae nihil est aliud quam quaedam rationis ordinatio ad bonum commune, ab eo qui curam communitatis habet, promulgata," ibid., q. 90, art. 4.

29. "Unde cum omnia quae divinae providentiae subduntur a lege aeterna regulentur et mensurentur, ut ex dictis patet, manifestum est quod omnia participant aliqualiter legem aeternam, inquantum scilicet ex impressione eius habent inclinationes in proprios actus et fines. Inter caetera autem rationalis creatura excellentiori quodam modo divinae providentiae subjacet, inquantum et ipsa fit providentiae particeps, sibi ipsi et aliis providens. Unde et in ipsa participatur ratio aeterna per quam habet naturalem inclinationem ad debitum actum et finem, et talis participatio legis aeternae in rationali creatura "lex naturalis" dicitur," ibid., q. 91, art 2. That Aquinas was aware of Augustine's view that the eternal law is "impressed" on us is evident from ibid., q. 93, art. 2, *sed contra,* "Augustinus dicit quod aeternae legis notio nobis impressa est." For the controlling text of Augustine, cf. *supra,* n. 13. The influence of Augustine's insistence on *ordo* is also

pervasive in Aquinas's entire treatment of law, with notable support from Aristotle. "Rationis enim est ordinare ad finem, qui est primum principium in agendis secundum Philosophum," ibid., q. 90, art 1.

    30. Ibid., q. 94, art 2, discussing whether natural law contains only one precept or a multiplicity.

    31. Ibid., q. 94, art. 4.

    32. Cf. *infra*, p. 183.

    33. In Jedin and Dolan, op. cit., vol. vi, p. 346.

    34. *DS* 2956; 2967. On the role of the future Leo XIII, cf. *DS* 2901, proem.

    35. *DS* 2786.

    36. *DS* 3772.

    37. *DS* 3266.

    38. *DS* 3272; 3156.

    39. *DS* 3165.

    40. *DS* 3172.

    41. *DS* 3152. Cf. 3132.

    42. *DS* 3247–51. On Aquinas, *DS* 3140.

    43. Cf. *DS* 3267–71, 3956, 3970.

    44. *DS* 3780.

    45. *DS* 3781.

    46. *DS* 2715, 2758, 2795, 2791. Pope Paul VI, *Humanae Vitae,* no. 11. Pope John Paul II, *Familiaris Consortio,* no. 34 (cf. nos. 29, 33).

    47. *DS* 3763.

    48. *DS* 3323.

    49. *DS* 3323, proem.

    50. Gilson, op. cit., p. 240.

    51. Ibid., p. 239.

    52. "non in eo tamen penitus exstincta est quaedam velut scintilla rationis, in qua factus est ad imaginem Dei," *De civ. Dei,* XXII, 24 (trans. Bettenson, p. 1071); *PL* 41, 789. Cf., ibid., XIX, 12 (*PL* 41, 639): "Nullum quippe vitium ita contra naturam est, ut naturae deleat etiam extrema vestiga."

    53. In the preface to Book five of the *City of God* Augustine posed the question "videamus qua causa Deus, qui potest et illa bona dare, quae habere possunt etiam non boni, ac per hoc etiam non felices, Romanum imperium tam magnum tamque diuturnum esse voluerit," *PL* 41, 141. This will remain his position, that the Romans were "non boni."

    54. Bettenson, pp. 201–2; "per quosdam paucos, qui pro suo modo boni erant," "non quidem iam sancti, sed minus turpes sunt," *PL* 41, 152–3.

55. Chap. 15; Bettenson, pp. 204–5; *PL* 41, 160, "De talibus enim, qui propter hoc boni aliquid facere videntur, ut glorificentur ab hominibus, etiam Dominus ait, *Amen dico vobis, perceperunt mercedem suam* (Matt. 6; 2)."

56. Chap. 18; Bettenson, p. 208; *PL* 41, 162, "Haec sunt duo illa, libertas et cupiditas laudis, quae ad facta compulere miranda Romanos."

57. Chap. 20; Bettenson, pp. 214–15; *PL* 41, 167, "Licet enim ista gloria delicata mulier non sit, inflata tamen est, et multum inanitatis habet."

58. Chap. 19; Bettenson, p. 213; *PL* 41, "Romanos secundum quamdam forman terrenae civitatis bonos . . . ; potest tamen et alia causa esse latentior, propter diversa merita generis humani, Deo magis nota quam nobis."

59. Ibid: "dum illud constet inter omnes veraciter pios, neminem sine vera pietate, id est, veri Dei vero cultu, veram posse habere virtutem."

60. Book XIX, chap. 10; Bettenson, p. 865; *PL* 41, 636, "Sed tunc est vera virtus, quando et omnia bona quibus bene utitur, et quidquid in bono usu bonorum et malorum facit, et se ipsam ad eum finem refert, ubi nobis talis et tanta pax erit, qua melior et major esse non possit."

61. Ibid., chap. 21; Bettenson, p. 883; *PL* 41, 649, "Serviens autem Deo animus, recte imperat corpori, inque ipso animo ratio Domino Deo subdita, recte imperat libidini vitiisque caeteris. Quapropter ubi homo Deo non servit, quid in eo putandum est esse justitiae; quandoquidem Deo non serviens, nullo modo potest juste animus corpori, aut humana ratio vitiis imperare?"

62. Book XXI, chap. 16 (Bettenson, p. 994); *PL* 41, 730, "Nonnumquam sane apertissima vitia aliis vitiis vincuntur occultis, quae putantur esse virtutes, in quibus regnat superbia et quaedam sibi placendi altitudo ruinosa."

63. Book XIX, chap. 26 (Bettenson, p. 891); *PL* 41, 656, "Nam qualis corporis atque vitiorum potest esse mens domina, veri Dei nescia, nec eius imperio subiugata, sed vitiosissimis daemonibus corrumpentibus prostituta? Proinde virtutes, quas sibi habere videtur, per quas imperat corpori et vitiis ad quodlibet adipiscendum vel tenendum, nisi ad Deum retulerit, etiam ipsae vitia sunt potius quam virtutes. Nam licet a quibusdam tunc verae et honestae putentur esse virtutes, cum ad se ipsas referuntur, nec propter aliud expetuntur; etiam tunc inflatae ac superbae sunt: et ideo non virtutes, sed vitia iudicanda sunt. Sicut enim non est a carne, sed super carnem, quod carnem facit vivere: sic non est ab homine, sed super hominem, quod hominem facit beate vivere."

64. Book XV, chap. 22 (Bettenson, p. 636); *PL* 41, 467, acknowl-

edges that female beauty is a good which is a gift of God, "sed propterea id largitur etiam malis, ne magnum bonum videatur bonis." In succumbing to it (Gen. 6: 2), the sons of God chose an "infimum bonum"; "Ita se habet omnis creatura. Cum enim bona sit, et bene potest amari, et male: bene, scilicet ordine custodito; male, ordine perturbato. . . . Unde mihi videtur, quod definitio brevis et vera virtutis, Ordo est amoris; propter quod in sancto Cantico canticorum cantat sponsa Christi, civitas Dei, *Ordinate in me charitatem (Cantic.* II, 4)."

65. Book V, chap. 19 (Bettenson, pp. 213–4); *PL* 41, 166, "Illi autem qui vera pietate praediti bene vivunt . . . virtutes suas, quantascumque in hac vita possunt habere, non tribuunt nisi gratiae Dei, quod eas volentibus, credentibus, petentibus dederit."

66. *Supra,* n. 63.

67. Gilson, p. 152.

68. Cf. the influential study which helped to rehabilitate the moral theology of Aquinas; G. Gilleman, *The Primacy of Charity in Moral Theology* (London, 1960). On "caritas forma virtutum," cf. *STh* 2a 2ae, q. 23, a. 8.

69. J. P. Kenny, "Supernatural," *NCE* 13, p. 812. Cf. H. de Lubac, *Surnaturel* (Paris, 1946), p. 327.

70. Cf. Aquinas, *STh* 1a 2ae, q. 63, a. 3 on infused moral virtues; a. 4, on how they differ from acquired moral virtues. "Patet igitur ex dictis quod solae virtutes infusae sunt perfectae, et simpliciter dicendae virtutes, quia bene ordinant hominem ad finem ultimum simpliciter. Aliae virtutes, scilicet acquisitae, sunt secundum quid virtutes, non autem simpliciter. Ordinant hominem bene respectu finis ultimi in aliquo genere, non autem respectu finis ultimi simpliciter. Unde, super illud, *Omne quod non est ex fide, peccatum est* [Rom. 14: 23], dicit Glossa Augustini, *Ubi deest agnitio veritatis, falsa est virtus etiam in optimis moribus,"* ibid., q. 65, art. 2. The thought is clearly Augustinian, although the quotation is not, in fact, from Augustine but from his friend and defender, Prosper of Aquitaine, *Sent.* 106; *PL* 51, 441. (Cf. *Summa Theologiae,* vol. xxiii, ed. W. D. Hughes, OP (London, 1969), p. 186.)

71. H. de Lubac, *Augustinisme et théologie moderne* (Aubier, 1965), p. 59. Cf. *supra,* pp. 52–3.

72. For a typically irrepressible and enjoyable account of the controversy, cf. James Brodrick, SJ, *The Life and Work of Blessed Robert Bellarmine,* 1542–1621 (London, 1928), vol. i, pp. 1–67. Cf. also *DS* 1997, proem.

73. "Omnia opera infidelium sunt peccata, et philosophorum virtutes sunt vitia," *DS* 1925. On Baius, cf. *supra,* p. 52.

74. Palmer, op. cit., p. 262.

75. The famous "Five Propositions," *DS* 2001–5, concluding with the comprehensive statement (*DS* 2007) "by this declaration and definition on the five aforesaid propositions we do not intend in any way to approve other opinions contained in the work referred to of Cornelius Jansen." Jansenist reception of this papal bull was devious, Antoine Arnaud introducing his celebrated distinction between the question of law (*de jure* the propositions were heretical) and the question of fact (*de facto* they were not what Jansen meant). The Sorbonne expelled Arnaud for propounding this subtlety, which may be thought typical of the worst type of "Jesuitical" casuistry which Arnaud found so repulsive, and at the request of the French bishops Pope Alexander VII issued in 1656 another bull which aimed to remove any further doubt. "We declare and define that those five propositions were excerpted from the book *Augustinus* of Cornelius Jansen, bishop of Ypres, and were condemned in the sense intended by Cornelius Jansen, and we again condemn them as such . . ." (*DS* 2012; for the historical details, cf. *DS* 2001, proem; 2010, proem.). Ten years later, Louis XIV obtained from the Pope a formula of submission to be accepted within three months by all, accepting the papal condemnations and rejecting and condemning "sincero animo" "the five propositions excerpted from the book *Augustinus* of Cornelius Jansen and in the sense intended by the author" (*DS* 2020; cf. proem.). Jansenist opposition survived, however, and public debate on a "case of conscience" on whether absolution could be given to anyone professing only external submission and not internal assent to the formula of submission (*DS* 2390, proem) led to yet a further authoritative clarification from Rome in the bull of 1705 entitled "The Vineyard of the Lord of Hosts." "To prevent any occasion of error in future, and so that all the sons of the Catholic Church may learn to listen to the Church, not simply in silence (for the wicked also are silent in darkness, I Kgs. 2: 9 [Vulg.]), but also submitting interiorly (*interius obsequendo*), as is the true obedience of an orthodox person; We decree, declare, lay down and ordain by Apostolic authority in this Constitution which will be forever in force that: the obedience owed to the previous Apostolic Constitutions is in no way satisfied by that submissive silence (*obsequioso illo silentio*); but that all the faithful ought to reject and condemn as heretical, not only with their lips but also in their hearts, the meaning condemned in the five propositions of Jansen's book which the words express, as it is expressed; and that the

formula may not be subscribed to in any other intention, mind or acceptance; so that whoever thinks, holds, preaches, teaches, or asserts in word or
writing, otherwise or to the contrary with regard to each and every one of
these points falls completely under each and every censure . . ." (*DS* 2390).
Not even this attempt to block all loopholes was successful, however. Cf. *DS*
2400, proem. Apart, of course, from the immediate interest of Roman reactions to Jansenism, two important questions of principle for moral theology
which emerge from the controversy are the possibility of even interior dissent from Roman teaching and whether papal infallibility can extend to
what, in the light of the five Jansenist propositions, came to be termed
"dogmatic facts." On these cf. *infra,* p. 148.

    76. De Lubac, p. 51. A clear guide to the whole tangled tale is readily
available in G. R. Cragg, *The Church and the Age of Reason* (London,
1972), ch. 2 and 13. It may not be over-simplifying the intellectual movements which mingled with religious and moral movements, and with political ambitions, to identify them as summed up in a confrontation between
Jansenism, with its fierce loyalty to Augustine and its roots in Platonism,
and the Society of Jesus, attracted to the cool and rational, even humanist,
optimism of Aquinas rooted in Aristotelianism.

    77. Jedin and Dolan, op. cit., vol. vi, pp. 5–10.

    78. Ibid., pp. 21–2; de Lubac, op. cit. p. 53.

    79. Louis Cognet, in Jedin and Dolan, vi, p. 28.

    80. Ibid., pp. 29–30. Among 101 (!) propositions excerpted from the
writings of Quesnel—who succeeded Arnaud as leader of the Jansenists—
and condemned by Rome, is the statement that "it is a wise, enlightening
and loving way of acting to provide souls with time to bear with humility
and to experience the state of sin, to seek a spirit of repentance and contri-
tion, and at least to begin to satisfy God's justice before they are reconciled"
(*DS* 2487).

    81. Op. cit., p. 25.

    82. Quoted in M. Hay's spirited attack, *The Prejudices of Pascal*
(London, 1962), p. 20, n. 1. For the events, cf. Jedin and Dolan, vi, p. 37.

    83. Quoted in Hay, ibid.

    84. Jedin and Dolan, vi, p. 31.

    85. Cf. Cognet, "Jansenism," *NCE,* 7, p. 820; K. Heckler, art. "Jan-
senism," in *Sacramentum Mundi* (London, 1969), vol. iii, pp. 171–2.

    86. Matteucci, "Jansenistic Piety," in *NCE* 7, p. 825; de Lubac, p.
51.

    87. Matteucci, ibid. For some indication of Jansenist influence in
England, cf. Bossy, op. cit., p. 290. Pope Pius X was not exaggerating when,
in 1910, his Decree lowering the age for reception of Communion and

encouraging even daily Communion pointed out how Jansenism especially had brought it about that very few were considered worthy to receive Communion daily and were content to receive less frequently, even annually. "In fact, severity reached such lengths that whole classes were excluded from frequenting the heavenly table, such as merchants or married people" (*DS* 3376).

88. The fifth of Jansen's condemned propositions was "it is semi-Pelagian to say that Christ died or shed his blood for absolutely all men" (*DS* 2005). On the restriction of grace to obey God's commands, cf. *DS* 2001 (the first Jansenist proposition) and *supra,* p. 53.

89. "Tametsi daretur ignorantia invincibilis iuris naturae, haec in statu naturae lapsae operantem ex ipsa non excusat a peccato formali," *DS* 2302. "Omnis humana actio deliberata est Dei dilectio vel mundi: si Dei, caritas Patris est; si mundi, concupiscentia carnis, hoc est, mala est," *DS* 2307. "Necesse est, infidelem in omni opere peccare," *DS* 2308. "Omne, quod non est ex fide christiana supernaturali, quae per dilectionem operatur, peccatum est," *DS* 2311. "Ubi quis invenerit doctrinam in Augustino clare fundatam, illam absolute potest tenere et docere, non respiciendo ad ullam Pontificis Bullam," *DS* 2330.

90. "tametsi in eis liberum arbitrium minime exstinctum esset, viribus licet attenuatum et inclinatum," *DS* 1522 (Trent), echoing Arles, "libertatem voluntatis humanae non existinctam, sed adtenuatam et infirmatam" (*DS* 339). Cf. *DS* 336.

91. "divinae legis doctrinam defendendo, quae a regno Dei non solum infideles excludit . . ." *DS* 1544.

92. "Si quis dixerit, opera omnia, quae ante iustificationem fiunt, quacumque ratione facta sint, vere esse peccata vel odium Dei mereri . . . : anathema sit," *DS* 1557.

93. Cf. *DS* 2401–5, 2438–49; 2619, 2623–4.

94. Cf. M. Flick and Z. Alszeghy, *Il Vangelo della grazia* (Florence, 1964), pp. 40–67.

95. "spoliatus a gratuitis et vulneratus in naturalibus," ibid., p. 183, n. 48. On Augustine, cf. *supra,* p. 49.

96. Cf. Karl Rahner, "Concerning the relationship between nature and grace," *Theological Investigations,* vol. i (London, 1961).

97. Cf. the encyclical of Pope Pius XII, *Humani generis,* "Alii veram 'gratuitatem' ordinis supernaturalis corrumpunt, cum autument Deum entia intellectu praedita condere non posse, quin eadem ad beatificam visionem ordinet et vocet" (*DS* 3891).

98. Cf. Flick and Alszeghy, op. cit., pp. 180–2, 190–1.

99. J. Alfaro, art. "Nature," *Sacramentum Mundi,* vol. iv, p. 174.

100. Ibid., p. 173. As a translation of *Restbegriff* here, "remainder" appears better than "vestigial," the latter implying "traces" of the supernatural in "nature."

101. *Nature and Grace* (London, 1963), p. 5.

102. Ibid., p. 7.

103. Ibid., p. 31 (italics in original).

104. Ibid., pp. 32, 35.

105. Rahner, "Concerning the relationship . . ." *Theological Investigations,* vol. i, pp. 314–15.

106. Cf. Vatican II, *Lumen Gentium,* no. 16, *Gaudium et Spes,* no. 22, *Ad Gentes,* no. 7. Cf. also, *infra,* p. 202.

107. K. Rahner, "Anonymous Christians," in *Theological Investigations,* vol. vi (London, 1969), p. 395.

108. Ibid., pp. 393–4.

109. *Idem,* "Christianity and the non-Christian Religions," in *Theological Investigations,* vol. v (London, 1966), p. 125.

110. "Anonymous Christians," ibid., p. 394. On Rahner's response to the difficulties raised against his thesis, cf. *idem,* "Observations on the problem of the 'anonymous Christian,' " in *Theological Investigations,* vol. xiv (London, 1976), pp. 280–94.

111. Justin, *First Apology,* ch. 44 (trans. Dods, p. 45), "For Moses is more ancient than all the Greek writers. And whatever both philosophers and poets have said concerning the immortality of the soul . . . or doctrines of the like kind, they have received such suggestions from the prophets as to enable them to understand and interpret these things. And hence there seem to be seeds of truth among all men," *PG* 6, 396. Cf. Tertullian, *Apol.,* chap. 19 (*PL* 1, 440–1). Augustine, *civ. dei,* viii, 11 (*PL* 41, 235) mentions entertaining the suggestion, but he later rejected it (trans. Bettenson), p. 314, n. 23.

112. Justin, ibid., ch. 46 (Dods, p. 46); *PL* 6, 397. On the espousal of this view by Pope John Paul II, cf. *Redemptor Hominis,* n. 11; *AAS* 71 (1979), p. 276. Cf. also the striking missionary passage in Vatican II, *Ad gentes,* 9; *AAS* 58 (1966), p. 958.

113. Justin, *Second Apology,* chap. 8 (Dods, p. 78); *PG* 6, 457. He ascribes the admirable moral teaching of the Stoics to "the seed of reason (τὸ σπέρμα τοῦ λόγου) implanted in every race of men," ibid.

114. Ibid., ch. 10 (Dods, p. 79); *PG* 6, 460. "Christ . . . was partially known even by Socrates (for he was and is the Word (λόγος) who is in every man)," ibid., p. 80; *PG* 6, 461. ὅσα οὖν παρὰ πᾶσι καλῶς εἴρηται, ἡμῶν τῶν χριστιανῶν ἐστι, ibid., ch. 13 (Dods, p. 83); *PG* 6, 465.

115. Justin, *Dialogue with Trypho,* chap. 45 (Trans. G. Reith), ibid.,

p. 144; *PG* 6, 572 ('Ἐπεὶ οἱ τὰ καθύλου καὶ φύσει καὶ αἰώνια καλὰ ἐποίουν, εὐάρεστοί εἰσι τῷ θεῷ).

116. Ronald Knox, *The Belief of Catholics* (London, 1927), p. 34.

117. Augustine, *de civ. dei*, xxii, 22; *PL* 41, 784 (Bettenson, p. 1065).

118. Cf. *supra*, n. 52.

119. *STh* 3a, q. 61, art. 3 ad 2.

120. *STh* 1a, 2ae, q. 91, art 4.

121. "Quia homo ordinatur ad finem beatitudinis aeternae, quae excedit proportionem naturalis facultatis humanae (cf. 1a, 2ae, q. 5, a. 5), ideo necessarium fuit ut supra legem naturalem et humanam dirigeretur etiam ad suum finem lege divinitus data', ibid. 'Ut ergo homo absque omni dubitatione scire possit quid ei sit agendum et quid vitandum, necessarium fuit ut in actibus propriis dirigetur per legem divinitus datam, de qua constat quod non potest errare," ibid.

122. Cf. *supra*, p. 79.

123. Cf. O. Lottin, *Principes de morale*, t. ii (Louvain, 1947), pp. 37–54, especially p. 49, n. 1.

124. "Derivantur ergo quaedam a principiis communibus legis naturae per modum conclusionum: sicut hoc quod est "non esse occidendum," ut conclusio quaedam derivari potest ab eo quod est "nulli esse faciendum malum,' " *STh* 1a, 2ae, q. 95, art. 2.

125. "Principia communia legis naturae non eodem modo applicari possunt omnibus propter multam varietatem rerum humanarum," ibid., ad. 3.

126. *STh* 1a 2ae, q. 94, a. 6.

127. "Ipsa naturalis cognitio boni in [malis] obtenebratur per passiones et habitus peccatorum," ibid., q. 93, a. 6. Cf. *STh* 3a, q. 61, a. 3 ad 2.

128. *STh* 1a 2ae, q. 94, a. 4, which may be seen as summing up Aquinas' view on the applicability and the "knowability" of natural law. "Sic igitur dicendum est quod lex naturae, quantum ad prima principia communia, est eadem apud omnes et secundum rectitudinem et secundum notitiam. Sed quantum ad quaedam propria, quae sunt quasi conclusiones principiorum communium, est eadem apud omnes ut in pluribus et secundum rectitudinem et secundum notitiam: sed ut in paucioribus potest deficere et quantum ad rectitudinem, propter aliqua particularia impedimenta —sicut etiam naturae generabiles et corruptibiles deficiunt ut in paucioribus propter impedimenta—et etiam quantum ad notitiam; et hoc propter hoc quod aliqui habent depravatam rationem ex passione, seu ex mala consuetudine, seu ex mala habitudine naturae; sicut apud Germanos olim latrocinium non reputabatur iniquum, cum tamen sit expresse contra legem naturae, ut refert Julius Caesar in lib. *de bello Gallico* [vi, 23]."

129. "Cum moralia praecepta sint de his quae pertinent ad bonos mores, haec autem sunt quae rationi congruunt, omne autem rationis humanae judicium aliqualiter a naturali ratione derivatur, necesse est quod omnia praecepta moralia pertineant ad legem naturae," *STh* 1a 2ae, q. 100, a. 1.

130. "Illa duo praecepta sunt prima et communia praecepta legis naturae, quae sunt per se nota rationi humanae, vel per naturam vel per fidem. Et ideo omnia pracepta decalogi ad illa duo referuntur sicut conclusiones ad principia communia," ibid., a. 4 ad 3. "Illa ergo praecepta ad decalogum pertinent quorum notitiam homo habet per seipsum a Deo. Huiusmodi vero sunt illa quae statim ex principiis communibus primis cognosci possunt modica consideratione: et iterum illa quae statim ex fide divinitus infusa innotescunt," ibid., art. 3. The precepts which, for Aquinas, result immediately from divinely infused faith are those which refer to one's conduct toward God himself.

131. "Illa [praecepta] quae sunt prima et communia, continentur in eis sicut principia in conclusionibus proximis: illa vero quae per sapientes cognoscuntur, continentur in eis, e converso, sicut conclusiones in principiis," ibid.

132. "Praecepta novae legis dicuntur esse majora quam praecepta veteris legis, quantum ad explicitam manifestationem; sed quantum ad ipsam substantiam praeceptorum Novi Testamenti omnia continentur in Veteri Testamento," q. 107, art. 3 ad 2. Cf. q. 108, art. 2 ad 1.

133. "lex nova, quae praeter praecepta legis naturae paucissima superaddit in doctrina Christi et Apostolorum," q. 107, art. 4.

134. "Consilia vero oportet esse de illis per quae melius et expeditius potest homo consequi finem praedictum," q. 108, art. 4, which proceeds to show how reasonable are the counsels given by Jesus, always depending on the aptitude of individuals (*idoneitate hominum*), ibid., ad. 1.

135. "Ad ea etiam quae de Deo ratione humana investigari possunt necessarium fuit hominem instrui revelatione divina. Quia veritas de Deo per rationem a paucis, et per longum tempus, et cum admixtione multorum errorum homini proveniret. . . . Ut igitur salus hominum communius et securius [*al.* convenientius et certius] proveniat necessarium fuit quod de divinis per divinam revelationem instruantur," *STh* 1a, q. 1, a. 1.

136. Op. cit., p. 172.

137. *DS* 2850–2. Pius IX was clear enough on the value of a "true and healthy philosophy" in diligently seeking truth and in cultivating human reason, "which has been darkened but in no way extinguished" by original

sin (*DS* 2853). Trent had applied this description to man's free will, as had the Council of Arles, Cf. *supra,* n. 90.

138. "Huic divinae revelationi tribuendum quidem est, ut ea, quae in rebus divinis humanae rationi per se impervia non sunt, in praesenti quoque generis humani condicione ab omnibus expedite, firma certitudine et nullo admixto errore cognosci possint. Non hac tamen de causa revelatio absolute necessaria dicenda est, sed quia Deus ex infinita bonitate sua ordinavit hominem ad finem supernaturalem, ad participando scilicet bona divina, quae humanae mentis intelligentiam omnino superant," *DS* 3005.

139. "Ecclesiam enim constituit ipse Christus Dominus magistram veritatis, in his etiam quae ad mores pertinent regendos ordinandosque, etsi in his multa humanae rationi impervia non sunt', *AAS* XXII (1930), 580. 'At nemo non videt, quot fallaciis aditus aperiretur et quanti errores admiscerentur veritati, si res singulis relinqueretur solo rationis lumine exploranda . . ." ibid., p. 579.

140. *Supra,* pp. 81–2.

141. "Licet humana ratio, simpliciter loquendo, veram et certam cognitionem . . . naturalis legis a Creatore nostris animis inditae, suis naturalibus viribus ac lumine assequi revera possit. . . . Humanus autem intellectus in talibus veritatibus acquirendis difficultate laborat. . . . Quapropter divina "revelatio" moraliter necessaria dicenda est, ut ea, quae in rebus religionis et morum rationi per se impervia non sunt, in praesenti quoque humani generis condicione, ab omnibus expedite, firma certitudine et nullo admixto errore cognosci possint," *DS* 3875–6, the final words being from Vatican I, *supra,* n. 138.

142. "The Thomistic natural law concept vacillates at times between the order of nature and the order of reason," C. E. Curran, *Contemporary Problems in Moral Theology* (Notre Dame, Indiana, 1970), p. 106. On the following reflections, cf., however, Aquinas, *de Malo,* q. 2, a. 4 (*Quaestiones disputatae* (Rome Marietti), 1965), vol. ii, p. 474), "bonum et malum in actibus humanis consideratur secundum quod actus concordat rationi informatae lege divine, vel naturaliter, vel per doctrinam, ver per infusionem."

143. Cf. *STh* 3a, q. 61, a. 2 ad 2: "Eadem est natura hominis ante peccatum et post peccatum, non tamen est idem naturae status." Sin does not affect the constitutive principles of nature or its powers, but it does affect its predisposition to virtuous action (*STh* 1a 2ae. q. 85, a. 1). And it is well known that he viewed the institution of private property as necessary for man only after the Fall, due, no doubt, to sin's affecting man's natural

predisposition to live in social harmony (1a, q. 98, a. 1; cf. 2a 2ae, q. 66, a. 2). It may also be noted that he considered man's original justice before the fall as accidental to his nature (1a, q. 100, a. 1), such that changes in the state of human nature are all equally accidental. Moreover, Aquinas distinguishes between nature in general (*natura universalis*) and nature in particular individuals (*natura particularis*) (1a, q. 99, a. 2 ad 1), and it appears that it is in this sense that he can refer to nature being changeable in individuals on account of particular circumstances. "Natura autem hominis est mutabilis, ideo id quod naturale est homini potest aliquando deficere," as in the case of a madman or a public enemy demanding the return of his sword (2a 2ae, q. 57, a 2 ad 1). Cf. *de Malo* (Marietti, op. cit., p. 477) q. 2, a. 5 ad 13, "mutabilitatem naturae humanae et diversas conditiones hominum et rerum, secundum diversitatem locorum et temporum." On the immutability of natural law, as a consequence of the immutability of nature, cf. Lottin, *Principes,* vol. ii, pp. 40–2.

144. Cf. *infra,* p. 206.

145. Condemning the view that "ab Adam usque ad Christum nullos ex gentibus per primam Dei gratiam, id est per legem naturae, in adventum Christi esse salvatos eo quod liberum arbitrium ex omnibus [= *ex toto*] in primo parente perdiderunt" (*DS* 336).

146. "principia moralis doctrinae de matrimonio, quae in lege naturali, divina Revelatione illustrata ditataque, nititur," *Humanae Vitae,* n. 4 (*AAS* 60 (1968), p. 483).

147. "Unde homo nova efficitur creatura, quae in caritate germanaque libertate superno sui Creatoris et Salvatoris consilio respondeat . . ." ibid., n. 25 (*AAS,* pp. 498–9).

148. "facere autem non potest, quin legem doceat, quae reapse propria est vitae humanae ad eius germanam veritatem restitutae, atque a Spiritu Dei actae," ibid., n. 19; *AAS* 60 (1968), p. 495.

149. "obiectivis criteriis, ex personae eiusdemque actuum natura desumptis," *Gaudium et Spes,* n. 51; *AAS* 58 (1966), p. 1072. An earlier draft ran "obiectivis criteriis, in eadem personae humanae dignitate fundatis," *Acta Concilii Vaticani Secundi,* vol. iv, 6 (Rome, 1978), p. 478.

150. W. M. Abbott, *The Documents of Vatican II* (London, 1966), p. 674.

151. "Dignitatis humanae personae homines hac nostra aetate magis in dies conscii fiunt," *Declaration on Religious Freedom,* n. 1; *AAS* 58 (1966), p. 929.

152. Abbott, op. cit. pp. 673, 672.

153. Cf. *infra,* pp. 194–202.

154. *Familianis Consortio,* n. 31, *AAS* 74 (1982), p. 117.

155. "Human dignity is the dignity of the grace of divine adoption and at the same time the dignity of the truth within the human race," *Redemptor hominis,* n. 11, *AAS* 71 (1979), p. 277. Cf. ibid., n. 12 (p. 280): "the dignity of the human person" is part of the Gospel, and freedom is the condition and foundation of the true dignity of the human person.

156. *Supra,* n. 58.

157. *Nature and Grace,* p. 42.

158. "De homine ideo hic agitur, in tota eius veritate, in universa eius amplitudine. Non agitur de homine *abstracto,* sed vero, ut est, de homine *concreto,* historico, ut aiunt. De quolibet homine agitur, cum quivis comprehenditur mysterio Redemptionis et huius mysterii gratia in omne tempus cum eo Christus se coniunxerit," *Redemptor hominis,* n. 13 (*AAS,* p. 283).

List of Contributors

Franz Böckle is Professor Emeritus of Moral Theology at the University of Bonn.

Michael B. Crowe was Professor of Philosophy at the University College, Dublin.

Charles E. Curran is the Elizabeth Scurlock University Professor of Human Values at Southern Methodist University.

John Finnis is Reader in Law, Oxford University, and Fellow of University College, Oxford.

Joseph Fuchs, S.J., is Professor of Moral Theology at the Gregorian University in Rome.

Richard M. Gula, S.S., is Professor of Moral Theology at St. Patrick's Seminary, Menlo Park, California.

Stanley Hauerwas is Professor of Theological Ethics at Duke University.

Gerard Hughes, S.J., is Professor of Moral Theology at Heythrop College, University of London.

Terence Kennedy, C.SS.R., teaches moral theology at the Alfonsianum in Rome.

Richard A. McCormick, S.J., is John A. O'Brien Professor of Christian Ethics at the University of Notre Dame.

Ralph McInerny is Michael P. Grace Professor of Medieval Studies at the University of Notre Dame.

John Macquarrie has retired from the chair of the Lady Margaret Professor of Divinity at the University of Oxford.

John Mahoney, S.J., is Frederick Denison Maurice Professor of Moral and Social Theology at King's College, University of London.

Jacques Maritain was an eminent Thomistic philosopher.

William E. May is Michael J. McGivney Professor of Moral Theology at the Pope John Paul II Institute for Studies on Marriage and Family in Washington, D.C.

John Courtney Murray, S.J., was a distinguished Professor of Systematic Theology and a *peritus* at Vatican II.

Bruno Schüller, S.J., is Professor of Moral Theology at the University of Münster.

READINGS IN
MORAL THEOLOGY NO. 2
THE DISTINCTIVENESS OF CHRISTIAN ETHICS

CONTENTS

Foreword *Charles E. Curran and Richard A. McCormick, S.J.* • Is There a Specifically Christian Morality? *Joseph Fuchs, S.J.* • Is There a Christian Ethics? *Dionigi Tettamanzi* • Is There a Catholic and/or Christian Ethic? *Charles E. Curran* • Christian Ethics: Distinctive and Specific? *James J. Walter* • Christ and Morality *Norbert Rigali* • Rethinking Natural Law *John Macquarrie* • Can Ethics be Christian? Some Conclusions *James Gustafson* • Does Religious Faith Add to Ethical Perception? *Richard A. McCormick, S.J.* • Magisterium of the Church, Faith, Morality *Joseph Ratzinger* • Nine Theses in Christian Ethics *Hans Urs von Balthasar* • The Debate on the Specific Character of a Christian Ethics: Some Remarks *Bruno Schüller* • Questioning the Specificity of Christian Morality *Ph. Delhaye* • The Grounding For the Moral Norm in Contemporary Theological Reflection *Enrico Chiavacci*

READINGS IN
MORAL THEOLOGY NO.5
Official Catholic Social Teaching

CONTENTS

Foreword *Charles E. Curran and Richard A. McCormick, S.J.* • **PART ONE: HISTORICAL DEVELOPMENT** • The Catholic Social Movement: Historical Aspects *Edward Cahill, S.J.* • The Rights and Duties of Labor and Capital *Richard L. Camp* • Toward a New Society *George G. Higgins* • The Drafting of Quadragesimo Anno *Oswald von Nell-Breuning, S.J.* • Forty Years Later: Reflections and Reminiscences *John F. Cronin, S.S.* • Pope John XXIII—A New Direction? *Donal Dorr* • Human Rights in Roman Catholicism *John Langan, S.J.* • Looking Back on Populorum Progressio *Barbara Ward* • Action for Justice as Constitutive of the Preaching of the Gospel: What Did the 1971 Synod Mean? *Charles M. Murphy* •

PART TWO: OVERVIEWS AND CONTEMPORARY DISCUSSIONS • Development of Church Social Teaching *John Coleman, S.J.* • The Changing Anthropological Bases of Catholic Social Ethics *Charles E. Curran* • Laborem Exercens and Social Morality *Richard A. McCormick, S.J.* • John Paul II's Encyclical on Labor *Gregory Baum* • Laborem Exercens: Toward a New Solidarity *Bartolomeo Sorge* • John Paul II: Continuity and Change in the Social Teaching of the Church *J. Bryan Hehir* • The Popes and Politics: Shifting Patterns in Catholic Social Doctrine *Peter Hebblethwaite* •

PART THREE: EVALUATIONS AND PERSPECTIVES • Methodological Differences: The Holy See and the World Council of Churches *Thomas Sieger Derr* • The Problem of Poverty and the Poor in Catholic Social Teaching: A Marxist Perspective *József Lukács* • From Catholic "Social Doctrine" to the "Kingdom of Christ on Earth" *James V. Schall* • The Bias Against Democratic Capitalism *Michael Novak* • Economic Systems, Middle Way Theories, and Third World Realities *Denis Goulet* • Global Human Rights: An Interpretation of the Contemporary Catholic Understanding *David Hollenbach, S.J.* • From Rerum Novarum to Laborem Exercens: A United States Labor Perspective *Thomas R. Donahue* • Feminist Themes and Laborem Exercens *Andrea Lee, I.H.M. and Amata Miller, I.H.M.* • Major Differences: Liberation Theology and Current Church Teaching *Christine E. Gudorf* •

READINGS IN
MORAL THEOLOGY NO. 4
The Use of Scripture
in Moral Theology

CONTENTS

Foreword *Charles E. Curran and Richard A. McCormick, S.J.* • Jesus, Ethics and the Present Situation *Richard H. Hiers* • Biblical Revelation and Social Existence *James H. Cone* • The Question of the Relevance of Jesus for Ethics Today *Jack T. Sanders* • Commands for Grown-Ups *Richard J. Mouw* • The Actual Impact of Moral Norms of the New Testament: Report from the International Theological Commission *Text by Hans Schürmann, Introduction and Commentary by Philippe Delhaye* • Scripture: The Soul of Moral Theology? *Edouard Hamel* • The Changing Use of the Bible in Christian Ethics *James M. Gustafson* • The Place of Scripture in Christian Ethics: A Methodological Study *James M. Gustafson* • The Role and Function of the Scriptures in Moral Theology *Charles E. Curran* • The Use of Scripture in Ethics *Allen Verhey* • The Moral Authority of Scripture: The Politics and Ethics of Remembering *Stanley Hauerwas* • Scripture and Christian Ethics *James F. Childress* • Scripture, Liturgy, Character and Morality *Richard A. McCormick, S.J.* • The Biblical Hermeneutics of Juan Luis Segundo *Alfred T. Hennelly* • A Critical Appraisal of Segundo's Biblical Hermeneutics *Anthony J. Tambasco* • Exodus and Exile: The Two Faces of Liberation *John Howard Yoder* • Toward a Feminist Biblical Hemeneutics: Biblical Interpretation and Liberation Theology *Elisabeth Schüssler Fiorenza*

READINGS IN

MORAL THEOLOGY NO.6

Dissent in the Church

CONTENTS

Foreword, Charles E. Curran and Richard A. McCormick, S.J. ● **PART ONE: THEOLOGICAL DISSENT IN GENERAL** ● The Rights and Responsibilities of Theologians, Jon Nilson ● Theology and Magisterium, Karl Rahner ● The Authority of the Magisterium on Questions of Natural Moral Law, Francis A. Sullivan, S.J. ● Infallibility and Specific Moral Norms, Germain Grisez ● Authority and Conscience, Avery Dulles ● Dissent in the Church, Michael Novak ● Statements of the Bishops on Dissent ● Dissent and the Catholic Religion Teacher, William Levada ● Dissent in the Church, Daniel Pilarczyk ● The Magisterium and Theological Dissent, Roger Mahony ● Thoughts on Freedom, Conscience and Obedience, Michael Pfeifer, O.M.I. ● The Price of Orthodoxy, Rembert G. Weakland, O.S.B.

PART TWO: CANONICAL ASPECTS ● Church Teaching Authority in the 1983 Code, John P. Boyle ● Reflections on the Text of a Canon, Ladislas Orsy, S.J. ● Theological Pluralism and Canonical Mandate, John Strynkowski

PART THREE: ACADEMIC ASPECTS ● Academic Freedom and Catholic Institutions of Higher Learning, Charles, E. Curran ● Statement of Presidents of Leading Catholic Universities on the Schema for a Proposed Document on the Catholic University ● The Catholic College Versus Academic Freedom, Edward J. Berbusse ● On Defending Catholic Higher Education in America, Mark D. Jordan

PART FOUR: MORAL THEOLOGY IN PARTICULAR ● The Drama of Morality and Remarks on Dissent, Joseph Ratzinger ● On the Other Hand, John Mahoney, S.J. ● Teaching Morality: The Tension Between Bishops and Theologians Within the Church, Joseph Fuchs, S.J.

PART FIVE: THE CURRAN CASE AND ITS AFTERMATH ● Letters to Curran, Joseph Ratzinger ● Response of Charles E. Curran ● The Vatican Moves to Repress Dissent, John C. Bennett ● The Ecumenical Impact of the Curran Case, J. Philip Wogaman ● Dissent in Moral Theology and Its Implications, Richard A. McCormick, S.J. ● The Curran Case: Conflict Between Rome and a Moral Theologian, Bernard Häring ● Public Dissent in the Church, Charles E. Curran ● L'Affaire Curran, Richard A. McCormick, S.J. ● The Search for Truth in the Catholic Context, Richard A. McCormick, S.J. ● Curran and Dissent: The Case for the Holy See, David Fitch, S.J. ● How to Deal with Theological Dissent, Germain Grisez ● Comments on the Curran Case: Pro, Kevin Kelly, Richard McBrien, Christine Gudorf ● Comments on the Curran Case: Con, James Hitchcock, Thomas P. Melady, Christopher Wolfe, Philip Lawler